Professional Windows GUI Programming using C#

Wahid Choudhury

Richard Conway

Jay Glynn

Zach Greenvoss

Shripad Kulkarni

Csaba Török

Neil Whitlow

Wrox Press Ltd. ®

Professional Windows GUI Programming
using C#

© 2002 Wrox Press

11-14-02

Published by Wrox Press Ltd,
Arden House, 1102 Warwick Road, Acocks Green,
Birmingham, B27 6BH, UK
Printed in USA
ISBN 1-86100-766-3

Trademark Acknowledgments

Credits

Authors
Wahid Choudhury
Richard Conway
Jay Glynn
Zach Greenvoss
Shripad Kulkarni
Csaba Török
Neil Whitlow

Technical Reviewers
Neil Avent
Mitchell Denny
Damien Foggon
Slavomir Furman
Andrew Krowcyk
Simon Robinson
David Schultz
Morgan Skinner
Gavin Smyth
Larry Schoeneman
Helmut Watson
Donald Xie

Managing Editor
Louay Fatoohi

Commisioning Editor
Julian Skinner

Technical Editors
Helen Callaghan
Gerard Maguire
Julian Skinner

Project Manager
Christianne Bailey
Charlotte Smith

Author Agent
Charlotte Smith

Production Coordinator
Abbie Forletta

Production Assistants
Sarah Hall
Neil Lote
Rachel Taylor
Pippa Wonson

Indexing
Andrew Criddle
Adrian Axinte

Proof Reader
Chris Smith

Illustrations
Natalie O'Donnell

Cover
Natalie O'Donnell

About the Authors

Wahid Choudhury

I first programmed with Fortran 77 and enjoyed solving physics problems with it. This fascination with Fortran stayed on and reached a peak when I decided to research in computational solid state physics (Fortran being a special favorite of physicists) after my first degree. At around this time I learned C++ and immediately dumped Fortran! C++ led to Win32, MFC, and COM. I was hooked, and like many physicists, jumped into the fast life of programming! I have been programming Win32/MFC and COM for about three years professionally now. When .NET came to the scene, I kept reading up articles and started experimenting on it as soon as I got my hands on the SDK. I have had the wonderful luck of being part of a company that is a member of the Compact Framework EAP and the .NET My Services EAP. Thus, my initial experimenting with C# soon turned in to full time professional work – which gives you the justification to waste time on a lot of things that you would like to try out in programming.

When I am not programming, I spend time with my lovely wife watching movies, at theatres and looking for good places to eat. I spend a lot of my free time reading books and dreaming of the coming mango season in Bangladesh.

Richard Conway

Richard Conway is an independent software consultant who lives and works in London. He has been using Microsoft technologies for the last five years, and has architected and built enterprise systems for the likes of IBM, Merrill Lynch, and Reuters. He has focused his development on Windows DNA, including using various tools and languages such as COM+, VB, XML, C++, J++, Biztalk, and, more recently, Data Warehousing. He has been involved in EAP trials with Microsoft for .NET My Services and the .NET Compact Framework. He has spent the last 18 months, since the release of the technical preview (of VS.NET), programming and doing proof-of-concepts in C#. His special area of interest is Network Security and Cryptography. Richard is a contributor to CSharptoday.com and ASPToday.com. He is currently finishing a Masters degree in Computing at the OU. Richard can be contacted at techierebel@yahoo.co.uk.

Jay Glynn

Jay started developing software in the late 1980's, writing applications for the Pick operating system in Pick BASIC. Since then he has created applications using Paradox PAL and Object PAL, Delphi, Pascal, C/C++, Java, VBA, and Visual Basic. Currently, Jay is a Project Coordinator and Architect for a large insurance company based in Nashville TN. For the past five years he has been developing software for pen-based computers and, more recently, for ASP and server-based systems. When not sitting in front of a keyboard, Jay is busy restoring a house in Franklin TN, playing a round of golf whenever possible, and watching Disney movies with his wife and three year old son. Jay can be reached at jlsglynn@hotmail.com.

I would like to thank my wife Lydia and my son Samuel for being patient and understanding of all the late nights. They are my motivation and inspiration.

Zach Greenvoss

Zach Greenvoss is a Senior Consultant with Magenic Technologies, a Microsoft Gold Certified Solution Provider and industry leader in providing custom business solutions utilizing the latest Microsoft technologies. He specializes in middle-tier architecture and implementation, utilizing various technologies including COM+, MSMQ, BizTalk, XML, and the .NET Framework. Zach's hobbies include traveling, caving, and playing his new XBox. He can be reached at zachg@magenic.com.

I would like to thank my wife Amanda for being patient and understanding of all the long hours.

Shripad Kulkarni

I have an MCP certification from Microsoft with around 10 years of IT experience. Currently I am working as a Sr. Analyst with Compuware Corporation in Milwaukee, Wisconsin. Over the years, I have worked on Databases, Unix systems, Windows, and Web development. I consult in Visual C++, MFC, Visual C#, Windows programming with .NET/COM/ActiveX, JAVA, and JSP. Most of my consulting experience has been oriented towards the Windows environment. I have contributed a number of articles on the Web in C# and other .NET technologies.

I live with my wife Vasanti and my one-year-old son Siddharth in the Village of Pewaukee, which is a suburb, west of Milwaukee. Currently most of my spare time is involved playing with my son, taking him outdoors to parks and lakes around Pewaukee. Taking care of a year old can be very handful so I would like to thank my wife for being so kind and considerate in taking care of him and giving me all the free time to concentrate on my work.

I like traveling, watching movies, football, and cricket.

I want to thank my friends and family members for their support and enthusiasm in co-authoring this book for Wrox.

Thanks to the Wrox Team. I am a regular reader of Wrox books and never imagined that I would one day write for them. I want to thank Julian Skinner for giving me this great opportunity to write for Wrox publications. Also many thanks to Christianne Bailey and Cilmaria Lion for their patience and support in replying to my frequent e-mails.

Csaba Török

Dr Csaba Török is a developer and consultant specializing in Microsoft Products and Internet scripting languages. He has experience as a project leader with a wide range of clients, ranging from insurance to the energy industry and nuclear research. He focuses on developing database-driven data mining applications, using statistical and graphical techniques.

When he is not sitting in front of his PC, he teaches programming languages and stochastic analysis for university students or tries to solve numerical or theoretical problems. His research interests include SDE, approximation theory, and wavelet analysis. He resides in Kosice and can be reached at csaba.torok@tuke.sk.

Neil Whitlow

Neil Whitlow is currently working as a Senior Systems Analyst developing software for pen-based computers with a large insurance company in Nashville, Tennessee.

Table of Contents

Table of Contents

Table of Contents

Introduction

Although web programming has been the hot topic in recent years, Windows programming is undergoing something of a rejuvenation under .NET. This is partly because web services allow us to take advantage of the Internet even in Windows applications, but it's also a belated recognition that Windows programs offer a much richer experience to the user than browser-based applications.

Perhaps the most exciting aspect of the .NET Framework is the fact that it combines the sort of power previously available only to C++ programs with the simplicity we associate with Visual Basic. In fact, with Visual Studio .NET, it's just as easy to create functional Windows applications in C# as it was in VB6. But the drag-and-drop simplicity of Visual Studio .NET shouldn't obscure the fact that .NET gives us much greater power than VB did. For example, it's now a relatively straightforward matter to customize the visual appearance of controls, so that we can still take advantage of their functionality while making them conform to our own look and feel. Even creating controls from scratch is now easy enough to be a worthwhile investment of time.

True, if we want to take advantage of these features, we need to do a little bit more work, but it's an effort that's amply repaid. In this book, we'll try to show you the capabilities of Windows Forms, and how to take advantage of them. The beauty of .NET is that it allows us to choose exactly the level of complexity that we need. Wherever we want to take control ourselves, that option exists (right down to the level of processing Windows messages ourselves); but where we just require the standard behavior, .NET obliges and does the hard work for us. This book aims to give you an understanding both of what .NET does for us, and of what we can achieve by taking control ourselves.

What do you need to use this book?

A prerequisite for this book is to have a machine with the .NET Framework installed upon it. This means that you'll need to be running either Windows 2000 Professional (or better), or Windows XP. The screenshots used in this book reflect the fact that either OS is compatible with the examples that we explore.

The .NET Framework itself is available as a free download from http://msdn.microsoft.com/netframework/downloads/howtoget.asp. It comes in two versions:

❑ The .NET Framework Redistributable – the full framework on its own. This includes everything you need to run any .NET application. Its approximate size is 20Mb.

❑ The .NET Framework SDK (Software Development Kit) – the full framework, plus tools for creating .NET applications, documentation, samples, and tutorials that you can refer to in order to learn more about .NET. Approximate size: 130Mb

This book is designed to be 'editor neutral'. All of the examples can be created, run, and understood using a simple text editor such as Notepad. You do not *need* Visual Studio .NET in order to use this book, although we do point out where it would be beneficial to use it. Chapter 10 discusses deploying Windows applications specifically using the tools shipped with Visual Studio .NET, although the latest versions of other installation applications (such as InstallShield) can be used with .NET.

Conventions

We've used a number of different styles of text and layout in this book to help differentiate between different kinds of information. Here are examples of the styles we used and an explanation of what they mean.

Code has several fonts. If it's a word that we're talking about in the text – for example, when discussing a for (...) loop, it's in this font. If it's a block of code that can be typed as a program and run, then it's also in a gray box:

```
Graphics g = CreateGraphics();
```

Sometimes we'll see code in a mixture of styles, like this:

```
protected override void OnPaint(PaintEventArgs e)
{
    Graphics g = e.Graphics;
    g.DrawString("Professional Windows GUI Programming",
            new Font("Arial", 10f),
            new SolidBrush(Color.Red),
            20f, 20f);
}
```

In cases like this, the code with a white background is code we are already familiar with; the line highlighted in gray is a new addition to the code since we last looked at it.

Advice, hints, and background information comes in this type of font.

Important pieces of information come in boxes like this.

Bullets appear indented, with each new bullet marked as follows:

❑   **Important Words** are in a bold type font.

❑   Words that appear on the screen, or in menus like the Open or Close, are in a similar font to the one you would see on a Windows desktop.

❑   Keys that you press on the keyboard, like *Ctrl* and *Enter*, are in italics.

Customer Support

We always value hearing from our readers, and we want to know what you think about this book: what you liked, what you didn't like, and what you think we can do better next time. You can send us your comments, either by returning the reply card in the back of the book, or by e-mail to feedback@wrox.com. Please be sure to mention the book title in your message.

How to Download the Sample Code for the Book

When you visit the Wrox site, http://www.wrox.com/, simply locate the title through our Search facility or by using one of the title lists. Click on Download in the Code column, or on Download Code on the book's details page.

When you click to download the code for this book, you are presented with a page with three options:

❑   If you are already a member of the Wrox Developer Community (if you have already registered on ASPToday, C#Today, or Wroxbase), you can log in with your usual username and password combination to receive your code.

❑   If you are not already a member, you are asked if you would like to register for free code downloads. In addition you will also be able to download several free articles from Wrox Press. Registering will allow us to keep you informed about updates and new editions of this book.

❑   The third option is to bypass registration completely and simply download the code.

Registration for code download is not mandatory for this book, but should you wish to register for your code download, your details will not be passed to any third party. For more details, you may wish to view our terms and conditions, which are linked from the download page.

Once you reach the code download section, you will find that the files that are available for download from our site have been archived using WinZip. When you have saved the files to a folder on your hard drive, you will need to extract the files using a de-compression program such as WinZip or PKUnzip. When you extract the files, the code is usually extracted into chapter folders. When you start the extraction process, ensure your software (WinZip, PKUnzip, etc.) is set to use folder names.

Errata

We've made every effort to take sure that there are no errors in the text or in the code. However, no one is perfect and mistakes do occur. If you find an error in one of our books, like a spelling mistake or a faulty piece of code, we would be very grateful for feedback. By sending in errata you may save another reader hours of frustration, and of course, you will be helping us provide even higher quality information. Simply e-mail the information to support@wrox.com; your information will be checked and if correct, posted to the errata page for that title, or used in subsequent editions of the book.

To find errata on the web site, go to http://www.wrox.com/, and simply locate the title through our Advanced Search or title list. Click on the Book Errata link, which is below the cover graphic on the book's detail page.

E-mail Support

If you wish to directly query a problem in the book with an expert who knows the book in detail then e-mail support@wrox.com, with the title of the book and the last four numbers of the ISBN in the subject field of the e-mail. A typical e-mail should include the following things:

❑ The **title of the book**, **last four digits of the ISBN** (7663), and **page number** of the problem in the Subject field.

❑ Your **name**, **contact information**, and the **problem** in the body of the message.

We won't send you junk mail. We need the details to save your time and ours. When you send an e-mail message, it will go through the following chain of support:

❑ Customer Support – Your message is delivered to our customer support staff, who are the first people to read it. They have files on most frequently asked questions and will answer anything general about the book or the web site immediately.

❑ Editorial – Deeper queries are forwarded to the technical editor responsible for that book. They have experience with the programming language or particular product, and are able to answer detailed technical questions on the subject.

❑ The Authors – Finally, in the unlikely event that the editor cannot answer your problem, they will forward the request to the author. We do try to protect the author from any distractions to their writing; however, we are quite happy to forward specific requests to them. All Wrox authors help with the support on their books. They will e-mail the customer and the editor with their response, and again all readers should benefit.

The Wrox Support process can only offer support to issues that are directly pertinent to the content of our published title. Support for questions that fall outside the scope of normal book support is provided via the community lists of our http://p2p.wrox.com/ forum.

p2p.wrox.com

For author and peer discussion join the P2P mailing lists. Our unique system provides **programmer to programmer**™ contact on mailing lists, forums, and newsgroups, all in addition to our one-to-one e-mail support system. If you post a query to P2P, you can be confident that it is being examined by the many Wrox authors and other industry experts who are present on our mailing lists. At p2p.wrox.com you will find a number of different lists that will help you, not only while you read this book, but also as you develop your own applications.

To subscribe to a mailing list just follow these steps:

1. Go to http://p2p.wrox.com/.

2. Choose the appropriate category from the left menu bar.

3. Click on the mailing list you wish to join.

4. Follow the instructions to subscribe and fill in your e-mail address and password.

5. Reply to the confirmation e-mail you receive.

6. Use the subscription manager to join more lists and set your e-mail preferences.

Why this System Offers the Best Support

You can choose to join the mailing lists or you can receive them as a weekly digest. If you don't have the time, or facility, to receive the mailing list, then you can search our online archives. Junk and spam mails are deleted, and your own e-mail address is protected by the unique Lyris system. Queries about joining or leaving lists, and any other general queries about lists, should be sent to listsupport@p2p.wrox.com.

1

.NET and Windows

Over the last several years there has been shift in the thinking of developers about how an application should be architected. Once upon a time, the usual practice was to develop a Windows application that contained all of the GUI code as well as most of the business logic, or at least what we couldn't make fit in a stored procedure. This was called **client-server** architecture, and at the time it was thought that it would replace mainframe systems. Then we got the capabilities to execute that business logic in a component (possibly hosted on a different machine) that lived between our data and us. Technologies such as MTS, MSMQ, and MQSeries gave the developer a new way of thinking about how an application should be architected. By separating the business logic and the presentation logic, changes in business rules could be implemented more easily. Code that implemented pure business logic has a better chance of being reused than something that is tangled with presentation code. Now most of the business logic lived in that "middle tier", and so multi-tier programming was born. It was thought that this would surely replace mainframe systems. As multi-tiered programming was evolving, so was this thing called the World Wide Web. As web development became more sophisticated, the client became thinner and thinner until we finally reached the point where it was declared by certain industry pundits that the PC would become obsolete; it was expected that everything would run from the Internet, intranet or local network. The client would be nothing more then a terminal-type device to render HTML. Instead of replacing mainframes, we were regressing back to becoming mainframe-like systems – very thin "dumb" clients working against centralized systems. This really didn't work out so well, and we stepped back a little. Thin client was still the way to go, but it should be a PC-based browser. This allowed scripts or applets to be downloaded to the client on demand and executed. One of the main reasons for this type of architecture was that Windows-based applications were notorious for being difficult to install and maintain. This was true especially if you had a network of a couple of thousand client PCs to manage. "DLL hell" would rear its ugly head and make applications inoperable. It made sense to try to execute as much as possible from the server and not the client. If you don't install anything on the client then you don't have anything to manage.

The problem with this architecture is that for the most part we were just rendering HTML on the client. It was difficult to give the user a rich user experience with just the browser. We either had to rely on scripts or applets, or had to make round trip after round trip to the server. Neither was a very appealing option from either a performance or from a security standpoint. The designers of the .NET Framework realized this and made sure that the high-fidelity, smart-client application was not forgotten. The Web will always be an important part of application development; however, not every application can live in a browser, nor should it. PCs today have processing power that was unthought-of just a few short years ago. It seems a waste to use them for rendering HTML and little else. The System.Windows.Forms namespace in the .NET Framework allows the developer to take advantage of this processing power.

Windows-based applications (or "smart-client applications", as Microsoft now calls them) are making a comeback. The same industry pundits who declared the PC dead are now saying just the opposite. Over the next few years, it is expected that a majority of the applications created will be smart-client applications. Some things can simply be done better with a smart client application: maintaining state, displaying complex graphics, and performing field-level entry validation are just a few areas where browser-based applications have severe limitations. .NET gives the client a new set of features as well. Client applications can call web services, for example. This can open up a completely new architecture for your enterprise applications. Deployment has been enhanced, so you no longer have to worry about DLL Hell – multiple versions of a component can be installed on a single machine. You can even deploy your application from a web server. Another big advantage is that a rich-client application can take advantage of all of the Win32 APIs. With the .NET class libraries, you probably won't need to call Windows API functions too often, but there are occasions when they're very useful. Finally, there are the graphics capabilities of GDI+. Irregular shaped forms, shading, translucency, and font manipulation are available through easy-to-use .NET classes that wrap the unmanaged GDI+ library.

This book will give you the basis for developing those high-fidelity client applications, both using the Visual Studio .NET IDE (VS.NET), and without it. (Even if you do have access to VS,NET it's a good idea to understand the code that VS generates in your applications, as it's often necessary to make adjustments to this code.) Some of the things we will be looking at in this book are:

❑   The basics of Windows Forms

❑   MDI forms

❑   Menus

❑   Predefined controls

❑   Data Binding

❑   Getting input from the user

❑   Drawing in .NET using GDI+

❑   Printing

❑   Building your own custom controls

❑   Deploying your Windows Forms application

If you're a Visual Basic programmer or an MFC programmer you will find some aspects of Windows forms programming familiar. Other parts will be new and exciting. VB features that MFC developers have been hoping for and vice versa have been combined in Visual Studio .NET, and are now available for everyone to use.

Windows Applications and .NET

So just exactly what does .NET have to offer a developer for creating Windows-based applications? We can start with the Forms Designer. This is actually part of Visual Studio .NET and not part of the .NET Framework itself, but we'll include it anyway. VB developers in particular will feel at home with the VS Forms Designer. It allows drag-and-drop form design in a very similar way to what we have been used to all these years.

The `System.Windows.Forms` namespace contains many classes that facilitate the creation and management of Windows applications. There are classes for creating the form itself and controlling its appearance and behavior. The `Form` class represents what a VB developer would call a form, and what an MFC or C developer would call a window. The two terms will be used interchangeably in this book. The `Application` class controls the application by handling much of the interaction with the Windows operating system, starting and stopping the application, and so on.

The .NET Framework ships with a number of controls for use in Windows applications, similar to the Windows Common Controls libraries we're already familiar with. All of these controls are classes in the `Windows.Forms` namespace; this allows us to inherit from these classes and extend them, adding our own functionality or overriding default behavior. The controls provided by Microsoft with the .NET Framework include the `TextBox`, `ListBox`, `ToolBar`, `GroupBox`, `ImageList`, and so on. These controls are built from the ground up to support the .NET Framework. This is what makes it easy for us to inherit from them. Since all of the controls derive from the same class hierarchy, they all have a very similar and consistent programming model.

If we want to create our own control from scratch, we can still take advantage of the control class hierarchy. This is the same class hierarchy that the included controls use, so we will be able to give our controls the same level of functionality as the included controls. We will look at some of the most widely used of the included controls in Chapter 3, and at creating our own customer controls in Chapter 8.

Another new feature is **visual inheritance**. Since all forms are really nothing more than classes themselves, it would make sense that we can inherit from them. This feature gives us the ability to develop a framework for our applications. We can develop a base form with the functionality and visual style that we want every form of the application to have, and then use this form as the base class for the other forms in the application. When we start a new form in the designer, the base form's controls will automatically be placed on the form. This allows us to give our users a consistent look and feel, and the other developers in our group a consistent interface to code against.

The event model in the .NET Framework is very powerful and flexible. One of the big drawbacks to VB programming is that the events were wired up as soon as the control or form was instantiated. In .NET, we can control when the events get wired up. This means we can wait until a certain condition is met before we hook up the event handlers to a button or to the click event of a grid control. The ability to get several controls to use the same event handler can also simplify quite a bit of code. We can also get a single event to call several different event handlers.

How it Used to be Done

One of the most successful and most widely read books in the Windows programming field would have to be *Programming Windows* by Charles Petzold (Microsoft Press). It is currently in its fifth edition and has been around since 1988. The Petzold style of programming has been used by developers since that first edition hit the bookshelves. In a moment, we will take a quick look at the Petzold style of programming so that we may see how .NET has evolved. If you have developed Windows applications using C or C++ using the Petzold style, you probably will want to skip this section. However, if you are a VB programmer, you will want to stick around. Understanding how a Window is created and how messages are processed will make you a better Windows developer, even in the brave new world of .NET.

Messages, Handles, and Windows

Before we get any further into the world of messages and handles, let's take a moment to explain what exactly messages and handles are.

Windows applications are event-driven. This means that a Windows application will wait for the system to deliver input; the application will then react to the input and return control back to the system. The system and the application communicate via **Windows messages**. Whenever the user moves the mouse, or when keyboard strokes are entered, the system sends messages to the application. The application has a special function (called the **window procedure**) to process the messages received in order to react to user input. This function is traditionally named WndProc(), although it doesn't have to be called this. However, user interaction isn't the only thing that can create messages for an application to process. Another example would be power management. A message is sent to all open applications just before a system goes into sleep mode. If an application is not ready to go into sleep mode, it can send a message back to the system that says, "Do not go into sleep mode at this time."

There are two types of message routing. One is to send the message to a first-in first-out queue called the message queue. There is a system message queue and a thread-specific queue for each user interface thread that is created. When the user moves the mouse, the associated message is placed in the system message queue. The system examines the message to determine which window is supposed to process the message, and then sends the message to the proper queue. The window's message queue then examines the message and tells the system to send it to the window's WndProc() function for processing. Mouse and keyboard messages are examples of queued messages. The other way for messages to be routed is for the system to send the message directly to the window procedure. Non-queued messages are usually sent to notify the window of an event that directly affects the window. Messages such as resizing and window activation messages would be sent as non-queued messages.

Each application may be made up of several forms or windows. Each window will have a window procedure to process the messages sent to it. The window procedure will examine each message and determine what needs to be done with the message. The process that sends the messages to the window procedure is known as the message pump. The message pump resides in the WinMain() function, which is the entry point of the application (similar to the Main() method in C#). We will look at this function in detail later in the chapter. Some messages are ignored completely; others are acted upon. There are two types of messages, system-defined and application-defined. System-defined messages are predefined messages that the system generates. Application-defined messages are, of course, defined by the application. In order to identify the message, four parameters are sent with it. They are:

❑   Window handle

❑   Message identifier

❑   Two message parameter values generally know as `lParam` and `wParam`

The window handle is a long value that is used to identify a specific window to the system. Every window that is created has a handle associated with it. This handle is sometimes referred to as the `hWnd`. The `hWnd` is generated by the system when the window is created, and stays constant as long as the window is not destroyed. The handle sent by the message is the handle of the window that the message is intended for.

The message identifier is a named constant that identifies what the message is. A common message that is dealt with is the `WM_PAINT` message. This is a system-defined message that tells the window that it needs to repaint itself. System-defined messages are divided into 30 different categories. Each category is defined by the two- or three-character prefix of the message. In the case of the `WM_PAINT` message, `WM` means general windows message. Other categories include `EM` for edit control, `CDM` for common dialog box and `TCM` for tab control. Each message identifier has a corresponding symbolic identifier that is defined in the Windows SDK.

The two message parameters `lParam` and `wParam` can contain almost anything. They could contain bit flags, integer values, object references, structure references, references to callback functions, and so on. If a message does not use either parameter, it is generally set to `null`.

This will start to make more sense if we take a look at a very simple example. Below is the listing for a very basic Windows application in the Petzold API-style of C programming (notice that I said C, not C++):

```c
#include <windows.h>

long FAR PASCAL WndProc (HWND, unsigned int, unsigned int, LONG);

int WINAPI WinMain(HINSTANCE hInstance, HINSTANCE hPrevInstance,
                LPSTR lpszCmdLine, int nCmdShow)
{
    static char szAppName[] = "Welcome2";
    HWND        hWnd;
    MSG         msg;
    WNDCLASS    wndclass;

    if (!hPrevInstance)
    {
        wndclass.style          = CS_HREDRAW | CS_VREDRAW;
        wndclass.lpfnWndProc    = WndProc;
        wndclass.cbClsExtra     = 0;
        wndclass.cbWndExtra     = 0;
        wndclass.hInstance      = hInstance;
        wndclass.hIcon          = LoadIcon(NULL, IDI_APPLICATION);
        wndclass.hCursor        = LoadCursor(NULL, IDC_ARROW);
        wndclass.hbrBackground  = static_cast<HBRUSH>
                                        (GetStockObject(WHITE_BRUSH));
        wndclass.lpszMenuName   = NULL;
        wndclass.lpszClassName  = szAppName;
```

```
    if (!RegisterClass (&wndclass))
            return FALSE;
    }

    hWnd = CreateWindow (szAppName,           /* window class             */
                    "Welcome to Windows",     /* window caption           */
                    WS_OVERLAPPEDWINDOW,      /* window style             */
                    CW_USEDEFAULT,            /* initial x position       */
                    0,                        /* initial y position       */
                    CW_USEDEFAULT,            /* initial x size           */
                    0,                        /* initial y size           */
                    NULL,                     /* parent window handle     */
                    NULL,                     /* window menu handle       */
                    hInstance,                /* program instance handle  */
                    NULL);                    /* create parameters        */

    ShowWindow (hWnd, nCmdShow);
    UpdateWindow (hWnd);

    while (GetMessage (&msg, NULL, 0, 0))
    {
        TranslateMessage (&msg);
        DispatchMessage (&msg);
    }

    return msg.wParam ;
}

long FAR PASCAL WndProc (HWND hWnd, unsigned int iMessage,
                        unsigned int wParam, LONG lParam)
{
    switch (iMessage)
    {
        case WM_DESTROY:
            PostQuitMessage(0);
            break;
        default:
            return DefWindowProc(hWnd, iMessage, wParam, lParam);
    }

    return 0L;
}
```

Bear in mind that this application does nothing but show a window. If you use Visual Studio .NET and create a new Win32 project in C++, you will end up with something similar. It will be a little more complex because of additional wizard-generated code, but if you look closely at it, you will see it is essentially the same code.

Let's take a look at what is going on in all of this mess so that we can have a better understanding of what makes up a window.

Every Windows application needs an entry point. In C# that entry point is the Main() function. It has the syntax of static void Main(string[] args). In a Petzold-style application, the entry point was called WinMain(). WinMain() takes four parameters; the first two are handles to the current instance and to a previous instance of the application, which is always null. The third parameter is a pointer to the command-line string, minus the program name. This will contain any additional parameters that were entered when starting the application. The last parameter is an integer that specifies how the window will be shown. This parameter corresponds approximately to the WindowState property of the Form class. Choices here include minimized, maximized, hide, and normal.

WinMain() is responsible for accomplishing three tasks. The first is to initialize the application; the next is to create the application's main window, and the final task is to start the message pump for the application. Initialization could be a number of things. Items such as reading configuration or .ini file information, opening files, establishing network connections and so on. In our sample application there really weren't any special initialization tasks.

The next two tasks are the ones that we will be looking closely at. For each of the Windows API functions and structures we will look at, we will look at only a few of the parameters. All of the calls that are made in this code snippet are fully documented in MSDN. The first task is creating the main window. The process for creating a window is a three-step process. The first step is to fill in a WNDCLASS structure. The instance of WNDCLASS in our example is called wndclass.

```
wndclass.style         = CS_HREDRAW | CS_VREDRAW;
wndclass.lpfnWndProc   = WndProc;
wndclass.cbClsExtra    = 0;
wndclass.cbWndExtra    = 0;
wndclass.hInstance     = hInstance;
wndclass.hIcon         = LoadIcon(NULL, IDI_APPLICATION);
wndclass.hCursor       = LoadCursor(NULL, IDC_ARROW);
wndclass.hbrBackground = static_cast<HBRUSH>
                                   (GetStockObject(WHITE_BRUSH));
wndclass.lpszMenuName  = NULL;
wndclass.lpszClassName = szAppName;
```

This structure includes items such as the name of the window procedure (we'll look at this later), the class name of the window, the icon for the window, the cursor to use, the menu name and the style of the window. There is a list of a dozen or so styles that can be applied. Multiple styles can be applied by ORing the styles together. In the examples above, the CS_HREDRAW and CS_VREDRAW styles are combined. This indicates that whenever the window is resized either horizontally or vertically, the complete window will need to be redrawn.

Once the WNDCLASS structure is populated, we register the window's class:

```
if (!RegisterClass (&wndclass))
    return FALSE;
```

This is a different process from what you might expect from the term "registering the class". Every window that is created belongs to a class of windows that share similar attributes. This is what is meant by windows being of the same class. Windows that are in the same class share a common window procedure. For example, all windows that belong to the Edit class (edit boxes) all share the same window procedure. When we register a new window, we are creating a new window class and telling Windows that we want the new window that we are about to create to belong to this class. Any window we create that has the same class name will also use the same window procedure as this window. This is done with the `RegisterClass()` API function. `RegisterClass()` takes a single parameter, the `WNDCLASS` structure we just filled out. Once the window class has been registered, we can call the `CreateWindow()` function. `CreateWindow()` takes eleven parameters:

```
hWnd = CreateWindow (szAppName,            /* window class           */
                "Welcome to Windows",      /* window caption         */
                WS_OVERLAPPEDWINDOW,       /* window style           */
                CW_USEDEFAULT,             /* initial x position     */
                0,                         /* initial y position     */
                CW_USEDEFAULT,             /* initial x size         */
                0,                         /* initial y size         */
                NULL,                      /* parent window handle   */
                NULL,                      /* window menu handle      */
                hInstance,                 /* program instance handle */
                NULL);                     /* create parameters      */
```

The first parameter is the name of the window class that we just registered. The other parameters are items such as the text in the title bar, the start up position's x and y coordinates, the height and width of the window, and a style parameter, which specifies how the window will look. These styles determine the basic behavior of the window, such as whether the control box and the min and max buttons appear on the window, the border style, whether it is a child window, and so on. Again, the styles can be ORed together. It is also important to note that this style is different from the style that we used in the `WNDCLASS` structure. The styles in the `CreateWindow()` function are related to the visual appearance of the window. Most of these style settings are properties of the `Form` class. If you're a VB programmer you will also notice that these are properties on a VB form as well. Now you can see how VB is hiding the complexity from you. The return value of `CreateWindow()` is the `hWnd` or handle of the window. This is another property that you may have seen before. It should be noted that `CreateWindow()` does not actually show the window. You will also need to call `ShowWindow()` for the window to be painted on the screen.

```
ShowWindow (hWnd, nCmdShow);
UpdateWindow (hWnd);
```

The `UpdateWindow()` function sends a `WM_PAINT` message to the window with the specified `hWnd` (window handle). This makes sure that the window is updated.

After the window is created and displayed on the screen, `WinMain()` starts into what is the most important step, and that is to start message processing. Remember that we discussed the message pump and message queues earlier in the chapter. This is an example of what the message pump code will look like:

```
while (GetMessage (&msg, NULL, 0, 0))
{
```

```
      TranslateMessage (&msg);
      DispatchMessage (&msg);
   }
```

The message pump will typically have three functions called from it. It will use `GetMessage()`, `TranslateMessage()`, and `DispatchMessage()`. `GetMessage()` is responsible for retrieving the message from the queue. `DispatchMessage()`, as you may guess, is responsible for sending the message to the window procedure. `TranslateMessage()` translates virtual key messages into the proper character message. Messages such as `WM_KEYDOWN` and `WM_KEYUP` that involve input from the keyboard contain a virtual key code that represents the key pressed. The `TranslateMessage()` function generates a `WM_CHAR` message that contains the ANSI or Unicode value (as appropriate) of the pressed key. This character message is then posted back to the queue to be processed.

Now that the messages are being processed, we need to have somewhere for them to go. This is where the window procedure comes in. If you look back at the code examples, we defined the name for our window procedure in the `WNDCLASS` member `lpfnWndProc`. Typically the name of this function will be `WndProc()`. `WndProc()` is called for each message that is handled in the message pump. The structure of a `WndProc()` is generally a `switch` statement based on the message. For each message for which we want special processing to be done, we add a case in the `switch` statement. In very large applications, it would not be uncommon for this procedure to become huge with nested `switch` statements. For messages that we did not want to process ourselves, we would call `DefWindowProc()`. This is the default window procedure, and provides basic functionality for a window.

Now why are we looking at all of this C code? VB did a wonderful job of hiding this stuff from the programmer, but perhaps it actually did too good a job. Sometimes you need to be able to process certain messages. Looking back at the power management example we mentioned earlier, if your VB application needed to trap the `WM_POWER` message and respond to it, this became difficult to do without resorting to third-party controls or performing tricks with the `AddressOf` operator. Unfortunately, the `AddressOf` operator had some baggage of its own – it had a tendency to be unstable. Code that used this technique to get to the `WndProc()` (sometimes called subclassing a window) could not be debugged easily.

Windows forms in .NET also do a wonderful job of hiding this complexity. The big difference is that if we need to get down to this level of message processing, we can. In fact we can do it rather easily, without sacrificing stability or having to rely on third-party controls, since .NET has provided us with easy access to the `WndProc()` function for each Windows form that we have in our application.

Spy++

To see how messages are always flying around in Windows, there is a utility that ships with Visual Studio called Spy++. Spy++ has been around for a long time in one form or another, and shows us all of the open windows, all of the processes, and all of the threads. For each one of these items, it will also show us a detail window that can provide us with a great deal of information. It will also capture and log all of the messages for a particular window. If you have Visual Studio .NET installed, you should see Spy++ under Visual Studio .NET Tools in the Microsoft Visual Studio .NET group on the Start menu. After starting Spy++, select Spy | Log Messages (*Ctrl + M*) from the menu, and the Message Options dialog will appear:

You can set various options on this dialog box. We won't go into all of them, but most are fairly self-explanatory. The **Messages** tab allows us to specify what messages we want to log. The default is to log all messages. To start logging, grab the icon next to **Finder Tool**, drag it over a window and release it. In this example, we are using Notepad. If you move the mouse a little over the target window, you will see a flurry of messages appear in the Spy++ log window. Every action that a user takes is represented by a message. Type a few words, and you will see what each keystroke generates. Typing a single letter generates three messages in Spy++: WM_KEYDOWN, WM_KEYUP, and WM_CHAR. The WM_KEYDOWN and WM_KEYUP messages are self-explanatory; WM_CHAR is the message that the TranslateMessage() function re-posted to the queue. Here is a screen snapshot of the messages captured by typing a sentence into Notepad:

Along with the ability to handle all of these messages and react to them, it became apparent that writing sophisticated applications would become tedious very quickly. Writing WndProc() after WndProc() with monstrous switch statements would also become rather difficult to maintain and to debug. A framework was needed: something that would abstract this tedious coding. And so the Microsoft Foundation Class Library (MFC) was born.

MFC

As you may have noticed, the API-style of writing code was not very object-oriented in its design. MFC is an object-oriented library built using C++ that represents basic objects that are used to build Windows-based applications. Some of the objects include menus and windows, but the entire API for Windows is not encapsulated in MFC.

MFC is organized into a class hierarchy similar to the .NET Framework. A large majority of the classes in MFC are derived from the CObject class, just as in the .NET Framework all classes are derived from System.Object. (However, it should be noted that this is where the similarity between CObject and System.Object ends.) Along with the basic windows classes, MFC had classes for ODBC and DAO, collection classes, file services, and internet protocols. However, MFC is geared to Windows development, and is meant to be used for creating client-side Windows applications. Each release of MFC saw it grow larger and more inclusive in the functionality it provided (and, of course, more complex). However, it still does not come close to the functionality of the .NET Framework.

Now what about WndProc(), the message loop and all that other stuff we just talked about? Well, it's in there; the MFC developer just doesn't need to deal with it directly. When an MFC application is created by the App Wizard in Visual Studio, there are several things that are already done and ready to go for the developer. One of these things is something called a message map. A message map is a data structure that maps the messages to the functions that will be processing the message. For something to receive messages in MFC it needs to be derived from the CCmdTarget class. When a message is sent to a window in MFC, the MFC window procedure, CWnd::WindowProc(), searches the message map and then executes the message handler if one is defined.

Since this isn't a book on MFC programming, we won't go into any more detail on MFC, but let's just say that MFC is a popular framework, very powerful, and very complex. One of the downsides to MFC programming is that in order to be really proficient you had to really understand what all of the MFC classes were doing and how they worked. MFC was able to remove some of the tedious coding that needs to be done, but it certainly did not make writing a Windows application any easier.

Visual Basic

For ease of programming, Visual Basic (VB) is hard to beat. VB made it possible for non-programmers to actually produce working applications, and experienced developers to reach new heights of productivity. VB was one of the first development tools to make use of the visual form designer. In VB you don't have to worry about creating the WNDPROC structure and registering the class. You select New Form from the menu and set a few properties in the property grid. If you need a couple of textboxes and a button or two, just drag them from the toolbox and drop them on the form. Run the application and you had a new window. No message pumps, no CreateWindow() call, no message maps or CWnd class. All of that is hidden "behind the curtain". The developer could concentrate on writing the business logic. This is what enabled VB to make developers so productive. You didn't have to wade through all of the window plumbing code for each window and control that you created.

All of this came at a price, however. You had a difficult time getting to that plumbing if you needed to. Up until version 5 of VB there were several Windows API functions that you could not call. The reason was that the call required a function pointer as a parameter (sometimes known as a callback function). VB does not directly support pointers, so there was no way of calling the API. Version 5 added the `AddressOf` operator, so finally we could create a callback function.

VB was partly responsible for popularizing another trend in software development – the predefined control or component. Taking a set of functionality and packaging it up in an ActiveX control or COM component made developing software that much more efficient. It is what code-reuse is all about. An industry was born just supplying controls and components for VB and VC++ application development. Most were visual components, such as grid controls or list boxes. It was not until version 5 of VB that you could actually create a control using VB (before then you had to use C++). As you will see later in this book, .NET has taken control and component creation to new levels of functionality and ease of development.

We have spent a fair amount of time looking at how Windows programming was done before .NET. The list of technologies that we have discussed is by no means complete. There are Delphi and OWL from Borland and WTL and ATL from Microsoft as well as others. The point of this book is to explore how it is now done. However, in order to fully understand how .NET makes Windows forms such a powerful tool, you really need to understand how windows are created and how the messages are processed. You can create sophisticated and complex Windows applications without going to this level of detail, but you can only really take full advantage of the technology by understanding it. You will be able to use Windows forms without understanding these concepts, but the better you understand them, the more functionality you will be able to incorporate into your applications. Let's take a look at how .NET is going to provide us with this functionality.

Windows Forms Namespace

The .NET Framework isn't built with a random selection of classes and functionality. It is a huge class hierarchy where each class builds on the functionality of its parent class. The `System.Windows.Forms` namespace follows this concept. The `Form` class has the following hierarchy:

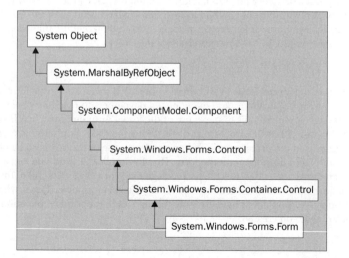

Each class inherits the functionality of its parent class. So
`System.Windows.Forms.ScrollableControl` has all of the functionality of all of the classes above it in the hierarchy. This is an important concept to understand, and it becomes particularly important when you design your own controls. You will see how this works in a later chapter. This diagram only shows the direct inheritance chain for the `Form` and `UserControl` classes. `ComonentModel.Component`, for example, is the base class for over 40 classes. Let's take a look at each of the classes in the hierarchy and discuss what functionality is included in the class.

System.Object

This is the root of all classes in .NET. Every class in .NET is derived from `Object`.

System.MarshalByRefObject

This class is important when you need to talk to another window that is not in the same application domain. An application domain is something that the Common Language Runtime (CLR) uses to isolate applications. This allows applications to have different security contexts, and if one application causes an exception, other applications will not be affected by it. We'll discuss application domains in a bit more detail in Chapter 9. If an object derives from `MarshalByRefObject` (or from a class that is derived from it), it can communicate with another application domain by way of a proxy. This means that only the request and result are actually passed between the application domains; otherwise, a complete copy of the object would be created and passed to the other application domain. This becomes an issue when the other application domain is on a different computer and the objects need to be copied across the wire – it is much more efficient just to send the request and the result, rather than sending the complete object back and forth across the wire.

System.ComponentModel.Component

The `Component` class is the base class for all components and controls. A component is a class that can be placed on a design surface; however, it does not have a visual representation. An example would be the `Timer` component (we'll look at this in Chapter 3). The `Component` class is mainly responsible for the communication between a component and the component's container. `Component` implements the `IComponent` interface. `IComponent` has a `Site` property that will return an `ISite` object. Objects that implement the `ISite` interface manage the communication between a component and the container.

System.Windows.Forms.Control

A control is a component with a visual representation. Textboxes, buttons, and listboxes are examples of controls. The `Control` class implements the base functionality to display information and to handle user input, typically through a keyboard and pointing device (such as a mouse). One interface that is implemented by `Control` is `IWin32Window`. It has one property – the `Handle` property, which returns the handle for the window. This is the hWnd that we created earlier in the chapter. If you're wondering – yes, this does mean that all controls are windows that are created in exactly the same way we discussed earlier in the chapter. Another interesting method is the `WndProc()` method. `WndProc()` takes a `Message` structure that represents a Windows message as a parameter. This is the window procedure for this particular window instance. Notice that you didn't have to do anything to create this method. It is available for the developer to override and use if the functionality is needed. We can override `WndProc()` if we want to handle Windows messages ourselves, so we can still write Petzold-style code if we want to process a message that can't be processed by more conventional .NET methods:

```
protected override void WndProc(ref Message m)
{
    switch (m.Msg)
    {
        case 0x0010:
            // Process WM_CLOSE message
            break;
        case 0x0048:
            // Process WM_POWER message
            break;
    }

    // Call WndProc() on the control's parent for default message handling
    base.WndProc(ref m);
}
```

System.Windows.Forms.ScrollableControl

This class adds scrolling capabilities. Typically, you would not inherit directly from this class but from one of its derived classes, `ComponentTray`, `Panel`, or the next one we will look at – `ContainerControl`.

System.Windows.Forms.ContainerControl

This enables a control to act as a container for other controls. The container control provides a boundary for the child controls in the container's `Controls` collection. The boundary is the screen region that the control is contained in.

System.Windows.Forms.Form

Finally, we come to the `Form` class itself. The `Form` class represents a window in your application. Instead of creating the WNDCLASS structure, or setting the parameters to a `CreateWindow()` call, we create an instance of a `Form` class, set a few properties, and call the `Show()` method of the form. We can use the Form Designer in Visual Studio .NET to create the form, but – as we'll see shortly – we can also create the source code for the `Form` class without the designer.

Notice that `Form` is derived from the same class as all of the controls that you will be using with `Form`. `Textbox` and `Button` both derive from `Control`, just as `Form` does. Understanding this relationship will help you design better controls and components of your own – knowing which class to inherit from and understanding what each class offers in functionality will make the controls that you design more flexible and robust.

Point and Size Structures

There are a few structures that will be used with almost every form that you create. The two most important ones are `Size` and `Point`. Both `Size` and `Point` are in the `System.Drawing` namespace. `Size` represents the size of a control or form. The `Size` structure's two important properties are `Height` and `Width`. These are both `int` values, but if you need `float` values, you can use the `SizeF` structure. It provides the same functionality, but uses `float`s instead of `int`s. There are a couple of methods in `Size` that will help in converting a `SizeF` to a `Size` if needed. `Ceiling()` and `Round()` will convert by either rounding to the nearest integer (`Round()`) or by rounding up to the next higher integer (`Ceiling()`).

The + and − operators have been overloaded so that you can easily add to or subtract from Size structures and return a new Size structure. The == and != operators have also been overloaded to compare two Size structures.

The other important structure is the Point structure. Point is used to represent the location of a control. It works in a very similar way to Size, except that instead of Height and Width, it has X and Y properties, which represent the top left corner of the control or form. Otherwise, it is very much like the Size structure, and also has the +, −, == and != operators overloaded.

Form Creation Without Visual Studio .NET

Visual Studio .NET is a great tool, and it can greatly increase the productivity of developers who use it. However, there is no requirement that you develop your applications using Visual Studio .NET. The .NET SDK, which you can download from Microsoft's web site, is free, and it contains command-line compilers for C# and Visual Basic .NET. These compilers, together with a good code editor, will allow you to develop any application that you can in Visual Studio .NET. In fact, most of the commercially available programmer's editors now include C# support. There is also a small market for specialized C# editors appearing. Some of the best known of these third-party editors are:

- ❑ CodeWright (http://www.starbase.com/products/CodeWright/)

- ❑ SharpDevelop (http://www.icsharpcode.net/OpenSource/SD/)

- ❑ Antechinus (http://www.c-point.com/csharp.htm)

- ❑ JEdit (http://www.jedit.org/)

We are going to create a very simple Windows application that will contain one form. The form will contain one textbox and one button. The source for this example is in the WinFormNonVS subfolder under the Chapter01 folder in the downloadable code. This code can be entered in any simple text editor; in the next section we will see how to compile from the command line and execute this application.

Here is the source code (we have named the file frmLogin.cs), although you could name it anything you wish:

```
using System;
using System.Drawing;
using System.ComponentModel;
using System.Windows.Forms;

namespace Wrox.7663.Chapter01.WinFormNonVS
{
    public class frmLogin : Form
    {
        System.Windows.Forms.TextBox txtUser;
        System.Windows.Forms.Button btnOK;
        System.Windows.Forms.Button btnCancel;

        public frmLogin()
        {
```

```
txtUser = new System.Windows.Forms.TextBox();
        txtUser.Location = new Point(30, 15);
        txtUser.Size = new Size(250, 20);
        txtUser.Text = "";
        txtUser.Name = "txtUser";
        this.Controls.Add(txtUser);

        btnOK = new System.Windows.Forms.Button();
        btnOK.Location = new Point(40,
            (txtUser.Location.Y + txtUser.Size.Height + btnOK.Size.Height));
        btnOK.Text="OK";
        btnOK.Name="btnOK";
        this.Controls.Add(btnOK);

        btnCancel = new System.Windows.Forms.Button();
        btnCancel.Location = new Point((this.Size.Width -
                                    btnCancel.Size.Width) - 40,
            (txtUser.Location.Y + txtUser.Size.Height + btnOK.Size.Height));
        btnCancel.Text = "Cancel";
        btnCancel.Name = "btnCancel";
        this.Controls.Add(btnCancel);

        this.Size = new Size(this.Size.Width, btnCancel.Location.Y +
                            btnCancel.Size.Height + 60);

        btnCancel.Click += new System.EventHandler(btnCancelHandler);
        btnOK.Click += new System.EventHandler(btnEventHandler);
    }

    private void btnEventHandler(object sender, System.EventArgs e)
    {
        MessageBox.Show(((Button)sender).Name);
    }

    private void btnCancelHandler(object sender, System.EventArgs e)
    {
        MessageBox.Show("The second handler");
    }

    [STAThread]
    static void Main()
    {
        Application.Run(new frmLogin());
    }
  }
}
```

In this example, all of the initialization happens in the form's constructor. This really isn't the best pattern to use – the better design would be to create a method much like the InitializeComponent() method that Visual Studio .NET creates for us, and then call it from the form's constructor. We will see how this looks in the next example.

If you have ever looked at the code in `InitializeComponent()` from a project created in Visual Studio .NET, and now look at the code in the constructor, you can see that they look similar. The reason is simple – this is what needs to happen to initialize the controls. The only difference that needs to be pointed out is that Visual Studio .NET puts in absolute `Size` and `Location` numbers. For example, as we will see in the next example, the size and location properties for the password textbox are set like this:

```
this.txtPassword.Location = new System.Drawing.Point(128, 56);
this.txtPassword.Size = new System.Drawing.Size(128, 20);
```

In this non-VS example, we use a relative method of sizing and location. This means that the size and location of the controls is relative to either another control or to the form itself. Take a look at how the `btnOK` button is located in this example:

```
btnOK.Location = new Point(40,
             (txtUser.Location.Y+txtUser.Size.Height + btnOK.Size.Height));
```

Notice that the location is relative to the `txtUser`. One reason for doing this is that since you don't have a designer to draw the form, there is a lot of trial and error involved in making the form look well designed. If the size and position of controls are based on those of other controls, then making a change to one control will have the effect of changing other controls. For example, if we change the location of `txtUser`, the location of `btnOK` will change as well.

Compiling Windows Applications from the Command Line

Now that we have the source already to go, how do we generate the compiled code? The C# command-line compiler is called `csc.exe` and it is located in the Windows\Microsoft.NET\Framework\v1.0.3705 folder. v1.0.3705 is the version number of the first release of the Framework.

There are several parameters that we can use with the compiler. We won't go into the complete list here, but I do suggest looking at the documentation so that you may become familiar with them. The only one that we will concern ourselves with is the `/target` or `/t` parameter. This informs the compiler what format to use in the compiled file. The options are:

❑ `/target:exe`. This creates a console application. Whenever this application starts, a command window will open for the duration of the application, even if it's a form-based application.

❑ `/target:library`. This will create a DLL. This would be what you would use for a control or class library, for example.

❑ `/target:module`. This creates a module that can be used in a multi-file assembly.

❑ `/target:winexe`. This creates a Windows application.

Here we use the `/target:winexe` option. The complete command used to create the `frmLogin` example would be:

```
csc.exe /target:winexe frmLogin.cs
```

The output of this will be an executable named `frmLogin.exe`. When you run this EXE, you should see a simple form with two buttons and a textbox:

If you click on either button, the event handler will execute, and a message box will appear telling you which button you pressed.

Creating a Form in Visual Studio .NET

We have seen how to create a very simple Windows application using a text editor and the command-line compiler, so now let's take a look at simple application created using Visual Studio .NET. We will see what code the designer implements for us, and what we have to do to add functionality.

Our example is going to be of a simple login form. It will accept a user name and a password. When the OK button is pressed, we will show a message box with the user name and password. The code for this example is located in the example download in the **Chapter01\WinFormVS** folder. This is what the application will look like when finished:

To create this project yourself, follow these steps:

❑ Create a new C# Windows Application. You can name it anything you wish, but we've called this example **WinFormVS**.

❑ Add two labels, two textboxes, and two buttons by dragging them from the toolbox onto the form.

❑ Change the names of all of the controls. In our example, we've called the textboxes `txtUserName` and `txtPassword`; the labels `lblUserName` and `lblPassword`; and the buttons `btnOK` and `btnCancel`. You should also set the `PasswordChar` property of `txtPassword` to '#'.

❑　Add the code to show the message box in the **OK** button's `Click` event. The easiest way to set up the event handler is to double-click on the button in the Form Designer. This will automatically set up the method definition for the event handler. We just need to add the code to the body. For the `btnOK` event handler, add the line:

```
MessageBox.Show(txtUserName.Text + " - " + txtPassword.Text);
```

and for the `btnCancel` handler:

```
Application.Exit();
```

Here is the complete source for the login example (the comments added by VS.NET have been removed to save space):

```
using System;
using System.Drawing;
using System.Collections;
using System.ComponentModel;
using System.Windows.Forms;
using System.Data;

namespace WinFormVS
{
    public class frmLogin : System.Windows.Forms.Form
    {
        private System.Windows.Forms.Label lblUserName;
        private System.Windows.Forms.Label lblPassword;
        private System.Windows.Forms.TextBox txtUserName;
        private System.Windows.Forms.TextBox txtPassword;
        private System.Windows.Forms.Button btnOK;
        private System.Windows.Forms.Button btnCancel;
        private System.ComponentModel.Container components = null;

        public frmLogin()
        {
            InitializeComponent();
        }

        protected override void Dispose( bool disposing )
        {
            if (disposing)
            {
                if (components != null)
                {
                    components.Dispose();
                }
            }
            base.Dispose(disposing);
        }

        #region Windows Form Designer generated code
```

```
private void InitializeComponent()
{
    this.lblUserName = new System.Windows.Forms.Label();
    this.lblPassword = new System.Windows.Forms.Label();
    this.txtUserName = new System.Windows.Forms.TextBox();
    this.txtPassword = new System.Windows.Forms.TextBox();
    this.btnOK = new System.Windows.Forms.Button();
    this.btnCancel = new System.Windows.Forms.Button();
    this.SuspendLayout();

    this.lblUserName.Location = new System.Drawing.Point(24, 16);
    this.lblUserName.Name = "lblUserName";
    this.lblUserName.TabIndex = 0;
    this.lblUserName.Text = "User Name:";
    this.lblUserName.TextAlign =
                        System.Drawing.ContentAlignment.MiddleRight;

    this.lblPassword.Location = new System.Drawing.Point(24, 56);
    this.lblPassword.Name = "lblPassword";
    this.lblPassword.TabIndex = 1;
    this.lblPassword.Text = "Password:";
    this.lblPassword.TextAlign =
                        System.Drawing.ContentAlignment.MiddleRight;

    this.txtUserName.Location = new System.Drawing.Point(128, 16);
    this.txtUserName.Name = "txtUserName";
    this.txtUserName.Size = new System.Drawing.Size(128, 20);
    this.txtUserName.TabIndex = 2;
    this.txtUserName.Text = "";

    this.txtPassword.Location = new System.Drawing.Point(128, 56);
    this.txtPassword.Name = "txtPassword";
    this.txtPassword.PasswordChar = '#';
    this.txtPassword.Size = new System.Drawing.Size(128, 20);
    this.txtPassword.TabIndex = 3;
    this.txtPassword.Text = "";

    this.btnOK.DialogResult = System.Windows.Forms.DialogResult.OK;
    this.btnOK.Location = new System.Drawing.Point(56, 112);
    this.btnOK.Name = "btnOK";
    this.btnOK.TabIndex = 4;
    this.btnOK.Text = "OK";
    this.btnOK.Click += new System.EventHandler(this.btnOK_Click);

    this.btnCancel.DialogResult =
                        System.Windows.Forms.DialogResult.Cancel;
    this.btnCancel.Location = new System.Drawing.Point(160, 112);
    this.btnCancel.Name = "btnCancel";
    this.btnCancel.TabIndex = 5;
    this.btnCancel.Text = "Cancel";
    this.btnCancel.Click += new
                        System.EventHandler(this.btnCancel_Click);

    this.AcceptButton = this.btnOK;
```

```
        this.AutoScaleBaseSize = new System.Drawing.Size(5, 13);
        this.CancelButton = this.btnCancel;
        this.ClientSize = new System.Drawing.Size(280, 163);
        this.Controls.AddRange(new System.Windows.Forms.Control[] {
                                            this.btnCancel,
                                            this.btnOK,
                                            this.txtPassword,
                                            this.txtUserName,
                                            this.lblPassword,
                                            this.lblUserName});
        this.Name = "frmLogin";
        this.Text = "Login";
        this.ResumeLayout(false);
    }
    #endregion

    [STAThread]
    static void Main()
    {
        Application.Run(new frmLogin());
    }

    private void btnOK_Click(object sender, System.EventArgs e)
    {
        MessageBox.Show(txtUserName.Text + " - " + txtPassword.Text);
    }

    private void btnCancel_Click(object sender, System.EventArgs e)
    {
        Application.Exit();
    }
    }
}
```

Now there is a fair amount of code here, but we actually only added two lines ourselves (the two highlighted lines). The rest was created by the Form Designer. Let's take a close look at the code that is generated. At the very start are the using directives. The default for Visual Studio .NET is to import the System, System.Drawing, System.Collections, System.ComponentModel, System.Windows.Forms, and System.Data namespaces. We are not using anything from some of these namespaces, but it doesn't hurt to keep the using statements. The compiler resolves these names at compile time, so neither the size nor the performance of the application is affected by retaining the using directives that are not used.

The next thing in the code is the namespace declaration. In this case, we have left the default generated by VS.NET: namespace WinFormVS. The default namespace on a new project is the project name; however, this can be changed on the **Properties** window for the project to anything you wish. You need to think carefully about namespace names when you start dealing with larger projects, as namespaces can be very beneficial in organizing a project. Thinking this through up-front will save some headaches, as you get farther into the project. Next comes the class declaration. We have named the class frmLogin. Notice that we are inheriting from System.Windows.Forms.Form. If we didn't add a single thing, we would still have all of the functionality implemented in the Form class, since we inherit from it.

Next come the field declarations. Here we declare variables for all of the controls that we add to the form. Notice that they are all declared as `private`:

```
private System.Windows.Forms.Label lblUserName;
private System.Windows.Forms.Label lblPassword;
private System.Windows.Forms.TextBox txtUserName;
private System.Windows.Forms.TextBox txtPassword;
private System.Windows.Forms.Button btnOK;
private System.Windows.Forms.Button btnCancel;
```

Why point this out? Well if you're a VB programmer, it's very likely that you have referred to a control on another form or window to get some property value or to call a method. You were able to do this since the controls were public in a VB form. This won't work any more unless you change the access level for the control. The easy way would be to change the declaration to `public`, or maybe `internal`. This may be the easy way, but it is certainly not the correct way. Good object-oriented principles dictate that we make something public only if it needs to be. By making the control public, we not only expose the property or method that we need, but we also expose the entire control and all of its methods and properties. The better way to do this would be to add a property to our form that exposes only the property or method that we are interested in. For example, if we wanted to have read access to the `txtUserName.Text` property in our example, we should create a property called `UserNameText`. It would look something like this:

```
public string UserNameText
{
    get { return txtUserName.Text; }
}
```

If we needed to be able to write to the property, we could add the `set` accessor as well.

The following line of code is interesting in that if you look carefully at the rest of the code, `components` is never used, except within the `Dispose()` method. So we create a `Container` object, never use it for anything, and then dispose of it. It does serve a purpose; just not in our example.

```
private System.ComponentModel.Container components = null;
```

If we were to add a component to our form, the component would be added to the `components` container. Notice that in the `Dispose()` method there is a check to see if `components != null`. If it doesn't, `components.Dispose()` is called. This will ensure that all of the components on your form will be disposed of properly.

The class constructor comes next. Since forms are classes in .NET, they come with constructors like any other class. In addition, constructors can of course have parameters. VB programmers had no way to pass in parameters when we instantiated an object – in order to seed any values in a form, we first had to create the form and then set individual properties. Now we can pass in parameters to the constructor when we instantiate the form. Suppose we want to pass in a default username to fill in the textbox so the user doesn't have to type it in. We could add the parameter to the current constructor:

```
public frmLogin(string UserName)
{
    InitializeComponent();
    txtUserName.Text = UserName;
}
```

The problem with this is that we would always have to supply a parameter when we created this form. A better solution would be to create an overload of the constructor and pass the parameter in there. This constructor will call the parameterless constructor and set the `Text` property of the **User Name** textbox:

```
public frmLogin(string UserName) : this()
{
    txtUserName.Text = UserName;
}

public frmLogin()
{
    InitializeComponent();
}
```

Now we have two different constructors that we can use to create the form. If we have a username to pass in, we can use the new constructor that we created, or we can use the default constructor that takes no parameters. Notice that the parameterless constructor is called before the parameterized one, so the code to update the **User Name** textbox is executed after the call to `IntializeComponent()`.

`InitializeComponent()` is the main initialization process for the form. It is very important that you never add code to it, since the designer can rewrite this code at any time. If it does this, your changes will be lost, so the best thing is to just stay out. If you refer to any of your controls in the constructor, you also need to wait until after this method has executed. You can also see that `InitializeComponent()` is wrapped up in a `#region` called "**Windows Form Designer generated code**". Regions are new to Visual Studio .NET, and allow us to mark off sections of code and collapse them so that only the region name is displayed. By default, this section of code is collapsed.

The first thing that happens in `InitializeComponent()` is that all of the controls are actually instantiated with the `new` keyword, so we now have newly created and functioning controls. The next line after the controls are created is `this.SuspendLayout()`. This method suppresses the `Layout` event from firing for the controls on the form. The `InitializeComponent()` method changes the size and location of every control that we have added, and each of these changes causes the `Layout` event to be raised. This would cause the form to be redrawn, but we can suppress these events by calling `SuspendLayout()`. We then call `ResumeLayout()` when we've finished laying out the controls, and one event will be raised at the end of the initialization process for all of the controls. Notice that we call **this**.`SuspendLayout()`; this means that `SuspendLayout()` is being called for the form (`this`). This causes the suppression of the `Layout` event for all child controls added to or modified on the form.

After the `SuspendLayout()` method is called, there are several sections in the code, one section for each control on the form. If we go back and change a property on any control, that property change will be reflected in this section. For example, if we look at the `txtPassword` section, there is the line:

```
this.txtPassword.PasswordChar = '#';
```

This line sets the password character property to `'#'`. This is what will display on the textbox when the user types in their password. If you go back to the designer, look in the property grid for the **Password Character** property and set it to `'*'`, and then look back at the code, you will see that this line of code has changed to reflect the change you made in the property grid. Any property that is not set to its default value will be added to this section for each control.

Another line of code that may be of interest is in the btnOK and btnCancel sections. This is where you will see the event delegates added:

```
this.btnOK.Click += new System.EventHandler(this.btnOK_Click);
```

This line of code adds the System.EventHandler delegate to the btnOk.Click event handler. In this case the delegate points to this.btnOK_Click. This is the name of a method in the frmLogin class that will be executed when the btnOK button is clicked. Note that you can have more than one event point to the same function, and you can add more than one handler to the event as well. This offers you a great deal of flexibility on how you handle events. This is another big step up for the VB programmer.

This brings us to the final sections in InitializeComponent(). This line of code is one of the more important ones in the section:

```
this.Controls.AddRange(new System.Windows.Forms.Control[] {
                                        this.btnCancel,
                                        this.btnOK,
                                        this.txtPassword,
                                        this.txtUserName,
                                        this.lblPassword,
                                        this.lblUserName });
```

This line adds the controls that we have just created to the form's control array. By doing this, we establish the parent-child relationship between the controls and the form.

The final few lines in the InitializeComponent() set a couple of properties for the form and then call the ResumeLayout() method. The false parameter indicates whether to execute any pending layout requests. In this case we are saying that we do not want to execute the requests.

The rest of the code in the form consists simply of the two event handlers that were created when we added the Click events to the two buttons. The other section of code is just the main entry point into the application:

```
[STAThread]
static void Main()
{
    Application.Run(new frmLogin());
}
```

Since there is only one form (window) in our example, we need to have an entry point. This is not the form's entry point, but the application's entry point – the Main() method that is the starting point for every C# application. The [STAThread] attribute sets the threading model to apartment threading. Windows forms-based applications will always run in a single-threaded apartment. The Application.Run() method is responsible for starting the message pump for the current thread. We'll look a bit more at this method in the next chapter.

Most of the forms that you will create using Visual Studio .NET will look very similar to this in structure. The `InitializeComponent()` method could become very large if you have a lot of controls on a form. By default, you won't even see this code since it is wrapped up in a region. Remember that the code in `IntializeComponent()` should never be edited. You will risk the loss of any changes that you do in this section since the Form Designer rewrites this code on occasion. The better pattern to use is to create your own initialization method and call it immediately after `InitilizeComponents()` in the form constructor. Be sure to call it *after* `InitilizeComponents()`, or you won't have any controls instantiated to modify!

Summary

This chapter provided a very quick look at what the .NET Framework has to offer for developing Windows-based applications. There is a definite move back to rich-client applications, and .NET makes developing them easy and yet highly functional. The important thing to remember as you go through the rest of this book is how all of the classes in the `Windows.Forms` namespace relate to each other. Understanding this relationship will in turn make it easier for you to extend the functionality of any given component or control. It is fundamental to creating your own controls from scratch.

The rest of this book will show you how to create your own controls and components. You will see how data binding works and how you can take advantage of it. The controls that come already defined in the `Windows.Forms` namespace will be explained, along with their public properties and methods. Since you are able to extend any of the controls in the framework, understanding what a particular control does is essential to creating your own custom version. We will also see how to use GDI+ to achieve interesting visual effects and to print out documents.

Working with Windows Forms

In the previous chapter, we looked at some of the background information we need to understand to have a good, in-depth knowledge of how Windows Forms work. Now we will take a more detailed look at forms and other related objects such as menus and dialog boxes that almost any form-based application uses. We will build up our picture of Windows Forms by progressively building a text editor that has a multiple document interface (MDI). As we investigate commonly used items, we will add those items to our application's form and discuss the code. We will also discuss alternatives to the code we have used. We will add the code without the help of VS.NET's designers and wizards, but discuss briefly how similar results can be achieved using the designers. This approach will hopefully give us a better understanding of the issues involved in creating Windows applications in C#, and give us more control over the code.

In this chapter, we will see how to:

- ❑ Create and customize forms
- ❑ Handle form events
- ❑ Create menus and set up handlers for menu items
- ❑ Develop MDI forms
- ❑ Use the common dialogs provided with .NET
- ❑ Add toolbars and status bars to our form

Creating a Form-Based Application

As we saw in the previous chapter, .NET provides the Form class in the System.Windows.Forms namespace for creating Windows GUI applications. The Form class represents a single window, and contains the code that handles messages received from the system. These message handlers handle all common user interactions such as dragging the window, maximizing and minimizing, drawing and re-drawing the window when it's exposed, and so on. If we are writing an application that has some kind of GUI, the Form class is one class that we absolutely must use. Given this fact, it is only fitting that we start our investigations on building GUI applications with C# with an introduction to the Form class. We briefly saw how to create a simple Windows application in C# in the previous chapter, but we'll take a more systematic look now at how the Form class works, by building up from the simplest possible example.

Instantiating a Form is straightforward; there is just one constructor that takes no parameters. So all we have to do is add the single line inside the Main() in the following code:

```
using System.Windows.Forms;

namespace Chapter2App
{
    public class MyForm
    {
        static void Main()
        {
            Form myForm = new Form();
        }
    }
}
```

We can compile this using the command-line compiler with the following command:

csc /t:winexe /r:System.Windows.Forms.dll chapter2app.cs

The target switch /t:winexe specifies that the EXE generated by the compiler will be Windows or based (as opposed to console based). Windows-based executables don't pop up the console when we run them, and so they are the most appropriate choice for Form-based applications. However, sometimes it's useful to use the console when we are building the application, since we can write any string on the console to help us debug the application. We can always compile it as Windows-based when the application is ready for release. The /r (reference) switch points to the DLL that contains the Form class so that the compiler can find it (in fact, this DLL is so commonly used that we can leave this out and the compiler refers to it by default). If we are using Visual Studio .NET (VS.NET) starting from an empty project then we just build the project. If we want to make it a Windows-based application (and get rid of the DOS console that pops up when we run it) then we would need to get to properties of the project and set the **Output Type** to **Windows Application** instead of the default **Console Application**.

However, if we compile the above code and run it – we get nothing. The reason we don't see the Form we have created is that we need to call the Show() method on the Form object to make it visible; the Form is hidden by default:

```
...
static void Main()
{
    Form myForm = new Form();
    myForm.Show();

    // Alternatively, we can set the Form's Visible property to true:
    // myForm.Visible = true;
}
...
```

When we run the resulting application, we may notice (on a slow machine) that a window pops up and then goes away. To those of you who have played with Windows programming a bit, the reason is obvious; the code above creates the Form and makes it visible, but then execution reaches the end of the Main() method, so the program exits and the Form that it had just shown is killed.

What we need is some way to keep the program alive by preventing it from reaching the end of the Main() method. But we also want to have the ability to make it reach the end of Main() when we want to stop the program, or we won't have a way of closing down the application. This is where the Application class comes to our rescue. This class has a static Run() method, which starts up a message loop on the thread it is called on and so prevents a program from exiting prematurely. One of the overloads for this method takes a Form object as its parameter. The Run() method starts up the message loop and calls the Show() method of the Form to make it visible. It also adds an event handler for the Closed event on the Form and from this event handler calls the static Application.ExitThread() method, which stops the application loop and makes the call to Run() return, so that the program reaches the end of the Main() method, and therefore closes. The Closed event on a Form is raised by default when we click on the close button of the Form, so if we use the Application.Run() method, we can stop the program by clicking on the close button of the Form. Let's modify our code again:

```
...
static void Main()
{
    Form myForm = new Form();
    Application.Run(myForm);
}
...
```

Notice that we have removed the call to Show(), because we know that the Application.Run() will do it anyway. When we compile and run the program this time, we find that the Form stays visible, and when we close the form, the Form closes and the program exits (we can use Task Manager to see if the program really exits or not). The Form stays visible because the call to Application.Run() doesn't return until we click on the close button of the Form.

This is the standard core of a Windows Forms application. The `Form` object we pass to `Application.Run()` is the main `Form` that governs the lifetime of the application. We will usually create other forms to do different things in the application; we can just instantiate those forms and call `Show()` to make them visible – they will stay visible because the application itself stays alive.

If we are using VS.NET wizards to generate the code and select the standard C# Windows application option we will end up with exactly the same sort of `Main()` function for the application. We shall investigate the wizard-generated code as we progress through the chapter.

Customizing the Form

The `Form` that we get from the application we have created above behaves exactly as a normal window should do, thanks to the code in the `Form` class. We can drag it, maximize and minimize it, and so on, but it is rather bland. What we need to do is add new features to it and change its properties.

The `Form` class has many different properties that are available to us. We will look at some of the more interesting ones and leave the rest for you to explore. We will start by giving the form a title and changing its size. We use the `Text` property to set the title of the form, and use the `Size` property to change the size of the form from the default of 300 pixels by 300 pixels (alternatively, we could have used the `Height` and `Width` property to do the same):

```
...
static void Main()
{
    Form myForm = new Form();

    // Set the title
    myForm.Text = "Hello world";

    // Set the size
    myForm.Size = new System.Drawing.Size(500,500);

    Application.Run(myForm);
}
...
```

The `Size` property of the `Form` must be set to an instance of the `Size` struct, defined in the `System.Drawing` namespace. The constructor we use here takes the width and the height as `int`s. We can make all kinds of changes to the form using different properties. For instance, if we want a form without any maximize-minimize buttons (because we don't want the user to ever maximize our form), all we would do is add the following bit of code:

```
myForm.MaximizeBox = false;
myForm.MinimizeBox = false;
```

Similarly, we can control the placement of the form with properties like `StartPosition`, `TopMost`, `ShowInTaskbar`, etc. Properties such as `FormBorderStyle`, `BackColor`, and `BackgroundImage` change the look and feel of the form.

Better Forms by Inheritance

Although we can change the properties of a Form to the needs of our application, we can gain greater control over the behavior of the form if we create our own specialized form derived from the Form class. The derived class would be able to add its own customization on top of the defaults provided by the Form class. Using a derived class also makes it easy to add custom event handling code on top of the handling provided by the Form class.

Let's modify our existing code and create our own class derived from Form. We want to set some default properties for the form – the form's caption, size, and border style. It's good design to make the property changes in the constructor; this ensures that the appropriate properties are set during instantiation, and a separate method does not need to be called by the object creating the form:

```
using System.Windows.Forms;
namespace Chapter2App
{
    public class MyForm : System.Windows.Forms.Form
    {
        // Constructor
        public MyForm()
        {
            // Set the title
            this.Text = "Hello world";

            // Set the default size
            this.Size = new System.Drawing.Size(500, 500);

            // Make the form non-resizeable with sunken edges
            this.FormBorderStyle = FormBorderStyle.Fixed3D;
        }
```

Apart from setting different properties of the form according to our needs, we would also need to add different controls onto the form. Controls such as buttons, edit boxes, checkboxes, etc., are UI elements that the user uses to interact with our code. The .NET Framework ships with many such controls ready-made for us to use. We can also build our own more specialized controls when the need arises. We'll have a look at some of the most commonly used controls in the next chapter, and custom controls will be discussed in Chapter 8. For the moment, we'll just look at the basics of adding a control (such as a button) to a form. To do this, we instantiate the appropriate object (in this case, a Button object), set any relevant properties for the object, and then add the instance to the form by adding it to the form's Controls collection.

The encapsulation of inherited forms becomes very noticeable when we have to use multiple instances of a customized form. In preparation for our ultimate plan of building a text editor, let's create the customized form that is going to be the window where we type in text. We will soon be using this class in the next section. To make things simple, all we want in our customized form is a RichTextBox control (this is an edit control on steroids) and we want this control to fill the entire area of the form. Adding the RichTextBox control is again similar to adding other controls such as buttons on a form. The trick of filling up the entire area of the form with the control is achieved by setting the Dock property of the control to the DockStyle.Fill enumeration value. This property sets the docking behavior of the control and takes one of the DockStyle enumeration values defined in the System.Windows.Forms namespace. Here is what the class looks like:

```
public class EditorForm : System.Windows.Forms.Form
{
    // The RichTextBox control
    private RichTextBox editingSurface;

    // Constructor
    public EditorForm()
    {
        // Instantiate the richTextBox member
        this.editingSurface = new RichTextBox();

        // Set the Dock style so that the control fills the Form
        this.editingSurface.Dock = DockStyle.Fill;

        // Add the RichTextBox to the Form
        this.Controls.Add(this.editingSurface);
    }
}
```

Wiring Events on the Form

This is a good time to look at the members of the Form class in the MSDN documentation to find what else is available. Apart from the public properties and the methods there are the public events of the Form class. For instance, looking at the documentation we find that there is a public event called Closing that is raised when the form is closing. When the user clicks on the close button, the Closing event is raised, and if there are any event handlers for this event those handlers are called. To connect a particular event handler to an event is known as **wiring** the event. This is done with delegates – which can be thought of as type-safe function pointers. When we wire the event with the delegates, the framework knows which methods should be called when the event is raised. Let's see all this with an example; let's wire the Closing event of the form.

The documentation shows that the Closing event has to be handled by a delegate of type CancelEventHandler. The definition of the CancelEventHandler is given below:

```
public delegate void CancelEventHandler(object sender, CancelEventArgs e);
```

What this means is that the CancelEventHandler can only point to methods that have the same definition (the same return type and parameter types). In other words, when we write our handler for this event, it must return void, and must take two parameters of type object and CancelEventArgs respectively.

All events in .NET have such delegates defined and we have to look up the documentation to find out which delegate (and so the method's definition) we need to use to wire the event. In our present case we know that we can only wire the Closing event with a method that matches the method definition of the CancelEventHandler delegate. Let's write a method with the same definition; we shall make the method static so that it is easier for us to access the function (we will not need to instantiate the object to access the method):

```
static void HandleClosing(object sender,
                        System.ComponentModel.CancelEventArgs e)
{
    // MessageBox.Show() creates a form with the text passed in
    // as the parameter and an OK button (by default).

    MessageBox.Show("The form is closing");
}
```

This method has the right signature for the `CancelEventHandler` delegate, so we can create a `CancelEventHandler` delegate that points to this method. To create an instance of the delegate we need to use the following code:

```
new System.ComponentModel.CancelEventHandler(HandleClosing);
```

The name of the method that we want to point to in the delegate becomes the parameter to the constructor. To wire the event to this delegate we just use the += operator on the event. The += operator is overloaded for the event so that it adds a delegate to a list of delegates for the event that the framework keeps. When the event is raised, the framework goes through the list and calls each of the methods wired to the event through its delegate on that list. Similarly, the -= operator removes a delegate from the event handler list for an event. It is good practice to detach event handlers from an event when the object that contains the event handler is going out of scope (otherwise the object is not garbage-collected because of the reference in the event handler list, and the handler keeps getting called). Delegates can be removed from the list with the -= operator, just as they are added with +=. The following code wires the `Closing` event to the `HandleClosing()` method in our example:

```
...
static void Main()
{
    MyForm myForm = new MyForm();

    // Code to set Form properties ...

    myForm.Closing +=
        new System.ComponentModel.CancelEventHandler(HandleClosing);

    Application.Run(myForm);
}
...
```

If we compile and run the application now, when we click on the closing button, instead of just closing the form, a dialog box (itself a Form) is shown, and we need to OK this box to close the original Form:

We know we can wire more than one method to an event. We can easily see this by creating similar methods to HandleClosing() and adding them to the Closing event with the += operator. If we do that, we will find that the framework calls the methods in the order that we added (wired) them to the event.

Modal and Modeless Forms

As the application stands, clicking the Close button doesn't close the form instantly, but instead pops up the form that MessageBox.Show() creates; it is only after we have clicked on OK that both forms close. We know that if we didn't have the MessageBox.Show() call, the form would have closed instantly. So MessageBox.Show() actually *blocks* the execution of the program to show the new form. Forms such as the MessageBox are called **modal** forms; a modal form needs to be closed to access any other form in an application. This is because the modal form takes over the execution of the program and returns only when it is closed.

A **modeless** form in contrast does not block the execution of the program. If we look back at the second code listing of this chapter, we see that that example was a modeless form – it did not block the execution of the program, so the program reached the end of the Main() function and exited.

We know how to create a modeless form, and we also know how to create a modal form using the MessageBox.Show() method. But the modal form we get from MessageBox.Show() is very restrictive; we can only do a fixed set of things with that form. What if we want the full-blown flexibility of the Form class on a modal form? That would allow us to put our application-specific behavior on the form. For instance, we could put our own brand logo on the form, or (for an application like the text editor we are planning to build) add a pane that shows the files that have been changed but have not been saved. For the moment, we won't go into such things, since we only want to see how to get a modal form without the MessageBox. We will be content with using a form that has a Yes and a No button (admittedly, this is something that the MessageBox could have done for us with the right set of parameters, but it's better to illustrate the principle with a simple example). When the user clicks on the close button, we want our modal form to pop up to make sure that the user does want to close the form. If the user clicks on the Yes button we carry on and close the form (and thus the program), and if the user clicks on the No button we close only the modal form but keep the original form up (thus keeping the program running).

Let's start by creating our "warning" form:

```
public class WarningForm : System.Windows.Forms.Form
{
    // Constructor
    public WarningForm()
    {
        // Create two buttons to use as the Yes and No buttons.
        Button yesButton = new Button();
        Button noButton = new Button();

        // Set the text of yes button.
        yesButton.Text = "Yes";
        // Set the position of the button on the form.
        yesButton.Location = new System.Drawing.Point(10, 10);

        // Set the text of no button.
        noButton.Text = "No";
        // Set the position of the button based on
        // the location of the yes button.
        noButton.Location = new System.Drawing.Point(yesButton.Right + 10,
                                                     yesButton.Top);

        // Set the caption bar text of the modal form.
        this.Text = "Are you sure you want to close?";

        // Set the size
        this.Size = new System.Drawing.Size(300, 100);

        // Add the buttons to the form.
        this.Controls.Add(yesButton);
        this.Controls.Add(noButton);
    }
}
```

To show a form modally, we need to call the ShowDialog() method of the Form class instead of the Show() method we have been using up to now. Here is the code for our all-new HandleClosing() method:

```
static void HandleClosing(object sender,
                          System.ComponentModel.CancelEventArgs e)
{
    WarningForm modalForm = new WarningForm();

    // Display the form as a modal dialog box.
    modalForm.ShowDialog();
}
```

The code is simple – we create the warning form and then show it modally with ShowDialog() method. Of course, we haven't got the code for implementing the behaviors for the **Yes** and **No** clicks yet. But before we do that, we have to think about how to detect which button has been clicked. As the code stands, we can compile and run it, and when we click on the **Close** button of the main form, we get our new form with its buttons. This form is modal, so we cannot access the main form when this form is displayed, but our problem is that the **Yes** and the **No** buttons do nothing. They just behave as buttons (they are clickable, and so on) by the virtue of the code within the Button class.

One way of making them do something is to wire the buttons' events to methods that carry out what we want to do, just as we wired the Closing event of the main form to our HandleClosing() method. This is definitely possible, and in fact this is the standard route for modeless forms (this is what VS.NET does when you add a method for a button click). However, for modal forms, where we want the click on a button to close the form and do something depending on which button was clicked, there is a simpler route.

The return type of the ShowDialog() method of the Form class is DialogResult. The DialogResult is an enumeration defined in the System.Windows.Forms namespace. We can use the Button.DialogResult property of the Button class to specify the button's value. When we do this, we get two things:

1. Clicking on the button closes the form that contains the button.

2. The DialogResult value of the button clicked is returned on the ShowDialog() call that created the modal form.

That is just what we wanted – a perfect example of killing two birds with one stone! So let's add two appropriate DialogResult values for our **Yes** and **No** buttons. There are eight values available in the enumeration, but the two we need are obvious. Remember we could have chosen any two of the values, since all of their behaviors are the same and as long as we know which button sends which, we are fine. We need to add these lines to the constructor of the warning form:

```
// Constructor
public WarningForm()
{
    // ...

    // Add DialogResult values of the button
    yesButton.DialogResult = DialogResult.Yes;
    noButton.DialogResult = DialogResult.No;

    // ...
}
```

Here is the code in the end part of our HandleClosing() method after our changes:

```
...

WarningForm modalForm = new WarningForm();

// Display the form as a modal dialog box.
```

```
    if(modalForm.ShowDialog() == DialogResult.No)
    {
        // Setting the Cancel property of the CancelEventArgs cancels
        // the event and keeps the Form open
        e.Cancel = true;
    }
    else
    {
        // The Yes button was clicked so we don't need to do anything -
        // the Form will close itself.
    }
    ...
```

The change is straightforward. The only new trick is stopping the form from closing when the modal dialog returns `DialogResult.No` (that is, the **No** button was clicked). This is done by setting the `Cancel` property of the `CanceEventArgs` sent by the framework to `true`, and thus letting the framework know of our intentions. This is a common way of communicating with the framework. Event delegates in the .NET Framework have two parameters; the first parameter is the source that raised the event and the second parameter contains data for the event and is used to communicate data between the event consumer and the framework.

Handling Events on Inherited Forms

Event handling can also take a new twist for inherited forms. Although it will work if we wire the `Closing` event in exactly the same way on the inherited form, there is a simpler way of handling some of the more frequently used events. This is done without a delegate and is only possible because the code behind the `Form` class calls specific methods to raise those events. For instance, when the user clicks on the **Close** button of the form, the `Form` class calls the `OnClosing()` protected method to raise the event. The way we were listening to the `Closing` event was: waiting for the `Form.OnClosing()` method to raise the event, and then relying on the framework to call our delegate. But now that we have inherited from the class, we can get into this event business a bit earlier on in the story. We can override the `OnClosing()` method and put our event handling code in there. So even before the event is raised, we can do our magic. However, we must remember to call the base class's method on our override so that the event does get raised and its receivers (if there are any) can handle the event. Most events have corresponding protected methods and these are documented in the MSDN documentation. For those events that do not have a corresponding method, our only option is to wire them with delegates.

So let's override the `OnClosing()` method of our form to handle the `Closing` event. The code within the `OnClosing()` method is exactly the same as our old `HandleClosing()` method, except for the call to the base class's method at the end. The positioning of the base class call on such an override is important. As a rule of thumb, events that involve initialization should be raised first by the base class call before other application-specific code in the override. In our case, since the event is for closing down the form, it's appropriate to call it as the last thing within the override:

```
    protected override void OnClosing(System.ComponentModel.CancelEventArgs e)
    {
        ...

        // Display the form as a modal dialog box.
```

```
        if(modalForm.ShowDialog() == DialogResult.No)
        {
            // Setting the Cancel property of the
            // CancelEventArgs to true cancels
            // the event and keeps the Form open
            e.Cancel = true;
        }
        else
        {
            // Yes button clicked so we need to do nothing
        }

        // Call the base method so that the event does get raised
        base.OnClosing(e);
    }
```

Using VS.NET Wizards to Create Forms

Up to now we have been doing all the coding by hand. In most cases, if we have VS.NET we would use its Form Designer to set up the form with its controls. The Form Designer makes it very easy to do this and saves a lot of time. So it is essential to describe how we would use VS.NET designers/wizards to simplify our coding and get to the point where we are now with our application.

To start off, we would select a new C# Windows Application project. This will create code very similar to our MyForm class code. If we look at the code, we will find that the wizard also hides the customization in the constructor of the derived Form class. The constructor calls an InitializeComponent() method that contains all the property setting and control addition code. Any change we make to the form from the Form Designer will generate the corresponding code in this method. The Form Designer overwrites the contents of the InitializeComponent() method, so any code we add should be outside of this method. We can put our code to wire up the Closing event directly in the constructor.

We can also wire up events from the Form Designer, particularly for controls that we add to a form. Usually the click event can be wired just by double-clicking the control on the Form Designer. If we look at the generated code, we will find that it holds no surprises and is exactly like our wiring. For more ambitious event wirings we need to select the form (or the control) and then on its **Properties** window click on the Events button (the button with the flash of lightning). This will present us with the list of events for that control; we need to double-click on the event we want to wire, and VS.NET will add the delegate and create the method definition – we just need to type our code into the method body.

To add new forms in the project, as we added the EditorForm, VS.NET provides the **Add Windows Form...** option in the context menu when we right-click on the project's name in Solution Explorer (and under the **Project** item on the main menu). This creates the skeleton of the derived Form class. To create our EditorForm class, we would drag a RichTextBox control from the Toolbox and drop it onto the form. We would then use the property viewer to change the Dock property – when we click on the Dock property it shows a visual representation of the DockStyle, and we just need to click on the central box to indicate DockStyle.Fill. All the code that the designer adds will look familiar to us because it's very similar to what we have written by hand. VS.NET just makes doing standard things such as this simpler and quicker – leaving us to concentrate on the more application-specific code.

Adding Menus to Forms

There are basically two kinds of menus in the standard Windows user interface:

1. The **main menu** of a window; this is the menu usually just underneath the title bar of a window. This menu is usually always visible and gives the user access to different functionalities of the application. For example, the menu with the File, Edit, etc., options in MS Word.

2. The **context menu**; this usually pops up when the user right-clicks on a UI item on the form. The contents of this menu are usually relevant to the UI item on which the user right-clicked. For example, the menu with Cut, Copy, Paste, and so on, that pops up when we right-click on an open document in MS Word.

The main menu and the context menu are provided by the MainMenu and ContextMenu classes of the System.Windows.Forms namespace. Both of these classes derive from an abstract class called Menu. There is another class that is derived from the Menu class, and that is the MenuItem class. A MenuItem represents an item that is contained within a menu. Let's see how it all works.

The Main Menu

First we will add a main menu to our myForm class. In our text editor application this menu will let the user create a new document, open an existing document, save a document, and so on. The Form.Menu property must be set to the MainMenu object we want to use as the main menu. Before we start coding, let's think about the issue for a moment. The main menu we see contains one or more items. These items are encapsulated in the MenuItem class. So we would expect the instance of the MainMenu class to contain an array of MenuItem objects. A quick look at the MainMenu documentation shows that there is indeed a constructor that takes an array of MenuItem objects as its parameter:

```
public MainMenu (MenuItem[]);
```

So we can use this constructor to pass in the MenuItem objects that should show in the main menu.

Now we know that each of the MenuItems in the main menu contains submenu items that show up in the drop-down menu (when the user clicks on the item). This indicates that the MenuItem objects themselves can have an array of MenuItem objects, which they use to show the submenu. Indeed, one of the constructors of the MenuItem takes an array of MenuItem objects as its parameter:

```
public MenuItem(string, MenuItem[]);
```

The first parameter of this constructor is a string that becomes the title of the menu item. This concept of a menu item within a menu item can go on and on, creating cascading submenus (although it's a good idea to limit the depth of such submenus to make them user-friendly). At the end node of such a submenu tree, we find the item that performs an action when clicked. This means that a MenuItem object can also have a delegate that points to the method that needs to be executed. This delegate is passed into either of the following MenuItem constructors:

```
public MenuItem(string, EventHandler);
public MenuItem(string, EventHandler, Shortcut);
```

The string still serves the purpose setting the title of the menu item. The EventHandler is the delegate and Shortcut is a type that allows us to pass keyboard shortcuts for the menu item (the user can use a keyboard shortcut to simulate a click on that menu item).

Now let's put all of these in use. We want a simple main menu in the form, which will have just one item called File. That item will have a submenu with three items – New, Open, and Save. These three will be the terminal nodes, so when these items are clicked some action will be taken by the application. To implement this scheme we have to start from the bottom; we create the three submenu items that point to three methods, and then create an array of menu items with the following code:

```
public MyForm()
{
   ...
   MenuItem miNew = new MenuItem("&New", new EventHandler(MenuNew_Click));

   // Adding a "-" titled menu item adds a divider on the menu
   MenuItem miDash = new MenuItem("-");
   MenuItem miOpen = new MenuItem("&Open", new
                                    EventHandler(MenuOpen_Click));
   MenuItem miSave = new MenuItem("&Save", new
                                    EventHandler(MenuSave_Click));

   // Create the array for the File menu item
   MenuItem[] fileMiArray = new MenuItem[] { miNew, miDash, miOpen,
                                    miSave };
   ...
```

Next, we create the File menu, passing it the array of menu items just constructed. Finally the array of MenuItem objects for the MainMenu object is created (containing just the File MenuItem object) and passed to the constructor of the MainMenu object. Once we have the MainMenu object we can use the Menu property of the Form class to assign the main menu for the form:

```
   ...
   MenuItem miFile = new MenuItem("&File", fileMiArray);

   MenuItem[] mainMiArray = new MenuItem[] { miFile };

   // Instantiate the MainMenu with the array of MenuItem crated
   this.mainMenu = new MainMenu(mainMiArray);

   // Set the Menu property to this instance of MainMenu
   this.Menu = this.mainMenu;
   ...
```

We obviously also need to add the methods associated with the delegates on terminal menu items. These methods must have the correct signature defined by the EventHandler delegate. We shall be putting in code into the menu handling function soon. Here is the present state of the code with only pertinent sections showing:

```
    ...
    // Constructor
    public MyForm()
    {
        // ... Initial property settings
        // ... All the Menu related code
        this.Menu = this.mainMenu;
    }

    void MenuNew_Click(object obj, EventArgs e) {}
    void MenuOpen_Click(object obj, EventArgs e) {}
    void MenuSave_Click(object obj, EventArgs e) {}
    ...
```

This is just one way of constructing the main menu of a form. There are other constructors and properties that can also be used to construct the menu. For instance, the `MainMenu.MenuItems` property holds a `MenuItemCollection` object that represents an array of `MenuItem` objects, and this can also be used to set the `MenuItem` objects of the `MainMenu`. The next code fragment will show this way of adding `MenuItem` objects to the `MainMenu` object.

VS.NET provides the Menu Designer for creating menus. We just need to drag a `MainMenu` control off the toolbox and insert it into the form. This shows an empty menu on the form. Then we can just double-click on this menu to add text and do the same to create submenus (whose placeholders show up when we create the top menu item). To attach methods to menu items we just double-click and the designer generates the necessary code with an empty method. Although the generated code is a bit different from the code we have used here, it is only a variation on how the `MenuItem` arrays are initialized and created.

VS.NET-generated code uses the parameterless constructor for `MenuItem`. It then sets different properties to do what we have done above. We can also do all sorts of interesting things to a menu item by changing its properties. Let's add a new top-level menu item on our main menu, next to the **File** menu, using this route. Here is the code we need:

```
    // Add the Help menu using a different route
    MenuItem aboutMenuItem = new MenuItem();
    aboutMenuItem.Text = "&About";

    // Wiring the menu handler to the Click event of the menu
    aboutMenuItem.Click += new EventHandler(MenuAbout_Click);

    MenuItem helpMenuItem = new MenuItem();
    helpMenuItem.Text = "&Help";
    helpMenuItem.MenuItems.Add(aboutMenuItem);

    // This is the way to add new top level items on the main menu
    mainMenu.MenuItems.Add(helpMenuItem);
```

The `MenuItem.Text` property sets the title of the menu, and we attach menu handlers by wiring the handler to the `Click` event of the menu item. This event wiring technique comes in very handy if we want to perform some non-standard behavior on the menu item using the different events available.

We would need to modify existing menu items through their properties if we wanted to make the main menu change depending on the context the application is in. One likely candidate for this in our application is the **Save** menu item. Since it only makes sense to have the **Save** menu item when there is a document to save, we should disable the menu item when there is no open document in our text editor. At this stage, we haven't yet written the code to open text documents, so we shall have to wait until we have developed the application a bit more for this magic in the menu. However, we'll have a sneak preview here: we will wire the `Popup` event on the **File** menu item and in the handler use the `MenuItem.Enabled` property of the `MenuItem` to enable or disable the item.

Another interesting property is the `MenuItem.Visible` property, which by default is `true`, but if we make that `false` the menu item doesn't show. A little bit of documentation lookup on the `MenuItem`'s properties and events can be very rewarding.

The Context Menu

The context menu is provided by the `ContextMenu` class in the `System.Windows.Forms` namespace. Constructing a context menu is very similar to creating a main menu. The main concept for context menus is that context menus are usually relevant to a particular UI item or control. So the context menu becomes a property of the control. This is facilitated by the `ContextMenu` property of the `System.Windows.Forms.Control` class that is the base class of all the controls, including the `Form` class. This means that, just as we set the `Form.Menu` property to a `MainMenu` object, we need to set the `ContextMenu` property of relevant controls to the `ContextMenu` object that relates to that control. When we do this, the context menu pops up when the user right-clicks on the control. It is also possible to manually force a context menu to pop up without the user clicking on the control.

Let's set up a context menu for our `myForm` object. We want the context menu to have two menu items, which the user can use to change the color of the form. As we can see, the code is very similar to the code for building our main menu. We create `MenuItem` objects using the constructor that takes the title string and the delegate for the `Click` event handler. Then we create the `ContextMenu` object using the constructor that takes the array of menu items, passing it an array of the `MenuItem` objects we have created. Finally, we set the `ContextMenu` property of our `MyForm` class to this `ContextMenu` object:

```
// Constructor
public MyForm()
{
    ...

    // Context Menu
    MenuItem redContext = new MenuItem("Make Form Red",
                                    new EventHandler(ContextRed_Click));
    MenuItem greyContext = new MenuItem("Make Form Grey",
                                    new EventHandler(ContextGrey_Click));

    ContextMenu colorContextMenu = new ContextMenu(new MenuItem[]
                                        { redContext, greyContext });
    this.ContextMenu = colorContextMenu;

    ...

}
```

```
void ContextRed_Click(object obj, EventArgs e)
{
    this.BackColor = Color.Red;
}

void ContextGrey_Click(object obj, EventArgs e)
{
    this.BackColor = Color.Gray;
}

...
```

In the above code, we also have some code in the Click event handlers for our menu. We just set the BackColor property to the right color (using the handy System.Drawing.Color enumeration). Notice that we just used two separate methods for setting the color; we could have devised a better scheme by using just one method. For instance, the method could use the object passed to it by the framework (the first parameter) to detect which menu item had been clicked.

We said earlier that the context menu can also be forced to pop up without a right-click. This is done using the ContextMenu.Show() method. This method takes two parameters; the first one specifies the control with which the menu is connected, and the second one specifies a Point object that specifies the co-ordinates where the menu should be displayed on the co-ordinate system of the control's client area. Let's put the following code on the handler of the Help | About menu item click:

```
void MenuAbout_Click(object obj, EventArgs e)
{
    // Forces the context menu for the main Form to pop up at
    // the given position.
    this.ContextMenu.Show(this, new Point(20, 100));
}
```

Now when we click on the About menu item, the context menu pops up at the location we specified. This isn't exactly what the user would expect, but it certainly proves that context menus are under our control!

Menu Handlers

It's time to put some meat on our menu-handling functions. The menu of an application usually provides access to all the functionality provided by that application. Hence, on a typical application, menu handlers provide the interface between the GUI code and the application service code. It is good design to pass the actual tasks to other objects/methods from the menu handlers, since this makes it possible to change the menu structures in the future, as well as access the tasks from other routes easily.

Let's start with the File | New menu item. In the context of our application, this should pop up a new edit window (form) for the user to start typing into. We know by now pretty well how to show a form, but the question is: should the form be modal or modeless?

If it's modal, we won't be able to access the main form and its menu items; for instance, we won't be able to use the Save menu item to save the text we have typed into the new form. Hence what we need is a modeless form. We will create this new modeless form on the handler for the File | New menu item click:

```
void MenuNew_Click(object obj, EventArgs e)
{
   // Instantiate our custom form and show it
   EditorForm editForm = new EditorForm();
   editForm.Show();
}
```

We create and show the derived `Form` class that we made earlier on in the chapter. The form just has a `RichTextBox` control filling the entire client area of the form, and this is where the user is supposed to type. Although we are using the `EditorForm` object as a local variable, the form stays alive even when the variable goes out scope (when the end of the method is reached), because .NET with its garbage-collected managed heap keeps objects alive by looking at references in the runtime.

When we run the application and click on File | New we find that our form pops up, and that we can also create multiple edit windows too. But things look a bit messy, since the forms show outside the main form – they look like they are completely independent of the main form (although if we close the main form all the editor forms close too). From the users' point of view this will be very confusing – they would find it difficult to remember that they need to click Save on a separate window to save their work. They are bound to run into all kinds of difficulty such as inadvertently closing all their editor windows by closing the main window that they thought was an unnecessary application. What we need is a main form that will create our editor forms inside its client area.

Multiple Document Interface Forms

A **Multiple Document Interface** (MDI) is the ability to show multiple forms within the context of a single parent form. For a Windows form with an MDI, there must be a parent form that becomes the container of one or more child forms.

To make our existing application MDI is extremely simple. First we have to set the `Form.IsMdiContainer` property of the main form to `true`. This lets the Framework know that the form can become the container for child forms. We set this property in the constructor:

```
// constructor
public MyForm()
{
   ...
   // Make this Form a MDI container
   this.IsMdiContainer = true;
}
```

With this done, all we need to do is tell our editor forms that they need to become child forms under the main form. We do this by setting the `Form.MdiParent` property of the editor form to the instance of the main form:

```
void MenuNew_Click(object obj, EventArgs e)
{
   // Instantiate our custom form and show it
   EditorForm editForm = new EditorForm();
   editForm.MdiParent = this;
   editForm.Show();
}
```

Now if we run the application and click on File | New, we find that the new editor forms created are all showing within our main form, and we can maximize and minimize these child forms within this main form. No doubt this is a great improvement, but there is a side effect – our right-click context menu no longer appears to change the color of the main form. This actually gives us a clue of what has happened when we have made our main form an MDI container. When we set the Form.IsMdiContainer property to true, a new form is created as a child of the main form, and this form fills up the entire client area of the main form with its client area. The new form doesn't have a non-client area – it has no title bars or borders. This new form actually has the ability to manage the child windows and this sits between our main form and the MDI child forms that we create.

Our right-click menu seems not to work because we only change the color of the main window that is now hidden behind the new MDI managing window. To fix this, we need to grab the new form that is covering the main form and change its color rather than the color of the main form. An easy way of grabbing the new form is to use the fact that it is a child control (a form is also ultimately derived from Control) of the main form. We can get the child controls of any control (including a form) by looking at the Controls property of the control. The Controls property holds a ControlCollection that is ultimately an array of child controls. Since there are no other child controls on the main form (such as buttons), the new form must be the first member of the ControlCollection. We use this and just set the BackColor property of the object. So here are the new context menu handlers with the old code commented out:

```
void ContextRed_Click(object obj, EventArgs e)
{
    // Grab the first child control of this form and set its color
    this.Controls[0].BackColor = Color.Red;

    // Doesn't work for an MDI container since this form is hidden
    // by a new MDI managing form
    // this.BackColor = Color.Red;
}

void ContextGrey_Click(object obj, EventArgs e)
{
    // Grab the first child control of this Form and set its color
    this.Controls[0].BackColor = Color.Gray;

    // Doesn't work for MDI ...
    // this.BackColor = Color.Gray;
}
```

To make the code safer we should have actually made sure that there are child controls of the main menu before we tried to access the first item (if there weren't any we would have ended up with a horrible crash with the present code). This particular technique might not prove to be very useful in real-life programs, but the philosophy this fix teaches us is rather important. In Windows programming, we are bound to come across situations where the standard routes do not provide us with a solution. In such cases we need to do a bit of investigation on what is exactly going on and then create our own solution, maybe bypassing some issues or going through a non-standard route. For investigating the forms an invaluable tool is the Spy++ tool that ships with the VS.NET, and which we looked at in the last chapter. You should fire it up once in a while and do some experimenting with it – it would not be time wasted. The following screenshot from Spy++ highlights the MDI managing window as a child of main form of our application:

Using Properties to Manage MDI Forms

The `Form` class provides us with quite a few properties, methods, and events that we can use to manage an application with MDI. The `Form.ActiveMdiChild` property will come in handy very soon when we want to save the active document – it retrieves the current active form. The Boolean `Form.IsMdiChild` and `Form.IsMdiContainer` properties reveal a form's identity in the MDI story.

To give the newly created forms default names, we will set up a member `int` variable, which will keep a count of how many times we have created new forms. We will use this to give each of the MDI child forms a default name. This can be very helpful to the user to distinguish newly created forms from each other. The obvious place to put this code is in the New menu handler, since this method actually creates the new form and thus changes the total number of MDI children of the main form. Here is the code for the New menu handler:

```
private int newDocCount = 1;

void MenuNew_Click(object obj, EventArgs e)
{
    // Instantiate our custom form and show it
    EditorForm editForm = new EditorForm();
    editForm.MdiParent = this;
    editForm.Show();


    // use the counter to set the title of the
    // main form and the newly created Form
    editForm.Text = "Document " + newDocCount.ToString();
    newDocCount++;
}
```

In this new handler for the **New** menu item, we get the length of the array of `MdiChildren` (and hence the number of child MDI forms), and use this number to set the `Text` property of the newly created form. Here is what the application looks like with three editor forms:

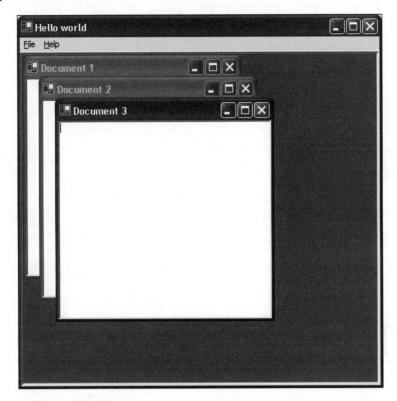

Changing the Menu

Now that we have setup the text editor with the basics of opening documents, we need to fulfill our promise of making the **Save** menu item more logical. The goal is to disable the **Save** menu item when there is no open document, but otherwise have it enabled. To do this, we need to wire the `Popup` event of the **File** menu item – which is raised when the user clicks on the **File** menu, and its submenu is about to pop up. In this handler, we cast the sender object to `MenuItem`, and then access the **Save** `MenuItem` within it, and set the `Enabled` property to enable or disable it. We use the `Length` property of the `Form.MdiChildren` to find out if there are any documents open. The `Form.MdiChildren` is an array of forms that are children of the main form.

```
// Constructor
public MyForm()
{
    ...

    // Create the File menu Item
```

```
    MenuItem miFile = new MenuItem("&File", fileMiArray);

    // Wire the Popup event
    miFile.Popup += new EventHandler(menuFile_Click);

    // Create the array of menu items for the main menu
    MenuItem[] mainMiArray = new MenuItem[] { miFile };

    // Create the main menu
    this.mainMenu = new MainMenu(mainMiArray);

    ...
}

void menuFile_Click(object sender, EventArgs e)
{
    // Cast the sender object to menuitem
    MenuItem miFile = (MenuItem)sender;

    // Set the Enabled property of the Save menu item (4th in the array)
    if(this.MdiChildren.Length == 0)
        miFile.MenuItems[3].Enabled = false;
    else
        miFile.MenuItems[3].Enabled = true;
}
```

Common Dialog Boxes

Now we turn our attention to the Open and Save menu items. We know that for these we have to provide the user with a friendly form that the user can use to point to a file to open or to a location where the file should be saved. These operations are so common that Windows provides predefined dialog boxes for them. The .NET Framework also provides classes that expose these common dialog boxes (and a few others). Hence, to implement the handlers for the Open and Save menu items, we shall use these classes to provide the standard file open and file save forms.

All the common dialog classes derive from an abstract base class called `CommonDialog`, which is defined in the `System.Windows.Forms` namespace and itself derives from the `Component` class. The hierarchies for these classes are shown below:

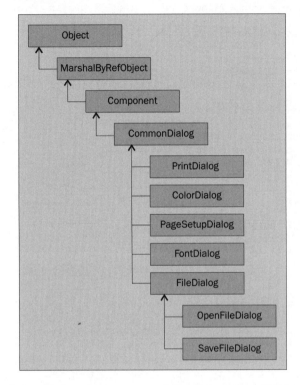

In this chapter, we will discuss the `FileDialog` and the `ColorDialog`. Other classes will be discussed elsewhere in the book.

The Open File Dialog

Let's start with the **Open** menu item. The class we need is the `OpenFileDialog` class. This manages the standard file open dialog. We need to use the `ShowDialog()` method to show the Windows **Open File** dialog box modally. Although the `OpenFileDialog` class does not derive from the `Form` class, the `ShowDialog()` method returns a `DialogResult`, just like the `ShowDialog()` method of the `Form` class. We can test this `DialogResult` to determine which button the user clicked, and then use properties of the `OpenFileDialog` object to get the information that we need. The property that we are particularly interested in is the `FileName` property, which returns a string containing the fully qualified path of the file selected by the user:

```
void MenuOpen_Click(object obj, EventArgs e)
{
    OpenDocument();
}
```

```
void OpenDocument()
{
    OpenFileDialog openDlg = new OpenFileDialog();
    openDlg.Filter = "Text Files|*.txt; *.text; *.doc|All Files|*.*";

    if(openDlg.ShowDialog() == DialogResult.OK)
    {
        // User click on Open
        // Open the file and get its content
        string txtFromFile = OpenFileAndReturnText(openDlg.FileName);

        // ...Code to handle empty file or file that failed to open

        // Instantiate our custom form and show it
        EditorForm editForm = new EditorForm();
        editForm.MdiParent = this;

        // Set the title of the Form
        editForm.Text = openDlg.FileName;

        // Set the contents of the Editor Form
        editForm.EditText = txtFromFile;
        editForm.Show();
    }
}

string OpenFileAndReturnText(string filename)
{
    // Open the file given by the filname param, read it,
    // and return its contents
    System.IO.StreamReader reader;
    try
    {
        reader = new System.IO.StreamReader(filename);
        return reader.ReadToEnd();
    }
    catch
    {
        MessageBox.Show("File could not be accessed");
        return "";
    }
}
```

We instantiate the OpenFileDialog class and then show it modally. If the user selects a file and clicks **Open** on the dialog, ShowDialog() returns with a DialogResult.OK enumeration value. In this case we call our OpenFileAndReturnText() method that opens the file and returns its content as a string. We then use that string to set the content of the RichTextBox control of our editor form. To do the last thing we had to set up a new property in our EditorForm class:

```
public class EditorForm : System.Windows.Forms.Form
{
    // The RichTextBox control
    private RichTextBox richTxtBox;
```

```
    // Constructor
    ...
    public string EditText
    {
        get
        {
            return this.editingSurface.Text;
        }
        set
        {
            editingSurface.Text = value;
        }
    }
}
```

The `EditorForm.EditText` property just sets and gets the `Text` property of the private `RichTextBox` control.

That's a very small amount of code to get such a lot of functionality. In fact, some of the functionality that we get is not immediately obvious. For instance, when a user navigates to a particular directory to open a file, Windows stores the directory path in the registry so that the next time the user clicks on **Open**, the file dialog box will display that directory. We can of course change this behavior, so that the file dialog always starts with a particular directory using the `InitialDirectory` property.

Our application can only deal with text files. Things get rather messy if the user tries to open other types of files. We also want the users of the application to find the appropriate files easily from all the other kinds of files that might be in a directory. We can use the `Filter` property of the `OpenFileDialog` class to set what types of file are shown to the user. To set up a filter we need to construct a string that has segments separated by the pipe character (|), and set the `Filter` property to this string. Each pair of segments in this string represents a file type filter, with the first part describing the filter and the second part being the actual filter. Here is an example:

```
openDlg.Filter = "Text Files|*.txt; *.text; *.doc|All Files|*.*";
```

Here, `Text Files` is the description of the file types given by the second segment of the pair – `*.txt; *.text; *.doc`. Notice that we can have multiple file types for a single description. The description is shown in the **File of types** combo box on the **File Open** dialog box. When the user selects one of the items in this combo box, the open dialog box runs the corresponding filter to show the files of that particular type:

We can also enable multiple file selection ability by setting the MultiSelect property to true. In this case we would need to use the FileNames property to access the array of strings that contains the fully qualified names of the files that the user selected.

The Save File Dialog

The class we need to bring up the standard dialog box for saving files is the SaveFileDialog class. Using this class is very similar to the OpenFileDialog described above. It is more user-friendly to suggest a file name with the correct extension on the save file dialog, and we can do this by setting the FileName property of the SaveFileDialog object before we display it. We can also use a filter, as in the open file dialog. The filter also has an extra function in this context – it provides a default file extension. If the user types just the name of the file, the currently selected item on the Save file as combo box adds the extension to the filename using the filter associated with the item. If there are multiple file extensions for a type description in the filter string, the first one is used to define the extension. To make this work we have to set the AddExtension property to true.

Two interesting properties of the SaveFileDialog class are the CreatePrompt and the OverwritePrompt properties. By default they are set to false and true respectively. The CreatePrompt property specifies if a prompt should be displayed when the user tries to create a new file that doesn't exist. The OverwritePrompt similarly specifies if a prompt should be displayed when the user is about to overwrite an existing file.

```
void MenuSave_Click(object obj, EventArgs e)
{
    SaveActiveDocument();
}
```

```
protected void SaveActiveDocument()
{
   // Get the active MDI child Form and cast it to the custom Form
   EditorForm activeForm = (EditorForm)this.ActiveMdiChild;

   if(activeForm != null)
   {
      // Instantiate the SaveFileDialog
      SaveFileDialog saveDlg = new SaveFileDialog();

      // Set the suggested name
      saveDlg.FileName = activeForm.Text;

      // Set the filter; this also sets the extension
      saveDlg.Filter =
            "Text Files|*.txt; *.text; *.doc|All Files|*.*";

      // Let the dialog set the extension
      saveDlg.AddExtension = true;

      if(saveDlg.ShowDialog() == DialogResult.OK)
      {
         // ... Code for saving the contents of the activeForm
      }
   }
}
```

When we run the code now and select **Save** on the menu, the following dialog will be displayed:

The Color Selection Dialog

The ColorDialog class lets the user pick colors from a standard dialog. We have an obvious place to use this dialog box – in our context menu for the main form to change its color. Currently the user can just select red or gray, but with a color selection box, we have unlimited possibilities. The use of the color selection box is very simple. We instantiate and show the box, and then use the DialogResult returned to determine if the user clicks on OK. If the user has clicked on OK, we just use the Color property of the object to find the selected color, and use that to set the color of the form (actually, we set the color of the MDI managing form that is the child of the main form). Delete the previous code for the context menu, and add this new code for the context menu and click handler for the only menu item that the new context menu contains:

```
// Constructor
public MyForm()
{
    ...

    // Context Menu
    MenuItem colorContext = new MenuItem("Change the color of the Form",
                                new EventHandler(ContextColor_Click));
    ContextMenu colorContextMenu =
        new ContextMenu(new MenuItem[] { colorContext });

    this.ContextMenu = colorContextMenu;

    ...
}

void ContextColor_Click(object obj, EventArgs e)
{
    ColorDialog colorDlg = new ColorDialog();
    if(colorDlg.ShowDialog() == DialogResult.OK)
    {
        // Grab the first child control of this Form and set its color
        this.Controls[0].BackColor = colorDlg.Color;
    }
}
```

The resulting color dialog box appears as shown below:

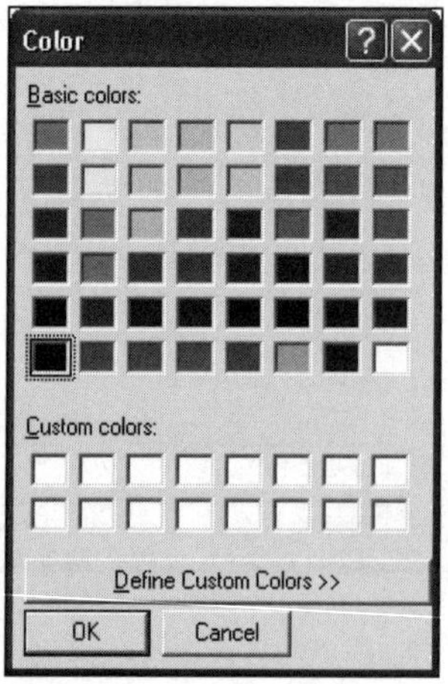

VS.NET and the Common Dialog Boxes

We can use the VS.NET Form Designer to add common dialogs to a form. We need to drag the appropriate dialog from the Toolbox (they are usually on the bottom part of the Windows Form Controls list). When we add the dialog we want to the form, it shows up in the tray at the bottom part of the Form Designer. This part of the designer contains the non-UI controls that we have added to the form, but which do not appear directly on the form when the form is shown. We can access the control's properties using the property viewer, and we can double-click on it to add the event handler for the click on the commit button (that is, the Open or Save button) of the form.

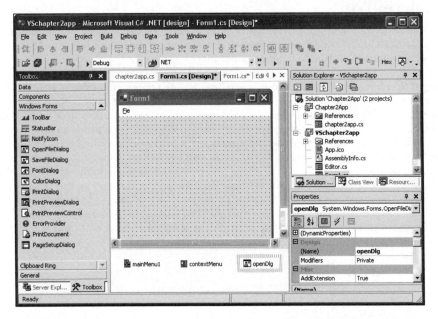

If we used VS.NET to add an open file dialog, we would just call ShowDialog() on the OpenFileDialog object to show it, and then process the file opening scenario in the menu handler that VS.NET sets up for us. We would not have to check the DialogResult enumeration that ShowDialog() returns. Using VS.NET for common dialogs makes it easier to set up a project with standard open/save file behavior quickly. One really helpful thing about using the designer for the common dialogs (as well as other things like menus and context menus) is that the designer shows these items, and it's easy for the programmer to spot what has been added to the project. It also makes it easier to change properties of different controls. The disadvantage of using VS.NET for these is that we lose some of the control. For common dialogs we are generally better off using VS.NET – it's simply quicker, and we tend to use them in very standard scenarios.

Toolbars

The toolbar is the band of buttons that usually sits just underneath the main menu. It provides users with easy access to commonly used functionality otherwise accessible through the menu items. Any self-respecting Windows application should have a toolbar, and that toolbar should have buttons carefully chosen to represent the most useful services of the application. For the application we are making, the choice is obvious – we just put the currently available menu items of the File menu.

Adding a Toolbar

A toolbar in the .NET Framework class library is represented by the ToolBar class, which predictably resides in the System.Windows.Forms namespace. Before we dive into using a toolbar on our form, let's reflect on what objects should be in a toolbar object.

A toolbar should have an array of buttons specialized for the context of toolbars. The members of this array of buttons show up in the toolbar. This array is represented by the Buttons property of the ToolBar object. This property represents a ToolBarButtonCollection object – which stores an array of specialized buttons of the type ToolBarButton. A toolbar also needs an array of images that show up on the buttons. This is provided by the ImageList property of the ToolBar object. This property holds an ImageList control that holds an array of images. The ToolBarButton object uses its ImageIndex property to know which image (referred to by its index in the ImageList) it should show on its face. So, to create a tool bar, the first thing we have to do is set up the ImageList. Then we instantiate the ToolBar object, set its ImageList property to the ImageList object we have created, and finally build up its array of buttons, by creating ToolBarButtons and adding them to the ToolBarButtonCollection. Here is our first shot at setting up a toolbar for our application:

```
// constructor
public MyForm()
{
    ...

    // Toolbar

    // The ImageList of the toolbar
    ImageList imageLst = new ImageList();

    // Create Bitmap objects to add to the ImageList
    // Need the actual bmp files in the directory of the app!
    Bitmap bmpNew = new Bitmap("New.bmp");
    Bitmap bmpOpen = new Bitmap("Open.bmp");
    Bitmap bmpSave = new Bitmap("Save.bmp");

    // Add the images created to the ImageList
    imageLst.Images.Add(bmpNew);
    imageLst.Images.Add(bmpOpen);
    imageLst.Images.Add(bmpSave);

    // Set transparent color so that background doesn't show
    imageLst.TransparentColor = Color.Red;
```

We have very laboriously created three separate `Bitmap` objects and added them individually to the `ImageList` object. We created the `Bitmap` objects by passing the filename to the `Bitmap` class constructor, so this will only work if the bitmap files are in the directory from which the EXE file is running. The bitmaps have a red background, and we use the `ImageList.TransparentColor` property to set the red color transparent – so that the actual images show nicely against whatever the system color for the form and toolbar is. Now we will create the `ToolBar` object and pass it the `ImageList` we created:

```
// Create the ToolBar object
ToolBar toolBar = new ToolBar();

// Toolbar belongs to this Form
toolBar.Parent = this;

// ImageList is the one we just created
toolBar.ImageList = imageLst;
```

We used the `Parent` property to attach the toolbar to our main form (in whose constructor this code belongs). Now that we have the `ToolBar` object with a proper `ImageList`, let's add the `ToolBarButtons`:

```
// Add 3 buttons
for(int i = 0; i < 3; i++)
{
    // Create the buttons
    ToolBarButton toolBtn = new ToolBarButton();

    // Show the image i from the ImageList of the toolbar
    toolBtn.ImageIndex = i;

    // Add the button to the ToolBar
    toolBar.Buttons.Add(toolBtn);
}

...
} // End of constructor
```

We create a `ToolBarButton` object, give it the right image reference and then add it to the `ToolBar` object's collection of buttons. We do this three times by means of the `for` loop, and thus add three buttons to the toolbar.

Obviously, this is just one way of setting up the toolbar. The objects don't have to be created in a particular order – as long as we can construct an `ImageList` and a `ToolBarButtonCollection` and pass them to the `ToolBar` object we should be fine.

The result of the above code is that we have a toolbar with the three buttons. They currently don't lead to any service, since we haven't added any event handler for them, but otherwise they behave visually just like buttons (they are clickable, and so on).

Although this works, and does what we want, adding separate images for each button is a pain. This is especially true when we have a lot of buttons on the toolbar. There is a very elegant solution to this; all we need to do is set up a bitmap file with all the images stuck next to each other, load the bitmap, and use the `ImageList.Images.AddStrip()` method to add this image. Since the images are of the same size, the `ImageCollection` class figures out the separate images from the strip. The trick is to make the width a multiple of the height (if we have square images for the buttons); alternatively, we can set the size of the images for the `ImageList` by the `ImageSize` property and then call `AddStrip()` (which would split the strip up according to the size). Here is the bitmap file we are using in this case:

With this trick in place, the code to create our `ImageList` becomes much more succinct:

```
// The ImageList of the toolbar
ImageList imageLst = new ImageList();

// Create Bitmap objects to add to the ImageList
Bitmap bmpStrip = new Bitmap("ToolBarStrip.bmp");

// For non-square images we would set the size for images
// imageLst.ImageSize = new Size(8,16);
imageLst.Images.AddStrip(bmpStrip);
imageLst.TransparentColor = Color.Red;
```

We again need to save our strip bitmap into a file (`ToolBarStrip.bmp`) in the directory from which the application is running. This is obviously a defect that we need to fix. The fix is simple; we embed the image in the resource file of the EXE, and create the `Bitmap` object from the resource. From the command line, we could use the following to embed the resource:

```
csc /resource:ToolBarStrip.bmp,Chapter2App.ToolBarStrip.bmp chapter2app.cs
```

The `/resource` option (which can be abbreviated to `/res`) specifies the file to embed and optionally the logical name for the resource. The logical name is the one used to access the resource from the code. In our case, since we have all the code under the namespace `Chapter2App`, we need to ensure that the logical name has `Chapter2App` as its first part.

It is also simple to embed the image from VS.NET – we need to add the bitmap file to the project by right-clicking on the project in Solution Explorer (or by clicking on the **Project** menu) and then selecting **Add existing item...**. If we were going to use VS.NET's image editor actually to construct the image, we would need to select the **Add new item...** option.

The next step is one that we have to remember to make things work. We need to set the **Build Action** property of the bitmap file just added to **Embedded Resource** – this actually embeds the image into the resource of the application. Once this is done, we can create our `Bitmap` object using the constructor of the `Bitmap` class that takes the name of a resource. Here is the new code for creating the bitmap:

```
// Create Bitmap objects to add to the ImageList
Bitmap bmpStrip = new Bitmap(GetType(), "ToolBarStrip.bmp");
imageLst.Images.AddStrip(bmpStrip);
imageLst.TransparentColor = Color.Red;
```

Now that we know how to get a basic toolbar up on the form, let's look at changing its look. The first thing we should do is to add tool tips to the buttons. It's as simple as setting the `ShowToolTips` property of the `ToolBar` object to `true` and assigning text for the `ToolTipText` property for each of the `ToolBarButton` objects.

We can also change the look of the toolbar by changing different properties of the `ToolBar` class. For example, we can give the toolbar a border using the `BorderStyle` property; we can change the style of the toolbar buttons by setting the `Appearance` property, and so on. We can also change the appearance of the buttons by changing the properties of the `ToolBarButton` class – we can add text to the button by setting the `Text` property, for instance.

There's one last thing to do before we move on to setting up handlers for the buttons. After we've added the toolbar to the form, we find that that our context menu that changes the color of the form is broken again. A quick investigation with Spy++ shows that now there are two child forms under the main form. The first child form is the tool bar, and the second one is the one we want to change the color of – the MDI managing form. So we need to change our fix to the context menu handler again, and change the index from 0 to 1 to get to the form we want:

```
void ContextColor_Click(object obj, EventArgs e)
{
    ColorDialog colorDlg = new ColorDialog();
    if(colorDlg.ShowDialog() == DialogResult.OK)
    {
        // Grab the second child of this Form and set its color
        this.Controls[1].BackColor = colorDlg.Color;

        // Doesn't work with toolbar, because toolbar becomes the
        // first child:
        // Grab the first child control of this Form and set its color
        // this.Controls[0].BackColor = colorDlg.Color;
    }
}
```

Handling Toolbar Events

The all-important event of the toolbar is obviously the event that is raised when the user clicks on a button on the toolbar. This is the `ButtonClick` event. Wiring to the event is of course no different from the other wiring we have done up to now. We need to define a suitable method that matches the signature of the delegate defined for the event. Then we use the += operator to wire the method to the event. The delegate that the event takes is of type `ToolBarButtonClickEventHandler`, which is defined as:

```
public delegate void ToolBarButtonClickEventHandler(
    object sender,
    ToolBarButtonClickEventArgs e
);
```

So the handlers we need to use should have the same method definition. We already have methods that perform the required action for each of the buttons of the toolbar from the implementation of the menu item handlers. All we need to do on the wired method is call the appropriate method. Notice that the click event belongs to the `ToolBar` class, and that individual `ToolBarButtons` do not have separate click events. Hence, the user's clicks on all the buttons of the toolbar need to go through the same handler, and the handler has to determine which button was clicked. This it can do with the help of the second `ToolBarButtonClickEventArgs` parameter. This type's `Button` property gives the `ToolBarButton` that was clicked. We can use this to find out what action to take on the handler. Since we have to identify buttons within the toolbar, let's make the `ToolBar` object a private member of the `MyForm` class, so that we can access it from anywhere within the class (alternatively we could have accessed the toolbar object within the handler from the first parameter of the method). So we move the declaration out from the constructor: to the top of the class

```
public class MyForm : System.Windows.Forms.Form
{
    private System.Windows.Forms.MainMenu mainMenu;
    private ToolBar toolBar;
```

The code in the constructor for setting up the toolbar can pretty much stay the same. We just need to add the following line that wires the ButtonClick event to the ToolBarClick() method (we shall define that method next):

```
// Constructor
public MyForm()
{
    ...
    // Wire the button click handler for the toolbar
    toolBar.ButtonClick += new
        ToolBarButtonClickEventHandler(ToolBarClick);
}
```

Finally, here is the implementation of the ToolBarClick() method. To identify the button clicked, we have used the Buttons property, using the IndexOf() method of the ToolBarButtonCollection class, passing it the ToolBarButton object given to us by the ToolBarButtonClickEventArgs.Button property. The IndexOf() method takes the object and then compares it with the members of its collection and returns the index of the object within the collection. Since we know the order in which we have added the buttons on the toolbar, we can use this index to identify the button that has been clicked and call appropriate functions. We use a switch statement to handle our three buttons:

```
void ToolBarClick(object sender, ToolBarButtonClickEventArgs e)
{
    // Find out which button is clicked by their position
    switch(toolBar.Buttons.IndexOf(e.Button))
    {
        case 0:
            // First button is the New button
            // Call the menu handler but passing null on 2nd param
            this.MenuNew_Click(sender, null);
            break;
        case 1:
            // Second button is the Open button
            this.OpenDocument();
            break;
        case 2:
            // Third button is the Save button
            this.SaveActiveDocument();
            break;
    }
}
```

Now our toolbar is fully functional. It does exactly what we expect. Now is the time to relax and reflect how we could have done things differently. This is what our application currently looks like:

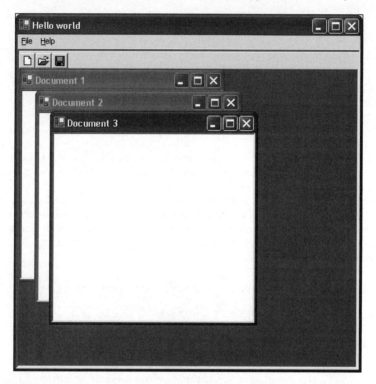

Obviously, there are other ways we could identify the buttons within the handler. If we had a unique Text property for the buttons, we could have used that text to identify the buttons; alternatively, we could have used the ImageIndex property, and so on. Let's look at an elegant alternative in which we use the Tag property of the ToolBarButton object. The Tag property holds an arbitrary object of the type Object, which means literally any object in the .NET Framework. In most applications, the toolbar buttons provide shortcuts to the menu item clicks, so if we store the appropriate MenuItem object in each of the ToolBarButton.Tag properties, we can just retrieve the MenuItem and call MenuItem.PerformClick() method on the object. The result will be exactly the same as the user clicking on the menu item. This is a clean implementation, which results in a much simpler handler for the toolbar. Of course, this will only work if the toolbar buttons only mimic the menu items (which is recommended practice). Here is our new code:

```
// Constructor
public MyForm()
{
    ...

    // Create the buttons
    ToolBarButton toolBtnNew = new ToolBarButton();
    ToolBarButton toolBtnOpen = new ToolBarButton();
    ToolBarButton toolBtnSave = new ToolBarButton();
```

```
    // Show the images from the ImageList of the toolbar
    toolBtnNew.ImageIndex = 0;
    toolBtnOpen.ImageIndex = 1;
    toolBtnSave.ImageIndex = 2;

    // Add the appropriate menu items
    toolBtnNew.Tag =  miNew;
    toolBtnOpen.Tag = miOpen;
    toolBtnSave.Tag = miSave;

    // Add the button to the ToolBar
    toolBar.Buttons.Add(toolBtnNew);
    toolBar.Buttons.Add(toolBtnOpen);
    toolBar.Buttons.Add(toolBtnSave);

    // Wire the button click handler for the toolbar
    toolBar.ButtonClick += new
            ToolBarButtonClickEventHandler(ToolBarClick);
}

void ToolBarClick(object sender, ToolBarButtonClickEventArgs e)
{
    MenuItem menuItemForButton = (MenuItem) e.Button.Tag;
    menuItemForButton.PerformClick();
}
```

Notice that we had to change our generic `for` loop for adding the buttons on to the toolbar to add different menu items onto the buttons. However, the `ButtonClick` handler for the toolbar is now much more succinct and much simpler to understand.

VS.NET and the Toolbar

As with most other things, if we're using VS.NET, we can just drag a toolbar control from the toolbox and drop it onto a form using the Form Designer. We end up with a blank toolbar on which we can add buttons by clicking on the `Buttons` property of the `ToolBar`'s property view. This brings up a dialog called the **ToolBarButton Collection Editor**. This form has **Add** and **Remove** buttons that let us add (remove) buttons on the toolbar. This form also has a property viewer for the buttons we add, so we can visually change the properties of the buttons:

ToolBarButton Collection Editor

Members:

| 0 | toolBarButton1 |

Add   Remove

toolBarButton1 Properties:

Configurations	
(DynamicProperti	
Data	
Tag	
Design	
(Name)	**toolBarButton1**
Modifiers	Private
Misc	
DropDownMenu	(none)
Enabled	True
ImageIndex	(none)
PartialPush	False
Pushed	False
Rectangle	0, 2, 23, 22
Style	PushButton
Text	
ToolTipText	
Visible	True

OK   Cancel   Help

To add an ImageList, we need to drag the ImageList control from the toolbox. We can then click on the Images property in the property viewer and add images to the ImageList. Once we have done this, we need to go back to the toolbar's properties, and set its ImageList property to our ImageList control. The drop-down box for this property figures out the ImageList we have just created and shows it. We just add it, and then we can add the ImageIndex property for each of the buttons. To add the event handler for the ButtonClick event, we just double-click on top of the ToolBar control in the Form Designer, and we are presented with the handler function.

The Status Bar

The status bar of an application is the control that usually stays at the bottom of a form with sections that have text pertinent to what the user is doing currently. For instance, Microsoft Word shows the page number, line number, and so on of the current document on the status bar. Let's add a status bar to the application we have been building. Since creating status bars is quite similar to creating toolbars, we shall keep this section short by giving a quick introduction to the code.

We need the StatusBar class of the System.Windows.Forms namespace to create the status bar. Like the ToolBar class, it has a property called the Parent, which specifies which form it belongs to. The Dock property of the StatusBar is by default set to DockStyle.Bottom, which makes it appear at the bottom of the form. The Text property sets the text that shows up in the actual control. Since we expect the status bar to be accessed from different parts of our class to set its text, we make the StatusBar a private field of the class. Here is the code to add the status bar with a bit of initial text in our form:

```
...
private StatusBar statusBar;

// Constructor
public MyForm()
{
    ...

    statusBar = new StatusBar();
    statusBar.Text = "I am a status bar";
    statusBar.Parent = this;
}
```

This adds the status bar with the text at the bottom of our MDI Form. The problem with this is that it only provides a place for a single string of text, whereas what we want is a segmented status bar with the possibility of adding different text in different sections.

The proper name for these segments in the context of status bars is **panels**. We create the panels in the StatusBar with the help of StatusBarPanel objects. To enable the StatusBar object to accept one or more panels within it, we need to set its ShowPanels property to true (by default it is set to false). After we have done that, we need to instantiate the StatusBarPanel objects and add them to the StatusBar by adding it to its StatusBarPanelCollection object exposed through the Panels property. Let's add two panels to our status bar. The first panel is where the application will put helpful comments depending on what the user is doing, and on the second panel we will just put today's date. Here is the code:

```
statusBar = new StatusBar();
statusBar.ShowPanels = true;
statusBar.Parent = this;

// Create the Help panel
StatusBarPanel statusPanelHelp = new StatusBarPanel();
statusPanelHelp.AutoSize = StatusBarPanelAutoSize.Spring;
statusPanelHelp.Text = "This is the place for help!";

statusBar.Panels.Add(statusPanelHelp);

// Create and add the Date panel
StatusBarPanel statusPanelDate = new StatusBarPanel();
statusPanelDate.AutoSize = StatusBarPanelAutoSize.Contents;

// Get today's date
DateTime dt= DateTime.Now;
statusPanelDate.Text = dt.ToShortDateString();

statusBar.Panels.Add(statusPanelDate);
```

We use the AutoSize property of the StatusBarPanel object to set the size of the panels. The StatusBarPanelAutoSize enumeration provides us with possible values for this property. Using the Contents value specifies size depending on the content, while Spring makes the panel take up available space on the bar.

As you might have expected, our context menu again fails to change the color of the form after adding the status bar. This is of course because the status bar is a child of the main form, so changing the MDI managing form's index in the main form's collection of child forms. We can again change the index, as we have done before to "fix" this issue – but in our heart of hearts we know that it is a hack, and like most other hacks it will only work for a special case. The following is a possible solution to this issue: let's iterate through the child forms of the main form and only change the color of the MDI managing form. This code only works because the ToString() method for the MDI managing form class returns the name of the class:

```
void ContextColor_Click(object obj, EventArgs e)
{
   ColorDialog colorDlg = new ColorDialog();
   if(colorDlg.ShowDialog() == DialogResult.OK)
   {
      // Iterate thorough the children
      foreach(Control ctrl in this.Controls)
      {
         // Only change color of the MDI managing form
         if(ctrl.ToString() == "System.Windows.Forms.MdiClient")
            ctrl.BackColor = colorDlg.Color;
      }
   }
}
```

Here is what our form looks like now:

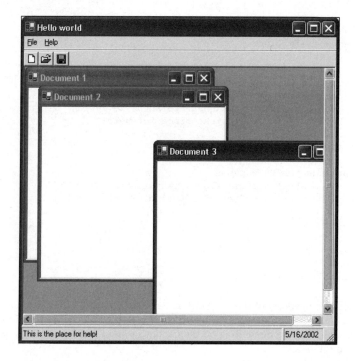

The MDI form's managing window has been giving us lot a trouble with our context menu, but it has given us a helping hand this time with the status bar. This isn't quite apparent at the moment, but if we were to use the same code for a status bar on an empty form (without any MDI managing form covering it) and had AutoScroll enabled, we would have run into a major problem. The problem would have been that the status bar would be treated by the scroll bars as another control, and the user would have been able to scroll away from the status bar. The standard way to prevent this is to use a Panel control on the form, which fills up the entire form and then add the status bar to the form. In this way the Panel would act very similarly to our MDI managing window, and the scroll bars would appear on it leaving the status bar static.

Summary

We have gone through the steps of creating a simple MDI text editor in this chapter. In this process, we have looked at creating forms and customizing the Form class. We then investigated MDI forms. We added a main menu and a context menu to the application, and looked at setting up menu item handlers. The menu handlers introduced us to the common file dialogs provided by Windows and how we access them from .NET. Finally, we added a toolbar and a status bar to the form. Hopefully, we've demonstrated that, although VS.NET is a very useful timesaving tool, it's not at all difficult to write this code manually. Even if you do use VS.NET, it's important to understand exactly what code it's adding to your application, and the only real way of doing this is to try your hand at writing it yourself.

Now we've seen how to work with Windows Forms in .NET, in the next chapter we'll go on to look in more detail at some of the most widely used controls that ship with the .NET Framework.

Windows Common Controls

Windows forms controls are reusable components that encapsulate user interface functionality. The .NET Framework provides many ready-to-use predefined controls in the System.Windows.Forms namespace. It also provides the infrastructure for developing our own controls using the System.Windows.Forms.UserControl class. We can combine existing controls, extend existing controls, or design our own controls from scratch. This chapter provides a quick overview of some of the common controls that it's vital to understand to start developing Windows applications. While most controls have a user interface that is displayed to the user, there are also certain controls that don't have a user interface. These controls are needed in for drag-and-drop development in Visual Studio .NET for tasks such as connecting to a database. When non user-interface controls are added to the Windows forms in Visual Studio .NET, they are added to the tray that appears below the form, instead of the form itself.

In this chapter, we'll look at some of the features common to all Windows controls, and then look in detail at using the most important individual controls. As in other chapters, we'll show you how to use the Visual Studio .NET IDE to simplify working with controls, but we'll concentrate on the actual code, so most of the discussion will be IDE-neutral.

The Control Base Class

The base class for Windows forms controls, System.Windows.Forms.Control, provides the plumbing required for visual display in client-side Windows applications. Every control provides handling for Windows messages, access to mouse and keyboard events, as well as many other user-interface events. It provides us with advanced layout manipulation such as docking and anchoring the control to the parent window. UI controls expose properties that enhance their appearance, such as ForeColor, BackColor, Height, Width, Dock, Font, and Anchor. Additionally, they may provide security, threading support, and interoperability with ActiveX controls.

Control Properties

Most of the properties for .NET controls can be set visually (via the Properties window) if you're using the Visual Studio .NET IDE. We can also set them at run time from your code; in fact, unlike VB6, any changes we make at design time are actually visible in the generated code. Generally, controls are initialized within the form's constructor, or (the option used by Visual Studio .NET) within an InitializeComponent() method called from the constructor.

To open the Properties window, right-click on the control in Design View and select Properties, or select the control and press either *Alt+Enter* or *F4*. The Properties window allows us to sort the properties either alphabetically, or by category, and to view the Events and Property Pages for the control:

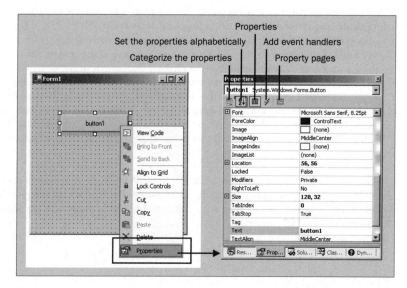

If you're not using Visual Studio .NET, the usual practice is to instantiate the control and to set any properties of the control we want to set within the constructor of the form to which the control belongs (or within a method called from the constructor). Controls are usually stored as private fields of the form. Once we've initialized a control, we need to add it to the parent control using that control's Controls.Add() or Controls.AddRange() method. For example, to initialize a simple Label control:

```
using System;
using System.Windows.Forms;
using System.Drawing;

public class MyForm : Form
{
    private Label textLabel;

    public MyForm()
    {
        this.SuspendLayout();

        textLabel = new Label();
        textLabel.Text = "I'm a label!";
        textLabel.Location = new Point(50, 50);
        textLabel.Size = new Size(100, 20);

        this.Controls.Add(textLabel);
        this.ResumeLayout();
    }

    public static void Main()
    {
        Application.Run(new MyForm());
    }
}
```

Some of the more advanced properties available with Windows controls in .NET, but not available with the equivalent pre-.NET controls, are:

Property	Type	Description
Anchor	AnchorStyles	Gets or sets which edges of the control are anchored to the edges of its container. This is a bitwise combination of one or more AnchorStyles enumeration values: Bottom, Left, None, Right, Top. If the property is set to AnchorStyles.Bottom | AnchorStyles.Right, the button will remain the same distance from the bottom and right edges of the form when it is resized.

Property	Type	Description
Dock	DockStyle	The **Dock** property describes to which edge(s) of the parent control a control is to fasten itself. This is very useful if the windows are resizing and you want controls to size accordingly. Again, this is a bitwise combination of enumeration values. The possible DockStyle values are: Bottom, Fill, Left, None, Right, Top. The DockStyle.Fill value indicates that the control is to fill the entire area of its parent control.
ContextMenu	ContextMenu	A short-cut menu to display when the right mouse button is clicked on the control. Context menus are discussed in Chapter 2.
DataBindings	ControlBindingsCollection	Holds details of how the properties of the control are bound to data sources. We look in depth at data binding in Chapter 4.

Control Containers

Each control also has a `Controls` property that returns a collection of the child controls contained in the control. We can add and remove controls within this collection. Since this is a property of the `Control` base class, in theory every control can act as a container for child controls. In practice, you are most likely to use this with controls such as tab controls, panels, and forms, which were specifically designed to group other controls together. But the fact that this is a property of `Control` also means that it's very easy to add controls to a parent control – we just call the `Controls.Add()` or `Controls.AddRange()` method, regardless of the type of control we want to add children to. We'll see an example of this when we look at panels in the first of our ActiveX control examples towards the end of the chapter. We should call `SuspendLayout()` and `ResumeLayout()` for each control that acts as a container for other controls.

Common Controls

In this section, we will take a quick tour of some of the common Windows controls. The topics discussed here should give you a quick overview of some of the common controls used in Windows applications. By the end of this chapter, you should be able to easily develop your Windows applications using the controls explained here. The controls we look at in this chapter are:

- ❑ TextBox
- ❑ ListBox
- ❑ ListView
- ❑ ComboBox

- ❏   Domain UpDown
- ❏   Button
- ❏   CheckBox
- ❏   RadioButton
- ❏   ScrollBar
- ❏   Timer
- ❏   DateTimePicker
- ❏   MonthCalendar
- ❏   TreeView

The TextBox Control

Let's begin our discussion with one of the simplest and most frequently used controls, the TextBox. The TextBox control is a rectangular box that allows the user to enter text in an application. Typically, a TextBox control is used to display or edit a single line of text. However, we can modify the properties to enable multiple lines of text to be displayed or entered using the MultiLine and ScrollBars properties.

Some of the most frequently used properties for a TextBox control are (note that a couple of these are inherited from Control or override Control implementations):

Property	Type	Description
AcceptsTab	bool	The tab character is used for editing instead of moving between fields
AcceptsReturn	bool	The return character is used for editing instead of signifying the end of input
MaxLength	int	The maximum number of characters that can be entered
PasswordChar	char	The masking character that appears when the user types a character into a password box.
ReadOnly	bool	The text is read-only
Font	System.Drawing.Font	The font used to display text
ForeColor	System.Drawing.Color	The color used to display the text
BackColor	System.Drawing.Color	The background color of the control
TextAlign	Horizontal Alignment	Alignment of the text within the control. This can be one of: Center Left Right

You can bind the `Text` property of a `TextBox` to a field name in a dataset using the `Binding` class. The following line binds the `Text` property of the `TextBox` to the `CustName` field in the `Customers` table in the dataset `myDS`:

```
text1.DataBindings.Add(new Binding("Text", myDSet, "Customers.CustName"));
```

We'll look at data binding in more detail in Chapter 4.

Textbox controls can also be used to accept passwords and other sensitive information. Use the `PasswordChar` property to mask characters entered in a single-line version of the control. The previous versions of the `TextBox` control in MFC can only use the `"*"` character as the password masking character. With the new `TextBox` control, we can specify our own masking character.

The RichTextBox Control

A `RichTextBox` can display a document in RTF (Rich Text Format). This kind of document can be used to display data in a very sophisticated fashion. It contains a number of formatting codes that control the way the document is displayed. Like the `TextBox` control, it derives from `TextBoxBase`; this abstract class defines the members common to both `TextBox` and `RichTextBox`, including all the properties mentioned above, except for `AcceptsReturn`, `PasswordChar`, and `TextAlign`. However, rich textboxes have far more powerful formatting features than standard textboxes, so they can contain text in many different fonts, colors, etc. This means that properties such as `Font` and `ForeColor` won't necessarily return the font or the foreground color for the entire text.

Text can be loaded into the control from an RTF file (`.rtf`), using the `LoadFile()` method. You can save the contents of the `RichTextBox` into an RTF file using the `SaveFile()` method:

```
richTextBox.LoadFile("c:\\temp\\RtfDoc.rtf");
richTextBox.SaveFile("c:\\temp\\RtfDoc.rtf");
```

The `RichTextBox` control can also be used to retrieve the RTF codes embedded into the document using the `Rtf` property. For example, if we have the following text in our `RichTextBox`:

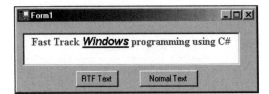

We can display the RTF text using the code:

```
string str = richTextBox1.Rtf;
MessageBox.Show(str, "RTF coded Text");
```

The output for this will look something like this:

As you can see, the `Rtf` property returns all the codes that are used to format the document. The `SelectedRtf` property gives us the RTF codes and text for the text that is selected or highlighted in the control. The `RichTextBox` control recognizes most of the RTF (Rich Text Format) codes; unrecognized RTF codes are ignored by the control when loading text. The basics of separating text from RTF controls are relatively simple, because all RTF controls begin with a backslash(\). Therefore, any incoming character that is not a backslash is text, and will be handled as text. To parse this text embedded with RTF codes, separating the codes from the text, we can use the `Split()` command:

```
string[] rtfCodes = str.Split('\\');
for (int i = 0; i < rtfCodes.Length; i++)
{
    // Separate the code from any following text
    string code = rtfCodes[i].Split(' ')[0];
    listBox1.Items.Add(code);
    // Compare rtfCodes[i] with a list of valid codes ..
}
```

Some of the most common codes used by RTF are:

Code	Description
\pard	Default Paragraph
\cf	Color Foreground
\ul	Begin Underline
\ulnone	Stop Underline
\i	Italic
\Ansi	CharSetAnsi
\pict	Picture
\picw, \pich	Picture Width and Height

A complete list of the RTF codes handled by the RichTextBox can be found at http://msdn.microsoft.com/library/default.asp?url=/library/en-us/rtfbox98/html/vbconsupportedrtfcodes.asp.

Writing an actual RTF parser is beyond the scope of this book, but a sample RTF reader can be found at http://msdn.microsoft.com/library/default.asp?url=/library/en-us/dnrtfspec/html/rtfspec_53.asp.

The RichEditTextBox also has various properties that enable us to handle the selected text in the control:

❑   SelectedText: Returns the current text selection in the control.

```
string selectedText = richEditText.SelectedText;
```

❑   SelectionColor: Sets or returns the Color of the selected text in the control. If more than one color is selected in the text, it returns Color.Empty.

```
Color c = richEditText.SelectedColor;
```

❑   SelectionFont: Sets or returns the Font of the selected text in the control. If more than one font is selected, it returns a null reference.

```
Font f = richEditText.SelectedFont;
```

One important property of this control is DetectUrl. When you type a link to a URL or a mailto: link, the control can detect the link automatically, and we can allow the user to navigate to the link by handling the LinkClicked event, for example by starting Internet Explorer in a new process:

```
private void richEditText_LinkClicked(object sender, LinkClickedEventArgs e)
{
    Process p = new Process();
    p.StartInfo.FileName = "C:\\Program Files\\Internet Explorer\\iexplore.exe";
    p.StartInfo.Arguments = e.LinkText;
    p.Start();
}
```

You can zoom the contents of the textbox using the ZoomFactor property. The scaling factor for zoom should be a number between 0.015625 and 64.0. A value of 1.0 indicates that no zoom is applied to the control, a value of 2.0 that the size of the text is doubled, and a value of 0.5 that the size is halved. The following screenshots show a textbox with normal sized text (ZoomFactor of 1.0), and with a ZoomFactor of 4.0:

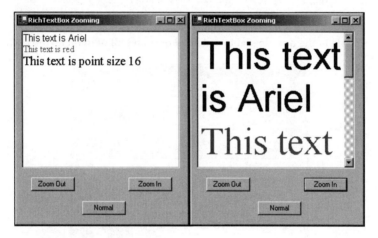

Single-Line and Multi-Line Textboxes

The TextBox control can be used in three different ways (these properties can be set either in code or in the control's **Properties** window):

❑   Editing or inputting a simple single line of text:

```
singleLine.ForeColor = System.Drawing.Color.DarkBlue;
singleLine.Location = new System.Drawing.Point(32, 40);
singleLine.Name = "single_line";
singleLine.Size = new System.Drawing.Size(408, 20);
singleLine.TabIndex = 0;
singleLine.Text = "textBox1";
```

❑   Editing or inputting a password (so that the characters are masked in the on-screen display). The password masking character can be set using the PasswordChar property. The following example sets the '^' character as your password masking character:

```
passwordLine.PasswordChar = '^';
```

❑   Multi-line edit style – additionally, the textbox can be used to edit or input multiple lines of text. You can add scrollbars to the control's view and set the maximum number of characters that the control can hold using the MaxLength property:

```
multiLine.Multiline = true;
multiLine.Name = "multiLine";
multiLine.ScrollBars = System.Windows.Forms.ScrollBars.Both;
multiLine.MaxLength = 5000;
```

The TextBox sample in the downloadable code demonstrates all of these textbox types:

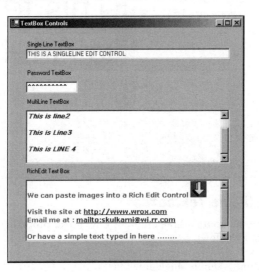

The ListBox Control

The ListBox control allows us to display a list of items to the user; the user can select one or more of these items by clicking on them. By default, only one item at a time can be selected, but we can modify the listbox to allow the user to select multiple items by setting its SelectionMode property. This can be one of the following SelectionMode enumeration values:

❑   MultiExtended – the user can select multiple values, and can also use the *Ctrl*, *Shift*, and arrow keys to select items.

❑   MultiSimple – multiple items can be selected by the user

❑   None – no items can be selected by the user

❑   One – only one item may be selected by the user at a time

If there's only one item selected, we can retrieve that item from the list (as an `object`) using the `SelectedItem` property, or we can retrieve its index position using the integer `SelectedIndex` property. We can also set these properties, if we want to select an item without the user's input.

If multiple items are selected, we can retrieve the selected items and their index positions using the `SelectedItems` and `SelectedIndices` properties respectively. These don't return arrays of objects and integers as we might expect (this would be problematic if we add items to the listbox), but return specialized collection classes – `ListBox.SelectedObjectCollection` and `ListBox.SelectedIndexCollection`. We can use the indexers of these collections to retrieve individual items/index values. For example, to retrieve the first selected item in a multi-select listbox, we could use:

```
object item = listBox1.SelectedItems[0];
```

Notice that these properties are read-only, so we can't use this to select specific items. Instead, we need to use the `SetSelected()` method:

```
public void SetSelected(int index, bool value);
```

Here, *index* is the index position of the item to select, and *value* specifies whether we want to select (`true`) or deselect (`false`) that item. There is also a corresponding `GetSelected()` method, which we can use to determine whether any particular item in the listbox is selected:

```
public bool GetSelected(int index);
```

Again, *index* is the index position of the item we want to test. This method returns `true` if the item is selected, or `false` if it isn't.

The `ListBox` also provides the Boolean `MultiColumn` property to enable the control to display items in columns, instead of a single vertical list. This property allows the control to display more items that are visible and avoids forcing the user to scroll to an item.

We can add items to the listbox by calling the `Add()` or `AddRange()` method of the listbox's `Items` collection. These work in exactly the same way as the methods we use to add controls to a form – the former takes a single object, the latter an array of objects. Additionally, `AddRange()` can take a `ListBox.ObjectCollection` (this is the type that the `Items` collection belongs to).

The `ListBox` also provides features that enable you to add items asynchronously to the listbox using the `BeginUpdate()` and `EndUpdate()` methods. The `FindString()` and `FindStringExact()` methods enable you to search for an item in the list that contains a specific search string.

We won't show a code example here, but there's an example containing several different styles of listbox in the downloadable code. As well as the different styles mentioned here, the sample also demonstrates custom drawing of listboxes (we'll look at custom drawing of controls towards the end of this chapter).

The ListView Control

The `ListView` control is a significantly enhanced listbox, but it is one of the more complex controls provided by .NET. This control supports four different views of the data:

- ❑ The `LargeIcon` view displays the data as icons. The icons have a multi-line title below them, and are large and easy to select. Far fewer data objects are represented in this view than can be displayed using the `SmallIcon` view.

- ❑ The `SmallIcon` view displays the data as small icons followed by a single line of text in horizontal lines.

- ❑ The `List` view is similar to the `SmallIcon` view, except that the data is displayed in vertical columns and the limitations on the text length are not that severe.

- ❑ The `Details` view lets the user see multiple columns of data, a bit like a spreadsheet. The user can sort on any column (if you implement this capability). The program can set the width of the columns, and the user can resize the column at any time. Optionally you can display an icon with each item to identify the type of item. You can also allow the user to drag columns to reorder the onscreen display.

An example of a `ListView` would be Windows Explorer. It allows the user to switch between the four views mentioned above (plus another one, **Thumbnail** view). Each item displays an icon indicating the type of item being displayed. A `ListView`'s display style can be set using the `View` property in the Form Designer or in our code.

You can add columns to a `Details`-style listview from the **Properties** tab, by selecting the **Columns (Collection)** property. You can also add columns at run time using the `Columns.Add()` method:

```
ColumnHeader ch;
ch = listView1.Columns.Add("Column", 100, HorizontalAlignment.Center);
```

The `ListView` provides a number of properties that provide flexibility in appearance and behavior. The `LargeImageList`, `SmallImageList`, and `StateImageList` properties allow you to specify the `ImageList` objects that contain the images displayed for items.

To associate icons with the `ListView` items, we need to create an `ImageList` object, just as we did to associate icons with the toolbar in Chapter 2:

```
// Create an image list of icons that you want to display for each item
ig.Images.Add(new Icon("flgusa01.ico"));
ig.Images.Add(new Icon("ctritaly.ico"));
ig.Images.Add(new Icon("flgcan.ico"));

// Set the Imagelist for SmallIcons
listView1.SmallImageList = ig;

// Set the ImageList for LargeIcons
listView1.LargeImageList = ig;
```

The `ListViewItem` class represents an item within a `ListView` control. The `ListViewItem` class can be used to add items to a listview using the `Add()` and `AddRange()` methods:

```
// Create a ListViewItem object for every item that you wish to add the ListView.
// The item can contain subitems - in this case, we can pass in an array of
// strings as a single item
string[] lv = new String[4];
lv[0] = "USA";
lv[1] = "Washington DC";
lv[2] = "New York";
lv[3] = "Los Angeles";

listView1.Items.Add(new ListViewItem(lv, 0));
// 0 indicates the index of the image in the ImageList that we want to
// display for this item
```

You can also use the `ListViewItem` to iterate through the sub-items within a single item:

```
// Iterate the items and sub items using ListView
for (int j = 0; j < listView1.Items.Count; j++)
{
   ListViewItem lvi = listView1.Items[j];
   for (int i = 0; i < lvi.SubItems.Count; i++)
      Console.Write(lvi.SubItems[i].Text + "\t");
   Console.WriteLine("\n");
}
```

By default, when you select an item in the `ListView`, the control will only highlight the first column in the view. To highlight the entire row, set `FullRowSelect` to `true`.

`ListView` supports single or multiple selections. The multiple selection feature lets the user select from a list of items in a way very similar to a `ListBox` control. This can be done using the `MultiSelect` property. You can also display checkboxes in a `ListView` using the `CheckBoxes` property.

Country	Capital	City_1	City_2
USA	Washington DC	New York	Los Angeles
Italy	Rome	Venice	Milan
Canada	Ottawa	Montreal	Quebec
Switzer...	Geneva	Zurich	Lucerne
United...	London	ChesterField	Wembly

Selected	Report	Small Icon	Checked	List	Large Icon

The `AllowColumnReorder` property allows the user to reconfigure (or move around) columns at run time.

When a column is added to the control, a `ColumnHeader` object is created. You can change the appearance of the column headers using the `HeaderStyle` property. Column headers can be:

❑ Clickable – Causes a `ColumnClick` event to be raised if the user clicks on one of the headers. We can use the handler for this event to sort the items in the `ListView`.

❑ NonClickable – The column headers are flat and don't react if the user clicks on them.

❑ None – No column headers are displayed for the 'details' view.

The ComboBox Control

A `ComboBox` displays an editing field combined with a `ListBox`, allowing the user to select from the list or to enter new text. The default behavior of a `ComboBox` is to display an edit field with a hidden drop-down list. The `System.Windows.Forms.ListControl` base class provides the core implementation for the `ListBox` and `ComboBox`.

The `ComboBox` control allows us to display the list in three styles using the `DropDownStyle` property:

❑ Simple – The textbox can be edited. The list containing the items is always visible.

❑ DropDown – The text portion is editable. The user must click the arrow button to display the list portion.

❑ DropDownList – Users cannot edit the text portion – they can only select one of the values in the list. The user must click the arrow button to display the list portion.

If you need to display a list that the user cannot edit, use a plain `ListBox` control (see above) instead of a combo box. You can add objects to the list at run time using the `Add()` or the `Insert()` method. Multiple objects can be added using the `AddRange()` method. Once populated, the list displays the default string value assigned with each object.

```
// Add an item
comboBox2.Items.Add("Sample String");

// Insert an item at position 9
comboBox2.Items.Insert(9 , "Sample String 9 ");

// Add a range of items
string[] countryList = new string[3];
countryList[0] = "USA" ;
countryList[1] = "UK" ;
countryList[0] = "India" ;

comboBox2.Items.AddRange(countryList);
```

To populate a combo box with a predefined list of items at design time, use the `Items (Collection)` property from the **Properties** menu. Alternatively, set the `Items` property to a `ComboBox.ObjectCollection` in the form's constructor.

You can search for an item in the list that contains a specific string or an exact matching string, using the FindString() and FindStringExact() methods.

```
MyComboBox.Items.Add("USA");
MyComboBox.Items.Add("UK");
MyComboBox.Items.Add("AUSTRALIA");
MyComboBox.Items.Add("ITALY");

// If a matching item is found, it returns the index of the item,
// otherwise it returns -1
int   Posa = myComboBox.FindString("AUS");       // Returns  2
int   Posb = myComboBox.FindString("GERMANY");   // Returns  -1

comboBox1.FindStringExact("ITALY");              // Returns 3
```

Normally, we would add multiple items to a ComboBox using the AddRange() method. However, if we need to add a large number of items to the list one at a time, we can prevent flickering by calling the BeginUpdate() method before adding the items, and EndUpdate() when we've finished. This prevents the control being repainted each time we add an item.

To retrieve the value of the currently selected item, use the SelectedIndex property (-1 is returned if no item is selected):

```
int pos = comboBox1.SelectedIndex ;
if (pos != -1)
    string str_value = comboBox.Items[pos];
```

We'll look at an example of using combo boxes later in this chapter, when we discuss custom drawing techniques for the predefined controls.

DomainUpDown Control

A DomainUpDown control displays a single string value that is selected from a collection of objects. You can select from the collection by clicking the up or down arrows of the control. If the ReadOnly property is false, the user can enter text in the control (however, the string typed in the edit control must match an item in the collection in order to be accepted). When an item is selected, the object is converted to a string value so it may be displayed in the control. You can add or remove items from the DomainUpDown control using the Add() and Remove() methods. The collection can also be sorted by using the Sorted property – setting this to true will sort the list in alphabetical order.

```
// Add Item
UPDOWN_DOMAIN.Items.Add("Visual C#");

// Remove Item
UPDOWN_DOMAIN.Items.RemoveAt(5); // Removes 5th item
```

The Wrap property makes the list work like a circular list – when the user navigates past the last item or before the first item, the list scrolls back to the first or the last item respectively.

The `UpdateEditText()` method is called whenever the up-down button is clicked or the `UpButton()` or `DownButton()` methods are called. If the `UserEdit` value is set to `true`, the string is matched to one of the values in the collection prior to updating the control's text display.

You can modify the appearance of the control by placing the up-down arrows on either the left or right side using the `UpDownAlign` property (this can be set to `LeftRightAlignment.Left` or `LeftRightAlignment.Right`):

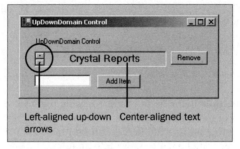

Left-aligned up-down   Center-aligned text
arrows

We can add custom processing for when the up-down button is clicked, by creating our own class that inherits from the `System.Windows.Forms.DomainUpDown` class (this itself derives from `UpDownBase`). This technique can actually be applied to any control, and we'll see how we can use it to create our own controls in Chapter 8. To add custom processing to the `DomainUpDown`, we need to override two methods. These methods are `abstract` methods that belong to the `UpDownBase` class, and must be implemented in the derived class:

❑   `public override void DownButton()`

❑   `public override void UpButton()`

When the down or up button is clicked, the `DownButton()` or `UpButton()` method is invoked. With every up or down event, call the `UpdateEditText()` method to update the text of the edit control:

```
public class MyUpDownControl : System.Windows.Forms.DomainUpDown
{
    public MyUpDownControl()
    {
        // Constructor code
        // Update the text
        UpdateEditText();
    }

    public override void DownButton()
    {
        // Custom processing code here
        // Update the text
        UpdateEditText();
    }

    public override void UpButton()
    {
```

```
      // Custom processing code here
      // Update the text
      UpdateEditText() ;
  }


  //If overridden, update the Text of the control
  protected override void UpdateEditText()
  {
      this.Text = "..."; // some text to display
  }
}
```

NumericUpDown Control

Similar to the DomainUpDown control, which consists of a collection of objects, .NET also provides a NumericUpDown control, which also inherits from the UpDownBase class. Instead of a collection of objects, this control provides a single numeric value that can be incremented and decremented using the up-down arrow keys. You can set the range of values in the numeric control using the Maximum and Minimum properties. Decimal values can be displayed using the DecimalPlaces property. This is an int value (by default set to zero) that specifies the number of decimal places to be displayed in the control. Numbers can also be displayed in hex format by setting the Boolean Hexadecimal property to true.

You can also use the up and down arrow keys on the keyboard to increment or decrement the values respectively when the control has input focus. This can be achieved by setting the InterceptArrowKeys property to true:

```
private void button3_Click(object sender, System.EventArgs e)
{
    // Enable the use of keyboard arrow keys with the numeric updown control
    // UP_KEY and DOWN_KEY
    numericUpDown1.InterceptArrowKeys = true;
    numericUpDown1.Focus();
}

private void button4_Click(object sender, System.EventArgs e)
{
    // Disable the use of keyboard arrow keys with the numeric updown control
    // UP_KEY and DOWN_KEY
    numericUpDown1.InterceptArrowKeys = false;
    numericUpDown1.Focus();
}
```

Button Control

Buttons are used very frequently within Windows applications. .NET provides us with different types of buttons – regular push buttons, RadioButtons and CheckBox buttons. A focused button (a button with a dotted rectangle within it) may be clicked on using the mouse or the *Enter* or *Spacebar* key on the keyboard. We can set the button as an AcceptButton (triggered by pressing the *Enter* key) or a CancelButton (triggered by pressing the *Esc* key). Buttons can also be used to set the return value from a dialog. If a dialog is displayed using the ShowDialog() method, the return value from the dialog can be set using the DialogResult property of the button. The various DialogResult values provided by .NET are shown in the screenshot below:

```
Form f = new Form();
f.ShowDialog();

if (f.DialogResult == DialogResult.Cancel)
    // Button returned Cancel result
else if (f.DialogResult == DialogResult.OK)
    // Button returned OK result
```

The Button control provides us with a wide variety of properties to control the appearance of the button, including ForeColor, BackColor, Font, ButtonStyle (Flat or Popup), TextAlignment, Image, ImageAlignment, and BackgroundImage. We can use these properties to enhance the look and feel of the button and of our application. We can also create our own class that derives from Button to do our own drawing and painting.

Subclassing the Button Control

The following section explains briefly how to subclass the control using our own Button class, but we'll look at subclassing controls in more detail in Chapter 8. The example class displays three different images for the following three different mouse events: MouseOver, MouseLeave, and MouseDown.

Create a Windows forms application and add a simple Button control onto the form. Create an ImageList object called ButtonImageList; add the three images we want to display for the three mouse events, as we did in the ListView example earlier in the chapter. Now set the Button's ImageList property to point to ButtonImageList: Set the Button's ImageAlign to TopCenter and TextAlign to BottomCenter to make sure that the image and text aren't placed on top of each other.

Next, create a new class called SMK_PictureButton, and derive this new class from System.Windows.Forms.ButtonBase.

Now add these three overridden methods in this new class. In each of the methods, we simply alter the text and the image, and then call the Invalidate() method to force the control to be repainted:

```
protected override void OnMouseDown (System.Windows.Forms.MouseEventArgs e)
{
    // Override the MouseDown function to set a new image
    // Display Image No 1 from ButtonImageList when mouse is clicked on the button
    ImageIndex = 1;
    Text = "SMILING FACE (MOUSE DOWN)";
    Invalidate();
}


protected override void OnMouseLeave (EventArgs e)
{
    // Override the MouseLeave function to set a new image
    // Display Image No 2 from ButtonImageList when mouse leaves the button
    ImageIndex = 2;
    Text = "HAPPY FACE (MOUSE LEAVE)";
    Invalidate();
}


protected override void OnMouseEnter(EventArgs e)
{
    // Override the MouseEnter function to set a new image
    // Display Image No 0 from ButtonImageList when mouse enters the button area
    ImageIndex = 0;
    Text = "SAD FACE (MOUSE ENTER)";
    Invalidate();
}
```

Now we just need to change the code to make sure that our button derives from this custom class, rather than from the standard `Button` class. First, in the form's field declarations, change the line:

```
private System.Windows.Forms.Button button1;
```

to:

```
private SMK_PictureButton button1;
```

Next, towards the start of the `InitializeComponent()` method, change the line:

```
this.button1 = new System.Windows.Forms.Button();
```

to:

```
this.button1 = new SMK_PictureButton();
```

And that's it! Compile and run the application; watch the image and text changing as you move the mouse over the button:

We'll extend this example later in the chapter, when we show how to take control of the drawing of the control, so we can modify the appearance of the predefined controls even more fundamentally, while still taking advantage of their functionality.

CheckBox Control

The `CheckBox` control allows the user to select one of two options, such as true/false or yes/no. The check box can also display an image, text, or both on the face of the control. `CheckBox` allows the user to pick a combination of options, unlike the `RadioButton` (which we'll look at next), where options are mutually exclusive. The control can appear either as a normal `CheckBox` or as a push button. This is done using the `Appearance` property. You can also display a flat button by setting the `FlatStyle` property to `Flat`:

```
flatCheckBox.FlatStyle = System.Windows.Forms.FlatStyle.Flat;
```

Since the `CheckBox` control can contain text and/or images as well as the box itself, the `CheckAlign` property is provided to position the location check box in the control:

```
this.checkBox1.CheckAlign = system.Drawing.ContentAlignment.MiddleRight;
```

The possible values for the ContentAlignment enumeration are:

- ❏ BottomCenter

- ❏ BottomLeft

- ❏ BottomRight

- ❏ MiddleCenter

- ❏ MiddleLeft

- ❏ MiddleRight

- ❏ TopCenter

- ❏ TopLeft

- ❏ TopRight

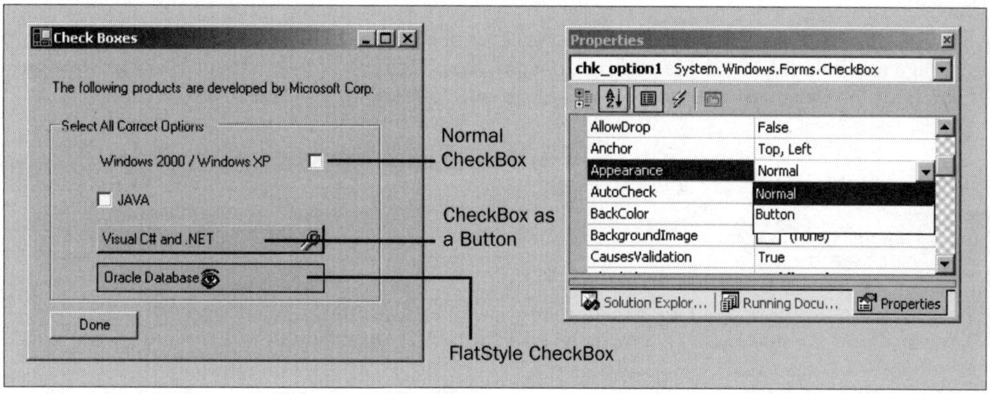

Use the Checked property to set the default state of the checkbox, or to determine its current state. A checkbox can actually have three states, if its ThreeState property is set to true. In this case, the exact state can be determined by the CheckState property. The various states are:

- ❏ CheckState.Checked – The control's check mark is visible (normal style), or the button is pressed (button style).

- ❏ CheckState.Unchecked – The control's check mark is not visible (normal style), or the button is raised (button style).

- ❏ CheckState.Intermediate – An intermediate state, where the control appears shaded (normal style), or the button is flat (button style).

In three-state mode, the Checked property will return true for either a Checked or Indeterminate state.

As we mentioned above, we can add images, text, or both to the CheckBox, using the Image property. The image can be any picture file such as an icon, .bmp, .gif, or .jpg image. You can control the alignment of the image using the ContentAlignment enumerated values:

```
// Load the Image that we want to display on the button
Image imga = Image.FromFile("WRENCH.ICO");

// Assign the Image for the checkbox
chk_option3.Image = imga;

// Align the image on the face of the checkbox
chk_option3.ImageAlign = ContentAlignment.MiddleRight;

// Select the background color for the checkbox
chk_option3.BackColor = Color.LightBlue ;

// Load the Image that we want to display on the button
imga = Image.FromFile("EYE.ICO");

// Assign the Image for the checkbox
chk_option4.Image = imga;

// Align the image on the face of the checkbox
chk_option4.ImageAlign = ContentAlignment.MiddleCenter;

// Select the background color for the checkbox
chk_option4.BackColor = Color.LightBlue ;
```

You can use events to determine the state of a CheckBox when it is clicked. This can be done via the CheckedChanged and CheckStateChanged events.

RadioButton Control

RadioButtons are usually placed in a group; when the user selects one radio button within a group, the others clear automatically, so only one button can be selected at any time. To create multiple groups within a Windows form, place each new group in its own container, such as a GroupBox or a Panel. The basic behavior of RadioButtons is just like that of a CheckBox. They allow the user to select a value from a group, except that you can select multiple values in a CheckBox, whereas RadioButtons within a group are mutually exclusive.

The Checked property can be used to get or set the state of a RadioButton. The Appearance property can be used to display the RadioButton in different styles, such as a push button or a regular RadioButton. To render a flat-style RadioButton, use the FlatStyle property. The AutoCheck property automatically changes the state of the RadioButton when it is clicked:

```
// Display the radio button as a Push buton
radioButton1.Appearance = System.Windows.Forms.Appearance.Button;

// Render the radio button flat
radioButton1.FlatStyle = System.Windows.Forms.FlatStyle.Flat;

// Set the default state of the radio button to checked
radioButton1.Checked = true;
```

We can add an image to the RadioButton using the Image property, and align the image position using the ImageAlign property. Set the background color of the control using the BackColor property. Similar to a CheckBox control, we can use the CheckedChanged event to determine the state of the RadioButton:

```
private void radioButton1_CheckedChanged(object sender, System.EventArgs e)
{
    if (radioButton1.Checked)
        // Now this option is selected
    else
        // Another option has been selected
}
```

We can set the default selected option by setting the Checked property of one of the buttons to true when we initialize the controls.

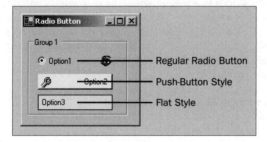

Scrollbar Controls

The ScrollBar control provides us with the basic functionality for scrolling data in a form. Most of the Windows controls provide us with their own scroll bars and do not require us to add this control explicitly. For example, multi-line textboxes, listboxes, and listviews all provide their own vertical and horizontal scroll bars. However, we can use the ScrollBar control in containers, which do not provide their own ScrollBars.

We do not inherit directly from the ScrollBar class. The ScrollBar class is the base class for subclasses representing horizontal (HScrollBar class) and vertical (VScrollBar class) scrollbars.

When using a ScrollBar control, and implementing its functionality, we need to use some or most the properties listed below:

❑   Minimum – Sets the minimum scrolling range.

❑   Maximum – Sets the maximum scrolling range.

❑   Value – Gets or sets the current numeric value for the ScrollBar.

❑   SmallChange – When the user clicks the arrow key, the Value associated with the control increments or decrements according to the value set by the SmallChange.

❑   LargeChange – When the user presses the *Page Up* or *Page Down* key, clicks in the scrollbar track on either side, or moves the scroll track by a very large amount, the Value property changes according to the value set in the LargeChange.

One example of a `ScrollBar` control implementation is a `NumericUpDown` control, as we saw earlier. Let's create our own numeric up-down control to see how we implement scrollbars in .NET. Create a new Windows application, and add a textbox and a `VScrollBar` to the form as below:

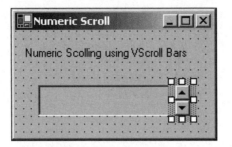

Set the minimum and maximum range of the scroll bar to 0 and 100 respectively, and create an event handler to handle the `VScrollBar`'s `Scroll` event.

The `ScrollEventArgs` passed into the handler for the `Scroll` event gives us access to the type of operation performed by the user. The various scrolling types are:

- ❑ `EndScroll` – The scroll box has stopped moving.
- ❑ `First` – The scroll box was moved to the minimum position.
- ❑ `LargeDecrement` – The scroll box moved back a large distance. The user clicked the scroll bar to the left of (horizontal) or above (vertical) the scroll box, or pressed the *Page Up* key.
- ❑ `LargeIncrement` – The scroll box moved forwards a large distance. The user clicked the scroll bar to the right of (horizontal) or below (vertical) the scroll box, or pressed the *Page Down* key.
- ❑ `Last` – The scroll box was moved to the maximum position.
- ❑ `SmallDecrement` – The scroll box was moved back a small distance. The user clicked the left (horizontal) or top (vertical) scroll arrow, or pressed the *Up Arrow* key.
- ❑ `SmallIncrement` – The scroll box was moved forward a small distance. The user clicked the right (horizontal) or bottom (vertical) scroll arrow, or pressed the *Down Arrow* key.
- ❑ `ThumbPosition` – The scroll box has been moved manually – the user moved the scroll box, but has now released it.
- ❑ `ThumbTrack` – The scroll box is currently being moved.

Within our handler for the scroll event, we'll increase or decrease a counter by the appropriate amount, and display the new value in the textbox:

```
private void vScrollBar1_Scroll(object sender,
                                System.Windows.Forms.ScrollEventArgs e)
{
    switch (e.Type)
    {
        // Check if the scroll is moved to maximum pos
```

```
        case ScrollEventType.Last:
          counter = 100;
          break;

      // Check if the scroll is moved to minimum pos
      case ScrollEventType.First:
          counter = 0;
          break;

      // Check if the scroll is moved up a small distance
      case ScrollEventType.SmallDecrement:
          counter--;
          break;

      // Check if the scroll is moved down a small distance
      case ScrollEventType.SmallIncrement:
          counter++;
          break;

      // Check if the scroll is moved up a large distance
      case ScrollEventType.LargeDecrement:
          counter-=5;
          break;

      // Check if the scroll is moved down a large distance
      case ScrollEventType.LargeIncrement:
          counter+=5;
          break;
  }
  if (counter > 100) counter = 100;
  if (counter < 0) counter = 0;

  textBox1.Text = counter.ToString();
}
```

Timer Control

A Timer allows us to execute a particular method after a specified time interval has elapsed. Microsoft .NET has provided the Timer control as part of the Component collections controls. The Timer control is a typical example of Windows non user-interface control.

To see how the Timer works, let's create a simple clock application.

MyClock

Create a new Windows application named `MyClock`. Add a `Label` to display the time to the form, and also add a `Timer` control, by dragging it onto the form using the Visual Studio .NET IDE, or by instantiating a `Timer` object in the form's constructor. Note that if you're using the IDE, you do not actually see any UI component on the form, since the `Timer` is not a UI control; instead, it appears in the tray beneath the form:

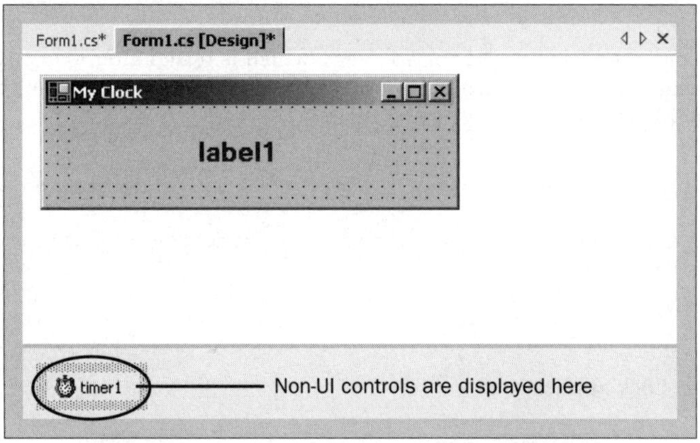

To get a `Timer` to display a new time every second, we need to set the `Timer` interval using its `Interval` property. The value for this property should be set in milliseconds, so we'll set this value to 1000:

```
// Set the interval time (1000 ms == 1 sec)
// after which the timer function is activated
timer1.Interval = 1000;
```

Next, we start the `Timer` by calling its `Start()` method:

```
// Start the Timer
timer1.Start();
```

After starting the `Timer`, set its `Enabled` property to `true`. The count starts at the time the `Enabled` property is set:

```
// Enable the timer. The timer starts now
timer1.Enabled = true;
```

If you wish to receive the `TimerEvent` only once, set the `AutoReset` property to `false`; otherwise, set the value to `true`.

> **If you have set the `Interval` to 10 seconds and you reset the `Interval` when the count is 5, the `Elapsed` event will be raised 15 seconds after `Enabled` was set – the event will first be fired `Interval` milliseconds after setting the `Enabled` property.**

We now need to handle the `Timer`'s `Elapsed` event, which is raised after every 1000 milliseconds (one second). Add an event handler, `OnTimerElapsed()`, for the `Timer` control. Within this method, we will simply display the date in a textbox:

```
private void OnTimerElapsed(object sender, System.Timers.ElapsedEventArgs e)
{
    // The interval has elapsed and this timer function is called after 1 second
    // Update the time now.
    label1.Text = DateTime.Now.ToString();
}
```

Here is the working clock application:

DateTimePicker Control

This control is used to display the Windows date and time in various formats. The control can be displayed as a combo box, which displays the month calendar when the down arrow is clicked (see the screenshot below). We can also change the appearance of the control to make it look like an up-down control. The various date time formats supported are contained in the `DateTimePickerFormat` enumeration (some of these formats vary according to the regional settings of the current user):

- ❑ `Long` – Displays the date in the format **Tuesday May 14 2002**
- ❑ `Short` – Displays the date in the format as **5/14/2002**
- ❑ `Time` – Displays the current time in the format set in the user's operating system (for example **1:32:11 PM**)
- ❑ `Custom` – Displays the date and time using a custom format string

We can also enhance the appearance of the control using various properties like `CalendarForeColor`, `CalendarFont`, `CalendarTitleBackColor`, `CalendarTitleForeColor`, `CalendarTrailingForeColor`, and `CalendarMonthBackground`.

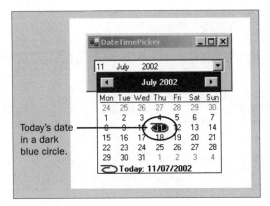

The control displays today's date at the bottom of the rectangle and highlights the day within a blue circle. The calendar also displays two arrows on the upper right and upper left corners of its rectangle that can be clicked to move up or down a month. The user can click on the Today field at any time to jump back to the current date.

If you need to change the year part of the date directly, click on the "year" item located on the top of the rectangle. The control immediately displays an up-down arrow next to the year. Click the up or down arrow to change the year:

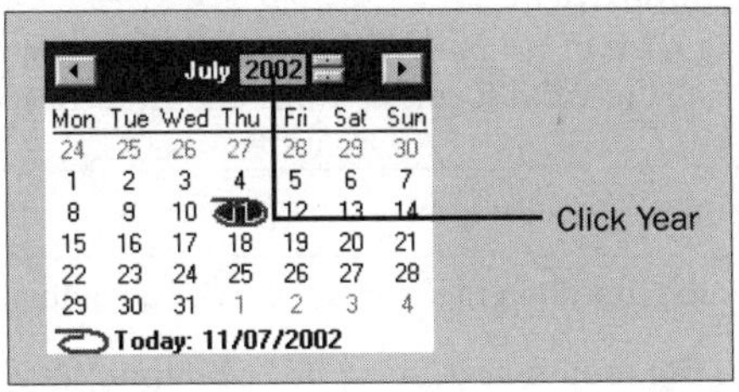

The control can also be modified to display an up-down control to adjust the date-time value, as shown in the figure overleaf. To set this format, set the ShowUpDown property to true. This style allows the user to change the month, day, or year portions of the date item individually. Click on the appropriate item (the display will change to select the item), and then click the up-down arrows to change values:

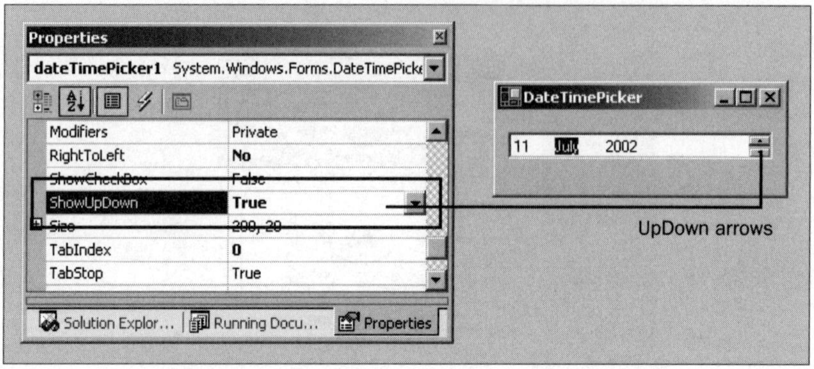

To retrieve the date and time displayed in the edit box of the control, use the `Text` property. To get or set the `Minimum` and `Maximum` dates set for the control, use the `MinDate` and `MaxDate` properties. The return values of these properties are of the type `DateTime`:

```
DateTime max_dt = dateTimePicker1.MaxDate;
DateTime min_dt = dateTimePicker1.MinDate;
```

Custom DateTime Formats

If we set the control's `Format` property to `DateTimePickerFormat.Custom`, the control allows us to display the date and time using custom formats. Use the `CustomFormat` property to define your own formats. The following table lists the valid format strings and their descriptions:

Format Name	Description
MM	Displays the month in the format 05 (with a leading zero for single-digit months)
MMMM	Displays the month as a string (for example, May)
dd	Displays the day as a number, (for example, 14)
ddd	The three-character abbreviation for the day of week (for example, Mon)
dddd	Displays the day as a string, for example, Tuesday)
yy	Displays the year as two digits (for example, 02)
yyyy	Displays year as four digits (for example, 2002)
tt	Displays AM or PM
h	Displays the hour in 12-hour format without leading zeroes (such as, 6)
hh	Displays the hour in 12-hour format as two digits (such as, 06)
H	Displays the hour in 24-hour format without leading zeroes (such as, 6)

Format Name	Description
HH	Displays the hour in 24 hour format as two digits (for example, 06)
m	Displays the minutes without leading zeroes (for example, 7)
mm	Displays the minutes as two digits (for example, 07)
s	Displays the seconds without leading zeroes (for example, 9)
ss	Displays the seconds as two digits (for example, 09)

The first example form in the DateTimePicker project in the downloadable code displays the current date and time in a number of different formats:

```
this.dateTimePicker1.CustomFormat = "hh:mm:s : MM/dd/yy";
this.dateTimePicker2.CustomFormat = "h/mm/ss : dd.MM.yyyy";
this.dateTimePicker3.CustomFormat = "HH-mm-ss : MMMM/dd/yyyy tt";
this.dateTimePicker4.CustomFormat = "tt hh/mm/ss : dddd.MMMM.yyyy";
this.dateTimePicker5.CustomFormat = "HH/mm/ss : ddd-MM-yy";
this.dateTimePicker6.CustomFormat = "hh/mm/ss : dddd MMMM yyyy tt";
```

MonthCalendar Control

The MonthCalendar control provides a simple yet intuitive way for a user to select a date from a familiar interface. It displays the calendar for the month in a rectangular window as opposed to the DateTimePicker control where the calendar is displayed in a drop-down control. Windows does not support dates prior to 1601. The MonthCalendar control is based on the Gregorian calendar, which was introduced in the eighteenth century. It will not calculate dates that are consistent with the Julian calendar that was in use prior to that.

You can use the keyboard to change the current month. Here is a summary of the keyboard commands you can use:

Key	Usage
Page Up	Move to the next month
Page Down	Move to the previous month
Home	Move to the first day of the current month
End	Move to last day of the current month
Ctrl + Home	Move to the first visible month
Ctrl + End	Move to the last visible month

You can change the calendar display to cause any day of the week to be displayed as the first day of the week, using the `FirstDayOfWeek` property:

FirstDayOfWeek is a "Thursday"

In applications you often need to select a range of dates. For example, assume you need to select a seven-day appointment schedule. You can set a range of dates for selection from the control, using the `MaxSelectionCount` property. This number indicates the continuous days you can select just by dragging the mouse. To retrieve the range of dates you have selected above, use the `SelectionRange`, `Start`, and `End` properties:

```
// Get the selection Range.
SelectionRange sr = monthCalendar1.SelectionRange;

// Get the start of Range
DateTime st = sr.Start;
```

```
// Get the end of Range
DateTime se = sr.End;
MessageBox.Show("RANGE START = " + st.ToString() + "\nRANGE END = " +
                se.ToString(), "Range Selection");
```

An interesting aspect of the `MonthCalendar` control is its ability to display a full calendar for the complete year using the `CalendarDimension` property:

```
// This will display the calendar in 4 columns and 3 rows.
monthCalendar1.SetCalendarDimensions(4, 3);
```

> The first parameter of the `SetCalendarDimensions()` method is the number of columns. The second parameter is the number of rows. A traditional `(x, y)` approach assigns `x` as the rows and `y` as the columns.

You can display the current week of the year as the first column within the control. This can be accomplished by setting the `ShowWeekNumbers` property to `true`:

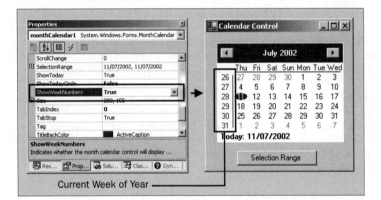

Current Week of Year

To change the month directly without having to click the right or the left arrow, click on the month name on the top of the calendar. This will display a context menu with the month names. Select an item from the menu to jump directly to the required month:

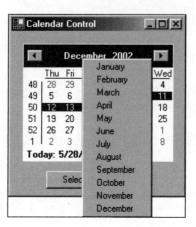

TreeView Control

A `TreeView` control displays data in a hierarchical fashion. A `TreeView` consists of a collection of nodes; every node is represented by a `TreeNode` object. The classic example of a tree view is Windows Explorer, which displays the hierarchy of folders and files within the file system. The versatile `TreeView` control is a good way of representing hierarchical data visually, and it's no coincidence that it uses the same family-based terminology as XML documents: the topmost node in a tree view is referred to as the root node. Any node that is subsequently added to the root node (or to another node) is called a child node, and child nodes with the same parent are called siblings.

As well as displaying text in a tree view, we can also display an image next to a node by using the `ImageList` object and referencing the index of the image in the list. Tree nodes can alternatively display a checkbox next to the node item. To do this, set the `CheckBox` property to `true`. We can associate data with each node of `TreeView` using the `Tag` property (alternatively, we can inherit from the `TreeNode` class, and add our own properties to contain the necessary data). We can edit the labels of `TreeNodes`, by setting the `LabelEdit` property to `true`.

Expanding and Collapsing Nodes

Nodes can be expanded to display any child nodes. Clicking on the + button next to the node (if one is displayed next to it) will expand the node. Alternatively, we can expand a node programmatically by calling the `Expand()` method on the node. To expand all the nodes in the `TreeView`, call the `ExpandAll()` method.

Similarly, any expanded node can be collapsed by clicking the − button next to the node, or we can call the `Collapse()` method to collapse a single node programmatically or use `CollapseAll()` to collapse all the nodes.

Apart from enhancing the appearance of the control using the standard properties such as `BackColor` and `Font`, the `TreeView` has some additional formatting properties of its own:

Property	Description
ShowLines	Set to true if lines are to be drawn between the nodes in the tree view.
ShowPlusMinus	Set to true to display the plus and minus signs for expanding and collapsing the nodes.
ShowRootLines	Set to true if lines are to be drawn between the nodes at the root of the tree view. If this is set to false, the plus and minus signs for expanding and collapsing the nodes won't be displayed.
HotTracking	If set to true, every time the mouse moves over a node, the node will be highlighted like a hyperlink in a web page.

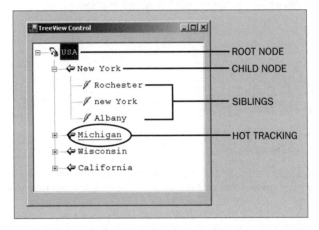

Let's take a quick look at the code to populate a TreeView. As in the screenshot above, we'll have a root node representing the USA; this will have a couple of child nodes representing some of the states, and each of these will have children representing some of the chief cities in that state.

First, we need an ImageList to store the images that will appear next to each node:

```
ImageList il = new ImageList();
```

We'll populate this ImageList within the form's Load event, and then set it as the ImageList for our TreeView:

```
private void Form1_Load(object sender, System.EventArgs e)
{
    il.Images.Add(new Icon("KEY04.ICO"));
    il.Images.Add(new Icon("ARW06LT.ICO"));
    il.Images.Add(new Icon("LITENING.ICO"));
    il.Images.Add(new Icon("ARW06UP.ICO"));
    treeView1.ImageList = il;
```

Next, let's add some nodes to the tree. We create each of the nodes by calling the `TreeView`'s `Nodes.Add()` method. This returns a reference to the created node. Once we've created each node, we can set its `ImageIndex` property to specify which image from our `ImageList` will be used for this node. First comes the root node representing the USA:

```
TreeNode rootNode = treeView1.Nodes.Add("USA");
rootNode.ImageIndex = 0;
```

Now we add the first of our second-level child nodes (this one representing New York State):

```
TreeNode states1 = rootNode.Nodes.Add("New York");
states1.ImageIndex = 1;
```

Once we have this node, we can give it some children of its own:

```
TreeNode child = states1.Nodes.Add("Rochester");
child.ImageIndex = 2;

child = states1.Nodes.Add("New York");
child.ImageIndex = 2;

child = states1.Nodes.Add("Albany");
child.ImageIndex = 2;
```

... and so on, for the remaining nodes.

Modifying the `ItemHeight`, `Indentation`, and `Font` properties, we can space the items apart further, and maybe display a large image next to the control. We can allow the user to edit labels in the control by setting the `LabelEdit` property to `true`.

The downloadable code also includes a more extensive `TreeView` example – an application that parses an XML file and displays its content as nodes in a tree view:

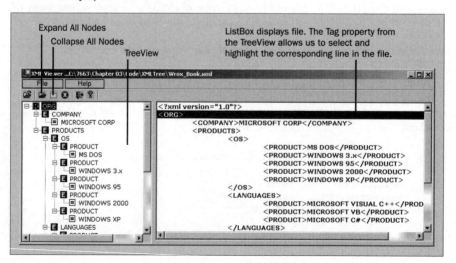

This example uses separate threads to populate the tree view that holds the visual breakdown of the XML file and the XML document itself in text format. We'll look at creating multi-threaded Windows applications in Chapter 9.

Custom Drawing

Certain .NET Windows controls allow us to perform custom drawing and painting. Custom drawing (or "owner drawing") allows us to modify the appearance of predefined controls by handling their drawing manually with GDI+ code. Other aspects of the control's behavior aren't affected. We'll look at two examples of custom drawing, the first using a ComboBox, and the second using buttons.

ComboBox Custom Drawing

We use the DrawMode property of the ComboBox to specify whether we want to handle drawing ourselves, or we want the control to draw everything for us. DrawMode supports three types:

❑   Normal – Displays the simple control. No additional drawing is done.

❑   OwnerDrawFixed – All the elements in the control are drawn manually and are of the same size.

❑   OwnerDrawVariable – All the elements in the control are drawn manually. Items may differ in size.

The custom drawing for the ComboBox is handled via two separate events:

❑   DrawItem – this event is raised when an owner-drawn ComboBox needs to be redrawn. We use the handler for this event to perform any custom drawing.

❑   MeasureItem – this event is raised before DrawItem if DrawMode is set to OwnerDrawVariable. We can use the handler for MeasureItem to specify the size of the item to be redrawn.

A more detailed description of working with fonts, brushes, colors, and the Graphics object can be found in Chapter 6.

Example Source Code

Let's see how this works in practice by looking at a simple example. This example will consist of a simple form with two combo boxes that allow the user to select a city and a color respectively. We'll add GDI+ code to draw each city item in a specific font, and an appropriately colored block with each color item. We won't go through every line of code, but we'll highlight the pertinent parts. The first combo box (for the cities) has its DrawMode property set to DrawMode.OwnerDrawVariable, so we'll handle both the DrawItem and MeasureItem events. Each item in the colors combo box will be of the same size, so we set its DrawMode to DrawMode.OwnerDrawFixed.

We have two arrays that are declared as private fields of the form to hold the list of colors and fonts. When the form loads, we'll populate these arrays, and add an item to the combo box for each color/city. The items in the color combo box will display the name of the color itself, so we'll add empty items for these:

```csharp
private void Form1_Load(object sender, System.EventArgs e)
{
    // Fill an array with the different colors you wish
    // to display in the ComboBox

    colorArray.Add(new SolidBrush(Color.Yellow));
    colorArray.Add(new SolidBrush(Color.Black));
    colorArray.Add(new SolidBrush(Color.Azure));
    colorArray.Add(new SolidBrush(Color.Firebrick));
    colorArray.Add(new SolidBrush(Color.DarkMagenta));

    // Add blank items to the list, since the text we will display
    // will be the name of the Color we are painting
    comboBox2.Items.Add("");
    comboBox2.Items.Add("");
    comboBox2.Items.Add("");
    comboBox2.Items.Add("");
    comboBox2.Items.Add("");

    // Fill an array with the different fonts that you will use to display
    // items in the other comboBox
    fontArray.Add(new Font("Ariel", 15, FontStyle.Bold));
    fontArray.Add(new Font("Courier", 12, FontStyle.Italic));
    fontArray.Add(new Font("Veranda", 14, FontStyle.Bold));
    fontArray.Add(new Font("System", 10, FontStyle.Strikeout));
    fontArray.Add(new Font("Century SchoolBook", 15, FontStyle.Underline));

    // Add the items that in the listBox
    comboBox1.Items.Add("Washington");
    comboBox1.Items.Add("Houston");
    comboBox1.Items.Add("Phoenix");
    comboBox1.Items.Add("Dallas");
    comboBox1.Items.Add("London");
}
```

Next, we'll add an event handler for the DrawItem event of our city combo box in order to display the items with different fonts and different colors. This consists primarily of GDI+ code, so we won't look at it in too much detail. Notice that we check to see whether the particular item is selected, and if it is we draw the city name in red with a blue background; otherwise we draw the text in black with a white background:

```csharp
private void comboBox1_DrawItem(object sender,
                        System.Windows.Forms.DrawItemEventArgs e)
{
    // Override this function to draw items in the Font comboBox

    // Get the Graphics Object (aka DC or Device Context Object)
```

```
    // passed via the DrawItemEventArgs parameter
    Graphics g = e.Graphics;

    // Get the bounding rectangle of the item currently being painted
    Rectangle r = e.Bounds;
    Font fn = null;

    if (e.Index >= 0)
    {
        // Get the Font object, at the specified index in the fontArray
        fn = (Font)fontArray[e.Index];

        // Get the text that we wish to display
        string s = (string)comboBox1.Items[e.Index];

        // Set the string format options
        StringFormat sf = new StringFormat();
        sf.Alignment = StringAlignment.Near;

        // Draw the rectangle
        e.Graphics.DrawRectangle(new Pen(new SolidBrush(Color.Black), 2), r);

        if (e.State == (DrawItemState.NoAccelerator | DrawItemState.NoFocusRect))
        {
            // If the item is not selected draw it with a different color
            e.Graphics.FillRectangle(new SolidBrush(Color.White), r);
            e.Graphics.DrawString(s, fn, new SolidBrush(Color.Black), r, sf);
            e.DrawFocusRectangle();
        }
        else
        {
            // If the item is selected draw it with a different color
            e.Graphics.FillRectangle(new SolidBrush(Color.LightBlue), r);
            e.Graphics.DrawString(s, fn, new SolidBrush(Color.Red), r, f);
            e.DrawFocusRectangle();
        }
    }
}
```

Next, we write the MeasureItem handler for the first combo box. We use this method to set the size of the item to be drawn; we alternate the heights of the items in the cities combo box, so that every second item has a height of 45, and the others have a height of 25:

```
private void comboBox1_MeasureItem(object sender,
                                   System.Windows.Forms.MeasureItemEventArgs e)
{
    // For the comboBox with OwnerDrawVariable property
    // Display every second item with a height of 45
    if (e.Index%2 == 0)
    {
        e.ItemHeight = 45 ;
        e.ItemWidth = 20 ;
    }
```

```
        else
        {
            // Display all other items with a height of 25
            e.ItemHeight = 25 ;
            e.ItemWidth = 10 ;
        }
    }
```

Next we handle the `DrawItem` event of the second combo box. Again, this consists mostly of GDI+ code that we won't examine too closely. The main point to notice is that each item in the colors combo box consists of two rectangles – a solid block filled with the appropriate color, and a block containing the name of the color.

```
private void comboBox2_DrawItem(object sender,
                                    System.Windows.Forms.DrawItemEventArgs e)
{
    // Override this function to draw items in the Color combo box

    // Get the Graphics Object (aka DC or Device Context Object)
    // passed via the DrawItemEventArgs parameter
    Graphics g = e.Graphics;

    // Get the bounding rectangle of the item currently being painted
    Rectangle r = e.Bounds;

    if (e.Index >= 0)
    {
        // Initialize the rectangle for the colored block.
        // We set it to the size of the bounds rectangle, and then
        // adjust its width, as the height and position will be the same
        Rectangle rd = r;
        rd.Width = 100;

        // Initialize the rectangle containing the name.
        // Again, we'll base this on the bounds rectangle, but set its
        // left edge to be the same as the right edge of the colored rectangle
        Rectangle rt = r;
        r.X = rd.Right;

        // Get the brush object, at the specified index in the colorArray
        SolidBrush b = (SolidBrush)colorArray[e.Index];

        // Fill a portion of the rectangle with the selected brush
        g.FillRectangle(b, rd);

        // Set the string format options
        StringFormat sf = new StringFormat();
        sf.Alignment = StringAlignment.Near;

        // Draw the rectangle
        e.Graphics.DrawRectangle(new Pen(new SolidBrush(Color.Black), 2), r);

        if (e.State == (DrawItemState.NoAccelerator | DrawItemState.NoFocusRect))
```

```
        {
            // If the item is not selected draw it with a different color
            e.Graphics.FillRectangle(new SolidBrush(Color.White), r);
            e.Graphics.DrawString(b.Color.Name, new Font("Ariel", 8, FontStyle.Bold),
                            new SolidBrush(Color.Black), r, sf);
            e.DrawFocusRectangle();
        }
        else
        {
            // If the item is selected draw it with a different color
            e.Graphics.FillRectangle(new SolidBrush(Color.LightBlue), r);
            e.Graphics.DrawString(b.Color.Name, new Font("Veranda", 12,
                            FontStyle.Bold), new SolidBrush(Color.Red), r, sf);
            e.DrawFocusRectangle();
        }
    }
}
```

That's it! This is how the combo boxes look when we execute the program:

Button Custom Drawing

The `ComboBox` control is unusual in having properties specifically designed to help out with custom drawing; for most other controls, we'll have to override the `OnPaint()` method. This method is called before the control is drawn, and we'll look at it in more detail in Chapter 6. To illustrate this technique, we'll extend our `Button` example from earlier in this chapter. We want to go a step further than our original example – we don't want the control to draw the text and picture for us. We want complete control over the `Graphics` object to do our own painting. What we want to achieve now is to have a flat button, with rounded edges, and to draw the text and picture where we want. To do this, we override the `OnPaint()` method. The signature for this method is:

```
protected override void OnPaint(PaintEventArgs e)
{
}
```

Add this method to the example from earlier in the chapter. Let's suppose for the moment that we do nothing here, and build the application as it stands. This is what the output looks like:

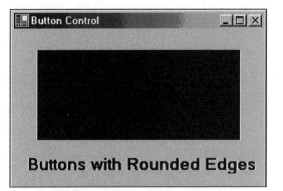

What you see is a black rectangle, since `OnPaint()` doesn't do any painting yet. We can still call the base class to do the painting, by calling the base class's `OnPaint()` method:

```
protected override void OnPaint(PaintEventArgs e)
{
    // Let the control do the painting
    base.OnPaint(e);
}
```

However, there's not much point overriding the method just to do this! Now let's do some custom drawing, such as creating the button with rounded edges.

To create a rectangle with rounded edges, we will use two unmanaged Windows API functions:

❏ `CreateRoundRectRgn()` from `gdi32.dll`

❏ `SetWindowRgn()` from `user32.dll`

To import these functions from the Windows API, we need to use the DllImport attribute. This attribute resides in the System.Runtime.InteropServices namespace, and is prefixed to the declaration of the method. Functions imported in this way must always be declared as static extern methods. The implementation is contained in the external DLL, so extern methods have no method body:

```
[DllImport("gdi32.dll", EntryPoint="CreateRoundRectRgn")]
private static extern int CreateRoundRectRgn(int x1, int y1, int x2, int y2,
                                             int x3, int y3);

[DllImport("user32.DLL", EntryPoint="SetWindowRgn")]
private static extern int SetWindowRgn(IntPtr hWnd, int hRgn, int bRedraw);
```

We cannot create a rounded rectangular region in the constructor of our Button control, since the control's size and dimensions are not yet defined. Instead, we create a new method called Init(), which will be invoked from the parent form when the form is loaded:

```
private void Form1_Load(object sender, System.EventArgs e)
{
    // Call the Button's Init() method here.
    // This is where the Rounded Rectangle Region is created
    // and the window is set to as this region
    button1.Init();
}
```

Within this Init() method, we create the rounded rectangular region:

```
public void Init()
{
    // Get the dimension of the client rectangle
    Rectangle rect = this.ClientRectangle;

    // Invoke the unmanaged DLL function here to create the
    // RoundRectangleRegion
    rg = CreateRoundRectRgn(rect.Left + 10, rect.Top + 10, rect.Right,
                            rect.Bottom, 100, 100);

    // Set the Window Region to a rectangle with rounded corners
    SetWindowRgn(this.Handle, rg, 1);
}
```

The OnPaint() Method

The OnPaint() method is called when a control needs to be redrawn. It takes one parameter – a PaintEventArgs class. This class has two public properties:

❑ Graphics – Encapsulates a GDI+ drawing surface (see Chapter 6 later in this book)

❑ ClipRectangle – Indicates the rectangle in which to paint

The Graphics object is the core object for working with graphics in .NET, and we'll see a lot more of it in Chapter 6. The ClipRectangle in this case is the rounded rectangle that we used the Windows API function to create.

Again, the OnPaint() method mostly contains GDI+ code, so we won't examine every line in detail:

```csharp
protected override void OnPaint(PaintEventArgs e)
{
    // Get the Graphics Object
    Graphics g = e.Graphics;

    // Get the Rectangle Object
    Rectangle rect = e.ClipRectangle;

    // Paint the rectangle with the color you want
    g.FillRectangle(new SolidBrush(Color.LightYellow), rect);

    // Define a StringFormat Object to display the string
    StringFormat sf = new StringFormat();
    sf.Alignment = StringAlignment.Center;
    sf.LineAlignment = StringAlignment.Center;

    // Get the current Image that we have set depending on
    // the location of the
    // mouse on the control as seen from
    // MouseDown, MouseEnter, MouseLeave events
    Image ig = this.ImageList.Images[ImageIndex];

    // Initialize the rectangle where you want the Image
    Rectangle rimg = rect;
    rimg.X += rect.Right/2 - 16;
    rimg.Y += rect.Bottom - 100;
    rimg.Width = 32;
    rimg.Height = 32;

    // Draw the Image
    g.DrawImage(ig, rimg, 0, 0, 32, 32, GraphicsUnit.Pixel);

    // Draw the String
    g.DrawString(Text, Font, new SolidBrush(Color.Blue), rect, sf);
}
```

Here's the result – completely distinctive buttons, which don't visually betray their dependence on the .NET Button control!

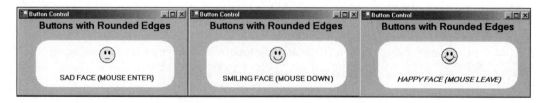

We haven't implemented every single feature possible – for example, we haven't implemented any code to deal with losing or gaining focus, but hopefully this short diversion into owner draw controls has given you a taste of what's possible, and has provided you with enough information to get started and to experiment with more ambitious techniques.

Consuming ActiveX Controls from .NET

As we've seen, the .NET Framework ships with a wide variety of controls, which will cover the most common situations where we need Windows controls. However, there is a much larger number of controls already written for use in VB6 and VC6 COM-based applications, and it's quite likely that there are custom controls you'll want to carry on using in .NET. In fact, even some of the existing Microsoft Windows Common Controls don't yet have .NET equivalents, so if you want to display web pages with an IE browser control, access inboxes using a MAPI control, or play video clips, you'll need a way of using your existing COM controls in .NET applications.

Thankfully, Microsoft foresaw this need and included an executable to import ActiveX controls into our .NET applications in the .NET Framework SDK. The ActiveX Control Importer, `AxImp.exe`, reads the type definitions in a COM type library for an ActiveX control, and generates a wrapper for the control, so that it can be used like a normal .NET Windows forms control. .NET controls derive from `System.Windows.Forms.Control`, so in order for an ActiveX control to be hosted on a form, it must be wrapped in a class that derives from `Control`. This class is the `Systems.Windows.Forms.AxHost` class; it acts as a Windows forms control wrapper from "outside", and acts as an ActiveX control container on "inside". The container hosts the ActiveX control and exposes the properties, methods, and events of the generated control.

We do not usually use the `AxHost` class directly – instead, `AxImp` does the work for us of generating a wrapper class derived from `AxHost`. This allows us to host the control in a Windows form and provides us with the same Visual Studio .NET support available to other Windows forms controls. As well as this wrapper control, `AxImp` generates a class library wrapper containing the type information for the methods, properties, and events exposed by the `ActiveX` control. This second assembly is called by the `AxHost`-derived class, and it in turn calls the runtime-callable wrapper (RCW) generated by the CLR, which itself calls the actual ActiveX control. A slightly simplified model of this process is shown overleaf:

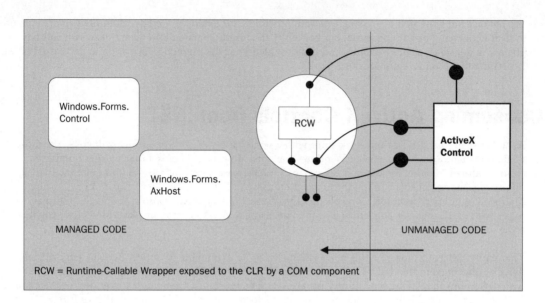

RCW = Runtime-Callable Wrapper exposed to the CLR by a COM component

Using AxImp

The AxImp executable resides in the \Program Files\Microsoft Visual Studio
.NET\FrameworkSDK\Bin folder. Before using this tool from the command line, it's convenient to add
this folder to the PATH environment variable.

The usage for AxImp.exe is:

```
AxImp [options] {file.dll | file.ocx}
```

Option	Description
file	The input file (.dll or .ocx) – the ActiveX control to convert
/delaysign	Used with /keyfile or /keycontainer
/help	Displays help and usage for the program
/keycontainer: <container name>	The name of a key container that holds the public-private key pair for signing the generated assembly
/keyfile: <filename>	A key file for signing the generated assembly with a strong name
/nologo	Suppresses the Microsoft start-up banner display
/out: <filename>	The file name of the assembly that AxImp generates

Option	Description
/publickey: <*filename*>	Specifies a file that holds the public-private key pair for signing the generated assembly
/silent	Prevents AxImp displaying a success message
/source	Generates C# source code for the Windows forms wrapper
/verbose	Specifies verbose mode (to display additional progress information)
/?	Displays the usage for the program (the same as /help)

> **There are two issues to be aware of when running** AxImp. **The first is that** AxImp **generates the wrapper DLL in the folder from which it's run; if this is the same folder as the original file, then** AxImp **will attempt to overwrite the original file. Also, if we create a wrapper for a control used by Windows or another program, there's a danger that that program will try to use the managed wrapper rather than the original ActiveX control.**

The assemblies generated by AxImp are named as follows:

❑ The CLR proxy for COM types: <*LibraryName*>.dll

❑ The Windows forms proxy for ActiveX controls: Ax<*LibraryName*>.dll This is the actual control that we add to our forms.

For example, if we run AxImp against the MS Agent Control (AgentObjects), the two assemblies generated will be AgentObjects.dll and AxAgentObjects.dll. These files appear like normal .NET assemblies, and so can be examined with tools such as the MSIL Disassembler, Ildasm.exe. This is what we see when we look at AgentObjects.dll:

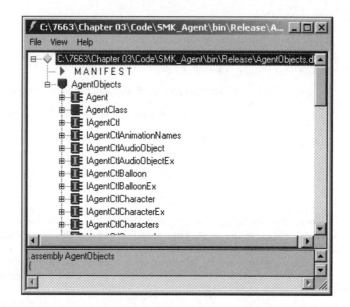

For each COM class in the library, AxImp generates a .NET interface with the same name, and a class called <ClassName>Class, for example Agent and AgentClass (for COM interfaces, only a corresponding .NET interface is generated). These are placed in a namespace with the same name as the control library, so the full names of the classes and interfaces are similar to COM ProgIDs. Just for the sake of comparison, here's the type library for the original ActiveX control as displayed in OLEView:

The `AgentClass` class in this assembly *doesn't* inherit from `AxHost`, so it can't be used as a Windows control – for that, we need to use the `AxAgent` class in the second assembly, `AxAgentObjects.dll`:

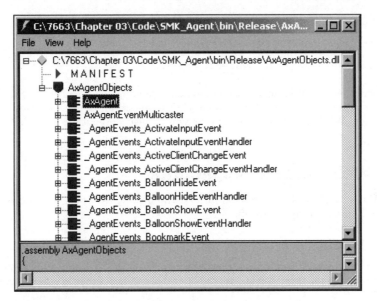

Notice that in this case, except for the `AxAgent` class, the generated .NET classes don't correspond to the COM classes and interfaces of the ActiveX control. Instead, the classes are used specifically to handle the events raised by the ActiveX control. For each event, a class named `<InterfaceName>_<EventName>Event` and a delegate named `<InterfaceName>_<EventName>EventHandler` are generated by AxImp. The delegates are used to hook up to the ActiveX control's events in .NET, just as we would hook up to a normal .NET event. Event delegates in .NET take two parameters – a `System.Object` instance representing the object that raised the event, and an `EventArgs`-derived object that contains any other arguments to be passed into the event handler. The `...Event` classes in our ActiveX control wrappers fulfill this function (but note that they *don't* derive from `System.EventArgs`).

For example, to hook up to the `AxAgent`'s BalloonShow event, we'll need to use an instance of the `_AgentEvents_BalloonShowEventHandler` delegate:

```
this.axAgent1.BalloonShow += new AxAgentObjects.
          _AgentEvents_BalloonShowEventHandler(this.axAgent1_BalloonShow);
```

The event handler will take an `_AgentEvents_BalloonShowEvent` object as its second parameter:

```
private void ax_Agent1_BalloonShow(object sender,
                          AxAgentObjects._AgentEvents_BalloonShowEvent e)
{
    // Event handling code here
}
```

Now that we've seen the theory, let's look at some examples in practice. Microsoft provides many COM components as ActiveX controls. Some typical examples are:

- ❑ Web Browser Control (C:\winnt\system32\shdocvw.dll)
- ❑ Media Player Control (C:\winnt\system32\mdxm.ocx)
- ❑ Agent Control (C:\winnt\system32\agentctl.dll)

We've included three examples in this section to help you understand AxImp. The first example will guide you step by step with using Visual Studio .NET to import an ActiveX control into your Windows Form application. We'll then look at creating the same project without the IDE. The other examples are built along the same lines.

A Simple Web Browser Application

In this example we will create a simple web browser by making use of the web browser ActiveX control (shdocvw.dll) provided by Microsoft.

Using Visual Studio .NET

Create a new C# Windows Application project in Visual Studio .NET and call it MyWebBrowser. Add two Panel controls to the form (a panel is container that can host other Windows controls):

- ❑ panel1 – to host a TextBox where the user can type the address of the site to go to, and a Button to tell the browser to navigate to that site. Set the Dock property for this panel to DockStyle.Top.
- ❑ panel2 – to host the ActiveX control itself. Set the Anchor property for this control to anchor to all edges of the form (AnchorStyles.Top | AnchorStyles.Bottom | AnchorStyles.Right | AnchorStyles.Left).

We will also add two simple Windows forms controls:

- ❑ A TextBox control (addressBox) to type the name of the website. Set the Anchor property to anchor this to the top, left, and right of the panel.
- ❑ A Button control to navigate to the site (goButton). Anchor this to the top and right of the panel.

Arrange the controls on the form so that they look something like this (we've added an image to the `goButton` for this example):

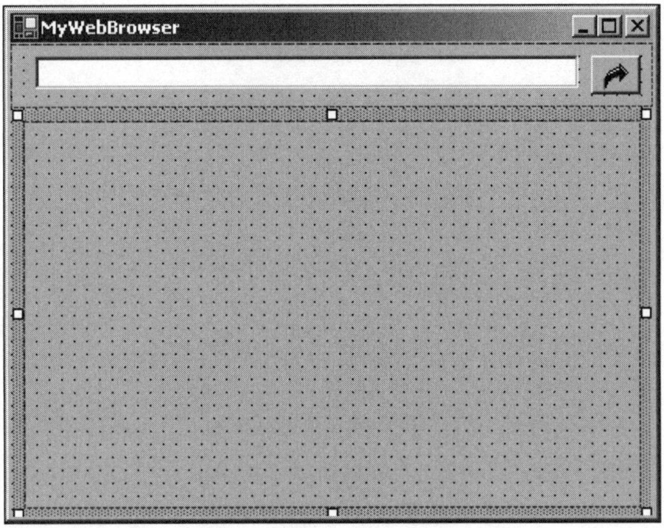

Before using the ActiveX control in our application, we need to make it available to our projects. The easiest way to do that is to add the control to our Toolbox. Open up the tab in the Toolbox where you want to add the control, right-click somewhere in that section, and select **Customize Toolbox...** from the context menu. This opens up the **Customize Toolbox** dialog:

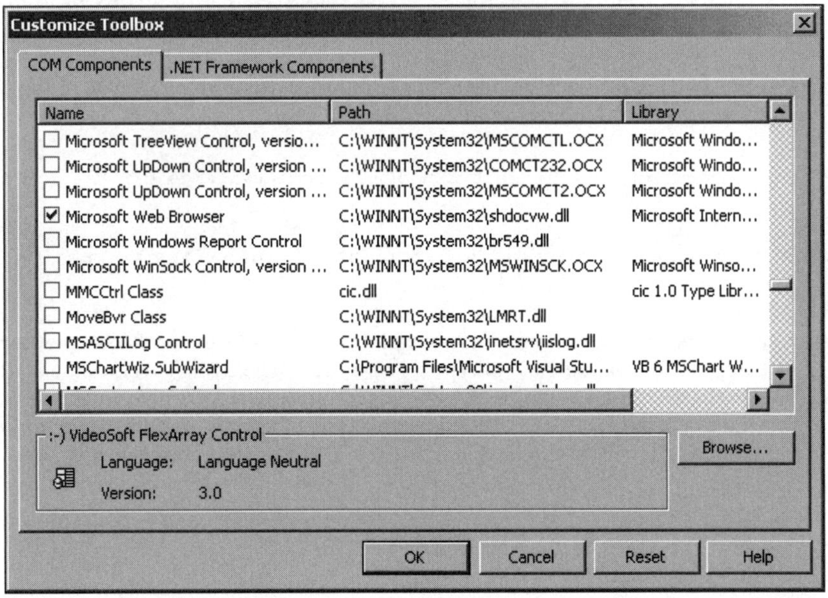

On the **COM Components** tab, scroll down the list to the **Microsoft Web Browser**, check the box next to this entry, and click on OK. The control will be added to the Toolbox, so we can drag it onto a form, just like a normal .NET Windows control (in this screenshot we've created a tab specifically for ActiveX controls):

Drag and drop the Explorer control onto `panel2`, and set its `Dock` property to `DockStyle.Fill`. When we add an ActiveX control to our project, Visual Studio .NET calls `AxImp` for us to generate local copies of the two assemblies. We don't need to call `AxImp` explicitly ourselves.

The next step is to add the click event handler for the button, where we'll navigate to the site in the textbox. Double-click on the button, and add the following code:

```
private void goButton_Click(object sender, System.EventArgs e)
{
    object o = null;
    axWebBrowser1.Navigate(addressBox.Text, ref o, ref o, ref o, ref o);
}
```

To navigate to a site, we call the web browser control's `Navigate()` method. This method takes five parameters: a string and four parameters of type `ref object`. The string specifies the URL for the page, so we pass in the text in the textbox as the first parameter. The other parameters contain information to send to the page, such as `POST` data and HTTP headers, and the frame to load the page in. We don't want to specify any of these, so we pass in a `null` object reference each time.

The last step is simply to navigate to the user's home page when the application loads. We'll do this in the form's constructor, after the call to `InitializeComponent()`, simply by calling the browser component's `GoHome()` method:

```
public Form1()
{
    InitializeComponent();
    axWebBrowser1.GoHome();
}
```

Build and execute the program, and there you go – you have your own web browser!

MFC provides us with the CHtmlView *class to display web pages. .NET does not have an equivalent to this, so if you need to develop an application in C# that displays web pages, this is the technique to use.*

Using the Command-Line Compiler

While using the Visual Studio .NET IDE makes it very easy to build this application, it's not very difficult even without it. The principal difference is that we have to call `AxImp` ourselves, rather than letting Visual Studio .NET do the work for us behind the scenes.

In this case, the command to generate the two .NET assemblies that act as wrappers for the ActiveX control is:

```
AxImp C:\WinNT\System32\System32\SHDocVw.dll
```

The path to SHDocVw.dll may vary, depending on the version of Windows you have installed. This generates the files SHDocVw.dll and AxSHDocVw.dll in the current directory.

Once we've run AxImp, we can start writing our code. AxImp places the wrapper for the control in a namespace called AxSHDocVw, so we'll include this in our using directives at the start of the file:

```
using System;
using System.Windows.Forms;
using System.Drawing;
using AxSHDocVw;
```

Next, we define the form. This will contain five controls as before, so we have five private field declarations:

```
public class WebBrowser : Form
{
    private AxWebBrowser browser;
    private Button goButton;
    private TextBox addressBox;
    private Panel panel1;
    private Panel panel2;
```

Within the form's constructor, we lay out the controls on the form and navigate to the user's home page. Firstly, we instantiate the panels and initialize the AxWebBrowser component. To do this, we need to call its BeginInit() method. ActiveX controls must be initialized before they are used, and calling this method starts this initialization process. We finish the process by calling EndInit(), when we're ready to start using the control:

```
public WebBrowser()
{
    panel1 = new Panel();
    panel2 = new Panel();
    browser = new AxWebBrowser();
    browser.BeginInit();
```

Now we've instantiated our panels, we can call SuspendLayout() on each of our container controls – the form and the two panels:

```
this.SuspendLayout();
panel1.SuspendLayout();
panel2.SuspendLayout();
```

Next we initialize the standard Windows controls – the textbox and button, and set the layout properties for the browser control. We also hook up the Button's Click event to an event handler. This code should be familiar by now:

```
this.Text = "MyWebBrowser";
panel1.Size = new Size(300, 30);
panel1.Dock = DockStyle.Top;
```

```
    panel2.Size = new Size(285,240);
    panel2.Location = new Point(5, 31);
    panel2.Anchor = AnchorStyles.Top | AnchorStyles.Bottom |
                    AnchorStyles.Left | AnchorStyles.Right;

    browser.Dock = DockStyle.Fill;

    addressBox = new TextBox();
    addressBox.Size = new Size(260, 20);
    addressBox.Location = new Point(5,5);
    addressBox.Anchor = AnchorStyles.Top | AnchorStyles.Right |
                        AnchorStyles.Left;

    goButton = new Button();
    goButton.Image = Image.FromFile("Arrow.ico");
    goButton.Location = new Point(270,5);
    goButton.Size = new Size(20,20);
    goButton.Anchor = AnchorStyles.Top | AnchorStyles.Right;
    goButton.Click += new EventHandler(goButton_Click);
```

Once we've initialized all the controls, we can place them on the panels, and we put the panels onto the form. Controls are placed onto panels (or other controls) in exactly the same way as they are placed onto a form: by calling the `Controls.Add()` method to add a single control, or the `Controls.AddRange()` method to add an array of controls:

```
    panel1.Controls.AddRange(new Control[] { addressBox, goButton });
    panel2.Controls.Add(browser);
    this.Controls.AddRange(new Control[] { panel1, panel2 });
```

Finally, we make the call to `EndInit()`, resume the layout of the controls, and call the `GoHome()` method to navigate the browser to the user's home page:

```
    browser.EndInit();
    panel1.ResumeLayout();
    panel2.ResumeLayout();
    this.ResumeLayout();

    browser.GoHome();
}
```

The event handler for the `Button` is identical to the VS version:

```
private void goButton_Click(object sender, EventArgs e)
{
    object o = null;
    browser.Navigate(addressBox.Text, ref o, ref o, ref o, ref o);
}
```

Lastly, we have the `Main()` method, which we use to launch our Windows application:

```
public static void Main()
{
    Application.Run(new WebBrowser());
}
}
```

Compile this as a Windows application using the command (assuming that the C# source file was saved as `WebBrowser.cs`, and that the wrapper assemblies generated by `AxImp` are in the same directory as this file):

csc /t:winexe WebBrowser.cs /r:AxSHDocVw.dll /r:SHDocVw.dll

This version of `MyWebBrowser` is very similar to the VS one, but there's one difference in the code that it's worth drawing attention to. If you look inside the `InitializeComponent()` method of the VS version and find the section where the web browser control is initialized, you'll see this line:

```
this.axWebBrowser1.OcxState = ((System.Windows.Forms.AxHost.State)
                               (resources.GetObject("axWebBrowser1.OcxState")));
```

The `OcxState` property of the `AxHost` class contains an object that represents the persisted state of the ActiveX control. VS creates a value for this which is stored in the resource (`.resx`) file for the project; this line of code reads that value from the resource file and initializes the control with it. The binary values used to represent the persisted state of ActiveX controls are beyond the scope of this book, but there is one issue we do need to draw attention to: ActiveX controls can't be resized until after the call to `EndInit()` if the `OcxState` property hasn't been set. However, docking and anchoring are effective – which is why we placed the browser control onto a panel, which we could resize.

Windows Media Player

We can use the same procedure to import the Windows Media Player ActiveX control (`msdxm.ocx`) for use in your Windows applications. This example also illustrates how to handle events raised by an ActiveX control.

The Media Player control allows us to view audio and video streams. The Media Player sends us numerous events that we can catch from our program. One such event handled by the control is `EndOfStream`. This event is sent when the control finishes playing the media file. Here is the code to initialize the Media Player:

```
mPlayer = new AxMediaPlayer.AxMediaPlayer();
mPlayer.BeginInit();
mPlayer.Size = new System.Drawing.Size(292, 273);
mPlayer.Location = new System.Drawing.Point(0, 16);
mPlayer.TabIndex = 0;
mPlayer.Dock = System.Windows.Forms.DockStyle.Fill;
this.panel2.Controls.AddRange(new System.Windows.Forms.Control[]{ this.mPlayer });
```

Handling Events from the Control

Suppose we need to know when the control completes playing the media file, so that you can open the next file to play. This can be achieved by handling the EndOfStream event. We saw when we looked at the AxAgentObjects.dll assembly in ILDasm that two classes are generated for each ActiveX event exposed by the control – a delegate to represent the event handling method, and a class to contain the arguments passed into this method. We hook into our event handler using the standard C# multicast delegate syntax:

```
mPlayer.EndOfStream += new
    AxMediaPlayer._MediaPlayerEvents_EndOfStreamEventHandler(this.streamEnded);
```

As soon as the media finishes playing the file, the control will invoke the streamEnded() method. Here we just stop the player, and set its position back to zero:

```
private void streamEnded(object sender,
                         AxMediaPlayer._MediaPlayerEvents_EndOfStreamEvent e)
{
    this.Show();
    mPlayer.Stop();
    mPlayer.CurrentPosition = 0.0;
}
```

Microsoft Agent

Let's have a last bit of fun with AxImp, and program the Microsoft Agent Control from C#. The Microsoft Agent Control allows us to program one of several cartoon characters with several predefined animation sequences, speech bubbles, etc., as a way of providing help to the user, much like the notorious Microsoft Office Assistant. Before you run the application, make sure that you have the data for the Genie agent character in the winnt\msagent\chars folder. You can download Microsoft agent characters from Microsoft's web site, at http://www.microsoft.com/msagent/characterdata.htm.

We'll program Genie to make a few gestures and speak a couple of sentences, and then allow the user to play any of the predefined animation sequences:

First, we need to declare the private fields that we will use in the form. As well as the controls that are placed on the form, we need fields to hold a collection of the available characters for the agent and the actual character we want to use:

```
private AxAgent agent;
private IAgentCtlCharacters agentChars;
private IAgentCtlCharacterEx actualChar;
private ListBox listBox1;
private Button playBtn;
private string file = "C:\\WinNT\\MsAgent\\Chars\\Genie.acs";
```

We initialize the AxAgent control in the normal way, in the InitializeComponent() method (this code is of course generated for us if we drop the control onto the form in Visual Studio .NET). However, there's a bit more work to do in the form constructor. First, we need to load the Genie character into our agentChars collection. We do this by calling the Load() method; this takes two parameters – a name by which we can refer to this character, and the filename where the character data is stored. This filename has to be cast to an object to be passed into the method. Finally, we call a method named ShowAgent() that will display and animate the agent:

```
public AgentExample()
{
    InitializeComponents();
    agentChars = agent.Characters;
    agentChars.Load("Genie", (object)file);
    ShowAgent();
}
```

Most of the work is done in this ShowAgent() method. First we get a reference to our Genie character (actualChar) from the agentChars collection. We iterate through the animation sequences available for this character, and add them to a listbox. The user will be able to select any of the sequences from this textbox to play. Then we show the character, move it across the screen, and play a couple of animation sequences and make the character speak a couple of sentences:

```
private void ShowAgent()
{
    actualChar = agentChars["Genie"];
    IEnumerator ie = actualChar.AnimationNames.GetEnumerator();
    while (ie.MoveNext())
    {
        listBox1.Items.Add(ie.Current.ToString());
        ie.MoveNext();
    }

    actualChar.Show(null);
    Rectangle r = this.Bounds;

    actualChar.Height = 200;
    actualChar.Width = 200;

    short x = Convert.ToInt16(this.ClientRectangle.Right / 2 +
                                        actualChar.Width / 2 + 100);
    short y = Convert.ToInt16(this.ClientRectangle.Bottom / 2 +
                                        actualChar.Height / 2 + 100);

    actualChar.MoveTo(x, y, 5);
    actualChar.Play("Congratulate");
    actualChar.Speak("Good morning to you my Master!", null);
    actualChar.SoundEffectsOn = true;
    actualChar.GestureAt(15, 50);
    actualChar.Speak("Your wish is my command !!", null);
}
```

The last piece of code is the event handler for our button. In this method, we want to play back the animation sequence selected in the listbox. If no sequence is selected, we return from the method; otherwise, we call the Play() method on actualChar passing in the name of the sequence:

```
private void playBtn_Click(object sender, System.EventArgs e)
{
    int sel = listBox1.SelectedIndex;
    if (sel < 0) return;
    actualChar.Play(listBox1.Items[sel].ToString());
}
```

Summary

We've covered quite a lot of ground in this long chapter. We've tried to present as quick a tour as possible through some of the most useful and widely used of the predefined controls that ship with the .NET Framework. We haven't hoped to cover every detail of every control, as this would make this chapter far larger than the entire book! Instead, we've tried to focus on the more interesting and advanced features, and particularly on those controls and features (such as owner drawing) that are either entirely new to .NET, or are greatly simplified.

After a quick introduction to using controls in general in Windows Forms applications, the bulk of the chapter consisted of overviews of the most useful controls. We then saw how we can draw controls manually, so that we can achieve effects not available as standard. Lastly, since there are many more ActiveX controls than there will be .NET controls for a long time, we saw how we can still use these within our Windows Forms applications, and we examined some of the issues involved in importing them into .NET projects.

4

Data Binding

One of the most obvious and valuable uses for a Windows application is to enter, display, and change data. One of the reasons that Visual Basic became so popular in the corporate environment is because a developer could create a Windows client application that worked as the front end to corporate data. The developer would drag a few textboxes and list boxes on a form, get the data and map it to the proper GUI element and you would have a functional application. With Visual Basic version 3.0, something called the Data Control was introduced. The developer could link the text box with data from the Data Control. The developer didn't have to write any code that kept the GUI elements on the form and the data in sync – the Data Control took care of that for us. It all sounded really good until you tried to use it on a high-volume client-server-type application. What we found out is that the Data Control couldn't keep up with the load. It was slow and prone to errors. It was also difficult to do any type of validation of the data. Developers didn't like the fact that they lost control of how data went from data base to screen. Most developers would use it to do simple prototyping but that was about it. When it came to writing the production enterprise-level applications, the Data Control generally was not used. One of the first things you did when creating a new form was to implement the data mapping functionality, getting the data from the database to the screen and from the screen back to the database.

In later versions of Visual Basic, the Data Control and data binding in general became a little better and a little more stable. However, now it was not an advantage from a design standpoint to have your GUI tied directly to the data in the form of a Data Control. Almost everyone was designing applications in a tiered environment. The data was the first tier, and then came various levels of business logic, and finally the client GUI. Some would even add layers such as messaging and transaction control (MSMQ and MTS, now incorporated into COM+). This isolated the data and the GUI even farther. So what would be the point of keeping data binding in .NET if nobody is really using it? What could possibly be gained from data binding? That is what this chapter will explore. We will look at how you can design a multi-tiered enterprise level application, and still take advantage of data binding.

Data Binding in .NET

Data binding in .NET has changed considerably from the first Data Control in VB 3.0. The first thing that you will (or rather won't!) see is that there isn't a data control any more. The Data Control was an ActiveX control that you had to place on each form that was going to utilize data binding. The Data Control would be responsible for mapping the data to the bound controls. Now data binding is built into the `System.Windows.Forms.Control` class. As you will recall, this is the base class for most of the `Windows.Forms` namespace. So, if you were to assume that this means that any control is bindable, you would be correct. Not only that, but almost any property of any control is `bindable`. What this means is that you can now bind data to properties such as `BackColor`, `Size`, `Location`, `Font`, etc. You will see how easy it is to create custom controls and user controls; it doesn't take much more to add advanced binding capabilities.

There are three classes that do a majority of the work for databinding:

- ❑   `BindingContext`
- ❑   `BindingManagerBase`
- ❑   `Binding`

First we'll talk about these three classes and how they relate to each other, and then we will look at several examples that show how they can be used. This discussion may seem a little confusing at first, but when we look at the examples things will clear up considerably.

BindingContext

Every object that has `Control` as its base class can have one `BindingContext` object. `BindingContext` is a collection class as it implements the `ICollection` and `IEnumerable` interfaces. `BindingContext` is responsible for managing a collection of `BindingManagerBase` objects for the control and any controls that may be contained by the control.

The only property that `BindingContext` has to use is the `Item` property. This will return a `BindingManagerBase` object. The `Item` property has two overloads. One that just takes the data source as a parameter of type `object` and the another takes the data source and the navigation path to the data member. The data source is the `list`, array, `DataSet`, or any other `Ilist`-based object (more on this later) that is being bound. The navigation path is a little trickier to explain. A **DataSet** can contain multiple **DataTables**. These `DataTables` can be linked using **DataRelations**. For example if you have two `DataTables`, `Customer` and `Orders`, and they are related with a `DataRelation` `custToOrder`, and you want to bind to the order number column, then the path would look like this:

```
Customer.custToOrder.OrderNumber
```

We will see more examples of this later in the chapter.

`BindingContext` has a couple of methods for us to use as well. As you might expect, they are related to managing the collection of objects that `BindingContext` contains. Some of these methods are protected, which means that they may not be available all the time. They are `Add`, `Clear`, `Contains`, and `Remove`.

BindingManagerBase

The objects that BindingContext manages are derived from BindingManagerBase. For each data source you bind to a form, there will be a BindingManagerBase object automatically created and associated with it. BindingManagerBase is an abstract class and there are two concrete classes that inherit from it. They are CurrencyManager (which doesn't, as it's name implies, only handle currencies) and PropertyManager. If the object that is being bound to (the data source) is a list of items (implements IList, IlistSource, or IBindingList) then a CurrencyManager is returned. If the data source object returns only a single property, then a PropertyManager is returned. For example, if the bound object is an array, this will be list-based, so a CurrencyManager object is used. Alternatively, if a TextBox is being bound to, it can only return a single property, so a PropertyManager is used. Most of the time you will be using a CurrencyManager.

When dealing with list-based data sources, the CurrencyManager's job is to keep the bound controls on a form in sync with each other for each data source. For example, if you are bound to a customer table, the BindingManagerBase object will make sure that you are looking at the firstName and lastName columns for the same row. Since most of the sources of data won't have a notion of position, it's the job of the CurrencyManager object to maintain position. A collection class or an array, for example, won't be able to tell you where in the list you are currently pointing. Two of the more important properties are Position and Current. Position is a zero-based integer index that tells you where in the list you're currently pointing, and Current returns the object at that position. The other properties are Count and Bindings. Count tells you how many items are in the list managed by the CurrencyManager and Bindings is a collection of Binding objects (we will look at these in a moment).

Here is the list of methods that BindingManagerBase contains:

Method	Description
AddNew()	Adds a new item to the underlying data list.
CancelCurrentEdit()	If the IEditableObject interface is implemented on the bound object, this will cancel the current edit and raise the Format event on the Binding object. Otherwise it is ignored.
EndCurrentEdit()	If the IEditableObject interface is implemented on the bound object, this will end the current edit. The difference between cancel and end current edit is that cancel will not save changes. If IEditableObject is not implemented, this is ignored.
GetItemProperties() GetItemProperties(dataSoure, listAccessors) GetItemProperties(listType, offset, dataSources, listAccessors)	Gets the list of property descriptors (more on these later) for the data source. Has three overloads: 1. No parameters 2. An arraylist of data sources and an arraylist of the bound properties 3. The type of the bound list, an int representing the number of recursive calls to make, and the two previously mentioned arraylists

Table continued on following page

Method	Description
GetListName(listAccessors)	Returns the name of the list that is the source of data for binding.
OnCurrentChanged(eventArgs)	Raises the CurrentChanged event.
PullData()	Pulls data from the control to the data source.
PushData()	Pushes data form the data source to the data control.
RemoveAt(index)	Removes the row at the specified index.
ResumeBinding()	Resume, binding after having suspended it.
SuspendBinding()	Temporarily suspends the binding. When binding is suspended, data can be manipulated and it will not raise any of the binding events.
UpdateIsBinding()	Updates the binding. After being suspended for example, calling this will make sure that the bindings are back in sync.

Binding Class

The last piece of the data-binding process is the Binding class. Binding is the class that actually binds or connects the property value of an object to the property value of a control. Remember that the BindingManagerBase object (either the CurrencyManager or PropertyManager) manages the collection of Binding objects for a form.

When you create a Binding object there are three things that you will need to know. First is the property on the control to be bound to. For example, this could be the Text property of a TextBox. The second thing to know is the data source or the object that will be bound to. The last thing that you will need is the navigation path, which we discussed earlier; this path will ultimately resolve to the list or property that contains the data you want to bind to.

Even though a CurrencyManager manages Bindings, and BindingContext objects manage CurrencyManagers, you don't need to create all three to bind data to a control. Every object inherited from Control contains a property called DataBindings; this returns an object of type ControlBindingsCollection, which is the collection class for the Binding objects. You can create the Binding objects and add them directly to this collection through the DataBindings property. For example, suppose you have a TextBox named txtLastName and you want to bind the Text property to the column lastName in the cust data table in the custList dataset. This is what the Binding creation code would look like:

```
txtLastName.DataBindings.Add("Text", custList, "cust.lastName");
```

Here you can see the three parameters that we just talked about. "Text" is the property to bind to, custList is the source of the data, and "cust.lastName" resolves to the lastName column. To put this another way, we want to display the data from the lastName column in the cust table that is in the custList dataset in the Text property of the txtLastName textbox.

The `Binding` class has six properties. They are:

Property Name	Description
BindingManagerBase	Returns the `BindingManagerBase` object that is managing this `Binding` object. It will be either a `CurrencyManager` or a `PropertyManager`.
BindingMemberInfo	Returns a `BindingMemberInfo` object. This is a struct that contains information about the binding such as the binding path and the binding member name.
Control	The control that the `Binding` object is associated with. Note that this returns a `Control` object, and not just the name of the control.
DataSource	The data source that is being bound to.
IsBinding	Returns `true` or `false` depending on whether the binding is active.
PropertyName	Gets or sets the name of the property that is being bound to on the control, the `Text` property of a `TextBox` for instance.

There are two events on the binding class that are most useful. They are `Format` and `Parse`. These two events are raised whenever the data is pushed from the data source to the control or when the data is pulled from the control to the data source. This allows you to do special validating or formatting of the data.

The `Format` event is used for formatting the data from the data source before it is displayed on the control. So when data is being pushed from the data source to the control, the `Format` event is raised and you can perform whatever data formatting or validation is necessary prior to displaying it. The `Parse` event is when the data is changed in the control and needs to go back to the data source. A classic example of this process would be data that is stored as a decimal, but displayed as a currency. The code in the event handler for the `Format` event would take the decimal value and format it for currency display, while the code in the `Parse` event handler will take the currency data and convert it back to decimal type.

Simple Data Binding

So far this all sounds rather confusing. Let's look at a few examples and maybe things will start to make sense. All of the examples are included in the code download available from http://www.wrox.com. The data for some of the examples is the pubs database in SQL Server or MSDE. Another source of data for some of the examples is the `address.xml` document that is included in the download. We'll start out with a couple of simple examples and work our way to the more advanced examples.

Just so that there isn't any question, the first example will be done without using Visual Studio .NET. We will go and get the all of the author information from the `authors` table in the pubs database and display it in a grid. This example is in the `SimpleDataBinding_1NoIde` folder of the example downloads. First here is the code:

```
using System;
using System.Windows.Forms;
using System.Drawing;
using System.Data;
using System.Data.SqlClient;

public class SimpleDatabinding : Form
{
    private DataGrid custGrid;

    public SimpleDatabinding()
    {
        this.Text = "Simple Databinding example";

        custGrid = new DataGrid();
        custGrid.Size = new Size(290,270);
        custGrid.Anchor = AnchorStyles.Top | AnchorStyles.Bottom |
                          AnchorStyles.Right | AnchorStyles.Left;
        custGrid.CaptionText = "Authors data";
        this.Controls.Add(custGrid);

        SqlConnection cn = new SqlConnection("Data Source=(local);Initial
                                  Catalog=pubs;User ID=sa;Password=");
        SqlDataAdapter da = new SqlDataAdapter("SELECT * FROM authors", cn);
        DataSet ds = new DataSet();
        da.Fill(ds);
        custGrid.DataSource = ds.Tables[0];
    }

    public static void Main()
    {
        Application.Run(new SimpleDatabinding());
    }
}
```

Not much to it. Looking at the code you can see that we create a new DataGrid object (custGrid) and set a couple of its properties, Size, Anchor, and Text. Next we go to the pubs database and retrieve our data. We create a new SqlConnection, a new SqlDataAdapter, and a new DataSet. After filling the dataset with the data from the authors table we set the DataSource property of the DataGrid to the DataTable that contains the authors information. As you might expect, Visual Studio .NET does make this process a little easier, but there isn't a single example in this chapter that cannot be done with Notepad and the command-line compiler.

The next example is by far the easiest. You really only have to write one line of code. The rest is merely clicking in the IDE. What we're going to do is create a simple Windows application. We will drop a datagrid on the form, add a data adapter component to the form and set the DataSource property of the grid to our new dataset. The complete process will take about two minutes form start to running the application. The completed application is in the SimpleDataBinding_1 folder of the example downloads.

The exact step-by-step process for creating this application is as follows:

1. Start Visual Studio .NET and create a new Windows application in C#.

2. From the Toolbox, select the datagrid and drag it to the blank form. Resize to your liking.

3. Select the Data tab of the Toolbox.

4. Select a `SqlDataAdapter` and drag it to the form. This will start the Data Adapter Configuration Wizard. Click Next.

5. Either select a current connection or create a new connection to a database. This example assumes you will be connecting to the `pubs` database in SQL Server. Once you have a connection, click Next.

6. Select the Use SQL statements option and click Next.

7. Enter `SELECT * FROM authors` in the box and click on Advanced Options...

8. Uncheck Generate Insert, Update and Delete statements. This will give us a read-only view of the data. We will look at updating data later in the chapter. Click OK.

9. You should see a message that `sqlDataAdapter1` was configured successfully. Click Finish.

10. At the bottom of the screen you should see two components, `sqlDataAdapter1` and `sqlConnection1`. Right-click on the `sqlDataAdapter1` component and select Generate DataSet.

11. Keep all of the defaults and click on OK.

12. You should now see another component named `dataSet11`. Right-click on the datagrid and select Properties. Change the `DataSource` property to `dataSet11.authors`. Notice that this is the navigation syntax that we discussed earlier.

13. View the code for the form and in the `Form1` constructor enter the following line of code after the call to `InitializeComponent`:

```
sqlDataAdapter1.Fill(dataSet11);
```

Now press *F5* and run you application. If you did everything correctly, you should be looking at a form with a grid full of data:

au_id	au_lname	au_fname	phone	address	city	state	zip	contract
172-32-1176	White	Johnson	408 496-7223	10932 Bigge	Menlo Park	CA	94025	☑
213-46-8915	Green	Marjorie	415 986-7020	309 63rd St.	Oakland	CA	94618	☑
238-95-7766	Carson	Cheryl	415 548-7723	589 Darwin L	Berkeley	CA	94705	☑
267-41-2394	O'Leary	Michael	408 286-2428	22 Cleveland	San Jose	CA	95128	☑
274-80-9391	Straight	Dean	415 834-2919	5420 College	Oakland	CA	94609	☑
341-22-1782	Smith	Meander	913 843-0462	10 Mississipp	Lawrence	KS	66044	☐
409-56-7008	Bennet	Abraham	415 658-9932	6223 Batema	Berkeley	CA	94705	☑
427-17-2319	Dull	Ann	415 836-7128	3410 Blonde	Palo Alto	CA	94301	☑
472-27-2349	Gringlesby	Burt	707 938-6445	PO Box 792	Covelo	CA	95428	☑
486-29-1786	Locksley	Charlene	415 585-4620	18 Broadway	San Francisc	CA	94130	☑

If you look at the form1.cs file that you just created, you'll notice that there isn't very much code apart from the one line that we added in the constructor. However, if we look at the declarations we do notice something rather interesting:

```
private System.Windows.Forms.DataGrid dataGrid1;
private System.Data.SqlClient.SqlDataAdapter sqlDataAdapter1;
private System.Data.SqlClient.SqlCommand sqlSelectCommand1;
private System.Data.SqlClient.SqlConnection sqlConnection1;
private SimpleDataBinding_1.DataSet1 dataSet11;
```

Everything looks OK until the last line. Shouldn't that be something like:

```
private System.Data.DataSet dataSet11;
```

What has happened is that Visual Studio.NET has generated a nicely typed dataset for you. If you look in your project folder you will see the file DataSet1.cs. If you have **Display All Files set** on the Solution Explorer then you will find it under the XML schema that was also generated for you. You can look at this file, but since this is a generated class, any changes you make may be overwritten. We won't get into the details of what is in DataSet1.cs, but if you look you can see that the class is derived from DataSet. The other interesting thing is that there are two nested classes – authorsDataTable, which is derived from DataTable, and authorsRow, which is derived from DataRow. If you look at these classes closely, you will be able to see why it is called a typed dataset. In the authorsDataTable class, DataColumn objects are created that have names and data types that match up with the columns from the database. The advantage of a typed dataset is that it provides better support in Visual Studio .NET, for example the ability to select column names with IntelliSense. This will obviously lead to fewer typographical errors in your code. You also reduce run-time errors because most of the type checking is done at compile time. As far as functionality and how it executes, there is little difference between a typed dataset and an untyped one, unless of course you add functionality to the typed DataSet.

This is without question the easiest way to display data on a form: a few clicks of the mouse and one line of code. But what if you don't want to display your data in a grid? Let's say you want to display data one row at a time. This can be done almost as quickly.

This example is in the SimpleDataBindings_2 folder of the examples download. We will take the same DataAdapter and DataSet components that we created in the first example, but instead of binding to a datagrid, we will bind to a series of textboxes and checkboxes.

The steps for this example are almost as simple as the previous example:

1. Start Visual Studio .NET and create a new Windows Application in C#

2. From the toolbox select and drag seven textboxes onto the form, and name the textboxes as follows:

- ❏ txtFirstName
- ❏ txtLastName
- ❏ txtPhone
- ❏ txtAddress
- ❏ txtCity
- ❏ txtState
- ❏ txtZip

3. Add a checkbox and give it the name cbContract

4. Add two buttons and name them btnPrev and btnNext

5. Complete Steps 3 to 13 as in the previous example

At this point you should have something that looks similar to this:

Now we need to set the bindings. Select the `txtFirstName` textbox. In the **Properties** window, find the **Data** category and click the plus next to **DataBindings**. You will see lines for **(Advanced)**, **Tag**, and **Text**. If you click on the **Text** property, a dropdown edit box will appear that should have the name of the dataset (**dataSet11**) that we just created. Click on the plus sign next to the dataset name, and **authors** should appear. If you click the plus sign next to **authors**, you will see the list of columns in the `authors` data table. For the `txtFirstName` text box, you should select au_fname. The complete line should read **dataSet11 – authors.au_fname**. Repeat this process for the rest of the textboxes, assigning the proper column to the proper textbox.

For the checkbox, you will see a different list of properties under the **DataBindings** property. The one that we are interested in is the `Checked` property. The `contract` column of the pubs database is defined as a `bit` data type. The column contains either 1 or 0, representing `true` or `false`. Since this is what the `Checked` property is looking for, we can bind directly to it. The list of properties that show up in the **DataBindings** section is not a complete list of properties that can be bound to. Remember we said that you can bind to nearly all of the properties of a control. The list here is just the most likely properties that you will want to bind to. If you click on the ellipsis on the **(Advanced)** line, the complete list of bindable properties will be displayed. We will look at binding to some of these other properties later in the chapter.

At this point you can run the example and you should see data in the textboxes. It should be the first row in the database. The problem is that this is the only row that you are able to view. We need to add some navigation capabilities. That is what our buttons are for. This is the code to place in the `btnPrev` click event handler:

```
private void btnPrev_Click(object sender, System.EventArgs e)
{
    this.BindingContext[dataSet11,"authors"].Position--;
}
```

That one line of code is actually doing quite a bit. We are asking the `BindingContext` object of the form (`this`) for the `CurrencyManager` that is assigned to the `dataSet11` data source. The navigation path for the data list of that data source is, in this case, just `"authors"`, which is the name of the data table that was created to store the results of our initial query. From the `CurrencyManager` object that is returned by the `BindingContext` object, we are decreasing the `Position` property by 1. Another way to write this would be like this:

```
private void btnPrev_Click(object sender, System.EventArgs e)
{
    CurrencyManager cm = this.BindingContext(dataSet11,"authors");
    cm.Position--;
}
```

The bottom line is that this is setting the current position of the data source to the row just before the current row. If we are at the first row, then nothing happens. We need to add the same code to the `btnNext` click event handler, except instead of decrementing; we will be incrementing (`++`). Now if you run the example you should be able to click the two buttons and navigate through the dataset.

There are a couple of other things we should look at in this example. If we look at the `InitializeComponent` method and find the section for `txtFirstName`, we will see the following line of code:

```
this.txtFirstName.DataBindings.Add(new System.Windows.Forms.Binding
                    ("Text", this.dataSet11, "authors.au_fname"));
```

This is where we are adding a new `Binding` object to the `DataBindings` collection of `txtFirstName`. Take a close look at the parameters that we pass in. The first one is the string `"Text"`; this is the property of `txtFirstName` that we want to bind to. The next parameter is the data source that is being bound to – in this case `dataSet11`. The last parameter is a string that uses that navigation syntax that we talked about before. Here the path to the data that should display in `txtFirstName` is `"authors.au_fname"`. We will be seeing this line of code quite often in the rest of this chapter.

Another thing to notice is that we never actually explicitly created a `BindingContext` object or the `CurrenyManager`. That was done automatically when we added `Binding` objects to the `DataBinding` collections of the controls. Another point to remember is that when we added the code navigation, we did not reference any of the controls directly; we didn't say something like `txtFirstName.MoveToTheNextRow`. We only referenced the `BindingContext` of the form, or more precisely the `BindingContext` object of the parent of the controls that we were binding to. That `BindingContext` object gave us a `CurrencyManager` to use for navigation. Remember that the `CurrencyManager` is responsible for keeping all of the controls that are bound to its data source in sync. Since all of the controls were bound to the same data source, we only had to deal with one `CurrencyManager`. This is an important concept to grasp if you want to understand data binding in .NET. Again you can see how different it is from previous versions of VB and how much more flexibility is available now.

Master/Detail Display

A very common request is to display data in a master/detail format. An example might involve taking a row from the `orders` table and showing all of the line items for that order. The easy way to do this would be to use a single data source on a form with multiple controls on it. In this example we will actually show a master/detail/detail display. This example is in the `DataBinding_3` folder of the code download.

The example will have three datagrids. Each grid should be big enough to see several rows of data. We'll be using the `Northwind` database as the source of data. Here is the source code for the form's constructor (the only place we need to add code for this example):

```
public Form1()
{
    //
    // Required for Windows Form Designer support
    //
    InitializeComponent();

    //
    // TODO: Add any constructor code after InitializeComponent call
    //

    SqlConnection cn = new SqlConnection(
                "data source=(local);uid=sa;password=;database=northwind");

    DataSet ds = new DataSet("CustOrders");

    SqlDataAdapter daCust = new SqlDataAdapter("SELECT * FROM Customers;" +
                "SELECT * FROM Orders; SELECT * FROM [Order Details]", cn);
    daCust.Fill(ds);

    ds.Relations.Add("CustOrder", ds.Tables["Table"].Columns["CustomerId"],
                            ds.Tables["Table1"].Columns["CustomerId"]);

    ds.Relations.Add("OrderDetail", ds.Tables["Table1"].Columns["OrderId"],
                            ds.Tables["Table2"].Columns["OrderId"]);

    grdCustomers.DataSource = ds;
    grdCustomers.DataMember = "Table";
```

```
        grdOrders.DataSource = ds;
        grdOrders.DataMember = "Table.CustOrder";

        grdOrderDetails.DataSource = ds;
        grdOrderDetails.DataMember = "Table.CustOrder.OrderDetail";
    }
```

We start out by making a new connection to the database. We then create a new `DataSet` object and give it the name `CustOrders`. Next, we create the `SqlDataAdapter` object. Notice the SQL command that we use – there are actually three separate SQL statements, each separated by a semi-colon. We select all of the rows from the `Customers` table, all of the rows from the `Orders` table, and all of the rows from the `Order Details` table. When we call the `Fill` method of the `SqlDataAdapter`, the dataset will contain three tables, one for each of the SQL statements. Since we didn't do anything to change the names, they will be `Table`, `Table1`, and `Table2`, the default names.

Now that we have the three tables, we need to set a couple of relationships between the tables. We need a relationship between the `Customers` table (`Table`) and the `Orders` table (`Table1`), with `CustomerId` as the key. We also need a relationship between the `Orders` table (`Table1`) and the `Order Details` table (`Table3`) with `OrderId` as the key. Notice that as part of the `Relations.Add` method we can give each relation a name:

```
ds.Relations.Add("CustOrder", ds.Tables["Table"].Columns["CustomerId"],
                            ds.Tables["Table1"].Columns["CustomerId"]);

ds.Relations.Add("OrderDetail", ds.Tables["Table1"].Columns["OrderId"],
                            ds.Tables["Table2"].Columns["OrderId"]);
```

As you can see in the code above, we give the names `CustOrder` and `OrderDetail` to the relations. These names are important, as we shall see in just a moment.

The next section of code is where we make the bindings:

```
grdCustomers.DataSource = ds;
grdCustomers.DataMember = "Table";

grdOrders.DataSource = ds;
grdOrders.DataMember = "Table.CustOrder";

grdOrderDetails.DataSource = ds;
grdOrderDetails.DataMember = "Table.CustOrder.OrderDetail";
```

We set the `DataSource` property and the `DataMember` property for `grdCustomers` first. Remember that the `DataMember` property is where the list of data for the control can be found. In the case of `grdCustomers`, it is `Table`, which is the `Customers` table. The settings for the other two grids are more interesting. We set the `DataSource` property for `grdOrders` and `grdOrderDetails` to the same data source as `grdCustomers`. We have to do this so that we have a common `CurrencyManager`. Once again, remember that you have one `CurrencyManager` assigned for each data source. However, the `DataMember` property for `grdOrders` is not set to `Table1` as you might expect; instead, it is set to the `CustOrder` relation that we added. If you consider this for a moment, you will see that it makes perfect sense. If we set the `DataMember` property on `grdOrders` to `Table1`, how would it know when `grdCustomers` has changed? How would it know what orders to display? By using the relation, we are saying that the only orders we want to see are the orders that have the same `CustomerId` as the current row in the `Customers` table. The same principle holds true for `grdOrderDetails`. However, notice that we are using the path starting from `Table`. This way everything stays in sync. When we select a different customer, `grdOrders` shows only orders for that customer, and `grdOrderDetails` shows details for the current order (the first one in the list until another one is selected). Here is what this example looks like:

You'll notice that as you click on the customer grid, the other two grids sync up with the current customer.

What if you don't want to display all of the customer data? Do we need to use a grid in order to see master-detail relationships? Of course not – here is the same example, but we have removed the customer grid and instead added a combo box and three textboxes. We will use the combo box to select the company name, and display the contact name, phone number and fax number, in the textboxes. Here is the modified code (located in `DataBinding_4`):

```
public Form1()
{
  //
  // Required for Windows Form Designer support
  //
  InitializeComponent();

  //
  // TODO: Add any constructor code after InitializeComponent call
  //

  SqlConnection cn=new SqlConnection(
                "data source=(local);uid=sa;password=;database=northwind");

  DataSet ds = new DataSet("CustOrders");

  SqlDataAdapter daCust = new SqlDataAdapter("SELECT * FROM Customers;" +
                "SELECT * FROM Orders; SELECT * FROM [Order Details]", cn);
  daCust.Fill(ds);

  ds.Relations.Add("CustOrder", ds.Tables["Table"].Columns["customerid"],
                                ds.Tables["Table1"].Columns["customerid"]);

  ds.Relations.Add("OrderDetail", ds.Tables["Table1"].Columns["orderid"],
                                ds.Tables["Table2"].Columns["orderid"]);

  //grdCustomers.DataSource = ds;
  //grdCustomers.DataMember = "Table";
  grdOrders.DataSource = ds;
  grdOrders.DataMember = "Table.CustOrder";
  grdOrderDetails.DataSource = ds;
  grdOrderDetails.DataMember = "Table.CustOrder.OrderDetail";

  cbCust.DataSource = ds;
  cbCust.DisplayMember = "Table.CompanyName";
  txtContact.DataBindings.Add("Text",ds,"Table.ContactName");
  txtPhoneNo.DataBindings.Add("Text",ds,"Table.Phone");
  txtFaxNo.DataBindings.Add("Text",ds,"Table.Fax");
}
```

The added code is in bold type. Also, notice that we commented out the lines of code that set the DataSource and the DataMember for grdCustomers. Looking at the code that is in bold, we can see that we set the same data source for the combo box (cbCust). Notice that the combo box doesn't have a DataMember property – instead it has a DisplayMember property. This property is inherited from ListControl. The reason for this is simple – a control that is derived from ListControl will only be able to display one property from the data source. A grid, for example can display the complete table; one column in the grid equals one property in the data source. So any control that is derived from ListControl will have a DisplayMember property. This property tells the data source which of its properties will be displayed. In this case, it is the CompanyName column from the Table table. Notice that we always give the complete navigation path; otherwise the combo box would not know where the CompanyName property was. Remember there are three tables in the dataset.

The textboxes that we add need to have a binding set as well. Here we will use the syntax that we saw the designer use in the earlier example. For each text box, we will add a new `Binding` object to the `CurrencyManager`'s `Bindings` collection:

```
txtContact.DataBindings.Add("Text", ds, "Table.ContactName");
txtPhoneNo.DataBindings.Add("Text", ds, "Table.Phone");
txtFaxNo.DataBindings.Add("Text", ds, "Table.Fax");
```

The parameters for the method tell the `Binding` object that is being added what bindings it is responsible for handling. In the first case (the `txtContact` textbox), we are saying that the `Binding` object is responsible for binding the `Table.ContactName` property from the `ds` data source to the `Text` property of the `txtContact` control. The same thing is repeated for the `txtPhoneNo` and `txtFaxNo` controls. When you run this example, you will see that it still works the same as before. When a new customer is selected, the orders grid and the order details grid stay in sync with the current customer. The only difference is that the user selects customers from a drop-down and not from a grid.

Instead of using a drop-down, we could have used another textbox for the contact name, and implemented the Prev and Next buttons as we did earlier. Here is what this example looks like:

The real point that we are trying to make is that it is not the controls that are managing the binding process. The controls are irrelevant for the most part. The `BindingContext` object and the `CurrencyManager` object are really managing the binding. As a little experiment, put the `grdCustomers` datagrid back on the form. Uncomment the two lines of code that set its `DataSource` and `DataMember` properties. Run the example and you will notice that you can select the customer from the grid, and the textboxes and drop-down list will reflect the change. Also, if you select the customer from the drop-down, the customer grid will reflect the change. We now effectively have two master resultsets and two details. But they all stay in sync because the `CurrencyManager` is doing its job.

Updating Data

We have the data bound to various controls on the form; everything is working great. However, most applications will require you to be able to modify and edit data as well as look at it. How can we make the changes on the form persist to the database? The answer is the same way you would if you weren't using databinding. Since the form is not maintaining an open connection with the database, any changes that you make on a form with bound controls will not be persisted to the database until you actually update the data adapter. Let's take one of the previous examples and add an **Update** button. This is in the `DataBinding_5` folder. We will be modifying the earlier example where we first added the **Prev** and **Next** buttons.

Updating the data to the database is actually not part of data binding. Data binding ensures that the data in your data source is current and in step with the data in the bound controls on the form. In this example, we will re-configure the data adapter component, and instead of unchecking the box that said **Generate Insert, Update and Delete statements**, we will check it this time. You will notice that there are now several more `SqlCommand` icons on the component tray of your form. There is a component for inserting (`sqlInsertCommand1`), one for deleting (`sqlDeleteCommand1`), and one for modifying (`sqlUpdateCommand1`). Here is the code for the **Update** button:

```
private void btnUpdate_Click(object sender, System.EventArgs e)
{
    DataRow[] dataRows = new DataRow[1];
    dataRows[0] = dataSet11.Tables[0].
                            Rows[this.BindingContext[dataSet11].Position];
    sqlDataAdapter1.UpdateCommand = sqlUpdateCommand1;
    sqlDataAdapter1.Update(dataRows);
}
```

The IDE created the commands for us, so all we have to do is tell the command which row(s) to update. In this example we create a `DataRow` array to pass into the update command. This will contain one row, which is the row that we are currently editing. Notice that we use the `CurrencyManager`'s `Position` property to determine the current row. The `sqlUpdateCommand1` has been set to the `sqlDataAdapter1.UpdateCommand` property by the wizard. We then call the `Update` method, passing in the array with the current row. Even though we used the `CurrencyManager` to determine which row to update, we could have very easily done it by iterating through the rows and looking for the rows with the `RowState` property set to `DataRowState.Modified`. Iterating through the rows of a grid can be slow if you have a large number of rows to process. Run the example and change a piece of data in one of the rows. Click the **Update** button and exit the example. Now restart the example, and you should see that the changes you made were indeed saved to the database.

What all of this means is that when it comes to updating, adding, or deleting data inthe database, you will have to manage the updates yourself. Data binding will keep the data in the data source and the bound controls in sync. You will have to make sure the data in the data source is persisted correctly. The example that we just looked at is but one way of persisting data to the database. You could for example allow the user to make changes to several rows or add several rows and then do an update of all the rows at once. In this case you might prefer to use the GetChanges method of the DataSet. GetChanges will create a dataset of the changes you just made. You can look at the framework documentation for more information on how to update data.

Complex Binding

We have seen how simple it can be to bind to a DataSet, but what if your data isn't in a DataSet? You could transform the data and put into a DataSet, DataTable, or DataView, but that isn't always practicable. Also, if you're designing a multi-tiered system, a DataSet may not be the best way to transmit data between tiers. Sometimes you need to have your data in a container that offers a little more functionality than a DataSet. You may have created classes to contain your data, and collection classes to contain those classes. You go through the design process and end up with a very nice, well-structured class hierarchy to manage your data in the business logic tier of your application. Does this mean you have to give up on data binding? The answer is no. As we will see, data binding can actually make the GUI code less complex. It also adds to encapsulation since more of the data manipulation logic will reside in the business tier.

Binding Requirements

The only real requirement to do any type of data binding with your classes is that you must implement the IList interface. This really isn't that difficult, especially if you're already building a collection class to manage you business objects. Here is what you must implement for IList:

IList Member	Description
IsFixedSize	Does the list have a fixed number of elements?
IsReadOnly	Is the list read-only?
Item	Gets or sets the element at the specified index.
int Add(object)	Adds a new element to the list. Returns the position that the new element is in.
void Clear()	Removes all elements from the list.
bool Contains(object)	Determines if the object passed in is already in the list.
int IndexOf(object)	Determines the index of the object passed in. If the object isn't found, returns -1.
void Insert(int, object)	Inserts the specified object at the specified location in the list.
void Remove(object)	Removes the object form the list.
void RemoveAt(int)	Removes the object at the specified location.

Most of the time you will also be implementing the `ICollection` interface. The reason is that you will generally be binding to something with a list of items. In the next example (`DataBinding_6` in the example downloads) we will create an address class and a collection class to hold the addresses. Here is the code for the `Address` class:

```
using System;
using System.Diagnostics;
using System.Xml;

namespace BindingTest
{
    public class Address
    {
        PhoneCollection _phones;
        string _name;
        string _add1;
        string _add2;
        string _city;
        string _st;
        string _zip;

        public Address() { }

        public string Name
        {
            get { return _name; }
            set { _name = value; }
        }

        public string AddressLine1
        {
            get { return _add1; }
            set { _add1 = value; }
        }

        public string AddressLine2
        {
            get { return _add2; }
            set { _add2=value; }
        }

        public string City
        {
            get { return _city; }
            set { _city = value; }
        }

        public string State
        {
            get { return _st; }
            set { _st=value; }
        }
    }
```

```
public string Zip
    {
        get { return _zip; }
        set { _zip = value; }
    }

    public PhoneCollection PhoneNumbers
    {
        get { return _phones; }
        set { _phones = value; }
    }
  }
}
```

This is a pretty straightforward class for maintaining address data. Notice that the PhoneNumbers property returns a PhoneCollection. This is another class, which holds a collection of Phone objects. The Phone class is as follows:

```
using System;
using System.Diagnostics;
using System.Xml;

namespace BindingTest
{
    public class Phone
    {
        string _type;
        string _number;

        public Phone() {}

        public string PhoneType
        {
            get  { return _type; }
            set  { _type=value; }
        }

        public string PhoneNumber
        {
            get { return _number; }
            set { _number = value; }
        }
    }
}
```

Now with these two classes we are going to create a simple form to display the data. The data for this example resides in an XML document called address.xml and it is located in the DataBinding_7 folder in the example download. Here is what address.xml contains:

```
<?xml version="1.0" ?>
<addressBook>
    <addressEntry>
```

```
    <name>Bugs Bunny</name>
        <phone type="home">123-555-1234</phone>
        <phone type="work">123-555-4444</phone>
        <address1>555 Some St</address1>
        <address2 />
        <city>Some City</city>
        <st>OH</st>
        <zip>12345</zip>
    </addressEntry>
    <addressEntry>
        <name>Porky Pig</name>
        <phone type="home">123-555-6543</phone>
        <phone type="work">123-555-4444</phone>
        <address1>555 Another St</address1>
        <address2>Apt #A5</address2>
        <city>Some City</city>
        <st>OH</st>
        <zip>12345</zip>
    </addressEntry>
    <addressEntry>
        <name>Daffy Duck</name>
        <phone type="home">123-555-9876</phone>
        <phone type="work">123-555-6546</phone>
        <phone type="cell">123-555-4567</phone>
        <address1>789 Main Ave</address1>
        <address2 />
        <city>Metro City</city>
        <st>NV</st>
        <zip>54321</zip>
    </addressEntry>
    <addressEntry>
        <name>Wile E Coyote</name>
        <phone type="home">123-555-9999</phone>
        <address1>987 1st St</address1>
        <address2 />
        <city>Small Town</city>
        <st>WY</st>
        <zip>65498</zip>
    </addressEntry>
    <addressEntry>
        <name>Elmer Fudd</name>
        <phone type="home">123-555-3578</phone>
        <phone type="work">123-555-4444</phone>
        <phone type="cell">123-555-9898</phone>
        <phone type="fax">123-555-8525</phone>
        <address1>654 Main Drag Ave</address1>
        <address2>Suite 123</address2>
        <city>Some City</city>
        <st>OH</st>
        <zip>12345</zip>
    </addressEntry>
</addressBook>
```

Well, now we have the ingredients for our sample application. What we will see is that we can bind the collection class for addresses to a straightforward form. First we need to look at how we are going to implement IList. Remember, in order for your class to be bindable, you need to implement IList. Here is a pretty basic and almost universal implementation that should work for a range of situations.

```csharp
using System;
using System.Diagnostics;
using System.Collections;
using System.ComponentModel;
using System.Xml;

namespace BindingTest
{
    /// <summary>
    /// Summary description for AddressCollection.
    /// </summary>
    public class AddressCollection : ICollection, IList
    {
        ArrayList _objList = new ArrayList();

        public AddressCollection() { }

        //ICollection
        public int Count
        {
            get { return _objList.Count; }
        }

        public bool IsSynchronized
        {
            get { return false; }
        }

        public object SyncRoot
        {
            get { return this; }
        }

        public void CopyTo(Array targetArray, int index)
        {
            _objList.CopyTo(targetArray, index);
        }

        //IList
        public bool IsFixedSize
        {
            get { return false; }
        }

        public bool IsReadOnly
        {
            get { return false; }
        }
```

```
public Address this[int index]
{
   get
   {
      if (index < _objList.Count)
         return (Address)_objList[index];

      return null;
   }
   set
   {
      if(index < _objList.Count)
         _objList[index] = value;
   }
}

object IList.this[int index]
{
   get
   {
      if(index < _objList.Count)
         return _objList[index];

      return null;
   }
   set
   {
      if(index < _objList.Count)
         _objList[index]=value;
   }
}

public int Add(object value)
{
   return _objList.Add((Address)value);
}

public void Clear()
{
   _objList.Clear();
}

public bool Contains(object value)
{
   return _objList.Contains(value);
}

public int IndexOf(object value)
{
   return _objList.IndexOf((Address)value);
}

public void Insert(int Index, object value)
```

```
{
        _objList.Insert(Index,(Address)value);
    }

    public void Remove(object value)
    {
        _objList.Remove((Address)value);
    }

    public void RemoveAt(int index)
    {
        _objList.RemoveAt(index);
    }

    public IEnumerator GetEnumerator()
    {
        return new AddressCollectionEnumerator(this);
    }

    /// <summary>
    /// Enumerator nested class
    /// </summary>
    class AddressCollectionEnumerator : IEnumerator
    {
        int _index = -1;
        AddressCollection _collection;

        internal AddressCollectionEnumerator(
                                AddressCollection collectionClass)
        {
            _collection = collectionClass;

            if(_collection._objList.Count == 0)
                _index = -1;
        }

        public bool MoveNext()
        {
            if(_index < _collection._objList.Count - 1)
            {
                _index++;
                return true;
            }
            return false;
        }

        public void Reset()
        {
            _index = -1;
        }

        public Object Current
        {
            get
```

```
        {
                    if (_index >= 0)
                        return _collection._objList[_index];
                    else
                        throw new InvalidOperationException("You can't do that");
                }
            }
        }
    }
}
```

We won't go over this in too much detail, but there are a couple of items worth looking at. First is the list that we are using to maintain our address objects:

```
ArrayList _objList = new ArrayList();
```

_objList is an ArrayList object that will hold our Address objects. We use ArrayList in this case because it is the most flexible to use. Most of the rest of the class is just implementing all of the required methods and properties to support both the IList interface and the ICollection interface.

There is one other interesting section. We have implemented this as a strongly typed collection. What this means is that when you access an address object using the indexer you will receive an Address object and not an object-based object. Here is the section of code that does this:

```
public Address this[int index]
{
    get
    {
        if(index < _objList.Count)
            return (Address)_objList[index];

        throw new ArgumentOutOfRangeException();
    }
    set
    {
        if(index < _objList.Count)
            _objList[index] = value;
    }
}

object IList.this[int index]
{
    get
    {
        if(index < _objList.Count)
            return _objList[index];

        return null;
    }
    set
    {
        if(index < _objList.Count)
```

```
_objList[index] = value;
    }
}
```

The first indexer returns an `Address` object, as we would want. However, we need to add the second one as well since the `IList` interface defines this as returning `object`. If we don't include this declaration we would receive a compile error that `AddressCollection` doesn't implement the `IList` interface properly. The `PhoneCollection` class looks identical to this except that where you see `Address` you would substitute `Phone`. You can create the `PhoneCollection` by making a copy of this class and doing a search and replace changing `Address` to `Phone`.

The last thing that we should look at is the nested `AddressCollectionEnumerator` class. This is what allows you to do a `foreach` iteration on your collection. Notice this method:

```
public IEnumerator GetEnumerator()
{
    return new AddressCollectionEnumerator(this);
}
```

This method returns the object in the iteration. For example, if we were to do a `foreach` on our `AddressCollection`:

```
AddressCollection addresses = new AddressCollection();
foreach(Address currentAddress in addresses)
{
    // Do stuff with currentAddress
}
```

`GetEnumerator` returns the next `Address` object (`currentAddress`) in the `AddressCollection` object (`addresses`). You should always try to implement this feature in your collections. It is a very efficient method of iterating through the collection.

In order to get the XML address data into the collection we add the following code to the constructor in the `AddressCollection` class:

```
public AddressCollection() {

  XmlDocument doc=new XmlDocument();
  doc.Load(@"..\..\..\address.xml");
  XmlNodeList nodes=doc.SelectNodes("addressBook/addressEntry");
  foreach(XmlNode node in nodes)  {
    Address tmpAdd=new Address();
    tmpAdd.Name=node.SelectSingleNode("name").InnerText;
    tmpAdd.AddressLine1=node.SelectSingleNode("address1").InnerText;
    tmpAdd.AddressLine2=node.SelectSingleNode("address2").InnerText;
    tmpAdd.City=node.SelectSingleNode("city").InnerText;
    tmpAdd.State=node.SelectSingleNode("st").InnerText;
    tmpAdd.Zip=node.SelectSingleNode("zip").InnerText;
    tmpAdd.PhoneNumbers=new PhoneCollection(node.SelectNodes("phone"));
    this.Add(tmpAdd);
  }
}
```

It's a matter of opinion if this is the best way of loading data into the data class (tmpAdd) and then adding the class to the collection, but it will work for our needs.

The only thing left is to make the GUI. This will be very simple and will look similar to the DataBindings_2 example. We will have a textbox and label for each of the following:

- **Name** (txtName)
- **Address Line 1** (txtAddress1)
- **Address Line 2** (txtAddress2)
- **City** (txtCity)
- **State** (txtState)
- **Zip** (txtZip)

We also need a datagrid for the PhonesCollection. In this example we will call it gridPhones. After you have the textboxes and datagrid laid out on the form, add two buttons for navigating through the data. Now come the important parts. In the field declarations for the form, add the following line of code:

```
AddressCollection _dataSource;
```

We need the data source variable to be class-level since we access it in several places. In the constructor of the form add the following:

```
public Form1()
{
    //
    // Required for Windows Form Designer support
    //
    InitializeComponent();

    //
    // TODO: Add any constructor code after InitializeComponent call
    //

    _dataSource = new AddressCollection();
    txtName.DataBindings.Add("Text", _dataSource, "Name");
    txtAddress1.DataBindings.Add("Text", _dataSource, "AddressLine1");
    txtAddress2.DataBindings.Add("Text", _dataSource, "AddressLine2");
    txtCity.DataBindings.Add("Text", _dataSource, "City");
    txtState.DataBindings.Add("Text", _dataSource, "State");
    txtZip.DataBindings.Add("Text", _dataSource, "Zip");
    gridPhones.DataBindings.Add("DataSource", _dataSource, "PhoneNumbers");

}
```

The code you need to add is highlighted. Does it look familiar? It should. All we are doing is adding new Binding objects to the CurrencyManager. The only difference from what we did before is that in this case the second parameter, the data source, is a collection class of our creation and not an ADO.NET object (DataView, DataTable, or DataSet). We have done the first step in making our own data structures bindable, which is a big step beyond what we could ever do before with data binding.

What we just did is not the only way to implement the ILIst and ICollection interface. The framework has another way that may be a bit easier. It is called the CollectionBase class. CollectionBase is an abstract class that you can inherit from to create your collection classes. You will want to use CollectionBase whenever you are able to; however, if you have a situation where you have another class that you need to derive from, you may not be able to use CollectionBase. Remember that you can only inherit from one class. You can implement as many interfaces as you want, however, so it's a good idea to be comfortable implementing ILIst and ICollection. Here is what the AddressCollection looks like using CollectionBase. You will find this code in DataBindings_8 folder:

```
using System;
using System.Diagnostics;
using System.Collections;
using System.ComponentModel;
using System.Xml;

namespace DataBinding
{
    public class AddressCollection : CollectionBase
    {
        public AddressCollection()
        {
            XmlDocument doc = new XmlDocument();
            doc.Load(@"..\..\..\address.xml");
            XmlNodeList nodes = doc.SelectNodes("addressBook/addressEntry");
            foreach (XmlNode node in nodes)
            {
                Address tmpAdd = new Address();
                tmpAdd.Name = node.SelectSingleNode("name").InnerText;
                tmpAdd.AddressLine1 = node.SelectSingleNode("address1").
                                                          InnerText;
                tmpAdd.AddressLine2 = node.SelectSingleNode("address2").
                                                          InnerText;
                tmpAdd.City = node.SelectSingleNode("city").InnerText;
                tmpAdd.State = node.SelectSingleNode("st").InnerText;
                tmpAdd.Zip = node.SelectSingleNode("zip").InnerText;
                tmpAdd.PhoneNumbers = new
                                PhoneCollection(node.SelectNodes("phone"));
                this.List.Add(tmpAdd);
            }
        }
    }
}
```

Well, that's a bit of a difference. We should note something here – this would not implement a strongly typed collection. In order to do that you will need to override the following methods:

❑ ICollection.CopyTo()

❑ ILIst.Add()

❑ ILIst.Contains()

❑ ILIst.IndexOf()

❑ ILIst.Insert()

❑ ILIst.Remove()

This will give you a strongly typed collection class. The implementation of Example_7 using CollectionBase as opposed to implementing IList and ICollection is in the Example_8 folder of the examples.

Another change that we made to Example_8 is the addition of a couple of events. If you need to do any type of formatting or data conversion from the list to the control the list is bound to, you will want to use the Parse and Format events of the Binding object. Here is the constructor with the additional code:

```
public Form1()
{
    //
    // Required for Windows Form Designer support
    //
    InitializeComponent();

    //
    // TODO: Add any constructor code after InitializeComponent call
    //

    _dataSource = new AddressCollection();
    txtName.DataBindings.Add("Text", _dataSource, "Name");
    txtAddress1.DataBindings.Add("Text", _dataSource,"AddressLine1");
    txtAddress2.DataBindings.Add("Text",_dataSource,"AddressLine2");
    txtCity.DataBindings.Add("Text",_dataSource,"City");
    txtState.DataBindings.Add("Text",_dataSource,"State");
    Binding zipBinding=new Binding("Text",_dataSource,"Zip");
    zipBinding.Format+=new ConvertEventHandler(AddPlusFour);
    zipBinding.Parse+=new ConvertEventHandler(RemovePlusFour);
    txtZip.DataBindings.Add(zipBinding);
    gridPhones.DataBindings.Add("DataSource",_dataSource,"PhoneNumbers");
}
```

The altered code is highlighted. We create a new Binding object with the same parameters that we have been using. The next couple of lines are what we want to look at. We just add handlers to a couple of events; in this case the events are Parse and Format. Format deals with the data as it goes from list to bound control, and Parse deals with data as it goes from bound control to list. ConvertEventHandler uses ConvertEventArgs as the event argument. ConvertEventArgs has two properties that we can use (above the standard event argument properties) – DesiredType and Value. Value is what you would expect, an object that represents the data that is going between the list and the control. DesiredType is the Type of the data. With these two properties, we can convert data types, alter data, or validate data. In our example we will be adding "-0000" to the zip code to match the 'Zip+4' zip code format of the United States Postal Service. Here is the code for the two event handlers:

```
private void AddPlusFour(object sender, ConvertEventArgs ev)
{
    string zip = ev.Value.ToString();
    if (zip.Length == 5)
        ev.Value = zip + "-0000";
}
```

```
private void RemovePlusFour(object sender, ConvertEventArgs ev)
{
    string zip = ev.Value.ToString();
    if (zip.Length > 5)
        ev.Value = zip.Substring(0, 5);
}
```

Very simply, if the data is going to the bound control from the list, AddPlusFour will append "-0000" to the data. When it is returned back from the bound control to the list, RemovePlusFour will strip off the all but the first five characters.

Implementing IList either directly or by deriving from CollectionBase is the absolute minimum requirement for binding your collection class. What that means is that there are other interfaces that you can implement that will give you added features to the objects that you want to bind with. Those interfaces include ITypedList, IBindableList and IEditable. We will talk about each of these interfaces next.

ITypedList

Let's take a look at binding our AddressCollection class to a datagrid. Since we implement the IList interface, you would think it would be a snap, and it almost is. If we take the last example and remove the textboxes and labels, and instead drop a datagrid onto the form and change the code in the forms constructor to this:

```
_dataSource = new AddressCollection();
gridNames.AllowNavigation = false;
gridNames.SetDataBinding(_dataSource, null);
gridPhones.DataBindings.Add("DataSource", _dataSource, "PhoneNumbers");
```

you will see that the AddressCollection data does indeed show up in the grid. However, do you notice something odd about the data? Here is how is looks:

Why is Zip the first column? AddressLine2 is the second column – why is that? Well, that's just the way they show up in the grid. The columns are properties that we implemented in the Address class, and there doesn't appear to be any default or preferred order. We can even change the order that they are implemented in our class, and there will not be a change in the order of the columns we could rearrange the grid columns, but that isn't the best solution. The better way of making the data show up in the grid the right way would be to implement ITypedList on the AddressCollection. What ITypedList does is to give you the ability to alter what the schema for binding is. We can have different public properties from those presented by the underlying list.

ITypedList has two methods that need to be implemented. They are GetItemProperties and GetListName. Each takes an array of PropertyDescriptor objects that represent the specific properties to return info for. GetListName returns a string that is the name of the underlying list of the collection, and GetItemProperties returns a PropertyDescriptorCollection for the collection.

A PropertyDescriptor is simply a description of a property in a class. In other words it is a class that contains information about a property. A PropertyDescriptor has properties such as IsReadOnly, Name, Description, and so on. Methods include SetValue, GetChildProperties, and CanResetValue. If you were to make a call to the static GetProperties method in the System.ComponentModel.TypeDescriptor class, you would receive the PropertyDescriptorCollection for a particular object. Instead of getting the PropertyDescriptors this way, in this example we will actually create our own, so that we may better see what it is that they do.

GetItemProperties is the method we are most concerned with. This will return the PropertyDescriptors for the specific properties of each Address object that we want to display. We will need to create each PropertyDescriptor for these properties. In order to do that, we will create a new class that inherits from System.ComponentModel.PropertyDescriptor. You can create a fairly generic version of this that will work for most of your needs using reflection. This is what we will do for this example. This example can be found in the DataBinding_9 folder. Here is the code for our PropertyDescriptor-based class:

```
using System;
using System.ComponentModel;
using System.Reflection;

namespace DataBinding
{
    /// <summary>
    /// Summary description for AddressPropertyDescriptor.
    /// </summary>
    public class AddressPropertyDescriptor : PropertyDescriptor
    {
        Type _type;
        PropertyInfo _pi;
        string _disName;

        public AddressPropertyDescriptor(string name, string componentType) :
                                         base(name,new Attribute[]{})
        {
            _type = Type.GetType(componentType);
            _pi = _type.GetProperty(name);
        }
```

```
        public override bool CanResetValue(object component)
        {
            return true;
        }

        public override Type ComponentType
        {
            get { return _type; }
        }

        public override object GetValue(object component)
        {
            return _pi.GetValue(component,null);
        }

        public override void SetValue(object component, object value)
        {
            _pi.SetValue(component,value,null);
        }

        public override bool IsReadOnly
        {
            get { return false; }
        }

        public override Type PropertyType
        {
            get { return _pi.PropertyType; }
        }

        public override void ResetValue(object component)
        {
            _pi.SetValue(component,null,null);
        }

        public override bool ShouldSerializeValue(object component)
        {
            return true;
        }
    }
}
```

This is the minimum that you will have to implement in the `PropertyDescriptor`-based class. Most of the properties and methods that we have implemented are pretty straightforward. The constructor in this case accepts that name of the property that we are making the `PropertyDescriptor` for, and the name of the parent object. So, for the `Name` property of the `Address` object, the code would look like:

```
AddressPropertyDescriptor apd = new
                AddressPropertyDescriptor("Name", "DataBinding.Address");
```

Notice that we need to pass in the entire parent object class name, including namespace. We call the base class (`PropertyDescriptor`) constructor, passing in the name string and an array of property attributes, if there are any. In this case there aren't any, so we construct an empty array and pass it in. Next in the constructor we get the `Type` of the parent object (`Address` in this case) and then retrieve a `PropertyInfo` class of the property of `Address` that we are building the `PropertyDescriptor` for. You can see that in the `PropertyDescriptor` class we use the `PropertyInfo` (`_pi` in the above source listing) in several places. This is basically passing the property info through the `PropertyDescriptor` class. Notice that we aren't changing anything. We could alter the value in the `GetValue` method if we wanted to. By putting a `switch` statement in and checking for a specific `Address` property, we could substitute in a different value, or format the data in a different way.

Another example is that for a particular property we can set the `IsReadOnly` property to `true`. Now when you bind this property to a grid or textbox, the user will not be able to alter the data. `PropertyDescriptors` can be a very powerful tool when used properly. Doing a little experimenting with the different methods and properties may turn up some interesting capabilities.

Now that we have an `AddressPropertyDescriptor` class, we can create the `PropertyDescriptorCollection` in the `AddressCollection` class. Here is what we have to add to the `AddressCollection`:

```
using System;
using System.Diagnostics;
using System.Collections;
using System.ComponentModel;
using System.Xml;

namespace DataBinding
{
    public class AddressCollection : CollectionBase, ITypedList
    {
        PropertyDescriptorCollection _pdc = new
                                    PropertyDescriptorCollection(null);

        public AddressCollection()
        {
            XmlDocument doc = new XmlDocument();
            doc.Load(@"..\..\..\address.xml");
            XmlNodeList nodes = doc.SelectNodes("addressBook/addressEntry");
            foreach (XmlNode node in nodes)
            {
                Address tmpAdd = new Address();
                tmpAdd.Name = node.SelectSingleNode("name").InnerText;
                tmpAdd.AddressLine1 = node.SelectSingleNode("address1").
                                                            InnerText;
                tmpAdd.AddressLine2 = node.SelectSingleNode("address2").
                                                            InnerText;
                tmpAdd.City = node.SelectSingleNode("city").InnerText;
                tmpAdd.State = node.SelectSingleNode("st").InnerText;
                tmpAdd.Zip = node.SelectSingleNode("zip").InnerText;
                tmpAdd.PhoneNumbers = new
                            PhoneCollection(node.SelectNodes("phone"));
                this.List.Add(tmpAdd);
            }
        }
```

```
        _pdc.Add(new AddressPropertyDescriptor("Name",
                                    "DataBinding.Address"));
        _pdc.Add(new AddressPropertyDescriptor("City",
                                    "DataBinding.Address"));
        _pdc.Add(new AddressPropertyDescriptor("PhoneNumbers",
                                    "DataBinding.Address"));
    }

    public PropertyDescriptorCollection GetItemProperties(
                            PropertyDescriptor[] arrDesctiptors)
    {
        return _pdc;
    }

    public string GetListName(PropertyDescriptor[] arrDescriptors)
    {
        return "List";
    }
```

```
//Rest of the class remains the same
```

The additions are highlighted. We create a `PropertyDescriptorCollection` object; then, after we load the collection, we add the properties that we want to get the collection object to display. In this case we are going to have only three properties – `Name`, `City`, and `PhoneNumbers`. The order that you add the `PropertyDescriptors` to the `ProperDescriptorCollection` will determine what order they appear in the grid. We will display `Name` and `City` in the grid, and of course `PhoneNumbers` is bound to the other grid on the form. Now if we run this example, this is what we should get:

Now we can see that the only two properties that the top grid displays are the two properties that we implemented the `PropertyDescriptor` objects for. This requires a little work up front, but it does add a greater level of control over your bound data classes. If you plan out you class hierarchy you will find that a great deal of the code required to implement the `PropertyDescriptors` for example, can be reused over and over again. Once you implement this in one place for one collection class, others become significantly easier.

IBindingList and IEditableObject

For the greatest level of control on your data source, you will want to implement the `IBindingList` on the collection class and `IEditableObject` on the data class of your data source. With these two interfaces implemented, you would have essentially the same functionality and notification capabilities that objects such as `DataView` and `DataTable` have. Implementing these two interfaces is not trivial, but it does add capabilities that are nice to have, such as sorting and change notification.

`IBindingList` has the following properties and methods (and events) that will need to be implemented:

Property, Method, or Event	Description
`AllowEdit` – property returns `bool`	Can the list be updated?
`AllowNew` – property returns `bool`	Can we add new items to the list?
`AllowRemove` – property returns `bool`	Can items be removed from the list?
`IsSorted` – property returns `bool`	Are the items in the list sorted?
`SortDirection` – property returns a `ListSortDirection` value	Is the list sorted in ascending or descending order?
`SortProperty` – property returns a `PropertyDescriptor`	What property is the list sorted on?
`SupportsChangeNotification` – property returns `bool`	Will the `ListChanged` event be raised when the list or items in the list are changed?
`SupportsSearching` – property returns `bool`	Is searching the list using the `Find` method supported?
`SupportsSorting` – property returns `bool`	Can the list be sorted?
`void AddIndex(PropertyDescriptor prop)`	Adds a `PropertyDescriptor` object to the indexes used for searching.
`object AddNew()`	Adds a new item to the list.
`void ApplySort(PropertyDescriptor prop, ListSortDirection dir)`	Sorts the list by `prop` in `dir` direction
`int Find(PropertyDescriptor prop, object key)`	Returns the list index of the object that contains `key` in property `prop`.

Table continued on following page

Property, Method, or Event	Description
`void RemoveIndex(PropertyDescriptor prop)`	Removes prop from the list of indexes.
`void RemoveSort()`	Removes any sorting from the list.
`event ListChangedEventHandler ListChanged`	Is raised when the list or an item ion the list changes. Receives a `ListChangedEventArgs` object.

The level of support that you want your data source to have would determine how much of the interface you actually have to implement. If you don't want to support sorting for example, you would set the `SupportsSorting` property to `false` and in the `IsSorted`, `SortDirection`, `SortProperty`, and `ApplySort` methods and properties, you would just throw a `NotSupportedException` exception.

In order to fully support the `ListChanged` event, you should implement the `IEditableObject` interface on the data class of your list. The `IEditableObject` interface has three methods that need to be implemented. They are `BeginEdit`, `CancelEdit`, and `EndEdit`. None of them returns anything or takes any parameters. After implementing this interface you will also have the ability to add commit and rollback functionality to your data object. In the `BeginEdit` method you can create a copy of the current object, and if the user decides to cancel the changes, you can easily roll back to the backup object that you saved.

To get the feel for how and when these methods are called, insert trace messages in each, and watch as you change an object in the collection. A common pattern is to have a `bool` flag to determine if `BeginEdit` has been called. This way, when an `EndEdit` or `CancelEdit` method is called, you can check the state of the flag and determine if you have to commit changes or not. It is at this point you would raise the `ListChanged` event in the collection class. This will let the list know that there has been a change. The `ListChangedType` in the `ListChangedEventArgs` will tell the list what type of change took place.

Let's take a look at how this works in our `AddressCollection` example. We won't implement all of the functionality of `IBindingList`, but you should get the idea of what you'll need to do. The complete example is in the `DataBinding_10` folder of the example downloads. First, let's look at the `Address` class and the implementation of `IEditableObject`.

We added two private fields:

```
AddressCollection _parent;
bool inEdit = false;
```

`_parent` gives us a reference to the `AddressCollection` when we need to raise the `ListChanged` event; `_inEdit` is the `bool` flag we talked about earlier.

Here is the rest of the code that was added to Address:

```
//Support for IBindingList
internal AddressCollection Parent
{
    get { return _parent; }
    set { _parent = value; }
}

private void OnAddressChanged()
{
    if (!inEdit && _parent != null)
        _parent.AddressChanged(this);
}


//IEditable implemetation

void IEditableObject.BeginEdit()
{
    if(!inEdit)
    {
        inEdit = true;
        //set backup data for restore
    }
}

void IEditableObject.CancelEdit()
{
    if(inEdit)
    {
        inEdit = false;
        //restore backup data
    }
}

void IEditableObject.EndEdit()
{
    if(inEdit)
    {
        inEdit = false;
        // Clear backup data
    }
}
```

In addition to the IEditableObject interface, we added a Parent property so that _parent can be set when a new item is added, and we created a private method for raising the ListChanged event on the AddressCollection class. Again you could add some trace statements in the BeginEdit, CancelEdit, and EndEdit methods to see when and how often these methods are called.

Next we have the IEditableObject implementation. Notice that this is not fully implemented, but you should be able to see what needs to be done from here. Also, notice that we don't make these public methods. There really isn't any need to. If you want to cancel an edit for example, you would call the CancelCurrentEdit method of the CurrencyManager, which in turn will execute the code in this method. If you don't implement IEditableObject, then the CancelCurrentEdit method of the CurrencyManager has no effect. The code in the CancelEdit method of your data class (Address in our example) will implement the code to roll the changes back to the original state. Lastly, you would want to call the OnAddressChanged method, which of course raises the OnListChanged event in the AddressCollections object. The process would be similar in the EndEdit method, except that you want to implement the code to persist the change back to the data store, again calling OnAddressChanged to notify the AddressCollection of the list change.

The changes to AddressCollection are a little more extensive. We declare three private fields:

```
bool _isSorted = false;
ListSortDirection _sortDir = ListSortDirection.Ascending;
PropertyDescriptor _sortProperty;
```

As you may have guessed, these are used to support sorting. We'll look at the sorting implementation shortly, but first we need to talk about the notification process. Remember that we need to implement the ListChangedEvent event for notification to work. Here is the code that starts that process:

```
ListChangedEventArgs resetEventArgs = new
                     ListChangedEventArgs(ListChangedType.Reset, -1);
ListChangedEventHandler listChangeHandler;
```

resetEventArgs is a predefined ListChangedEventArgs that we will be using in several locations in the class. The next line is where we establish the ListChangedEventHandler for the class. We declare the event just as you would any other event:

```
public event ListChangedEventHandler ListChanged
{
    add { listChangeHandler += value; }
    remove { listChangeHandler -= value; }
}
```

Here is the OnListChanged code that is executed when the event is raised:

```
protected virtual void OnListChanged(ListChangedEventArgs ev)
{
    if (listChangeHandler != null)
    {
        listChangeHandler(this, ev);
    }
}
```

As you can see, all we do is call the `listChangeHandler` with the proper parameters. The method that we exposed for the `Address` object to call for notification is:

```
internal void AddressChanged(Address changedAddress)
{
    int index = List.IndexOf(changedAddress);
    OnListChanged(new ListChangedEventArgs(
                            ListChangedType.ItemChanged, index));
}
```

This is again very simple – all we do is to get the index of the item that changed, and then call `OnListChanged` with a new `ListChangedEventArgs` object.

In order to fully support the notification process, we need to implement a couple of methods from `CollectionBase`:

```
protected override void OnClear()
{
    foreach (Address c in List)
    {
        c.Parent = null;
    }
}

protected override void OnClearComplete()
{
    OnListChanged(resetEvent);
}

protected override void OnInsertComplete(int index, object value)
{
    ((Address)value).Parent = this;
    OnListChanged(new ListChangedEventArgs(
                            ListChangedType.ItemAdded, index));
}

protected override void OnRemoveComplete(int index, object value)
{
    OnListChanged(new ListChangedEventArgs(
                            ListChangedType.ItemDeleted, index));
}

protected override void OnSetComplete(int index, object oldValue,
                                        object newValue)
{
    if (oldValue != newValue)
    {
        Address oldcust = (Address)oldValue;
        Address newcust = (Address)newValue;

        oldcust.Parent = null;
        newcust.Parent = this;
```

```
            OnListChanged(new ListChangedEventArgs(
                                    ListChangedType.ItemAdded, index));
        }
    }
```

The code in these methods is pretty much self-explanatory. When the `OnXxxComplete` method is called, we make sure that the `Parent` property is set on the item that is being changed, and then call `OnListChanged` with the proper `ListChangedType`. Remember `Parent` is holding a reference to the collection class (`AddressCollection`) in the `Address` class. We need this reference in order for the notification process to work. We could also implement the corresponding `OnXxx` method (`OnInsert`, `OnRemove`, etc.) for added functionality. The `OnXxx` method is called before the event takes place, whereas `OnXxxComplete` is executed after the event takes place. Now we have complete notification when an item is added, changed, or deleted. If we were to set up an event handler on the form for the `ListChanged` event, we could respond whenever an item is added, changed, or deleted.

So, for example if the user were to insert a new Address, the `CurrencyManager` would automatically call the `OnInsertComplete` method. Since we have the `OnListChanged` event called with the proper `EventArgs` added, the `ListChanged` event would be raised and the calling process would know that a new Address has been inserted. Since the `ListChanged` event is raised, the calling process would also know what event took place (`Add`, `Edit`, `Clear`, etc.) and what needed to be done next (persisting to the database etc.).

Implementing the sorting capability is a little more work. We start out by informing our `AddressCollection` object that sorting will be supported:

```
bool IBindingList.SupportsSorting
{
    get { return true ; }
}
```

Once again, notice that we didn't make this a public property, as it doesn't need to be public. The next thing is to implement the other sort properties and methods. Firstly there are a couple of properties that we need to work on. Here is the code for `IsSorted`, `SortDirection`, and `SortProperty`:

```
public bool IsSorted
{
    get { return _isSorted; }
}

public ListSortDirection SortDirection
{
    get { return _sortDir; }
}

PropertyDescriptor IBindingList.SortProperty
{
    get { return _sortProperty; }
}
```

Notice that we did make the `IsSorted` and `SortDirection` properties public. The reason is that sorting can be an expensive operation. By making these properties public, the calling application can ask the object if the sort operation has already been done. We could also have done something similar to the way the `DataView` implements the sort functionality. We could add a `Sort` property that takes a string with the name of the property to sort by with either `"ASC"` or `"DESC"` appended to the string. The `Sort` property would then be responsible for calling the next method that we implement, `ApplySort`. This is where we set the fields that we return in the other three properties. The implementation of `ApplySort` looks like this:

```
public void ApplySort(PropertyDescriptor property,
                      ListSortDirection direction)
{
    _sortProperty = property;
    _sortDir = direction;
    this.InnerList.Sort(new AddressComparer(_sortProperty));
    if (_sortDir == ListSortDirection.Descending)
        this.InnerList.Reverse();

    _isSorted = true;
}
```

As you can see, the two parameters to `ApplySort` are a `PropertyDescriptor` for the sorted property, and the direction to sort it in. From a design standpoint, it's a good idea to implement the `Sort` property, or at least a way for the calling program to specify a string with the property names. Your data source collection class would then create the `PropertyDescriptor` from the string.

The first couple of lines are just setting the class-level variables for property and sort direction. Then comes an interesting line of code:

```
this.InnerList.Sort(new AddressComparer(_sortProperty));
```

The `InnerList` property is from the `CollectionBase` class that we derived our collection class from. It returns an `ArrayList` of the items being held in the collection. This is the list that `CollectionBase` manages for us. We call the `Sort` property of the `ArrayList`. It takes an `IComparer` object as a parameter. `IComparer` does pretty much what the name suggests – it compares two objects and returns -1, 0, or 1, according to whether the first object is less than or greater than the second, or if they are equal. Here is the code for our `IComparer`, `AddressComparer`:

```
using System;
using System.ComponentModel;
using System.Collections;

namespace DataBinding
{
    /// <summary>
    /// Summary description for AddressComparer.
    /// </summary>
    public class AddressComparer : IComparer
    {
        PropertyDescriptor _sortProp;
```

```
        public AddressComparer(PropertyDescriptor sortProperty)
        {
            _sortProp=sortProperty;
        }

        public int Compare(object xObj, object yObj)
        {

            int retVal = ((string)_sortProp.GetValue((Address)xObj)).
                            CompareTo(_sortProp.GetValue((Address)yObj));
            return retVal;
        }
    }
}
```

Since we don't know which property may need to be sorted, we have to do a little reflection based on the PropertyDescriptor that is passed in. Using the GetValue method of the PropertyDescriptor to return a couple of strings, we can use the CompareTo method of the String object to compare the two strings. This is easy in our example, since all of the properties return strings, except for Phones, which returns a PhoneCollection object. A more complete implementation would check the type of the objects passed in to determine how the comparison should be made.

> You should be careful how you implement this comparison if you cannot use the CompareTo method. If you have a large list to sort, this method will be called a large number of times during the sort process. A poor implementation or a poorly designed algorithm could really cost you performance. It may be that you have to implement a couple of IComparer objects, one each for different types that may need to be sorted.

On our form we have added a couple of radio buttons so the user can select sort order, a combo box that we fill with the properties of an Address object so the user can select what property to sort on, and a button that executes the sort. Here is the code for the Sort button:

```
private void btnSort_Click(object sender, System.EventArgs e)
{
    ListSortDirection lsd;
    if (rbAsc.Checked)
        lsd = ListSortDirection.Ascending;
    else
        lsd = ListSortDirection.Descending;

    //Apply the sort and position on the first position
    _dataSource.ApplySort((PropertyDescriptor)cbProperties.
                                                SelectedItem,lsd);
    this.BindingContext[_dataSource].Position = 0;
    ((CurrencyManager)this.BindingContext[_dataSource]).Refresh();
}
```

We first check to see which radio button is checked – Ascending or Descending. Then we apply the sort to the data source's ApplySort method. As you can see, we pass in the PropertyDescriptor and the sort order in the form of a ListSortDirection object. The last couple of lines repositions us onto the first element in the collection, and then refresh the bound controls.

We have also implemented an AddNew method on the AddressCollection. The IBindingList interface has AddNew as one of the methods that should be implemented. We need to be able to create a new data object (Address in our example) and make sure that we raise the ListChanged event. It should be pointed out that AddNew is different from Add. With Add, we add an object that is passed in as a parameter to the method call. AddNew doesn't take any parameters – it creates the new object for us and adds it to the list.

The first thing we do is to create a public method called AddNew. It returns the new Address object that was created and added to the list. Here is the code for AddNew:

```
public Address AddNew()
{
    // Forward to the IBindingList implementation
    return (Address)((IBindingList)this).AddNew();
}
```

All we do is call the IBindingList version, which we have implemented as well:

```
object IBindingList.AddNew()
{
    Address newAddress = new Address();
    newAddress.Parent = this;
    int newPos = List.Add(newAddress);
    OnListChanged(new ListChangedEventArgs(
                              ListChangedType.ItemAdded,newPos));
    return newAddress;
}
```

So why not just put the implementation in the AddNew method? Type safety – notice that the IBindingList version returns an object. In the version we created, we return an Address object. If you were to try to set a Phone object to the result of this AddNew, you would receive a compile error and would be able to fix the problem easily.

In the IBindingList.AddNew implementation, we create a new Address object and set its Parent property. We add it to the list, making sure we have the index value of where in the list it was placed. We need this to pass to the ListChangedEventArgs object on the ListChanged event, which we raise after the item has been added to the list.

We have added a new button to the form named btnAdd. In the click event handler, we have the following code:

```
private void btnAdd_Click(object sender, System.EventArgs e)
{
    CurrencyManager cm = (CurrencyManager)this.BindingContext[_dataSource];
    Address newAdd = cm.AddNew();
```

```
   // Address newAdd = _dataSource.AddNew();
   // Do stuff with newAdd here
}
```

In this version, we use the `CurrencyManager` to add the new `Address` object, but as you can see from the commented line of code, we can use the data source and call the `AddNew` method from it.

We have now implemented the major interfaces for creating a bindable data source. The complete process may seem like a lot of work, but if you look closely at it, you should be able to define a couple of classes that encapsulate a lot of the implementation. This allows us to create a data source framework that you can reuse in other development projects.

Binding to a Custom Control

I know it's a bit mischievous to mention Custom Controls before we get to that chapter, but I just can't resist! Let's say that we have just built a really nice user control or custom control, maybe an `Address` custom control like the one that we will build in the Custom Controls chapter. Wouldn't it be nice to add a `DataSource` property to the control so we could bind our `AddressCollection` object to the control? It's not actually all that hard to do. We just have to add a couple of things to the `Address` control before this will work.

The first item that needs to be done is again related to type safety. If we had built a new and improved grid control, for example, we would not really care what type of `IList`-based object we were going to bind to. We could just read the `PropertyDescriptors`, create columns based on them and iterate through the list and load the data into the grid. However, the `Address` control is built to display one thing – addresses. It would not make much sense to try to display the final standings of a bowling league in a control built for addresses. So what we need to do is to implement a couple of interfaces in the control so that we always know what the data will look like. The two interfaces we need are one for the data objects (`Address`) and one for the collection class that contains the data object (`AddressCollection`). First, here is the `IAddress` interface (this code is in the `AddressControl` folder of the example download):

```
using System;

namespace Wrox.Samples.GUI
{
    /// <summary>
    /// Interface to use when binding to Address control.
    /// </summary>
    public interface IAddress
    {
        string AddressLine1
        {
            get;
            set;
        }

        string AddressLine2
        {
            get;
```

```
      set;
         }

         string City
         {
            get;
            set;
         }

         string State
         {
            get;
            set;
         }

         string Zip
         {
            get;
            set;
         }
      }
   }
```

We make sure that there are properties for AddressLine1, AddressLine2, City, State, and Zip. They all return strings and each one has both get and set accessors. The definition for IAddressCollection looks like this:

```
using System;

namespace Wrox.Samples.GUI
{
   /// <summary>
   /// Interface to use when binding to Address control.
   /// </summary>
   public interface IAddressCollection
   {
      IAddress this[int index]
      {
         get;
         set;
      }
   }
}
```

All we want to do is make sure that the collection class returns an object that is based on the IAddress interface. Otherwise, we won't know what we are binding to.

Now that we have a type-safe control, we can make a new property called DataSource. We can actually call it anything we want, but this would follow the same pattern as other controls. Here is the code for the DataSource property:

```
/// <summary>
/// Gets or sets the IAddress based datasource for the control.
/// </summary>
[Category("DataBindings"),
   Description("Source of data for DataBinding. Must Implement IAddress")]
public IAddressCollection DataSource
{
   get { return _dataSource; }
   set
   {
      if(value != null)
      {
         _dataSource = value;
         txtLine1.DataBindings.Add("Text", _dataSource, "AddressLine1");
         txtLine2.DataBindings.Add("Text", _dataSource, "AddressLine2");
         txtCity.DataBindings.Add("Text", _dataSource, "City");
         txtState.DataBindings.Add("Text", _dataSource, "State");
         txtZipCode.DataBindings.Add("Text", _dataSource, "Zip");
      }
   }
}
```

We also need to create an IAddressCollection-based field named _dataSource. The get accessor just returns the value of _dataSource. The set accessor does do a little more work. First we set _dataSource. Then we add the Binding objects for the five textbox controls; you have seen this code before. The important thing to make note of here is that the DataSource property is not of type object, but an IAddressCollection-based object. This guarantees that the data source will have the properties AddressLine1, AddressLine2, and so on. Otherwise we would not be able to add these binding objects – what would we be binding to? Now we can add the Address control to a project, create a data source that implements the IAddress and IAddressCollection interfaces, and have fully functional data-bound control!

Summary

Data binding has taken a big step forward with the .NET Framework. In this chapter we looked at how all of the various parts come together to allow you to develop robust bound controls and data sources. We looked at the three workhorses of data binding – the `BindingContext` class, the `BindingManagerBase` (and specifically the `CurrencyManager` implementation of `BindingManagerBase`), and the `Binding` class itself. These three classes control the binding process on the form, such as synchronization and position and as such are part of the `System.Windows.Forms` namespace.

We also looked at the interfaces that you will need to implement on your data source to provide full binding capabilities. The nice thing about how the framework has organized these interfaces is that we can implement as much or as little support as we need, from the basics of `IList` to the full support of `IBindingList`.

By careful analysis and planning you should be able to develop a framework of bindable data sources that can be used and reused in the various applications that you will develop. Scalability and performance are no longer issues that should keep you from creating such a framework based on data binding.

In the next chapter we will be looking at how we can make great use of keyboard and mouse events which will enhance our applications – so let's go!

User Input

This chapter is about capturing and responding to input from the user from within our C# programs. It focuses on the two most commonly used peripherals of a computer system – the keyboard and mouse. Many of the tasks that occur in the development of desktop applications use keyboard and mouse input without the need for handling of this input – for example, a textbox control uses a mouse click to gain focus and automatically puts the cursor to the far left corner of the textbox. The textbox also turns all keypresses into printed characters displayed in the textbox. This is obviously something that we don't have to worry about. In fact, development of Windows Forms applications doesn't necessarily require us to understand the underlying implementation. There are times, however, where the applications that we develop require a greater understanding of how we can use the keyboard and mouse directly in our applications.

The chapter begins with an in-depth look at using the keyboard and mouse in a computer program and looks at examples of how they can be used to enhance an application. Each distinct section in this chapter is supported by an application (included in the code download available from the Wrox web site). Code examples from these applications are used where required to support explanations on important topics.

Keyboard events are triggered every time a user taps a key on the keyboard, while mouse events are triggered when the user moves the mouse or clicks on one of its buttons. Most of this chapter will focus on how to respond to keyboard or mouse events in applications, so that keypresses and mouse actions will invoke custom event handling code.

A great deal of the MSDN documentation is devoted to the topic of the Windows API, and for many years this was the sole manner of development for desktop applications. One of the many good things about the Windows Forms model is that many of the features that formerly involved function calls to the Windows API have now been made redundant, and we're left with a single, all-encompassing set of class libraries.

In this chapter, we will cover:

- ❏ Responding to the `KeyUp` and `KeyDown` events
- ❏ Responding to the `KeyPress` event
- ❏ Using the `Key` enumeration
- ❏ Using the modifier keys
- ❏ Multilanguage support
- ❏ Retrieving device information
- ❏ Tracking the mouse
- ❏ Responding to mouse events
- ❏ Using the mouse wheel
- ❏ Responding to hover events

Introducing the Keyboard

Because we'll be concentrating on two devices, this chapter will be roughly divided into two halves, concentrating on the keyboard and the mouse respectively. Since the keyboard has traditionally been the main way for the user to input information to the computer, we'll start off our tour of processing user input in .NET Windows applications with a look at the keyboard.

A Word about Encoding

Before diving into the concepts and techniques needed to develop applications that process keyboard events, let's recap on how the operating system encodes characters (as this is key to understanding further concepts – such as internationalization).

Newer versions of Windows such as Windows NT/2000 and Windows XP use a character-encoding scheme called Unicode. Unicode stores character representations in a two-byte structure catering for large numbers of character sets. This means that Unicode can represent virtually all character sets worldwide, as well as other non-alphabetic characters. As each character has a number, alphabets normally have ranges of numbers that can be represented as a sequence of bits (between 0 and 15) to represent the character.

The following shows a short list of Unicode character sets (alphabets) and the corresponding number ranges:

- ❏ Basic Latin (33-127)
- ❏ Hebrew (1456-1524)
- ❏ Greek (894-974)

The Windows 9x operating systems all use ANSI internally; the version of ANSI used is MBCS, which can represent character sets of more than 256 characters (as opposed to SBCS or Single Byte Character Set, which uses a single byte to store the related character). C++ developers will need little explanation as to how to write applications that can support both character sets, as this is a key concept in Windows Application development (so much so that macros such as _UNICODE or _MBCS and functions such as MultiByteToWideChar() exist to convert between the formats).

The .NET Framework has an Encoding class that can be useful for converting between these different formats. It exposes a series of properties that can be used to return Encoding objects for specific encoding formats. The following standards are supported:

❑   ASCII

❑   BigEndianUnicode

❑   Default

❑   Unicode

❑   UTF7

❑   UTF8

ASCII (American Standard Code for Information Interchange) holds character numeric values in a single byte (like SBCS). BigEndianUnicode is a variation on Unicode. The Default property return's the systems default ANSI character encoding class. UTF8 format allows Unicode characters to be encoded with a variable number of bytes, and is extensively used through HTTP requests to web servers.

The class also supports a Convert() method, which enables the conversion of characters from one type of encoding to another.

The KeyboardSample Application

The first project we'll create will be used to demonstrate many of the functions of keyboard input and event handling. The project is called KeyboardSample, and consists of a simple Windows Forms project with one form. The form contains two group boxes, each of which contains a label and a textbox. The labels display information about the keys pressed, and the textboxes provide a place for the user to type. The first box monitors simple key presses; the second provides a way of monitoring key combinations such as *Ctrl + Alt + U*, to enter 'ú':

In order to capture the keypresses on the textboxes, we can handle the KeyDown event for our textboxes. This event is raised for the control that currently has the focus when the user presses a key. The KeyDown event is inherited from the Control class, so this event is raised for all controls, not just those where the user can enter text.

Instead of handling the event by wiring it up to a method using a delegate, we could create controls derived from the TextBox class, and override their OnKeyDown() method, in exactly the same way that we overrode the Form's OnClosing() method in Chapter 2. However, this would complicate the code unnecessarily, so we're wiring up the methods in the usual way for this example.

Keyboard Events

The KeyDown event handler for the top textbox is much the simpler of the two, so we'll look at that method first. The event handler for this method must be of type KeyEventHandler, so we wire the event handler with the code:

```
txtMonitor.KeyDown += new KeyEventHandler(txtMonitor_KeyDown);
```

Within the method, we just display the code for the key that the user pressed:

```
private void txtMonitor_KeyDown(object sender,
                              System.Windows.Forms.KeyEventArgs e)
{
    lblMonitor.Text = e.KeyValue.ToString();
}
```

Like other event handlers in .NET, the handler for the KeyDown event takes two parameters – the object for which the event was raised, and an object derived from System.EventArgs. This second parameter is of type KeyEventArgs, and allows us to ascertain the code value for the key through its KeyValue property. This returns an int, so we call its ToString() method before displaying it in the label.

The KeyDown event is one of three Control events that allow us to capture input from the keyboard. The others are:

- ☐ KeyUp – raised when the user releases the key.

- ☐ KeyPress – raised after the KeyDown event. Both KeyDown and KeyPress are raised at regular intervals if the user keeps the key pressed. The arguments object for the KeyPress event handler gives us easy access to the actual character value of the pressed key.

Each of these events has a corresponding method that we can override in classes that derive from Control:

```
void OnKeyDown(KeyEventArgs e);
void OnKeyUp(KeyEventArgs e);
void OnKeyPress(KeyPressEventArgs e);
```

These methods are called by the .NET Framework before the corresponding event is raised; in fact, the base implementations of the methods raise the event themselves. By overriding these methods, we can cut out one step of the event process – we don't need to wait for the event to be raised, as we can write the event-handling code in this method. If we still want the event to be raised, we can call the same method on the base class at the end of our implementation (for example, base.OnKeyDown(e);). See Chapter 2 for more information about this technique.

The Keys Enum

The KeyDown event handler for the second textbox demonstrates the use of the Keys enum (which resides in the System.Windows.Forms namespace). This enumeration provides intuitive names for key code values. We can use this to change the purpose of particular keys, which normally have a specific function in the application; for example, in the section of the KeyboardSample that we're just about to look at, we use the Keys enumeration to trap virtually every key press (and some combinations of key presses) on the keyboard. The Keys enumeration has a member for each key on the keyboard, so the *A* key is represented by Keys.A, and the right-hand *Shift* key is represented by Keys.RShiftKey.

There are several types of key that can easily be distinguished and categorized by their properties:

- ☐ **Character keys** – These keys are the normal printable character keys on the keyboard (alphanumeric characters, punctuation marks, and so on).

- ☐ **Modifier keys** – These keys modify the value of another key pressed simultaneously, and include *Alt*, *Ctrl*, and *Shift*.

- ☐ **Non-character keys** – Any keys which aren't printable, and don't have a function unless made to function in specific way in an application. Some of these have traditional uses, such as cursor keys and function keys.

- ☐ **Toggle keys** – These keys toggle between two states, such as *Caps Lock*, *Num Lock*, and *Scroll Lock*.

The KeyEventArgs

Before looking at the second event handler, we'll review some of the members of the `KeyEventArgs` and define their use with respect to processing keyboard events.

❏   `KeyCode` – Returns the numerical value of the key pressed as a member of the enumeration

❏   `KeyData` – Returns a bitwise combination of `Keys` enum values, which allows us to discern in a single step which combination of modifiers and other keys have been pressed

❏   `KeyValue` – Returns the `Keys` enum value for a single key pressed

❏   `Modifiers` – Returns the combinations of the modifier keys pressed (we'll show how to test for individual modifiers very shortly)

Now let's see how we can use the `Keys` enum and the `KeyEventArgs` object to discover which keys the user pressed. This is the purpose of our second textbox in the `KeyboardSample` application. The code below is the `KeyDown` event handler for this textbox, and we use it to check whether any modifier keys such as *Alt* have been pressed, whether any one of the characters in the word "Wrox" has been pressed, and to print appropriate messages in a label control:

```
private void txtKeys_KeyDown(object sender, Windows.Forms.KeyEventArgs e)
{
    StringBuilder sb = new StringBuilder();
    if(e.Shift) sb.Append("Shift, ");
    if(e.Alt) sb.Append("Alt, ");
    if(e.Control) sb.Append("Ctrl, ");

    if(e.KeyCode == Keys.W || e.KeyCode == Keys.R || e.KeyCode == Keys.O ||
        e.KeyCode == Keys.X)
    {
        sb.Append("Wrox Press!!");
    }
    else if(e.KeyCode == Keys.C && e.Modifiers == (Keys.Control | Keys.Alt))
    {
        sb.Append("©");
        txtKeys.SelectedText = "©";
        txtKeys.SelectionLength = 0;
    }
    else
    {
        sb.Append(Convert.ToString(e.KeyData));
    }

    lblKeys.Text = sb.ToString();
}
```

If we consider this from the top down, we can see that we're using a `StringBuilder` object to store a concatenated string value showing which keys have been pressed. The `StringBuilder` class resides in the `System.Text` namespace, and is far more efficient if we want to perform a number of modifications on a string. If we had used a normal string, a new `String` object would be created each time the string is modified, with enough memory to hold the new value. The `StringBuilder` class automatically allocates enough memory, and allows us to modify a string without creating a new object.

A series of `if` conditions is used to determine which modifier keys have been pressed. Examining this code shows how easy it is with `KeyEventArgs` to check whether these keys have been pressed. If the instance of `KeyEventArgs` is represented by e, then the Boolean `e.Control`, `e.Alt`, and `e.Shift` properties allow us to inspect whether each of these keys has been pressed. Each of these returns `true` if the value has been pressed.

Next, we check whether any one of the W, R, O, or X keys has been pressed, and if so we print the message `"Wrox Press !!"` in the label. Here we use the `Keys` enum – we check the `e.KeyCode` property against each enum value that we want to look for. In order to check for a key being pressed using the `Keys` enum, we can specify the key name, such as `Keys.W`, `Keys.Insert`, or `Keys.End`. So to check for any of the characters in the name Wrox, we'd use this line:

```
if (e.KeyCode == Keys.W || e.KeyCode == Keys.R || e.KeyCode == Keys.O ||
    e.KeyCode == Keys.X)
```

Modifier Keys

Modifier keys are used to modify the behavior of keystrokes. For example, pressing the *Ctrl*, *Alt*, and *Delete* keys simultaneously interrupts all running processes in Windows – the behavior of the *Delete* key has been modified by adding extra keys to the sequence. Or, to give another example, the *Shift* key alters the behavior of all other keys on the keyboard, such as toggling between lower and upper case for alphabetic characters. Modifier keys raise the `KeyDown` event, so any modifier key can be trapped in its own right if pressed by the user.

The next `if` condition tests whether the *Control*, *Alt*, and *C* keys have been pressed in tandem. If they have, we'll display a copyright sign (©) in the textbox and in our label. To test for the *C* key being pressed, we can use `Keys.C`, and we can use the `Modifiers` property of the `KeyEventArgs` class to tested whether *Ctrl* and *Alt* have been pressed simultaneously.

The modifier codes are bit values that can be combined; for example, we can trap simultaneous *Shift* and *Alt* keypresses using `Keys.Shift | Keys.Alt`. Pressing *Ctrl* + *Alt* + *C* doesn't by default display anything in the textbox, so as well as adding the copyright sign to the `StringBuilder` to be displayed in our label, we also need to set the selected text in the textbox to `"©"`. This will replace any text that is currently selected; if no text is selected, it will add the character at the current cursor position. We then set the `SelectionLength` property of the `TextBox` to zero, to move the cursor to the position immediately after the character we've just inserted:

```
else if(e.KeyCode == Keys.C && e.Modifiers == (Keys.Control | Keys.Alt))
{
    sb.Append("©");
    txtKeys.SelectedText = "©";
    txtKeys.SelectionLength = 0;
}
```

The `KeyData` property can be used for combined testing of non-modifier and modifier keys, so an expression like the following can be used to check whether *Ctrl*, *Alt*, and *C* have been pressed together:

```
if(e.KeyData == Keys.Shift | Keys.Alt | Keys.C) { ... }
```

We can calculate the value to test for in `KeyData` by ORing the `Keys` values for the individual keys.

193

The KeyPress Event

Using the KeyPress event allows a character to be retrieved from the keyboard input. On the other hand, the KeyPressEventArgs class has a KeyChar property that contains the char value of the keyboard character pressed. Printing it out as in the code below will result in printable characters in the messagebox or the familiar hollow square block in place of a non-printable character (this is dependent on the font used to display the message):

```
private void txtKeys_KeyDown(object sender, Windows.Forms.KeyEventArgs e)
{
    MessageBox.Show(e.KeyChar.ToString());
}
```

Remember that this event is raised *after* the KeyDown event.

The following table is derived from our KeyboardSample application – it shows some of the most widely used keyboard characters with their numerical equivalents:

Character	Value	Character	Value
A	65	0	48
B	66	1	49
C	67	2	50
D	68	3	51
E	69	4	52
F	70	5	53
G	71	6	54
H	72	7	55
I	73	8	56
J	74	9	57
K	75	*F1*	112
L	76	*F2*	113
M	77	*F3*	114
N	78	*F4*	115
0	79	*F5*	116
P	80	*F6*	117
Q	81	*F7*	118
R	82	*F8*	119

Character	Value	Character	Value
S	83	*F9*	120
T	84	*Escape*	27
U	85	*Insert*	45
V	86	*Delete*	46
W	87	*Page Up*	33
X	88	*Page Down*	34
Y	89	*End*	35
Z	90	*Home*	36

Accelerator Keys

Accelerator keys allow us to apply keyboard shortcuts to selections of some kind. We most commonly come across them in the form of a menu keyboard shortcut. For example, if you look at the menu options in Microsoft Office, there are underlined menu options that have default keyboard shortcuts of *Alt* followed by the underlined letter. For example, to open up the File menu, the user can press *Alt* followed by the *F* key. The menu options under one of the top-level menu items in Office contain shortcuts to each option (usually the shortcut key sequence is listed after the option). These shortcut keys normally consist of *Ctrl* plus another key.

A typical menu item in code exemplifies the use of shortcut keys.

```
MenuItem mnuOpen = new MenuItem("&Open", new EventHandler(Menu_OpenItem),
                                Shortcut.CtrlO)
```

This menu item will be created with the first letter (O) of the item underlined. The `Menu_OpenItem()` method will handle the click or keypress to the menu item and we create a shortcut for the key using the `Shortcut` enumeration. This enumeration offers an easy way to integrate shortcut keys into the program. Most of the key sequences represented by the enumeration involve simultaneous key presses of *Ctrl* and/or *Shift* and some other keyboard key. The enumeration resides in the `System.Windows.Forms` namespace. Some of the enumeration values are:

❑   `Shortcut.ShiftF10`

❑   `Shortcut.CtrlA`

❑   `Shortcut.CtrlShiftA`

The enumeration values are fairly explicit and need little explanation; suffice it to say that virtually every combination of keyboard shortcut key is covered by the enumeration. By default (if no other shortcut enumeration value is used), underlined menu items containing the `'&'` character have default shortcuts of *Alt* plus the following key. (If we want to display an actual ampersand character in a menu item, we need to escape the character by doubling it (`&&`)).

Menus are discussed in Chapter 2.

Developing a Keyboard Timer

In order to appreciate the use of the `OnKeyDown` and the `OnKeyUp` methods another project included with this chapter's downloadable code is the `Key Timer` project. There may be instances where the time that the key is held down for should reflect a changing value elsewhere in the program. For example, programming a music notation program where keyboard impression is monitored and the time for which a key was held down reflects the length of a note.

This application is much simpler, but it does demonstrate the two events functioning concurrently. In this program we'll call an external function from the Win32 API using Platform Invoke (P/Invoke). To enable this, we need to use the `DllImport` attribute from the `System.Runtime.InteropServices` namespace, so add the following `using` directive to the top of the source code:

```
using System.Runtime.InteropServices;
```

The project consists of a single Windows Form, with no controls belonging to it. It will simply display a message in a messagebox showing the length of time that a key has been held down for. Two private fields are declared to hold the start and stop times of the keypress:

```
private uint start = 0;
private uint stop = 0;
```

In order to import the external function, we can declare it as follows (this code can be placed immediately after the private field declarations):

```
[DllImport("kernel32.dll")]
public static extern uint GetTickCount();
```

The `DllImport` attribute allows us to import the function from `kernel32.dll`. An entry point for the function will be sought, and the function can then be referred to in the body of our code in the same way as an ordinary .NET method. The `GetTickCount()` method returns the time elapsed since Windows was booted up.

We'll override both the `OnKeyDown()` and `OnKeyUp()` methods of the form. In the `OnKeyDown()` method (called before the `KeyDown` event is raised), we set the value of our `start` field, based on the current tick count retrieved from the Win32 API function. Remember that we said earlier that the `KeyDown` event is raised periodically if the user presses a key for a long period; because of this, we first check to see whether `start` is equal to zero. If it is, we know that this event hasn't been raised for this keypress yet, so we set `start` to the current tick count. If `start` has already been set, we can just ignore this event:

```
protected override void OnKeyDown(KeyEventArgs args)
{
    if (start == 0) start = GetTickCount();
}
```

When the key is released, we call the GetTickCount() function again, and store the new value in the stop field. We then compare the two values, and display the difference in a message box. We also reset the start and stop fields to zero:

```
protected override void OnKeyUp(KeyEventArgs args)
{
    stop = GetTickCount();
    uint elapsed = (stop - start);
    MessageBox.Show(args.KeyData.ToString() + ", time elapsed: " +
                    elapsed.ToString() + " msecs");
    start = 0;
    stop = 0;
}
```

Checking Keyboard Modifiers

We've seen how we can use the Modifiers property of the KeyEventArgs class to determine whether a modifier key had been pressed. The problem is that we only have access to a KeyEventArgs object in the handler for a KeyUp or KeyDown event. However, it is possible to determine whether the modifier keys are still pressed, irrespective of the event occurring. The Control class (from which forms and other common graphical "widgets" derive) has a static property that can be used to retrieve the state of the modifier keys. The value returned from this property is a bitwise combination of Keys enumeration values that represent the real-time state of the modifier keys.

We can determine from this value whether a particular modifier is being pressed using standard bitwise arithmetic. For example, we could use this code to discover whether the *Ctrl* key is currently being pressed:

```
bool ctrl = ((Control.ModifierKeys & Keys.Control) == Keys.Control);
```

If the *Ctrl* key is being pressed, the bit for this key will be set in the Control.ModifierKeys value, so the result of ANDing this value with the Keys.Control value will be exactly the same as the value for Keys.Control itself.

Internationalizing the Keyboard

One of the essential tests for any Windows application is the internationalization of the keyboard. This means making sure that our program supports a variety of languages. Languages can be installed in Windows XP by selecting Regional Options from the Control Panel and choosing the Languages tab:

In Windows 2000, select Regional Options from the Control Panel, and on the General tab check the boxes next to any languages/character sets you want to install:

By default, you can switch between installed input locales be pressing *Shift* together with the left *Alt* key.

For this example, we will use the Hebrew language as it meets a few test criteria. These are:

❑   A different character set from English

❑   The language is written from right to left

So what does this mean for our application? Each control will have to process the characters from right-to-left instead of left-to-right. This doesn't change the nature of the textbox control, which will still write characters from the left hand side of the control, but the text will be read the other way around.

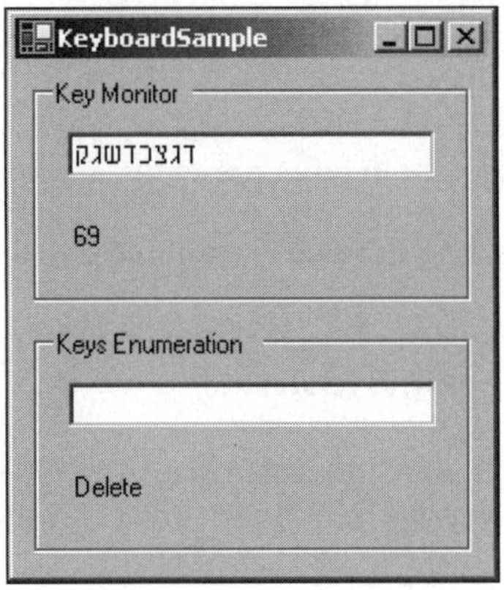

One of the things to note about the above example is that because the KeyDown event is used, we won't be able to retrieve the required information for the character code. When pressing a Hebrew character, the code is expected to be somewhere in the range 1400 – 1500 as a Unicode character value. As you can see from the above picture using the KeyDown event gives us results that show the underlying key code being pressed as opposed to the key value. This would be no good for us if we wish to obtain the Unicode character value.

To remedy this, we can just use the KeyPress event containing the property KeyChar we introduced earlier. KeyChar lets us access the value of the internationalized character (in this case, a Hebrew letter) in the form a of a char variable. The InternationalText application compensates for the problems encountered in the KeyboardSample application. We can take the text from the textbox and effectively reprint it into the text label, along with the Unicode character code:

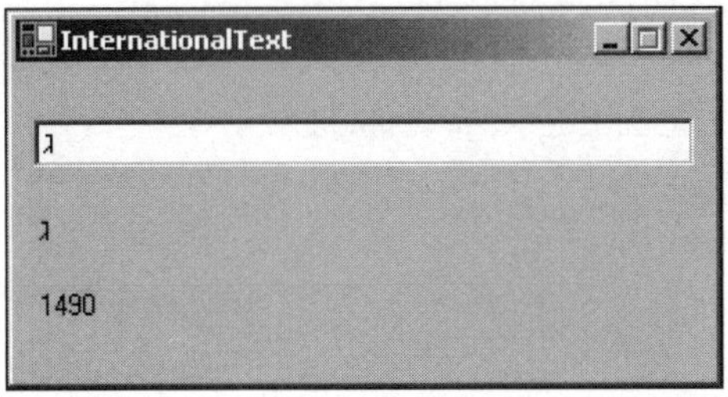

The Hebrew character *gimel* is shown in the above picture; when pressed, this reveals a Unicode value of 1490. We are using Hebrew as an example here, but the same technique can be applied to any international keyboard character set, such as Mandarin, Cantonese, or Arabic.

This program is quite simple and follows the same basic format as the previous programs. The form has one textbox, and two labels. We'll handle the `KeyPress` event for the textbox, so we can display the character and its Unicode code when a key is pressed.

```
private void txtInternational_KeyPress(object sender, KeyPressEventArgs e)
{
    lblInternationalText.Text += e.KeyChar.ToString();
    lblCharCode.Text = ((int)e.KeyChar).ToString();
}
```

The first label control, `lblInternationalText`, simply appends every character that is returned from the `KeyChar` property of the `KeyPressEventArgs` to the existing text in the label control.

As the `KeyChar` property returns a `char` value, we can retrieve the 16-bit Unicode character code from this just by casting to `int`:

```
lblCharCode.Text = ((int)e.KeyChar).ToString();
```

Once we've converted the Unicode `KeyChar` value to an `int` type, we can print the Unicode character code on the screen simply by calling the `int`'s `ToString()` method.

To complete our internationalization of applications, we also need a way of recognizing when the input locale has changed in an application. For example, an application may need to allow some sort of multilingual input and know when the base language has changed, so that a translation dictionary can be used on the new language.

The `Form` class has two events that can be used to detect language changes:

❑   `InputLanguageChanging`
❑   `InputLanguageChanged`

As with many other Windows Forms events, we can handle these by overriding related methods in a derived class, so we'll add these two methods to our form:

```
protected override void OnInputLanguageChanged(
                            InputLanguageChangedEventArgs e)
{
    MessageBox.Show("Input language changed to:" +
                            e.InputLanguage.Culture.Name);
    base.OnInputLanguageChanged(e);
}

protected override void OnInputLanguageChanging(
                            InputLanguageChangingEventArgs e)
{
```

```
      MessageBox.Show("Input language changing to:" +
                                    e.InputLanguage.Culture.Name);
      base.OnInputLanguageChanging(e);
}
```

Using the two classes `InputLanguage` and `CultureInfo` (in the `System.Windows.Forms` and `System.Globalization` namespaces respectively), the name of the language (or, more accurately, the language code followed by the county code) can be determined; for example, Hebrew is he-IL, and US English is en-US. Whenever the language changes and/or is changed message boxes will pop up displaying the name of the language in the format shown above.

Internationalized application development has become relatively easy with Windows Forms. It's always worth testing and building software for a variety of languages, although it can still entail a great deal of testing and further development consideration for larger projects (for example, possible changes in visual control layout to support different character sets). The keyboard events allow virtually any customized program to be able to process keyboard information of any form. In order to test internationalized applications, a keyboard map of characters will need to be known as each character set has a specific keyboard layout. This can be obtained from simple programs like the `KeyboardSample` above by mapping foreign key characters to keyboard characters and character codes, or by using the Windows Character Map utility, which can be used to inspect fonts and the Unicode values of those fonts. It can be found in the Accessories program menu.

Losing and Gaining Focus

No discussion of Windows Forms would be complete without an appreciation of keyboard focus and focus events. Focus needs to be set for a particular control if that control can accept input messages from the keyboard. Forms that currently have the focus have a highlighted caption bar – other forms will have a dull color effect on their caption bars to show that they do not have the focus. Different controls respond to focus in different ways; for example, a textbox contains a flashing cursor when focus is gained. Focus can be gained by either clicking the mouse on a control that can receive focus, or by pressing the tab key within an application. The controls that can gain focus in an application have a specific tab order that can be altered by changing the control's properties. In this way the *Tab* key can be used to move from textbox controls where the user has finished entering information to button controls that allow the user to submit the information just entered. Focus allows the developer to enable applications to respond to user input and changes in entered data. Keyboard input can be validated in the same way as before by using the focus events instead of the keyboard events.

Focus events can be used to:

❑ Validate user data

❑ Check if the application is no longer the current context window

The `FocusForm` application demonstrates the use of the focus events, properties, and methods available in .NET. The events are:

❑ GotFocus

❑ LostFocus

201

The `FormFocus` application uses these two events to track whether the form is the current context window. This example will demonstrate some of the design considerations when attempting to create forms that make use of the focus events. The application admittedly demonstrates an extreme case, but it is one that can occur with ill-thought out design.

To begin with, we set up handlers for the two focus events for our textbox:

```
txtFocusForm.LostFocus += new System.EventHandler(txtFocusForm_LostFocus);
txtFocusForm.GotFocus += new System.EventHandler(txtFocusForm_GotFocus);
```

This will mean that every time the textbox loses focus and gains focus, different methods will handle the event. The two methods simply display a message box with either "Hello!" or "Goodbye!" printed on it:

```
protected void txtFocusForm_LostFocus(object sender, EventArgs e)
{
    MessageBox.Show("Goodbye!");
}

protected void txtFocusForm_GotFocus(object sender, EventArgs e)
{
    MessageBox.Show("Hello!");
}
```

Rather predictably, an infinite loop will take place each time the message box pops up. When the form initially loads, the focus is set to the textbox, thus creating a textbox with the word "Hello!". When the button on the message box is pressed, focus is lost so the "Goodbye!" message box replaces this. This will continue, since the textbox will continually gain and lose focus while the user interacts with the message box. Form designs like this should be avoided at all costs! (One alternative to this would be to create a form with a label for displaying the messages. The label cannot receive user input, so won't gain focus, and the infinite loop can avoided.)

The `FocusForm` application uses the `Click` event for the button to display some information about the focus of the `TextBox` control on the form:

```
private void btFocusForm_Click(object sender, System.EventArgs e)
{
    bool canFocus = txtFocusForm.CanFocus;
    bool containsFocus = this.ContainsFocus;
    bool focused = txtFocusForm.Focused;

    MessageBox.Show("Textbox can focus: " + canFocus +
                    "\nForm children contain focus: " + containsFocus +
                    "\nTextbox has focus: "+ focused);
    txtFocusForm.Focus();
}
```

This method displays various properties and methods derived from `Control` that can be very useful in the application writing process. The first, `Control.CanFocus`, is a Boolean property that returns `true` if the control can take the focus at all. If, for example, the textbox were `disabled` then this property would return `false`, as the control would never be able to gain focus through tab keypresses or through the mouse.

`Control.ContainsFocus` is also a useful property revealing whether the control or any of its children has focus. This can be used at the form level (as here), or it could be used with other containers, such as group boxes.

The `Control.Focused` property also returns a Boolean value; this indicates specifically whether the requested control currently has focus. In this way, other methods can determine whether the control has the user's focus. One good use of this is to check the state of a form while a background thread does work behind the scenes; if the form is the current context window, then the process can gain control and print a message to the user; otherwise it will wait.

The `Control.Focus()` method is used to give focus to a particular control. In this example, after the button-handling code has been invoked and the message box has been shown, we call this method to transfer focus from the button to the textbox.

Focus can be toggled between visual objects on a form. When the *Tab* key is pressed, focus will move to the next visual object on the form. The order in which this is done is defined by the `TabIndex` property of each control. The `TabIndex` is an integer value that defines the order in which controls get focus when the user presses *Tab*. Controls with lower `TabIndex` values receive focus earlier than higher `TabIndex` values, and the lowest `TabIndex` property value is the first of the form's child controls to get focus. So to make the `txtFocusForm` control the first control to gain focus from a *Tab* key press, we would set its `TabIndex` to zero:

```
txtFocusForm.TabIndex = 0;
```

If another object had an identical `TabIndex` value, the control with the highest z-order would then be the first to gain the focus from a *Tab* key press (z-order is determined by which object is the topmost on the form, and can be set through the Bring to Front option in the control's context menu in the Form Designer).

The `TabIndex` property can effectively be disabled by setting the `TabStop` property on the control to `false`. When this is done, focus through tabbing will not occur on the specified control. Earlier we stated that `Label` controls cannot gain focus. This is not strictly true – they appear not to be able to gain focus, but in reality they can be focused like any other control – however, the `TabStop` property on this control is set to `false`, which renders any tabbing or clicks to gain focus useless.

Responding to the Mouse

Unquestionably, the keyboard's companion as the most useful input device is the mouse, as mouse clicks form an integral part of any Windows application. The rest of this chapter will focus on all of the uses of the mouse and the way that the developer can use the mouse in an application to enhance the user experience through the Windows Forms programming model.

A Windows Forms program should display mouse behavior consistent with user expectations. For example, while a form is "locked" processing a task, the mouse pointer should change to an hourglass or some equally familiar symbol to denote "busy". Similarly, the web browser has popularized the hand-pointing icon for moving the mouse over hyperlinks in an HTML document. These are features that the user will expect of any application we write (we'll look at some examples of this later in the chapter).

Mouse Capabilities

Until now, we haven't had to worry about trapping the mouse specifically, as each control has its own implementation of mouse handling code. To introduce the subject of the mouse as an input device we can start by displaying general information about the capabilities of the mouse (as each mouse is different, the application below may yield different results with different mouse models). The `SystemInformation` class has a great many uses, as it encapsulates most of the common information about the user's system. One such use is obtaining information about the user's mouse to use in our application. There are a variety of reasons for doing this, but more often than not we're interested in the capabilities of a mouse and the functions that we can ascribe to different click events. Does the mouse have scrolling capabilities (is a mouse wheel present)? Does it have a middle button?

The `MouseMovement` application uses this class to read and display general information about the capabilities of the user's mouse:

The code to do this is very simple; we just use a `StringBuilder` to concatenate a message containing a bit of descriptive text for each of the relevant static properties of the `SystemInformation` class, and the property's value:

```
StringBuilder sb = new StringBuilder();

sb.Append("Mouse Present: "+ SystemInformation.MousePresent + "\r\n");
```

```
sb.Append("Number of Mouse Buttons: " + SystemInformation.MouseButtons +
        "\r\n");
sb.Append("Mouse Wheel Present: " + SystemInformation.MouseWheelPresent +
        "\r\n");
sb.Append("Number of Mouse Wheel scroll lines: " +
        SystemInformation.MouseWheelScrollLines + "\r\n");
sb.Append("Native wheel support: " +
        SystemInformation.NativeMouseWheelSupport + "\r\n");
sb.Append("Mouse buttons swapped: " + SystemInformation.MouseButtonsSwapped +
        "\r\n");
```

Once we have this message, we just display it in a multi-line textbox (as in the screenshot above). The properties we display are:

❑ SystemInformation.MousePresent (bool)

❑ SystemInformation.MouseButtons (int)

❑ SystemInformation.MouseWheelPresent (bool)

❑ SystemInformation.MouseWheelScrollLines (int)

❑ SystemInformation.NativeMouseWheelSupport (bool)

❑ SystemInformation.MouseButtonSwapped (bool)

The MousePresent property simply indicates whether a mouse exists on the computer and whether it is active. The MouseButtons property returns an integer that is the number of mouse buttons present on the device. This number can vary considerably. As you can see from the screenshot on the previous page, I have a mouse with five buttons! The MouseWheelPresent property returns true if the mouse contains a scrolling wheel. The MouseWheelScrollLines property returns an integer based on the number of lines that the mouse wheel can scroll. Use notepad or Microsoft Word to verify this figure, allowing you to determine the number of scrollable lines. This number is configurable. Selecting **Mouse** in the **Control Panel** in Windows XP will display the following dialog (Windows 2000 doesn't have an equivalent to the **Wheel** tab):

Changing the value above on the Wheel tab results in the SystemInformation class returning a new value for the MouseWheelProperties. The NativeMouseWheelSupport property checks whether the operating system has support for the mouse wheel. Most new operating system such as Windows XP will have innate support of mouse wheels in generic drivers. The MouseButtonSwapped property returns true if the mouse buttons have been "virtually" swapped so that the right mouse button can be used for clicking and the left to call up context menus. This change can be made on the Buttons page of the Mouse Properties pages. It's worth changing a few of these properties on your own systems and seeing the data change in the MouseMovement application.

Tracking the Mouse

Tracking the mouse pointer is a very easy exercise with the Windows Forms programming model. Again, we can handle events using delegates in the normal way, or we can override On...() methods for our control. In this case, we override the OnMouseMove() method, which is called every time the user moves the mouse. Notice that this method is called very frequently, so in a real application you should be very careful to limit the amount of processing you do here.

The following code is from the MouseMovements application, and tracks the mouse pointer on the screen and displays its X and Y coordinates relative to the top left corner of the form. We can get these from the X and Y properties of the MouseEventArgs object that is passed into the OnMouseMove() method. We use a Boolean toggleMouse field (initially set to false) to determine whether the program actually responds to mouse movements by printing the coordinates on the form. This field is set to true or false when the user clicks on the Start Track Mouse or Stop Track Mouse button respectively:

```
private void btTrackMouseOn_Click(object sender, System.EventArgs e)
{
    toggleMouse = true;
}

protected override void OnMouseMove(MouseEventArgs e)
{
    if (toggleMouse) txtMouseInfo.Text = "x: " + e.X + ", y:" + e.Y;
}

private void btTrackMouseOff_Click(object sender, System.EventArgs e)
{
    toggleMouse = false;
    txtMouseInfo.Text = GetMouseInfo().ToString();
}
```

The above code shows how easy it is to trap mouse movement and turn it into something that the application can use to pinpoint the mouse's position. The MouseMovement program was created to be able to toggle between two states. The "On" state shows the position of the cursor on the form by showing the X and Y coordinates of the mouse pointer in the textbox. This is continually updated as the OnMouseMove() method is called every time the mouse pointer changes screen position. The **Stop Track Mouse** button stops tracking the mouse and displays the mouse properties from SystemInformation once again.

OnMouseMove() is another virtual method that can be used to track control information. In this case, it tracks mouse movement on the control. The only caveat to this, and drawback for the program, is that the control will only respond to mouse movement within the area of the control itself. A good test of this is to notice the X and Y position change with the mouse movement when the pointer is over an area of the form that is not part of the form control (such as the textbox or button controls). There are two ways around this:

❑   Track the screen position of the cursor on the screen independently of the control

❑   Track areas of the form that contain other controls, so we can work out the position over each control and add it to the top left position of the control on the form (this will give the position of the mouse pointer in relation to the top left corner of the control)

```
this.btTrackMouseOff.MouseMove += new
                           MouseEventHandler(this.Control_MouseMove);
this.btTrackMouseOn.MouseMove += new
                           MouseEventHandler(this.Control_MouseMove);
this.txtMouseInfo.MouseMove += new MouseEventHandler(this.Control_MouseMove);
```

We use the same method to handle the MouseMove event for the three different button controls on the form. The Control_MouseMove() method will track the position of the mouse on the control and work out the position relative to the top of the form by using the top and left properties of each control. Notice that the delegate System.Windows.Forms.MouseEventHandler is used instead of System.EventHandler.

Here is the revised code used to trap all mouse movements on the form. The OnMouseMove() method handles movement of the mouse on the form, and the Control_MouseMove() method responds to all mouse movements over the three button controls. Both methods call a helper method called CheckMousePosition(). This takes a MouseEventArgs object as the first argument so that the position of the mouse can be calculated. The second argument contains a reference to the control so that the top and left positions can be calculated. If the mouse is over the form itself, null is passed in place of the control reference (since the top and left position are effectively zero):

```
protected override void OnMouseMove(MouseEventArgs e)
{
    CheckMousePosition(e, null);
}

protected void Control_MouseMove(object sender, MouseEventArgs e)
{
    CheckMousePosition(e, sender);
}

private void CheckMousePosition(MouseEventArgs e, object control)
{
    if(control == null)
    {
        if (toggleMouse) txtMouseInfo.Text = "x: " + e.X + ", y:" + e.Y;
    }
    else
    {
        int left = e.X + ((Control)control).Left;
        int top = e.Y + ((Control)control).Top;
        if (toggleMouse) txtMouseInfo.Text = "x: " + left + ", y:" + top;
    }
}
```

Notice, however, that everything is done in the context of the form. Perhaps, though, the application will need to track mouse movement outside of the form and throughout the whole screen. Move the mouse pointer outside the form area, and you'll see the coordinate values stop updating. However, there is a very easy way to solve this problem:

The premise of tracking the mouse pointer across the screen is another simple concept and is implemented with great ease using the Windows programming model. The mouse tracking that we described previously was solely available using mouse events with particular controls on a form. Very quickly we discerned that it would be difficult to track the mouse pointer across the entire screen using this method, as we can only handle events for our own application.

Changes in the mouse movement application depicted by the new large button allow us to achieve our goal. Aside from the new button, we have a Timer control that can be used to execute code at specific intervals. We will use this to check the position of the mouse periodically.

```
private Timer tCheckMouse = new Timer();
```

In order to initialize the Timer object, we have to set a method to handle the Tick event and start the timer. When the form loads, the code below is invoked to initialize the Timer:

```
tCheckMouse.Tick += new EventHandler(Timer_Check);
tCheckMouse.Enabled = true;
tCheckMouse.Stop();
```

The code is very self-explanatory. First, we set the Timer_Check() method to handle the Tick event. Then we enable the timer and set its state to "stopped". The Start() method of the Timer object is called when the **Start Screen wide mouse tracking** button is clicked – we won't start the Timer until the user clicks on this button. At periodic intervals (the default is 100 milliseconds), the Tick event is raised, and the Timer_Check() method is called. We'll also update the Click event handler for our btTrackMouseOn button, to stop the timer again:

```
private void btTrackMouseOn_Click(object sender, System.EventArgs e)
{
    toggleMouse = true;
    tCheckMouse.Stop();
}

private void Timer_Check(object sender, EventArgs e)
{
    Point pMousePosition = Control.MousePosition;
    txtMouseInfo.Text = "x: " + pMousePosition.X + ", y:" + pMousePosition.Y;
}

private void btScreenTrack_Click(object sender, System.EventArgs e)
{
    toggleMouse = false;
    tCheckMouse.Start();
}
```

The btScreenTrack_Click() method (the event handler for the button that starts screen-wide mouse tracking) starts the timer and sets the toggleMouse flag to false, so that we don't attempt to display both the coordinates within the form and the screen-wide coordinates.

The Timer_Check() method is where we actually check the screen-wide coordinates. This method is called every 100 milliseconds, as this is the default Interval for a Timer (we could have set the Interval property, but this adequate for our needs). The Control.MousePosition() static method returns a System.Drawing.Point object (the same struct that we use to position controls on a form). We check the X and Y properties of this struct to retrieve the two 2D spatial values of the point. The X and Y values are respectively the position from the left hand side of the screen and the position from the top of the screen.

Drawing with the Mouse

No Windows GUI Programming book would be complete without a minor implementation of the "Scribble" application. For the purposes of this chapter, this application will provide good example material to illustrate the use of mouse clicks and mouse events. The Scribble application is a good tool for illustrating he synergy between the mouse events – how they can be used together to produce good effects.

The Scribble drawing application allows the user to draw on the screen. Holding down the mouse button (usually the left button) allows the user to draw freehand on the form, until the mouse button is released. To enable this to occur we have to override three methods:

- ❑ OnMouseMove()
- ❑ OnMouseDown()
- ❑ OnMouseUp()

It is the combination of these three events that lets us trace the mouse pointer across the screen, and track which button(s) the user has clicked on the mouse.

Five private variables are declared to track the state of the mouse and the current drawing color, and to help us draw on the screen:

```
private bool mouseDown = false;
private Point lastPoint = Point.Empty;
private string color = "black";
private Graphics g;
private Pen p;
```

The first is a Boolean value that is set to true if the mouse button is currently held down; the second represents a Point object that holds the position of the last point on the screen where we drew. The third variable is a string containing the color of the current pen being used. The default is "black", but later we'll have the option to change the color. The last two are GDI+ objects from the System.Drawing namespace. We'll look at GDI+ in the next chapter, but for now we'll just say that a Graphics object provides a surface for drawing on, and a Pen allows us to draw in a particular color on that surface. We initialize these two objects in the form's constructor, after the call to InitializeComponent(). A Graphics object is created by calling the Control's CreateGraphics() method. This method will return a Graphics object for use on the control (in this case the Form). We also create a Pen object with the currently selected color:

```
public frmScribble()
{
    InitializeComponent();
    g = CreateGraphics();
    p = new Pen(Color.FromName(color));
}
```

Within the overridden OnMouseDown() and OnMouseUp() methods, we just set the mouseDown Boolean flag to true or false as appropriate:

```
protected override void OnMouseDown(MouseEventArgs e)
{
  mouseDown = true;
}

protected override void OnMouseUp(MouseEventArgs e)
{
  mouseDown = false;
}
```

The OnMouseDown() method sets the mouseDown Boolean value to true, so the application can determine the current state of the mouse (whether the mouse button is being held down or not). In the OnMouseUp() method, the reverse must occur – we set mouseDown to false.

The OnMouseMove() method is where the real implementation takes place. Initially, there is a check to ensure that the lastPoint variable is set to something. The constant Point.Empty is used for this check. If the Point is empty then lastPoint is set to the current point. As the graphics method we use needs two points to plot on the form setting, this variable is very important. It will mean that the first time that this event is raised it will set the lastPoint and the current point to the same Point value:

```
protected override void OnMouseMove(MouseEventArgs e)
{
    if (lastPoint.Equals(Point.Empty)) lastPoint = new Point(e.X, e.Y);
    if (mouseDown)
    {
        Point pMousePos = new Point(e.X, e.Y);
        g.DrawLine(p, pMousePos, lastPoint);
    }
    lastPoint = new Point(e.X, e.Y);
}
```

If the mouse button is clicked and held down, the current point is obtained. A line is then drawn between the current and previous points. The points will normally be different aside from the first time that the method is raised (when the `lastPoint` value is not populated with anything other than an empty value).

The `DrawLine()` method is used to draw a line between the two points using the `Pen` object that we instantiated earlier.

The Scribble application will continue to work if the mouse is outside the form area. The `MouseUp` and `MouseDown` events will be raised if the mouse button state changes even outside this area. When the mouse returns to the area, it will have previously reset the `mouseDown` variable if the left mouse button has been raised.

There we have it – a Scribble program! However, suppose we want to add different `Pen` colors to the program? We'll do this by adding a context menu. This will appear when the right mouse button is clicked. In order to do this we add some extra code to the `OnMouseDown()` method:

```
protected override void OnMouseDown(MouseEventArgs e)
{
    mouseDown = true;
    if(e.Button == MouseButtons.Right)
    {
        ContextMenu m = new ContextMenu();
        m.MenuItems.Add(0, new MenuItem("black", new
                                    EventHandler(RightMouseButton_Click)));
        m.MenuItems.Add(1, new MenuItem("white", new
                                    EventHandler(RightMouseButton_Click)));
        m.MenuItems.Add(2, new MenuItem("red", new
                                    EventHandler(RightMouseButton_Click)));
        m.MenuItems.Add(3, new MenuItem("green", new
                                    EventHandler(RightMouseButton_Click)));
        m.MenuItems.Add(4, new MenuItem("blue", new
                                    EventHandler(RightMouseButton_Click)));
        m.Show(this, new Point(e.X, e.Y));
    }
}
```

This method checks whether the right mouse button has been clicked, and if so shows a context menu with color options. The `MouseEventArgs.Button` property returns a `MouseButtons` object that can be checked to determine which button has been clicked. In order to check that the right mouse button has been clicked, we can use the `MouseButtons.Right` enumeration value. If this is `true`, we create a `ContextMenu` and add five items to it. Each item represents a color. The colors chosen are:

❑   Black

❑   White

❑   Red

❑   Green

❑   Blue

Finally, we call ContextMenu.Show(), passing the current form and the current Point determined by the MouseEventArgs.X and MouseEventArgs.Y values. A right mouse click will now cause a menu to appear next to the pointer. The EventHandler for each of the MenuItems has been set to the RightMouseButton_Click() method.

This may seem like a long-winded way of generating a context menu. After all, we could have simply used the ContextMenu property of the control to refer to the ContextMenu. The code is written like this primarily to demonstrate the use of trapping the right mouse button click and manually generating a context menu. The idea is shown in its simplest form but can be extended to produce a custom control that acts as a graphical tablet whereby we can select the color we desire from a color swatch.

The RightMouseButton_Click() simply casts the sender from type object to type MenuItem and uses the Text property of the chosen MenuItem to populate the color variable. We then use this to create a new Pen object of the appropriate color:

```
protected void RightMouseButton_Click(object sender, EventArgs e)
{
    color = ((MenuItem)sender).Text;
    p = new Pen(Color.FromName(color));
}
```

MouseButtons

The MouseButtons application illustrates the ease with which mouse buttons and wheel movements can be trapped using Windows Forms. The MouseButtons application is a simple form that responds to different mouse events to determine the scope of mouse wheel movement or button presses.

```
protected override void OnMouseWheel(MouseEventArgs e)
{
    switch(e.Delta)
    {
        case -360:
            lblRightClick.Text = "One Rotation Reverse";
            break;
        case -240:
            lblRightClick.Text = "Two Thirds Rotation Reverse";
            break;
        case -120:
            lblRightClick.Text = "One Third Rotation Reverse";
            break;
        case 360:
            lblRightClick.Text = "One Rotation Forward";
            break;
        case 240:
            lblRightClick.Text = "Two Thirds Rotation Forward";
            break;
        case 120:
            lblRightClick.Text = "One Third Rotation Forward";
            break;
        default:
```

```
                lblRightClick.Text = "More Than One Rotation " +
                                    (e.Delta < 0 ? "Reverse" : "Forward");
            break;
    }
}
```

The integer `Delta` property of the `MouseEventArgs` represents the change in movement of the wheel in degrees. Overriding the `OnMouseWheel()` method allows us to trap movements of the mouse wheel, convert them, and check to see the number of degrees of movement the wheel has made. In this case, 360 degrees represents a full movement of the wheel whereas -360 degrees represents a full movement of the wheel in the reverse direction. A single turn of the mouse by the user is normally 120 or -120 degrees (one third of a full rotation).

```
protected override void OnMouseDown(MouseEventArgs e)
{
    switch(e.Button)
    {
        case(MouseButtons.Left):
            lblLeftClick.Text = "Left Click";
            break;
        case(MouseButtons.Middle):
            lblLeftClick.Text = "Middle Click";
            break;
        case(MouseButtons.Right):
            lblLeftClick.Text = "Right Click";
            break;
        case(MouseButtons.XButton1):
            lblLeftClick.Text = "XButton1 Click";
            break;
        case(MouseButtons.XButton2):
            lblLeftClick.Text = "XButton2 Click";
            break;
    }

    switch(e.Clicks)
    {
        case 1:
            lblMiddleClick.Text = "Single Click";
            break;
        case 2:
            lblMiddleClick.Text = "Double Click!";
            break;
        default:
            lblMiddleClick.Text = "Many clicks!";
            break;
    }
}
```

Overriding the OnMouseDown() method allows us to trap a click of any one of the mouse buttons. The mouse button clicked can be determined using the Button property of MouseEventArgs. This returns a MouseButtons enumeration value. The MouseButtons enumeration contains values that we can use to test against the MouseEventArgs.Button property value:

❑   MouseButtons.Left

❑   MouseButtons.Right

❑   MouseButtons.Middle

❑   MouseButtons.XButton1

❑   MouseButtons.XButton2

The first three should be self-explanatory. The last two represent buttons on the new four or five button mice that allow the user to navigate forward and backwards with a couple of mouse buttons on the side.

The Clicks property of the MouseEventsArgs object relates to the number of times that the mouse has been clicked. It is applicable to any of the buttons. If the user clicked the right button twice, the MouseEventArgs.Clicks property will return 2, allowing us to test for a double click in our application:

In the application, three labels show different aspects of what the mouse is doing; one label shows the wheel movements, another shows the number of clicks of the mouse button and a third shows which button has been pressed. The fourth label is used to introduce the hover events. There are three events that relate to the pointer being over a form object:

❑   MouseEnter

❑   MouseHover

❑   MouseLeave

`MouseEnter` is raised when the mouse pointer enters the client area; `MouseHover` is raised when a short time passes and the pointer is hovering over the control; and `MouseLeave` when the mouse pointer leaves the control. The `MouseHover` event is only raised once, so in order to check whether the mouse is still hovering at any one time we can use flags that are set when the mouse enters and leaves the control. Alternatively, we could use a timer started on the `MouseHover` event, and keep checking whether the mouse is still hovering.

We track these events by setting up delegates in the usual way:

```
lblHover.MouseEnter += new EventHandler(lblHover_MouseEnter);
lblHover.MouseHover += new EventHandler(lblHover_MouseHover);
lblHover.MouseLeave += new EventHandler(lblHover_MouseLeave);
```

The three events are wired up and each handler is implemented using a different method. We've only reproduced the code for one below as they are essentially the same (aside from the mouse pointer changing to different cursor types):

```
protected void lblHover_MouseHover(object sender, EventArgs e)
{
  lblHover.Text = "Hovering over label";
  Cursor = Cursors.Hand;
}
```

These methods can be overridden on controls in the way described throughout this chapter. This method is invoked when the `MouseHover` event is raised (effectively the mouse pointer hovers over the object – in this case the label control). In order to give it a web-like effect, the cursor is changed to a hand. The `Cursors` class contains a number of properties that we can use to change the type of mouse pointer on the screen. The three used in the code are:

- ❑ `Cursors.NoMove2D`
- ❑ `Cursors.Hand`
- ❑ `Cursors.Default`

We should also mention one more:

- ❑ `Cursors.WaitCursor` (not used in code but very useful to know)

These cursors respectively refer to a cross sign, a hand sign, whatever the system default is (usually a pointer), and the hourglass. However, there is a wealth of other system cursors that can be used from the enumeration. It's almost too easy to get carried away using obscure cursors and endlessly confuse users who would have no idea what the application is doing!

As we illustrated earlier with concurrent keystrokes in the first half of the chapter, it is also possible to click more than one button at a time using the mouse. As each `MouseButton` constant is simply a bit flag, each time combinations of buttons are clicked they can be tested for using the `&` operator on each pair or trio of enumeration values and checking to see if the result is equal to `MouseEventsArgs.Buttons`.

Using ToolTips

Tooltips are small pieces of text that pop up over controls to inform the user about the type of activity performed by a particular control or the level of interactivity required by the user. Tooltips are a standard of UI development and have been popularized in HTML documents that show alternative text tooltips in web browsers when the mouse hovers over an image. The following code is from the Tooltips application. This generates a tooltip when the mouse pointer hovers over a button or a textbox:

```
ToolTip forButton = new ToolTip();
forButton.SetToolTip(btnTooltips, "You are now over the button!!");
forButton.SetToolTip(txtTooltip, "You are now over the textbox!!");
forButton.AutomaticDelay = 2000;
```

A ToolTip object is created and the method SetToolTip() is used to set the tooltip text for a particular control. The single instance of this object can be used create tooltips for every control on the form. The RemoveAll() method will clear all the tooltip values from the object. Tooltips, by default, pop up after a short delay, so their impact on the screen is subtle (rather than abrupt). This delay is set through the AutomaticDelay property, an int value (in milliseconds), which is used to control the initial delay of the popup. This value is used by other property values to calculate defaults such as when the tooltip is removed or reshown to the user.

Summary

The .NET Framework offers an all-encompassing model that enables developers to use simple techniques such as control inheritance and method overriding to enable mouse checks and keyboard checks. The applications shown in this chapter reflect the minimum needed to establish an understanding of user input via the keyboard and the mouse. All of the programming techniques can be adapted to any Windows Forms application – either through control inheritance or event chaining. These simple techniques can be used in a variety of applications. Some suggestions to get you started could include:

- ❑ Drawing applications
- ❑ Multithreaded forms – checking for input changes while background processes change to reflect new input changes
- ❑ Validating user input
- ❑ Games programming

In this chapter we covered a variety of programming techniques to capture user input from the keyboard and mouse:

- ❑ Keyboard events
- ❑ Trapping specific key values and combinations of values
- ❑ Modifier keys
- ❑ Internationalization of an application
- ❑ Trapping mouse events
- ❑ Responding to button clicks (for example, by popping up context menus)
- ❑ Tracking the mouse
- ❑ Drawing using the mouse
- ❑ Detecting mouse hovers

6

Drawing in .NET

What should a chapter on graphics discuss? Imagine you are standing in northern Spain's Altamira cave, whose walls bear prehistoric paintings, and admiring the red bison. You might consider the following questions:

(The code to display this sketch of a red bison from Altamira is given in our first project.)

❑   What **tools and techniques** were used and applied by the ancient artists during the creation?

❑   What was the **function** or **purpose** of these cave paintings – communication?

❑   What **information** do the pictures contain?

❑   Do the compositions affect your **senses** – are they aesthetic?

When discussing drawing and painting the accent may be shifted in some direction depending on the topic and composition in question. However, it seems that the questions above remain the principal ones regardless of the time and place. This chapter deals with the **tools** and **techniques** that are provided by **GDI+**. It includes many pictures and examples in addition to the technical description of the main features and techniques of GDI+. We hope the examples not only give you an idea of what can be done and how it can be achieved in C#, but also encourage you to enhance our solutions and give you inspiration for further experimentation and creation.

Overview of GDI+

Let's begin with a very brief overview of **GDI+**. The name derives from its predecessor, the Graphics Device Interface or **GDI** that allows you to display graphical output on the screen, on a printer, or on a bitmap in memory too. GDI+ as a set of classes (gdiplus.dll) written in C++ is a subsystem of the Microsoft Windows XP and Windows .NET Server operating systems and can be used both in managed and unmanaged code. You can use GDI+ in managed code due to the wrapper classes of the System.Drawing namespace. The main difference between these two graphics device interfaces is that GDI+ is not based on the device context as GDI was, but on the Graphics object. The Graphics object may be associated with almost any part of a window such as the form or its controls.

GDI+ optimizes the functions of GDI and expands on the capabilities of GDI by providing new features such as:

❑ **Gradient Brushes** – GDI+ provides linear and path gradient brushes for filling shapes, paths, or regions and even drawing lines and curves with gradually changing colors

❑ **Alpha Blending** – enables us to specify the transparency of a fill color

❑ **Matrix Object** – allows us to perform transformation (translation, scaling, rotation) of objects

❑ **Scalable Regions** – unlike GDI, GDI+ stores regions in world coordinates and enables you to carry out transformations of regions

❑ **Independent Path Objects** – in GDI+ the GraphicsPath objects are separate from the Graphics object and are not destroyed after drawing and so can be reused

❑ **Cardinal Splines** – can connect array points not only with straight lines, but also with curves

❑ **New Image Formats** – through the Image, Bitmap, and Metafile classes, GDI+ supports the image formats BMP, GIF, JPEG, ICON, WMF, EMF, PNG, TIFF, and EXIF.

The GDI+ wrappers in the .NET Framework contains 95 classes, 3 interfaces, 8 structures, 12 delegates, and 59 enumerations in six namespaces that fall into the broad categories opposite:

GDI+ namespace	Classes	Interfaces	Structures	Delegates	Enums
System.Drawing	29	0	8	3	10
System.Drawing.Drawing2D	14	0	0	0	22
System.Drawing.Imaging	16	0	0	1	16
System.Drawing.Text	3	0	0	0	3
System.Drawing.Printing	22	0	0	3	7
System.Drawing.Design	11	3	0	5	1

❑ **2-D vector graphics** – GDI+ can draw and fill such basic building blocks as lines, polygons, rectangles, ellipses, arcs, and curves on the basis of coordinate points. It implements two special algorithms for drawing curves, the Bézier curves and cardinal splines. If you want to create complex shapes, pictures from the primitives, texts, and images, you can use the GraphicsPath, Region, Metafile, and Container classes.

❑ **colors** – You can draw and fill graphics shapes with Pen and Brush objects that take a Color argument. The 32-bit Color object contains the alpha, red, green, and blue components of a given color.

❑ **fonts** – You can draw text within GDI+ using the Graphics.DrawString method passing in a Font object.

❑ **images** – For painting and rotating images in GDI+ you can use the Image, Bitmap, and Metafile classes.

These topics will be covered in more detail in the forthcoming sections (another chapter is devoted to printing). You can download the book's support material before going through this chapter.

After this brief overview of GDI+, let us turn to our first project on graphics (see project P01Altamira in the downloadable code), which displays the sketch image of a red bison with a passe-partout, frame and the word **Altamira**. The project has two purposes. It is straightforward; however, unlike the other projects in this chapter that are devoted to special topics, it contains many relevant and different elements of GDI+ and so it can serve as a quick reference to how to define colors, pens, brushes, and fonts, and how to get a Graphics object, draw shapes, texts, and images (the concepts and techniques will be highlighted in the following sections). The project's second aim is to show how to manage the flicker of the application that occurs under some special circumstances.

```
using System;
using System.Drawing;
using System.Windows.Forms;

namespace Altamira
```

```
{
  public class Form1 : Form
  {
    Pen p;
    SolidBrush b, bT = new SolidBrush(Color.Black);
    string path = "Altamira5.bmp";  // change the path if needed
    Image im;
    Font f;

    public Form1()
    {
      InitializeComponent();
      MyIni();
    }

    private void InitializeComponent()
    {
      this.SuspendLayout();

      this.ClientSize = new System.Drawing.Size(290, 260);
      this.Text = "Altamira";

      this.ResumeLayout(false);
    }

    private void MyIni()
    {
      Color cP = Color.Gray;
      Color cB = Color.LightGray;

      p = new Pen(cP, 6);
      b = new SolidBrush(cB);
      im = Image.FromFile(path);
      f = new Font(new FontFamily("Times New Roman"), 10);
    }

    static void Main()
    {
      Application.Run(new Form1());
    }

    protected override void OnPaint(PaintEventArgs pea)
    {
      Sketch();
    }

    private void Sketch()
    {
      Graphics g = Graphics.FromHwnd(this.Handle);

      g.FillRectangle(b, 4, 4, 260, 220);  // passe-partout
      g.DrawRectangle(p, 4, 4, 260, 220);  // frame
      g.DrawImage(im, 33, 35, 200, 145 );  // image
      g.DrawString("ALTAMIRA", f, bT, 180, 190);  // text
```

```
        g.Dispose();
      }
    }
  }
```

The images for this chapter are included in the projects' base directory. So if you use VS.NET write
"..\\..\\Altamira5.bmp" or @"..\..\Altamira5.bmp", otherwise "Altamira5.bmp".
Compile the code with **csc Form1.cs** and run it. The following table shows the main steps of painting
graphic shapes, images, and texts:

Shape	Image	Text
Get a `Graphics` object	Get a `Graphics` object	Get a `Graphics` object
Define the shape's geometrical structure	Define the image's position	Define the text's position
Select a color	Load an image	Select a color
Create a `Pen` or `Brush`		Create a `Brush`
		Create a `Font`
Paint – draw, fill	Paint – draw	Paint – draw

We discuss the `Onpaint` method that ensures repainting in the next section. Repainting causes flicker
when resizing or covering the application window. If you did not paint the passe-partout and frame,
`FillRectangle` and `DrawRectangle` respectively, there would be no flicker. So let us paint the four
objects – passe-partout, frame, image, and text – to the screen simultaneously. First we paint everything
in a memory buffer, and then we paint the content of the buffer onto the form. This technique is called
double buffering. Replace the method `Sketch` with `SketchDBuf` that accomplishes double buffering,
painting first to a `Graphics` object created from an abstract `Image` object and then to the
form's surface:

```
private void SketchDBuf()
{
  int hh = 3, w = 260, h = 220;

  Graphics g;
  Bitmap bm = new Bitmap(w + 2*hh, h + 2*hh);
  g = Graphics.FromImage(bm);  // buffer graphics

  g.FillRectangle(b, hh , hh, w, h);  // passe-partout
  g.DrawRectangle(new Pen(Color.Gray, 2*hh), hh, hh, w, h);  // frame
  g.DrawImage(im, hh + 30, hh + 32, 200, 145);  // image
  g.DrawString("ALTAMIRA", f, bT, 180, 190);  // text

  g = Graphics.FromHwnd(this.Handle);  // real graphics
  g.DrawImage(bm, 1, 1);

  g.Dispose();
}
```

With regard to double-buffering, remember that in some situations the `DoubleBuffer`, `ResizeRedraw`, `UserPaint`, and `Opaque` members of the `ControlStyles` enumeration that are passed to the protected `Control.SetStyle` method can come in useful:

```
SetStyle(ControlStyles.DoubleBuffer | ControlStyles.ResizeRedraw, true);
```

You should also know that the form's controls, unlike the form itself, use double buffering for painting by default and implementing painting on the surface of the controls takes only a little longer than painting on the surface of the form.

Events and Painting

Every Windows application should know how to repaint itself when it is invalidated: when it is resized, restored from a minimized state, pushed outside the Windows area by a user, or covered and then uncovered by another application. A Windows application receives messages with painting information from the Windows operating system when the application's form or any part of it is invalidated and it needs to be updated. These messages are passed to the application form's `Paint` event. The `PaintEventArgs` class derived from `System.EventArgs` and defined in the `System.Windows.Forms` namespace provides data for the `Paint` event. A `PaintEventArgs` specifies the `Graphics` object used to paint the control and the `ClipRectangle` in which to paint. You usually provide rendering logic for painting by overriding the protected `OnPaintBackground` and `OnPaint` virtual methods with a `PaintEventArgs` argument or by defining a user `myPaint` event handler method (this name is arbitrary; the generated name in VS.NET is `Form1_Paint`) with the same arguments as the `PaintEventHandler` delegate and associate it with the `Paint` event method (you can define several handler methods).

Notice that since the virtual `OnPaint` and `OnPaintBackground` methods are protected, they are accessible only when your application form or its controls are derived from `Control` (in VS, the generated code for the Windows application `Form1` is by default derived).

So the process of overriding the methods `OnPaint` and `OnPaintBackGround` consists of one step (they handle the event without attaching a delegate):

```
protected override void OnPaint(PaintEventArgs pea)
{. . .}

protected override void OnPaintBackground(PaintEventArgs pea)
{. . .}
```

whereas user event handlers need two steps: association of the user's `myPaint` event handler with the public `Paint` event:

```
this.Paint += new
    System.Windows.Forms.PaintEventHandler(this.myPaint);
```

and definition of the static `myPaint` method:

```
private void myPaint(object sender, System.Windows.Forms.PaintEventArgs e)
{. . .}
```

You may ask where to invoke these event handlers. You need never call the event handlers directly. They are called by the system when a form is invalidated. If necessary, you can invoke them via the `Invalidate` method or some other methods that call `Invalidate`, such as `Update` or `Refresh`. There are six overloaded `Invalidate` methods. `Invalidate` can invalidate either the entire client area (the client area of a control represents the bounds of the control, minus the non-client elements such as scroll bars, borders, title bars, and menus) or a specific region of the control defined by `Rectangle` or `Range` parameters and causes a paint message `WM_PAINT` to be sent to the control.

Let us recap handling events for painting. The `Paint` event occurs when a control is redrawn. It is a message sent by an object to signal the occurrence of an action. The action could be caused by user interaction or it could be triggered by some other program logic. The painting tasks may be defined in one of the three event handler methods discussed.

Graphics Objects

Painting in GDI+ needs a surface of an object of type `Graphics`. A `Graphics` object may correspond to a form, control, image, printer, or even the Windows desktop. You can access a `Graphics` object in three standard ways:

❑   Using the `Graphics` property of various event arguments such as `PaintEventArgs`, `MeasureItemEventArgs`, `DrawItemEventArgs`, and `PaintPageArgs`

❑   Calling the static methods `FromHwnd`, `FromImage`, and `FromHdc` of the `Graphics` class

❑   Invoking the create methods `CreateGraphics` and `CreateMeasurementGraphics` of an object's form and printer settings respectively

The benefit of the second and third approaches is that they do not need the three event handlers for painting and you can use them for painting in triggered events, for example `Click` or `MouseMove`. Let us now see concrete examples of creating a `Graphics` object.

As you already know the `OnPaint`, `OnPaintBackGround`, and `myPaint` event handlers provide a `PaintEventArgs` parameter. This parameter enables access to a `Graphics` object through its `Graphics` property:

```
Graphics g = e.Graphics;  // 1.
```

Although the `Graphics` class cannot be instantiated, its static method `FromHwnd` returns a `Graphics` object. Use this method if you intend to paint on the form or its controls:

```
Graphics g = Graphics.FromHwnd(this.Handle);  // 2.
Graphics g = Graphics.FromHwnd(this.label1.Handle);  // 2.
```

Instead of `Graphics.FromHwnd(this.Handle)` you can also write:

```
Graphics g = this.CreateGraphics();   // 3.
```

If you want to paint on an image use the `Graphics.FromImage` static method:

```
Graphics g = Graphics.FromImage(img);   // 2.
```

The controls are system-drawn by default. A control is owner-drawn when the user manages exactly how the control should look. There are two special events `MeasureItemEvent` and `DrawItemEvent` that enable us to retrieve a `Graphics` object. The handler methods of these events provide parameters `MeasureItemEventArgs miea` and `DrawItemEventArgs diea` respectively so you can write:

```
Graphics g = miea.Graphics;   // 1.
Graphics g = diea.Graphics;   // 1.
```

There are two ways to access a `Graphics` object with a printer. The `OnPrintPage` and `myPrint` event handlers in the class `PrintDocument` have an argument `PaintPageEventArgs`. One of the six properties of `PaintPageEventArgs ppea` is `Graphics`:

```
Graphics g = ppea.Graphics;   // 1.
```

The `CreateMeasurementGraphics` method of the `PrinterSettings` class returns a `Graphics` object that contains information on a printer:

```
Graphics g = ps.CreateMeasurementGraphics;   // 3.
```

If you write code that uses classic GDI, you need to connect to a device context with a `Graphics` object. The static `FromHdc` method of the `Graphics` class creates a new `Graphics` object from the specified handle to a device context:

```
IntPtr hdc = pea.Graphics.GetHdc();
Graphics newGraphics = Graphics.FromHdc(hdc);   // 2.
```

Although you can rely on the **Garbage Collector** when writing managed classes, it is good programming practice and is highly recommended to dispose the objects that have `Dispose` methods, like the `Graphics` object.

A `Graphics` object can not only perform drawing and painting, but it also contains attributes that specify how the drawing is done. The **graphics state** stored in the `Graphics` object defines:

- ❑ **The clipping region** – clipping involves preventing drawing beyond a certain rectangle or region that applies to all items drawn by the `Graphics` object.

- ❑ **World and page transformations** – the `Graphics` object maintains these two transformations. The state of the translation, scale, rotate, reflect, and skew transformation is stored in the world transformation. The page transformation can carry out a change of units and also scaling.

❑ **Quality settings** – such as smoothing and interpolation mode (how to draw a curve segment between two points) or text rendering.

❑ The **interaction** between the `Graphics` object and its device context behind the scene. You make calls to methods provided by GDI+ classes that in turn make the appropriate calls to specific device drivers. Thanks to this interaction you can create device-independent applications.

You can temporarily change the `Graphics` state, clipping region, transformation, and quality settings in GDI+ using graphic containers that may be nested.

Colors, Pens, and Brushes

`Color` objects, which are instances of `System.Drawing.Color` struct, store a 32-bit value in a variable of type ARGB that contains four 8-bit components in the order: alpha, red, green, and blue. The `Color` object is used by the `Pen` and `Brush` objects. The `Pen` class stores information on the color, width, and style of the line. The five brush classes derived from the abstract base class `Brush` store information about the filling colors and patterns of shapes. The `SolidBrush` and `TextureBrush` classes are defined in the `System.Drawing` namespace. The `HatchBrush`, `LinearGradientBrush`, and `PathGradientBrush` classes are defined in the `System.Drawing.Drawing2D` namespace.

The functionality of `Pen`, `Brush` and `Color` is closely connected. Remember, however, that there is a considerable difference between them. While `Color` is a structure, `Pen` and `Brush` are classes. Similarly to the `Graphics` objects, `Pen` and `Brush` objects should be disposed.

The color value may be created by:

❑ The static `FromArgb` method

❑ The appropriate static color property of the `Color` structure

❑ The `ForeColor` and `BackColor` properties of an existing object such as `Form1`

❑ Using either the static `FromName` method or the static `FromKnownColor` method with a specified pre-defined system color argument (`FromKnownColor` is used in the first application of this section)

```
Color c1 = Color.FromArgb(128, 0, 0, 255);  // semitransparent blue
Brush b = new SolidBrush(c1);
Color c2 = Color.DarkGreen;
Pen p = new Pen(c2);
Color c3a = this.ForeColor;
Color c3b = this.BackColor;
```

c1 is a transparent blue `Color` structure defined with the four ARGB component values: alpha, red, green, and blue. `FromArgb` has four overloaded versions. If the alpha component is not given, then its default value is 255 (fully opaque). The closer the alpha component is to zero the more you see from the background through the shape. You can also use gamma correction (gamma-corrected colors are adjusted to take account of the monitor's input signal) when blending colors due to the `CompositingQuality` property of the `Graphics` object.

If you intend to draw or fill with standard colors use the static properties of the Pens and Brushes classes:

```
Pen p = Pens.Red;
Brush b = Brushes.Red;
```

Here the pen p has a default width of 1. When you need to set the pen's width instantiate a Pen object with an appropriate constructor:

```
Pen p = new Pen(Color.Red, 10);  // the pen's width is 10
```

Notice that you can create a pen from a brush, and a color from a pen:

```
p = new Pen(b, 5);
c = p.Color;
```

Transparency

You can create effects with transparent colors using the alpha component of the color or the form's Opacity and TransparencyKey properties. While the integer alpha value ranges from 0 (fully transparent) to 255 (opaque), the double value of Opacity ranges from 0.0 (fully transparent) to 1.0 (opaque).

The project P06_Transparency displays five yellow squares on a red background with various alpha values. The squares are transparent at different levels except the left one, which is opaque.

```
protected override void OnPaint(PaintEventArgs e)
{
    Graphics g;
    g = Graphics.FromHwnd(this.Handle);

    g.FillRectangle(new SolidBrush(Color.Red), 10, 10, 210, 50);

    // Five yellow squares with different alpha values
    Rectangle r = new Rectangle(40, 20, 30, 30);  // 1. rectangle
    Color c = Color.FromArgb(255, 255, 255, 0);
    g.FillRectangle(new SolidBrush(c), r);

    r.Offset(30, 0);  // 2. rectangle
    c = Color.FromArgb(200, 255, 255, 0);
    g.FillRectangle(new SolidBrush(c), r);

    r.Offset(30, 0);  // 3. rectangle
    c = Color.FromArgb(150, 255, 255, 0);
    g.FillRectangle(new SolidBrush(c), r);

    r.Offset(30, 0);  // 4. rectangle
    c = Color.FromArgb(100, 255, 255, 0);
    g.FillRectangle(new SolidBrush(c), r);
```

```
    r.Offset(30, 0);   // 5. rectangle
    c = Color.FromArgb(50, 255, 255, 0);
    g.FillRectangle(new SolidBrush(c), r);

    g.Dispose();
}
```

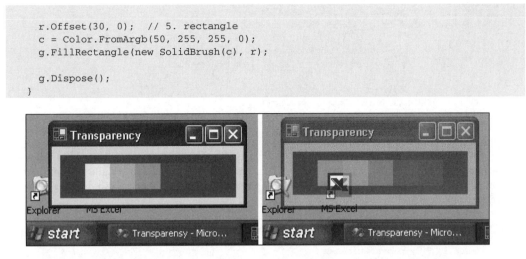

We used the following settings for the right-hand application form:

```
this.Opacity = 0.5;
this.TransparencyKey = System.Drawing.Color.Yellow;
```

Since the `TransparencyKey` is set to yellow, the yellow area on the form will be completely transparent. As you can see there is a hole in the place of the left yellow square. The effect of the `TransparencyKey` is more striking, if you comment the opacity code line (or set it to 1.0). Be careful! If you set the opacity to 0.0, the form will be invisible. Do not panic, you can close the application with *Alt+F4*.

Known Colors

If you write Windows applications, you can use both predefined known colors (custom, Web, and system colors such as `Red`, `IndianRed`, and `ControlDark` respectively) and user-defined colors via the static `FromArgb` method.

To construct a list of all predefined colors, use the `KnownColor` enumeration. The `NonSystemColors` method from the project `P07KnownColors` returns the known non-system colors `cAL` and their names `cNAL` as `ArrayList`:

```
   ...
cAL = new ArrayList();      // colors
cNAL = new ArrayList();     // strings
NonSystemColors(cAL, cNAL);
this.comboBox1.Sorted = true;
this.comboBox1.DataSource = cNAL; //set the combo's data source
...

private void NonSystemColors(ArrayList cAL, ArrayList cNAL)
{
```

```
    Array cA = Enum.GetValues(typeof(KnownColor));
    foreach(KnownColor knwnC in cA)   // cX.Length = 167
    {
        Color curC = Color.FromKnownColor(knwnC);
        if(!curC.IsSystemColor) // known but non-system color
        {
            cAL.Add(curC);
            cNAL.Add(curC.Name.ToString());
        }
    }
}
```

It would be sufficient to use only one ArrayList; however, we decided to include both of them to show how to extract not only the colors but their names too. The application also displays these known non-system colors and their names on the form:

```
protected override void OnPaint(PaintEventArgs pea)
{
    Graphics g = pea.Graphics;
    int wi = 70, hi = 12, rectNb = 8;
    int cALNb = cAL.Count;

    this.Width = (wi +2)*rectNb + 9;
    int y = (int)(cALNb / rectNb);
    this.Height = y*(2 + hi) + 60;

    DisplayKnownColors(g, cALNb, wi, hi, rectNb);
    g.Dispose();
}
private void DisplayKnownColors(Graphics g, int cALNb, int wi, int hi, int rectNb)
{
    Rectangle rec;
    Pen p = new Pen(this.ForeColor);
    Brush b;

    StringFormat strfmt = new StringFormat();
    strfmt.LineAlignment = strfmt.Alignment = StringAlignment.Near;

    int x, y;
    for (int i = 0; i < cALNb; i++)
    {
        x = (int)(i % rectNb);
        y = (int)(i / rectNb);
        rec = new Rectangle(1 + x*(2 + wi), 1 + y*(2 + hi), wi, hi);

        g.DrawRectangle(p, rec);
        b  = new SolidBrush((Color)cAL[i]);
        g.FillRectangle(b, rec);

        b  = new SolidBrush(Color.Black);
        g.DrawString((string)cNAL[i], this.Font, b, rec, strfmt);
    }
    x = (int)(cALNb % rectNb);
    y = (int)(cALNb / rectNb);
    this.comboBox1.Location = new Point(x*(wi + 2) + 2, y*(2 + hi) + 2);
}
```

In the picture you can find `Red` and `IndianRed`; however, `ControlDark` is absent.

Gradient Colors

GDI+ provides several techniques to enable continuous passing from one color to another. This section covers briefly the `LinearGradientBrush` and `PathGradientBrush` methods. The project `P08LinearGradient` illustrates the `LinearGradientBrush` and the settings of the `LinearGradientMode` enumeration.

```
protected override void OnPaint(PaintEventArgs e)
{
    Graphics g = e.Graphics;
    Font f = new Font(new FontFamily("Times New Roman"), 10);
    Brush fb = new SolidBrush(Color.Black);
    LinearGradientBrush lGB;   // namespace System.Drawing.Drawing2D;
    Color cR = Color.Red, cW = Color.White;
    int w = 100, h = 70;

    // Left upper rectangle:
    g.DrawString("Horizontal", f, fb, 10, 5);
    Rectangle rec = new Rectangle(10, 20, w, h);
    LinearGradientMode lGM = LinearGradientMode.Horizontal;
    lGB = new LinearGradientBrush(rec, cR, cW, lGM);
    g.FillRectangle(lGB, rec);

    // Right upper rectangle:
    g.DrawString("Vertical", f, fb, w + 20, 5);
    rec.Offset(w + 10, 0);
    lGM = LinearGradientMode.Vertical;
    lGB = new LinearGradientBrush(rec, cR, cW, lGM);
    g.FillRectangle(lGB, rec);

    // Left lower rectangle:
    g.DrawString("ForwardDiagonal", f, fb, 10, h + 25);
    rec.Offset(-w - 10, h + 20);
```

```
    lGB = new LinearGradientBrush(rec, cR, cW, lGM);
    g.FillRectangle(lGB, rec);

    // Right lower rectangle:
    g.DrawString("BackwardDiagonal", f, fb, w + 20, h + 25);
    rec.Offset(w + 10, 0);
    lGM = LinearGradientMode.BackwardDiagonal;
    lGB = new LinearGradientBrush(rec, cR, cW, lGM);
    g.FillRectangle(lGB, rec);
    fb.Dispose();
    g.Dispose();
}
```

Our linear gradient brush begins with red and ends with white. As you can see from the screenshot the Horizontal, Vertical, ForwardDiagonal, and BackwardDiagonal linear gradients begin on the left, at the top, in the upper left corner, and in the upper right corner, respectively:

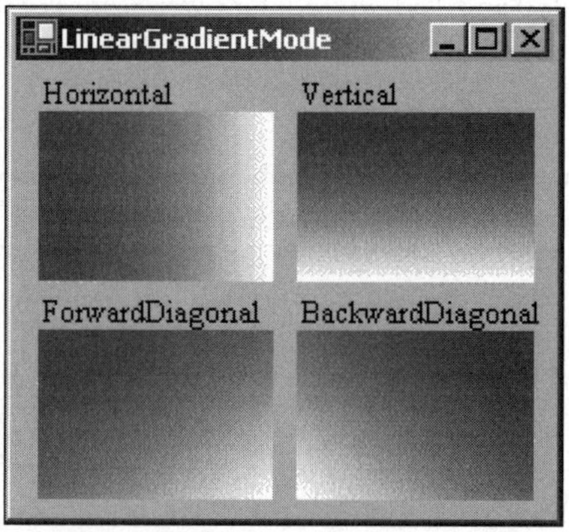

The project P09PathGradient demonstrates the PathGradientBrush and the use of its CenterPoint, CenterColor, and SurroundColors properties. The number of colors in the SurroundColors may be less than or equal to the number of vertices in the GraphicsPath object.

```
protected override void OnPaint(PaintEventArgs e)
{
    Graphics g = e.Graphics;
    Font f = new Font(new FontFamily("Times New Roman"), 10);
    Brush fb = new SolidBrush(Color.Black);
    GraphicsPath gp;
    PathGradientBrush pGB;  // namespace System.Drawing.Drawing2D;
    Rectangle rec;
    Color cR = Color.Red, cW = Color.White, cY = Color.Yellow;
    int w = 100, h = 70;

    // Left upper rectangle:
    g.DrawString("Center", f, fb, 10, 5);
    gp = new GraphicsPath();
    rec = new Rectangle(10, 20, w, h);
```

```
        gp.AddRectangle(rec);
        pGB = new PathGradientBrush(gp);
        pGB.CenterPoint = new Point(10 + w/2, 20 + h/2);
        pGB.CenterColor = cR;
        pGB.SurroundColors = new Color[1]{cW};
        g.FillRectangle(pGB, rec);

        // Right upper rectangle:
        g.DrawString("Center - 2 x 2 Colors", f, fb, w + 20, 5);
        gp = new GraphicsPath();
        rec = new Rectangle(20 + w, 20, w, h);
        gp.AddRectangle(rec);
        pGB = new PathGradientBrush(gp);
        pGB.CenterPoint = new Point(w + 20 + w/2, 20 + h/2);
        pGB.CenterColor = cR;
        pGB.SurroundColors = new Color[4]{cW, cY, cW, cY};
        g.FillRectangle(pGB, rec);

        // Left lower rectangle:
        g.DrawString("LefTopCenter", f, fb, 10, h + 25);
        gp = new GraphicsPath();
        rec = new Rectangle(10, h + 40, w, h);
        gp.AddRectangle(rec);
        pGB = new PathGradientBrush(gp);
        pGB.CenterPoint = new Point(10, h + 40);
        pGB.CenterColor = cR;
        pGB.SurroundColors = new Color[1]{cW};
        g.FillRectangle(pGB, rec);

        // Ellipse
        g.DrawString("Top", f, fb, w + 20, h + 25);
        gp = new GraphicsPath();
        rec = new Rectangle(w + 20, h + 40, w, h);
        gp.AddEllipse(rec);
        pGB = new PathGradientBrush(gp);
        pGB.CenterPoint = new Point(w + 20 + w/2, h + 40);
        pGB.CenterColor = cR;
        pGB.SurroundColors = new Color[1]{cW};
        g.FillRectangle(pGB, rec);

        g.Dispose();
        fb.Dispose();
}
```

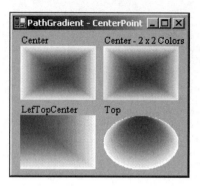

Hatch Brushes

You can make use of the 53 hatch styles such as `HatchStyle.Shingle` that are passed to the `HatchBrush` class:

```
Brush hb = new HatchBrush(HatchStyle.Shingle, cf, cb);
```

The project `P10HatchBrushesStyles` displays all the predefined hatch styles:

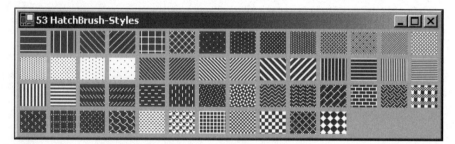

```
protected override void OnPaint(PaintEventArgs e)
{
    Graphics g = e.Graphics;
    Font f = new Font(new FontFamily("Times New Roman"), 10);
    Brush fb = new SolidBrush(Color.Black);
    Color cb = Color.Red, cf =Color.White;

    int wi = 30, hi = 25, rectNb = 14;
    int x, y;
    HatchBrush hb = null;
    for(int i = 0; i < 53; i++)
    {
        x = (int)(i % rectNb);
        y = (int)(i / rectNb);
        hb = new HatchBrush((HatchStyle)i, cf, cb);
        g.FillRectangle(hb, 2 + x*(5 + wi), 2 + y*(5 + hi), wi, hi);
    }
    fb.Dispose();    hb.Dispose();    g.Dispose();
}
```

Color Dialog

Finally, let us briefly look at the use of ColorDialog (covered in more detail in Chapter 2) from project P11_ColorFontDialog that unfortunately does not provide an Apply option.

```
private void button2_Click(object sender, System.EventArgs e)
{
    ColorDialog cd = new ColorDialog();
    cd.AllowFullOpen = true;   // allow custom colors
    //cd.FullOpen = true;      // shows custom colors automatically
    cd.Color = Color.DarkBlue; // sets the custom color
    //cd.Color = Color.Blue;   // set the basic color

    if(cd.ShowDialog() == System.Windows.Forms.DialogResult.OK)
        this.label1.ForeColor = cd.Color;
}
```

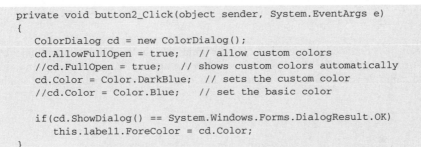

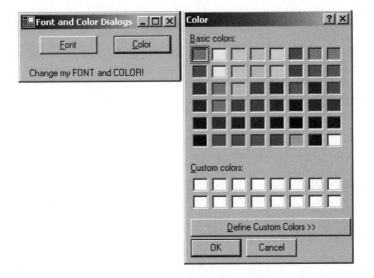

Shapes, Paths, and Regions

You can paint in GDI+ the following primitives based on coordinate points:

	Arc	Bezier(s)	Closed Curve	Curve	Ellipse	Line(s)	Pie	Ploygon	Rectangle(s)
Draw	Y	Y	Y	Y	Y	Y	Y	Y	Y
Fill			Y		Y		Y	Y	Y

It follows from this table that five GDI+ basic building blocks can be both drawn and filled. For example:

```
Graphics g = ...
Rectangle r = Rectangle(0, 0, 100, 100);  // square
g.FillRectangle(r);
g.DrawEllipse(r);  // circle
```

In GDI+, the rectangle is defined by its left upper corner point (left, top) and its width and height. As you can see, the DrawEllipse uses the same structure as DrawRectangle, and circles are not defined by the center and radius. If you want to draw a circle with a center [x, y] and radius r, then you have to use:

```
Rectangle(x-r, y-r, 2*r, 2*r);
g.drawEllipse(brush, rc);
```

By the Windows convention the world origin [0, 0] in pixels is in the upper left corner of the Graphics object's area. GDI+ involves three coordinate systems: world, page, and device coordinate systems, and a variety of measurement units such as Pixel, Point, Inch, Mm, or Cm. Passing from one system to another is managed by the Graphics class. The default world coordinate system uses pixels. We will consider only the world coordinate system, where the x-axis points and the x values increment to the right, and the y-axis points and the y values increment downward. The maximum available visible coordinates of the windows client's area along the x and y axis may be determined by calling the X and Y properties of the ClientRectangle of the underlying control:

```
this.button1.ClientRectangle.X;
```

Lines and Curves

Now we will draw two adjacent mountain peaks using different primitives (see project P02_Primitives). This simple task demonstrates the main differences between the methods Line, Lines, Polygon, Curve, ClosedCurve, Bezier, and Beziers.

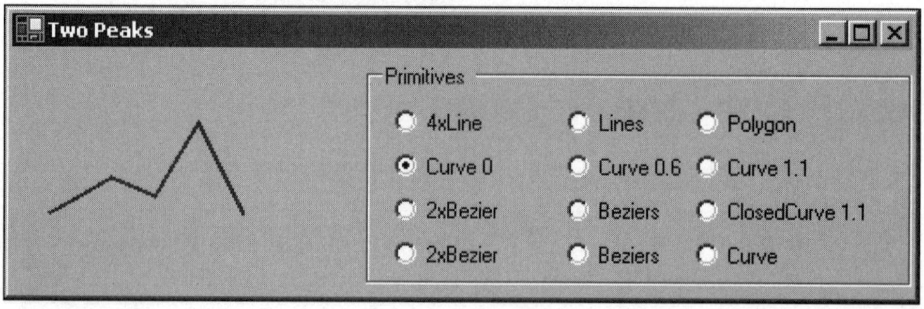

The position of the peaks from the next picture corresponds to the radio buttons' position.

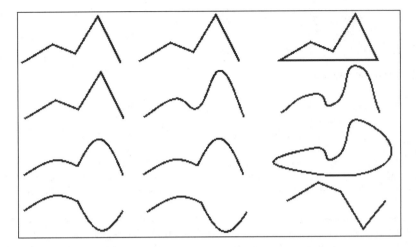

The event handler for the radio buttons calls `Refresh` and the invoked `OnPaint` method calls the different solutions:

```
radioButton1.CheckedChanged += new System.EventHandler(RBs_CheckedChanged);
...
radioButton12.CheckedChanged += new System.EventHandler(RBs_CheckedChanged);
...

private void RBs_CheckedChanged(object sender, System.EventArgs e)
{
    this.Refresh();
}

protected override void OnPaint (System.Windows.Forms.PaintEventArgs e)
{
    Graphics g = e.Graphics;
    g.Clear(this.BackColor);

    if (this.radioButton1.Checked) Ex01_4xLine(g);
    if (this.radioButton2.Checked) Ex02_Lines(g);
    ...

protected void Ex01_4xLine(Graphics g)
{
    Pen pn = new Pen(Color.Blue, 2);
    g.DrawLine(pn, 20, 90, 55, 70);
    g.DrawLine(pn, 55, 70, 80, 80);
    g.DrawLine(pn, 80, 80,105, 40);
    g.DrawLine(pn,105, 40,130, 90);
}

protected void Ex02_Lines(Graphics g)
{
```

```
          Pen pn = new Pen(Color.Blue, 2);
          g.DrawLines(pn, pnts);
      }
```

where `pnts` is a class member:

```
      Point[] pnts = { new Point(20, 90), new Point(55, 70),
            new Point(80, 80), new Point(105, 40),
            new Point(130, 90)};
```

The method `Ex01_4xLine` draws the two peaks calling the `DrawLine` method four times, and so three points (the inner ones) are used twice. The method `Ex02_Lines` draws the peaks invoking the method `DrawLines` that, due to the second array argument `pnts`, uses every point only once.

The `DrawPolygon`, `DrawCurve`, and `DrawClosedCurve` methods use the same `Point` array `pnts`. Unlike `DrawLine`, `DrawPolygon` draws a closed shape from line segments. The third tension argument defines the measure of curvature: the further the tension value is from zero, the more bent the curve is. Negative values result in hooks. You get straight segments if the tension is zero.

```
    g.DrawPolygon(pn, pnts);
    g.DrawCurve(pn, pnts, 0.0f);
    g.DrawClosedCurve(pn, pnts, 1.1f,
                      System.Drawing.Drawing2D.FillMode.Winding);
```

To draw Bézier curves, you need to define two additional control points for every shape segment. The segment is defined with the first and fourth points (the so called end points) and the second and third control points.

The `DrawBeziers` method assumes that each successive segment begins with the last point from the previous segment. So the number of points for `DrawBeziers` is 4 + 3k, where k is positive integer

```
    protected void Ex07_2xBezier(Graphics g)
    {
       Pen pn = new Pen(Color.Blue, 2);
       g.DrawBezier(pn, 20, 90, 50, 70, 60, 70, 80, 80);
       g.DrawBezier(pn, 80, 80,100, 40,110, 40,130, 90);
    }

    protected void Ex08_Beziers(Graphics g)
    {
       Pen pn = new Pen(Color.Blue, 2);
       Point[] pnts = {new Point(20, 90), new Point(50, 70),
            new Point(60, 70), new Point(80, 80),
            new Point(100, 40), new Point(110, 40),
            new Point(130, 90)};
       g.DrawBeziers(pn, pnts);
    }
```

In the next picture, the control points of three Bézier curve segments are shown. The relative position of the first set of control points (the odd ones) is the same; however, the second set of control points (the even ones) vary, and they result in three different shape segments:

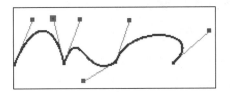

This drawing of a woman's head consists of several Bézier curves:

Transformations

To change the position, orientation, and size of geometrical objects you can use transformations. The basic types of transformations in the plane are:

❑ Shifting to a point A [x, y]

❑ Rotating by angle alpha around the origin O [0, 0]

❑ Reflecting with respect to a line or point

❑ Stretching (inflate, scale) and dilatation (offset, translation)

These and some more transformations are supported by the .NET Framework through the instances of the `Rectangle` structure, classes `Graphics`, `Matrix`, `GraphicsPath`, `Region` and their methods:

Rectangle	Offset, Inflate
Graphics	Transform, TranslateTransform, RotateTransform, ScaleTransform, MultiplyTransform, ResetTransformation, TranslateClip
Matrix	Translate, Rotate, RotateAt, Scale, Shear, TransformPoints, TransformVectors
GraphicsPath	Transform, Warp
Region	Transform, Translate

Of these transformations, `Offset` and `Inflate` are the simplest. We illustrate their use by building a pyramid from one `Rectangle` object, coded in the project P03_Pyramid:

```
protected void Pyramid(Graphics g)
{
   Pen p = new Pen(Color.Blue);
      int ten = 10;
      Rectangle rc = new Rectangle(50, 90, 150, ten);   // the base rectangle
      g.DrawRectangle(p, rc);
      for(int i = 1;i <= 7; i++)
      {
          rc.Offset(0,-ten);
          rc.Inflate(-ten, 0);
          g.DrawRectangle(p, rc);
      }
          p.Dispose();
}
```

The `Offset(x, y)` method shifts the upper-left corner of the `Rectangle` object by x units right, and by y units down. The positive and negative arguments in the `Inflate` method cause inflating and contracting respectively. Thus `Inflate(-10, 0)` means that the rectangle loses 5 units from both the left and right side, but does not change along the vertical axis as the second parameter is zero. We return to this example after introducing paths and show how to rotate the pyramid as a `GraphicsPath` object.

To make graphics and animation simpler, Microsoft introduced in the .NET Framework two types of transformations: **global** and **local**. Global transformations relate to the whole interface area so you can execute them by calling the appropriate methods of the `Graphics` class. A local transformation influences only one shape object, and may be used with either a `GraphicsPath` object or a `Rectangle` structure. The project P13_TextDirection from the section *Text Direction* uses both local and global transformations.

Consider the rotation by angle alpha about an arbitrary point [x, y]. To solve this task you have to make two transformations **before drawing**: shifting by x, y and rotating by alpha. Before giving several solutions we must introduce the class `Matrix`. Matrices give the mathematical representation of transformations. The picture illustrates some common transformations and their matrices T. One of the four constructors of `Matrix` has six arguments. The first two arguments of `Matrix` correspond to the first row of the transformation matrix T, and the third and fourth elements to the second row. The last two arguments represent a translation.

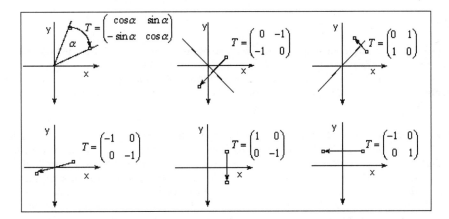

Let us now see the possible solutions.

```
Matrix m = new Matrix();  // or Matrix(1, 0, 0, 1, 0, 0)
m.Translate(x, y);
m.Rotate(alpha);
```

The first two code lines above can be combined:

```
Matrix m = new Matrix(1, 0, 0, 1, x, y);
m.Rotate(alpha);
```

Even the rotation can be expressed through the `Matrix`:

```
float c = (float)Math.Cos(alpha);
float s = (float)Math.Sin(alpha);
Matrix m = new Matrix(c, s, -s, c, x, y);
```

We must mention that in the case of global transformations you can also write:

```
g.TranslateTransform(x, y);
g.RotateTransform(alpha);
```

After doing the transformations you can write:

```
gp.Transform(m);  // gp is a GraphicsPath object, see the next section
g.DrawPath(Pens.Red, gp);
```

if you wanted a local transformation or:

```
g.Transform  = m;
g.DrawRectangle(Pens.Blue, r);
```

if you wanted a global transformation.

Chapter 6

Paths

If you want to create complex shapes from the basic building blocks and/or pictures you can use the GraphicsPath, Region, Metafile, and Container classes. GraphicsPath represents a series of lines, curves, and texts. You can use paths to draw outlines of shapes, fill their interiors, transform them, and create clipping regions. Region describes the area of a graphics shape constructed from rectangles and paths. The next section is devoted to regions.

Metafiles as images store a sequence of drawing commands and settings and can be stored in memory or a file in Enhanced Metafile **EMF** and **EMF+** format. EMF files contain only GDI records; EMF+ files may contain both GDI+ and GDI records. We recommend you to have a look at the very rich EmfPlusRecordType enumeration that specifies the methods available for use with a metafile to read and write graphic commands. Graphics state is stored in a Graphics object by default. You can temporarily change and store the state in a graphics container. You start a Container by calling the BeginContainer method of the Graphics class, and you end a container by calling the EndContainer method. Any state changes you make to the Graphics object between these methods belong to the container and do not overwrite the existing state of the Graphics object.

The GraphicsPath class is defined in the System.Drawing.Drawing2D namespace. You can create a unit of primitives and texts with a GraphicsPath object, and also apply transformation, clipping, and gradient brushes to such a unit. A path is a set of coordinate points that represent lines, curves, and texts. The points in a path may be connected or not. Connected points make up a **figure** or **subpath** that may be closed or open. You are provided with six constructors for instantiating a GraphicsPath object in GDI+. Primitives and texts are appended to a path by the corresponding Add methods. Figures within a path are created calling the method StartFigure and get closed applying the CloseFigure method. You can transform a path using its Transform method and paint it with the DrawPath and FillPath methods.

Let us return to our pyramid example and see how it is rotated by 45 degrees around the center denoted by a little red circle when you click the button:

```
private void button1_Click(object sender, System.EventArgs e)
{
   rot++;  // rot is a class member
   PyramidPathRotate(CreateGraphics());
   Refresh();
}

protected void PyramidPathRotate(Graphics g)
{
   GraphicsPath gP = new GraphicsPath();  // create an empty path
   Pen p = new Pen(Color.Blue);
   int ten = 10;
   Rectangle rc = new Rectangle(50, 90, 150, ten);  // the base rectangle
   gP.AddRectangle(rc);
   for(int i = 1;i <= 7; i++)
   {
      rc.Offset(0,-ten);
      rc.Inflate(-ten,0);
      gP.AddRectangle(rc);
   }
```

```
      Matrix m = new Matrix();
      m.RotateAt(45*rot, center, MatrixOrder.Append);
      gP.Transform(m);
      g.DrawPath(p, gP);  // draw the rotated path
      g.FillEllipse(Brushes.Red, center.X, center.Y, 3, 3);  // center point

      p.Dispose();
   }
```

Shade and Clipping

Our next example (project P04_ShadeClipping) provides two solutions for creating text shade with
the methods DrawPathTransform and DrawClip. The first approach uses only a transformation for
shifting a path.

```
   protected override void OnPaint(System.Windows.Forms.PaintEventArgs e)
   {
      Graphics g = e.Graphics;
      DrawPathTransform(g);
      //DrawClip(g);
      g.Dispose();
   }
   void AddStringToPath(string s)
   {
      int fSt = (int)FontStyle.Regular;
      Point xy = new Point(50, 10);
      FontFamily fF = new FontFamily("Times new roman");
      StringFormat sFr = StringFormat.GenericDefault;

      gP.AddString(s, fF, fSt, 100, xy, sFr);  // add the string to the path
   }
   void DrawPathTransform(Graphics g)
   {
      gP = new GraphicsPath();  // create a new path
      AddStringToPath("C#");
```

```
       g.FillPath(Brushes.Gray, gP);   // draw the path to the surface
       Matrix m = new Matrix();
       m.Translate(5, 5);
       gP.Transform(m);
       g.FillPath(Brushes.Yellow, gP);   // draw the path to the surface
       g.DrawPath(Pens.Red, gP);   // draw the path to the surface
   }
```

Clipping can play an important role in improving the painting performance when using the
ClipRectangle property of the PaintEventArgs class. We show its use in the second solution to
shading. The clip area is defined by the SetClip method that can take either a region or path
argument. The gray C# is displayed due to the gray rectangle and the C# text clip area:

```
   void DrawClip(Graphics g)
   {
      gP = new GraphicsPath();   // create a new path
      AddStringToPath("C#");

      g.SetClip(gP);
      g.TranslateClip(-5, -5);

      RectangleF rc = gP.GetBounds();
      rc.Offset(-5, -5);
      g.FillRectangle(Brushes.Gray, rc);   // results in gray C#

      g.ResetClip();
      g.FillPath(Brushes.Yellow, gP);   // draw the path to the surface
      g.DrawPath(Pens.Red, gP);   // draw the path to the surface
   }
```

Instead of setting the clipping region using:

```
   g.SetClip(gP);
```

We could use the Clip property of the Graphics class, which needs a region as described in the
next section:

```
   g.Clip = new Region(gP);
```

Regions

You use Region objects for managing clipping areas, hit testing (testing the position of the mouse
cursor) and due to operations Intersect, Union, Exclude, Xor for creating new regions. Rectangle
also has a Union method; however, the results of these methods are different. A region is a set of points
that represents a part of the Graphics object's area. It has five constructors. A path can be converted
into a region but not vice versa. However, the Region's GetRegionScans method returns an array of
RectangleF structures that approximate a Region object. You put regions into the area of a
Graphics object with its FillRegion method.

Region has several useful and powerful methods:

- ❑ IsInfinite and IsVisible test whether the region has an infinite interior or contains a specified rectangle

- ❑ GetBound returns a RectangleF structure that represents the region's bounds

- ❑ GetRegionScans returns an array of RectangleF structures that approximate the region

Now let us see how you can apply regions for hit testing:

```
// P05RangeHitTest project
void CreateFont()
{
   Graphics g = this.CreateGraphics();
   label1.Text = mes;
   string s = "I";
   int fSt = (int)FontStyle.Regular;
   Point xy = new Point(50, 10);
   StringFormat sFr = StringFormat.GenericDefault;

   gP = new GraphicsPath();  // gp is a class member
   gP.AddString(s, fF, fSt, 50, xy, sFr);  // add the string to the path
}

protected override void OnPaint(System.Windows.Forms.PaintEventArgs e)
{
  Graphics g = this.CreateGraphics();
  g.DrawPath(Pens.Black, gP);  // draw the path to the surface
  g.Dispose();
}

private void Form1_MouseMove(object sender, MouseEventArgs e)
{
  Region reg = new Region(gP);
  if(reg.IsVisible(new Point(e.X, e.Y)))
    mes = "You touched me ...";
  else
    mes = "Move to the big I!";
  CreateFont();
}
```

Here we hit test with the single letter I, but the code also works with a longer text. Hit is tested by the IsVisible method that takes the mouse position. The rectangle's Contains method can also be used for hit testing.

Drawing Texts – Fonts

To draw text within GDI+ with the `DrawString` method, you need a `FontFamily` and `Font` objects. GDI+ groups fonts with the same typeface but different styles into font families: the `Font` object defines the size, style, and units and the `FontFamily` the typeface having a similar basic design and certain variations in styles. While the `FontFamily` has three constructors, the `Font` class has thirteen constructors that enable us to create fonts in three ways. The following code lines create a font object using an existing font, a string name of a `FontFamily`, and a `FontFamily` object respectively:

```
Font f1 = new Font(this.Font, 10, FontStyle.Italic);
Font f2 = new Font("Arial", 10, FontStyle.Bold);
Font f3 = new Font(FontFamily.GenericSerif, 10, FontStyle.Bold);
```

Alternately:

```
Font f3 = new Font(new FontFamily(GenericFontFamilies.Serif), 10, FontStyle.Bold);
```

There are three `GenericFontFamilies`: `Monospace`, `SansSerif`, and `Serif`. To get information on a font use the `Font` members such as `Name`, `FontFamily`, `Style`, `Height`, `Size`, or `Bold`. To set the font style, use the `FontStyle` enumeration; this has `Bold`, `Italic`, `Regular`, `Strikeout`, and `Underline` members that allow bitwise combination.

Font Dialog

In Windows applications, you can use the `FontDialog` to offer a user a choice from a list of fonts that are installed on the system; see project `P11_ColorFontDialog`:

```
private void button1_Click_1(object sender, System.EventArgs e)
{
    FontDialog fd = new FontDialog();
    fd.ShowColor = true;
    fd.Color = Color.Blue;
    fd.ShowApply = true;    // ColorDialog does not provide this option!!!
    fd.Apply += new EventHandler(ApplyFont);
```

```
    if(fd.ShowDialog() != System.Windows.Forms.DialogResult.Cancel)
        ChangeFont(fd);
}

private void ApplyFont(object o, EventArgs ea)
{
    ChangeFont((FontDialog)o);
}

private void ChangeFont(FontDialog fd)
{
    this.label1.Font = fd.Font;
    this.label1.ForeColor = fd.Color;
}
```

Unlike the `ColorDialog`, `FontDialog` provides the option for applying the selected properties before the dialog is closed, so the user can choose other settings. From the picture you can see that the `FontDialog` the **Basic Sans Heavy SF** font supports only **Bold** and **BoldItalic** `FontStyle`, not `Regular` and `Italic`.

Installed Font Families

To list the font families, use either the `Families` and `GetFamilies` members of the `FontFamily` class, or the `InstalledFontCollection` and `PrivateFontCollection` classes defined in the `System.Drawing.Text` namespace. The `InstalledFontFamilies` method from the `P12_FontFamilies` project returns both the installed font families as a `FontFamily` array and the corresponding string names as an `ArrayList`:

```
FontFamily[] iFCF;
ArrayList iFCFN;

iFCF = InstalledFontFamilies(iFCFN);
this.comboBox1.Sorted = true;
this.comboBox1.DataSource = iFCFN;  //set the combo's data source
...

private FontFamily[] InstalledFontFamilies(ArrayList iFCFN)
{
    InstalledFontCollection iFC = new InstalledFontCollection();
    foreach(FontFamily ff in iFC.Families)
        iFCFN.Add(ff.Name);
    return iFC.Families;
}
```

The `FontFamily` array `iFCF` and the `ArrayList` `iFCFN` can be used as follows:

```
Font f = new Font(iFCF[i], 8, FontStyle.Regular, GraphicsUnit.Point);
Font f = new Font((string)iFCFN[i], 8, FontStyle.Regular,
                  GraphicsUnit.Point);
```

This line also displays the names of the installed font families with the corresponding fonts:

```
g.DrawString((string)iFCFN[i], f, b, rec, strfmt);
```

Fonts that do not have a Regular style are displayed with the style Strikeout. The picture confirms that **Basic Sans Heavy SF** does not support the Regular style:

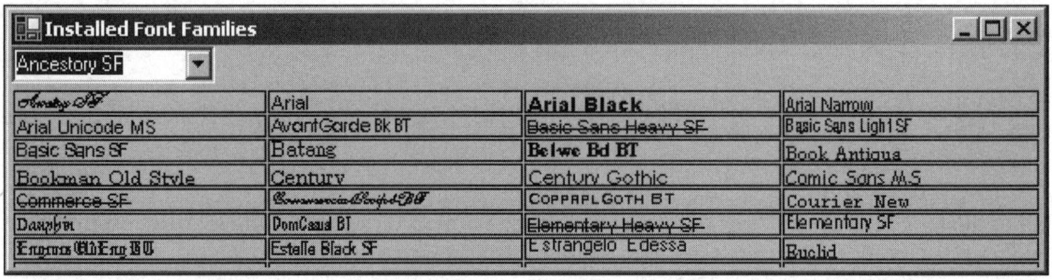

```
protected override void OnPaint(PaintEventArgs pea)
{
    Graphics g = pea.Graphics;
    int wi = 150, hi = 12, rectNb = 4;
    this.Width = (wi + 2)*rectNb + 9;
    int iFCFNb = iFCF.Length;
    DisplayInstalledFontFamilies(g, iFCFNb, wi, hi, rectNb);

    g.Dispose();
}

private void DisplayInstalledFontFamilies(Graphics g, int iFCFNb, int wi,
                                          int hi, int rectNb)
{
    Rectangle rec;
    Pen p = new Pen(this.ForeColor);
    Brush b = null;

    Font f;
    StringFormat strfmt = new StringFormat();
    strfmt.LineAlignment = strfmt.Alignment = StringAlignment.Near;

    int x, y;
    for (int i = 0; i < iFCFNb; i++)
    {
        x = (int)(i % rectNb);
        y = (int)(i / rectNb);
        rec = new Rectangle(1 + x*(2 + wi), 25 + y*(2 + hi), wi, hi);
        g.DrawRectangle(p, rec);

        try
        {
            f = new Font(iFCF[i], 8, FontStyle.Regular, GraphicsUnit.Point);
        }
```

250

```
        catch
        {
            // some fonts do not support Regular style
            f = new Font("Arial", 8, FontStyle.Strikeout, GraphicsUnit.Point);
        }

        b  = new SolidBrush(Color.Black);
        g.DrawString((string)iFCFN[i], f, b, rec, strfmt);
    }

    p.Dispose();   b.Dispose();
}
```

The code uses the StringFormat class to specify the text layout alignment. Its LineAlignment property gets or sets the line alignment. The StringAlignment enumeration specifies the alignment of a text string relative to its layout rectangle.

Text Direction

There are situations where you want to change the default horizontal text direction. You can do it in one of three ways: setting the StringFormat, using different combinations of global and local transformations such as the Graphics object's RotateTransform method or the GraphicsPath object's Transform method, and using the image's RotateFlip method.

The project P13_TextDirection illustrates the first two approaches (we discuss RotateFlip later in this chapter). The local and global rotations are made about the magenta center point:

```
protected override void OnPaint(PaintEventArgs e)
{
    Graphics g = CreateGraphics();
    string txt = "HELLO";
    float alpha = 45.0f;
    int fontSize = 24;
    Point center = new Point(90,20);

    // Vertical text:
    FontFamily ff = new FontFamily("Times New Roman");
    Font f = new Font(ff, fontSize, FontStyle.Regular);
    StringFormat sf = new StringFormat();
    sf.FormatFlags = StringFormatFlags.DirectionVertical;
    g.DrawString(txt, f, new SolidBrush(Color.Blue), center, sf);

    // Global shift of the origin:
    g.TranslateTransform(center.X, center.Y);   // X + fontSize/2
    g.DrawEllipse(Pens.Magenta, new Rectangle(0, 0, 1, 1));   // center

    // Local rotation of vertcal text (sf):
    GraphicsPath gp = new GraphicsPath();
    gp.AddString(txt, ff, (int)FontStyle.Bold, fontSize + 4,
        new Point(0, 0), sf);
    Matrix m = new Matrix();
```

```
    m.Rotate(alpha);  // clockwise
    gp.Transform(m);
    g.DrawPath(Pens.Red, gp);  //g.FillPath(Brushes.Black, gp);

    // Global rotation of vertical text (sf):
    g.RotateTransform(-alpha);  // anticlockwise
    g.DrawString(txt, f, new SolidBrush(Color.Black), 0, 0, sf);

    gp.Dispose();  g.Dispose();  m.Dispose();
}
```

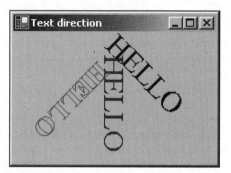

Setting the `DirectionVertical` member of the `StringFormatFlags` enumeration draws the vertical HELLO. The other two texts rotated by 45 degrees are much more interesting. The left hello is drawn with a graphics path. Its rotation is local and so does not affect the following global rotation executed on the `Graphics` object. If you put the local transformation after the local one, you will see that the global one influences the result of the local transformation.

Handling Images

This section briefly describes and illustrates the use of methods and classes designed for manipulating pictures. GDI+ provides techniques for handling images through the `Image`, `Bitmap`, `CachedBitmap`, `Icon`, and `Metafile` classes.

`Image` is an abstract class, so it cannot be instantiated. However its members `FromFile` and `FromStream` return an `Image` object. The `FromFile` method has two overloaded versions and you can use it as follows (we show how to load a picture from the Internet using the static `FromStream` method at the end of this section):

```
string path = @"..\..\szeret3.BMP";
Image im = FromFile(path);
```

To paint an image on a `Graphics` object g, simply use one of the 30 versions of the `DrawImage()` overloaded method defined in the `Graphics` class. To draw the image im at the location x, y write:

```
g.DrawImage(im, x, y);  // or:
g.DrawImage(im, x, y, im.Width, im.Height);
```

To fit an image into a rectangle or parallelogram destination area respectively, use:

```
DrawImage (Image im, Rectangle r);
DrawImage (Image im, point[] p3);
```

However, be aware of a possible image distortion. The point array p3 should contain the upper left, upper right and lower left vertices of the destination area. The fourth vertex is computed automatically. We applied this version of DrawImage to create a picture cube in project P14_ImageCube. For better orientation in code we denoted the corresponding vertices on the left cube.

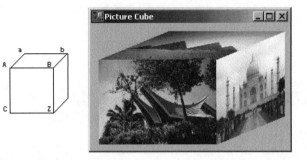

```
protected override void OnPaint(PaintEventArgs pea)
{
  CubeDBuf();
}
private void CubeDBuf()
{
  Graphics g;

  string path;
  int x = 100, y = 40;
  Point A = new Point( 10,  50);
  Point B = new Point(180,  50);
  Point C = new Point( 10, 170);

  Point a = new Point(A.X + x, A.Y - y);
  Point b = new Point(B.X + x, B.Y - y);
  Point Z = new Point(B.X, C.Y);

  Point[] p3Fro = {A, B, C};
  Point[] p3Top = {a, b, A};
  Point[] p3Rig = {B, b, Z};

  Bitmap bm = new Bitmap(B.X +x, C.Y + y);
  g = Graphics.FromImage(bm);

   path = @"..\..\IndonHouses.bmp";
  Image im1 = Image.FromFile(path);
  g.DrawImage(im1, p3Fro);
```

```
    path = @"..\..\Pyramids.BMP";
    Image im3 = Image.FromFile(path);
    g.DrawImage(im3, p3Top);

    path = @"..\..\TadjMahal.bmp";
    Image im2 = Image.FromFile(path);
    g.DrawImage(im2, p3Rig);

    g = Graphics.FromHwnd(this.Handle);
    g.DrawImage(bm, 1, 1);

    g.Dispose();
}
```

Zooming

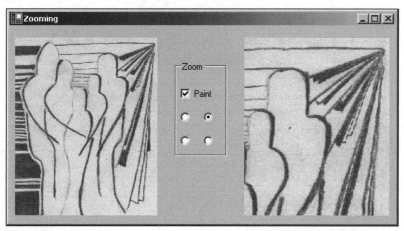

DrawImage can not only display the whole image, it also has versions for displaying only a rectangular part of the image. Let us see how you can use these methods for zooming. The project P15_ImageZoom draws on two labels. This approach enables us to set the size of the displayed picture manually. To fit the whole image into the label we pass the width and height of the label to the DrawImage method. To simplify the code we do not handle the flicker by double buffering.

```
protected void ImageZoom()
{
    Graphics g1 = Graphics.FromHwnd(this.label1.Handle);
    Graphics g2 = Graphics.FromHwnd(this.label2.Handle);
    Rectangle rec;
    Rectangle recPart;

    if (this.checkBox1.Checked)
    {
        if (im == null) ReadImage();
```

```
            rec = new Rectangle(0, 0, label1.Width, label1.Height);
            g1.DrawImage(im, rec);

            // Center part:
            recPart = new Rectangle(im.Width/4, im.Height/4, im.Width/2,
                                im.Height/2);
         if(this.radioButton1.Checked)  // Left-Top part
            recPart = new Rectangle(0, 0, im.Width/2, im.Height/2);
         if(this.radioButton2.Checked)  // Right-Top part
            recPart = new Rectangle(im.Width/2, 0, im.Width/2, im.Height/2);
         if(this.radioButton3.Checked)  // Left-Bottom part
            recPart = new Rectangle(0, im.Height/2, im.Width/2, im.Height/2);
         if(this.radioButton4.Checked)  // Right-Bottom part
            recPart = new Rectangle(im.Width/2, im.Height/2, im.Width/2,
                                im.Height/2);

            g2.DrawImage(im, rec, recPart, GraphicsUnit.Pixel);
      }
      else
      {
         Clear(g1);
         Clear(g2);
      }

      g1.Dispose();    g2.Dispose();
}
```

Rotating and Flipping

The project P16_RotateFlip shows how to rotate and flip an image. It uses the RotateFlip method that takes one of the 16 members of the RotateFlipType enumeration that specifies the direction of the image's rotation and the axis used to flip the image:

```
protected void RotateFlip()
{
  Graphics g = Graphics.FromHwnd(this.label1.Handle);
  Brush b = new SolidBrush(this.label1.BackColor);

  if (this.checkBox1.Checked)
  {
    if (im == null) ReadImage();

    Graphics g2 = Graphics.FromImage(im);   // For text "Himalaya"
    FontFamily ff = new FontFamily("Times New Roman");
    Font f = new Font(ff, 25, FontStyle.Bold);
    g2.DrawString("HIMALAYA", f, new SolidBrush(Color.Yellow), 170, 210);
    g2.Dispose();

    im2 = (Image)im.Clone();
```

```
    int w2 = label1.Width/2, h2 = label1.Height/2;
    g.DrawImage(im, 0, 0, w2, h2);

    if(this.radioButton1.Checked)  // Rotate180FlipY
    {
      im2.RotateFlip(RotateFlipType.Rotate180FlipY);
      g.DrawImage(im2, w2, 0, w2, h2);
    }
    else g.FillRectangle(b, w2, 0, w2, h2);  // Clear old

    if(this.radioButton2.Checked)  // Rotate180FlipX
    {
      im2.RotateFlip(RotateFlipType.Rotate180FlipX);
      g.DrawImage(im2, 0, h2, w2, h2);
    }
    else g.FillRectangle(b, 0, h2, w2, h2);  // Clear old

    if(this.radioButton3.Checked)  // Rotate180FlipNone
    {
      im2.RotateFlip(RotateFlipType.Rotate180FlipNone);
      g.DrawImage(im2, w2, h2, w2, h2);  // Clear old
    }
    else g.FillRectangle(b, w2, h2, w2, h2);

    im2.Dispose();
  }
  else Clear(g);

  b.Dispose();  g.Dispose();
}
```

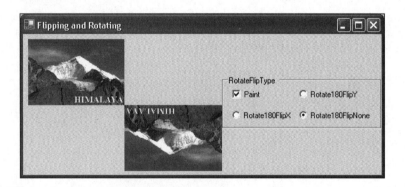

PictureBox Control

There is a special Windows control with some extra features that can hold images – it is `PictureBox`. Its `SizeMode` property can be set by the values of the `PictureBoxSizeMode` enumeration:

- ❑ `CenterImage` – center the picture within the control

- ❑ `Normal` – align the picture's upper left corner with the control's upper left corner

- ❑ `StretchImage` – the size of the image is adjusted to the size of the control

- ❑ `AutoSize` – the size of the control is adjusted to the size of the image to fit the picture it displays

When the `SizeMode` is set to `CenterImage` or `Normal` and the image is larger than the control, the image's corresponding edges are clipped. The following code snippet is from project P17_PictureBox.

```
private void SetPictureBoxSizeMode()
{
    string path = @"..\..\Dobos3.BMP";  // Change the path if needed.

    pictureBox1.SizeMode = PictureBoxSizeMode.CenterImage;
    pictureBox1.Image = Image.FromFile(path);

    pictureBox2.SizeMode = PictureBoxSizeMode.Normal;
    pictureBox2.Image = Image.FromFile(path);

    pictureBox3.SizeMode = PictureBoxSizeMode.StretchImage;
    pictureBox3.Image = Image.FromFile(path);

    pictureBox4.SizeMode = PictureBoxSizeMode.AutoSize;
    pictureBox4.Image = Image.FromFile(path);
}
```

Scrolling

If the application's form contains too many controls, text rows, or a large picture that can not be displayed within the form's client area, you may make use of scrolling. Scroll bars can be put on the form either by instantiating the HScrollBar and VScrollBar classes that represent the Windows horizontal and vertical scroll bars respectively, or using the form's AutoScroll and AutoScrollMinSize properties, which add the scroll bars to the form automatically if they are needed.

The default value of AutoScroll is true and the default Width and Height of AutoScrollMinSize equal zero. The client area of the form is defined by its bounds, minus the non-client elements such as scroll bars, borders, title bars, and menus. If a form contains a control that is outside the client area, the code line

```
this.AutoScrollMinSize = new Size(1, 1);
```

automatically adds the appropriate scroll bar. If a form contains a large picture that cannot be displayed as a whole, to get the scroll bars you can write:

```
this.AutoScrollMinSize = new Size(image.Width, image.Height);
```

We used this approach in project P18_Scrolling

```
protected override void OnPaint(PaintEventArgs e)
{
    Graphics g;
    g = Graphics.FromHwnd(this.Handle);
    GraphicsUnit units = GraphicsUnit.Pixel;
```

```
        string path = "..\\..\\MonetZsu.jpg";
        Image im = Image.FromFile(path);
        this.AutoScrollMinSize = new Size(im.Width, im.Height);
        //this.AutoScroll = true;

        Point P = this.AutoScrollPosition;
        Rectangle dstR = this.ClientRectangle;
        RectangleF srcR = new RectangleF(-P.X, -P.Y, dstR.Width, dstR.Height);
        g.DrawImage(im, dstR, srcR, units);
        g.Dispose();
}
```

What else can you do with images in GDI+? If you want to change the resolution of a bitmap or need access to the bitmap's pixel data use the `Bitmap` class derived from the `Image`. For instantiating or loading a bitmap object you can apply twelve constructors of the `Bitmap` class. We used this class for double buffering. You can set the compression rate of JPG files too.

We demonstrate in our last simple project `P19WebIconThumbNail`, how to display icons, build thumbnails from images and load a picture from the Internet. Note that the code needs the `System.Net` and `System.IO` namespaces.

```
protected override void OnPaint(System.Windows.Forms.PaintEventArgs e)
{
    // Icon 3 times:
    string p = @"C:\Program Files\Microsoft Visual Studio
.NET\VC#\CSharpProjectItems\icon.ico";
    Icon ic = new Icon(p);
    this.Icon = ic;   // Icon 1
    Graphics g = e.Graphics;
    g.DrawIcon(ic, 0, 0);  // Icon 2
    Image i = ic.ToBitmap();
    g.DrawImage(i, 50, 0);  // Icon 3

    // Thumbnail:
    p = @"..\..\MonetZsu.JPG";
    i = Image.FromFile(p);
    Image tn = i.GetThumbnailImage(50, 50, null, IntPtr.Zero);  // (IntPtr)0
    g.DrawImage(tn, 100, 0, tn.Width, tn.Height);

    // Picture from Internet:
    p = "http://www.kosice.sk/newimg/kolazx4.jpg";
    WebRequest wReq = WebRequest.Create(p);  // using System.Net;
    WebResponse wRes = wReq.GetResponse();
    Stream strm = wRes.GetResponseStream();  // using System.IO;
    Image im = Image.FromStream(strm);
    g.DrawImage(im, 0, 50);
    strm.Close();

    g.Dispose();
}
```

Summary

This chapter introduced you to the .NET Framework graphics. It described the basic techniques and concepts of GDI+ such as double buffering, invalidating, paths, regions, transformations, clipping and hit testing. You learned how to use colors, pens, and brushes, how to paint images, texts, single and complex shapes, and how to handle painting events and flicker. We discussed briefly transparent colors, scrolling, and changing the text direction.

7

Printing

Printing is an important component of any good Windows application, but it is often an overlooked and misunderstood piece of most enterprise systems. The .NET Framework contains support for working with printers, printing, and print previewing, and understanding how to utilize this functionality is crucial for building robust and complete Windows applications.

This chapter will focus on the following topics:

- ❑ The `System.Drawing.Printing` namespace and the major classes contained within
- ❑ How printing is handled within the .NET Framework
- ❑ Querying installed printers and obtaining their current settings
- ❑ How to send text and graphical output to a printer
- ❑ Utilizing the Windows common dialogs for page setup and print preview functionality
- ❑ How to implement a real-world printing solution

System.Drawing.Printing

This namespace contains the various .NET classes used to implement printing functionality. The vast majority of classes in this namespace are utility classes, and are utilized only when configuring and setting various aspects of the printing process. These classes include: `Margins`, `PaperSize`, `PaperSource`, and `PrinterResolution`. The other classes that are key to the printing process are the `PrintDocument` class and the `PageSettings` and `PrinterSettings` classes.

The `PrintDocument` class is the key to printing in the .NET Framework, as it is the only class required when any printing is performed. This class interfaces with the printer and acts as an intermediary between your custom application code and the Windows printing API. We will examine how to utilize its various properties and objects to write text and graphics out to a printer, and how the .NET Framework makes this process very similar to writing out to the screen.

The `PageSettings` and `PrinterSettings` classes are both key utility classes that are used to configure the document being printed and the printer, respectively. In many cases the user can modify these classes directly through the use of the Windows printing common dialogs – without too much work on your part. However, understanding how these classes work will allow you to create robust custom printing solutions.

If you are coming from a MFC background, the printing support provided by the .NET Framework may seem lacking. The .NET Framework does not natively support a document/view architecture, and therefore the automatic support for printing and print-previewing that such a design pattern provides is not available. This is not to say such things are impossible in .NET, quite the opposite, as we will see in this chapter. However, there will be more work writing the "plumbing" than you are used to with MFC. Note that if you are coming from a VB6 background, the printing support is vastly improved, both in terms of capabilities and ease of use.

Printing in .NET

In the last chapter we discussed how the `Graphics` class is used to draw to the screen. The `Graphics` class is akin to a device context in the Win32 API. Much as GDI in the Win32 API provides a device context for a printer, thus maintaining the same abstraction for writing to a printer as writing to the screen, the .NET Framework also provides a `Graphics` object that refers to the printer, making it relatively easy to write to the printer. This `Graphics` object is used to produce printed output in the same manner as writing to the screen or an off-screen buffer.

Under the hood, the `Graphics` class is interacting with the Windows API and the printer driver, which in turn talks to the **Hardware Abstraction Layer (HAL)** within Windows. This makes it possible to write to any printer because Windows converts the printing instructions into the specific device dependent instructions before sending them to the physical printer. This is why applications do not need to worry about printer drivers and specific printer formats – Windows handles all of these tasks.

We will discuss the general outline for printing in the .NET Framework, and then examine a simple "Hello Printer" application before investigating the various classes in detail. To send output to the printer, first an application must create a `PrintDocument` object. We will discuss this object in great detail next; for now just know it is the object used to access the printing capabilities of Windows. Printing is handled through events of the `PrintDocument` class, so event handlers must be assigned and managed by the application itself. The most important of these is the `PrintPage` event, which is invoked for every printed page. When the `Print` method is called on the `PrintDocument` object, the printing events will be fired off, allowing custom application code to respond and write out content to the printer through the `Graphics` object passed to the event.

Here is a bare bones application to get us started looking at printing in .NET. This is a basic console application that prints a simple message to the printer.

> This application and all the other examples for this chapter can be found on
> http://www.wrox.com. This example is in the **BasicPrint** directory of the Chapter
> 7 folder.

```csharp
using System;
using System.Drawing.Printing;
using System.Drawing;

namespace BasicPrinting
{
  class PrintSample
  {
    [STAThread]
    static void Main(string[] args)
    {
      PrintSample oSample = new PrintSample();
      oSample.RunSample();
    }

    public void RunSample()
    {
      Console.WriteLine("Printing to the default printer...");
      try
      {
        PrintDocument pd = new PrintDocument();
        pd.PrintPage += new PrintPageEventHandler(this.PrintPageEvent);
        pd.Print();
      }
      catch(Exception ex)
      {
        Console.WriteLine("Error printing -- " + ex.ToString());
      }

      //Read input - to delay the closing of the DOS shell
      Console.ReadLine();
    }

    //Event fired for each page to print
    private void PrintPageEvent(object sender, PrintPageEventArgs ev)
    {
      string strHello = "Hello Printer!";
      Font oFont = new Font("Arial",10);
      Rectangle marginRect = ev.MarginBounds;

      ev.Graphics.DrawRectangle(new
          Pen(System.Drawing.Color.Black),marginRect);
      ev.Graphics.DrawString(strHello,oFont,new
          SolidBrush(System.Drawing.Color.Blue),
          (ev.PageBounds.Right/2), ev.PageBounds.Bottom/2);
    }
  }
}
```

This application runs from the console, but it prints to the default Windows printer. Because it references the drawing libraries, a reference must be added to the `System.Drawing.dll` as it is not included by default in console applications. This is accomplished in the **Add Reference** dialog on the Visual Studio .NET IDE. When we create Windows Forms applications next this will be included automatically, so there will be no need to add it manually.

The application itself is very simple. It merely creates a `PrintDocument` object and assigns an event handler for the `PrintPage` event. It then calls the `Print` method on the object, which causes the `PrintPage` event to be raised. It is within the `PrintPage` event that the actual magic happens, as this is where the custom code is placed to control what is printed to the page. In this example we draw a rectangle around the margins of the page and output the words "Hello Printer!" in the following two lines:

```
ev.Graphics.DrawRectangle(new Pen(System.Drawing.Color.Black),marginRect);
ev.Graphics.DrawString(strHello,oFont,new SolidBrush(System.Drawing.Color.Blue),
    (ev.PageBounds.Right/2), ev.PageBounds.Bottom/2);
```

Note that we access the `Graphics` object contained as a member property of the `PrintPageEventArgs` class to perform our GDI calls to the printer. We will be discussing this extensively in the next section. The `marginRect` variable is obtained from the `MarginBounds` property of the `PrintPageEventArgs`; as should be obvious by the name, this property represents the margin boundary on the page. Our code first draws a box around the margins, and then prints the text to the center of the page, using the `PageBounds` property, which represents the actual boundary of the page. Note that the text will not be exactly centered as it must be adjusted for the width and height of the text itself, but this is only an introductory example. We will examine more complete examples later.

Note that the call to the `Print` method is enclosed in a `try...catch` block. Therefore if an error occurs, it will be reported to the user after being caught, thus ensuring the application doesn't terminate without warning. This is important in a printing situation, because it can be common for the printer to be offline or paper to be missing. In this way writing to a printer is very different from writing to a screen, and care must be taken to ensure you provide the user with a convenient manner to recover from printing errors and mistakes. Note that in a production application you would want to explicitly handle exceptions and not just have an all-purpose handler for every exception.

Graphics

The `Graphics` class is used to draw and write to the printer. This `Graphics` class is the same class used to draw to the screen, and due to the flexibility of device contexts and a well-written framework, all of the same drawing operations are available. This means that if written correctly, your application should have to do very little modification to change from writing to the screen to writing to the printer. However, Windows applications are often composed primarily of controls and not GDI calls, and the printer functionality is most commonly used for printing things like reports and summary information, which is often displayed in grid controls on the screen. Because of this, frequently the printing logic will have to be completely written from scratch.

The `Graphics` object used to write to the printer is accessed within the `PrintPage` event of the `PrintDocument` object, as we saw previously. By writing code in this event, your application can send custom output to the printer. There are some considerations that must be taken into account, however, due to the fact that you are writing to a paper medium instead of a vacuum tube or LCD display. Some of the important things to consider are page breaks – what do you do about them? Will you apply a header and footer to each page? What happens if your text wraps too far? You can't just add a scrollbar to the page. All these things and more make printing a more complex endeavor than simply routing GDI calls to the printer.

PrinterSettings

Because of the challenges associated with writing output to a fixed media format, it is important to know what tools are at our disposal. The `PrinterSettings` class provides the ability to query installed printers and give our application an idea of the available capabilities. Let's examine this class in more detail. While it does contain some methods, the large numbers of properties available provide the most usefulness. These properties are explained below.

PrinterSettings Properties

❑   `CanDuplex` – Boolean flag indicating if the printer supports double-sided printing.

❑   `Collate` – Boolean flag indicating if the document should be collated.

❑   `Copies` – The number of copies of the document to print.

❑   `DefaultPageSettings` – The default `PageSettings` object for the printer.

❑   `Duplex` – Boolean value, indicating if this printing job should perform duplex (double-sided) printing.

❑   `FromPage` – Value indicating the first page to print in this print job.

❑   `InstalledPrinters` – `String` collection containing the names of all installed printers on this computer.

❑   `IsDefaultPrinter` – Boolean value indicating if the referenced printer is the Windows default printer.

❑   `IsPlotter` – Boolean flag indicating if the referenced printer is a plotter.

❑   `IsValid` – Boolean flag indicating if the printer referenced by `PrinterName` is a valid printer on this system.

❑   `LandscapeAngle` – The angle, in degrees, that the portrait orientation is rotated to produce the landscape orientation for this printer.

❑   `MaximumCopies` – Value indicating the maximum number of copies this printer can print at one time.

❑   `MaximumPage` – Value indicating the maximum `From` and `To` pages that can be set from a `PrintDialog`. This can be used to keep the users from selecting a value above the max number of pages in the dialog box.

❑ MinimumPage – Value indicating the minimum From and To pages that can be set from a PrintDialog.

❑ PaperSizes – Returns a collection of PaperSize objects that indicate the valid paper options for the referenced printer.

❑ PaperSources – Returns a collection of PaperSource objects that indicate the valid paper source trays for this printer.

❑ PrinterName – The name of the printer to use. Can be set to change the referenced printer.

❑ PrinterResolutions – Returns a collection of PrinterResolution objects that indicate the valid resolutions supported by the referenced printer.

❑ PrintRange – A PrintRange enumeration that indicates if this print job should print the entire document, only the selected sections, or only a range of pages.

❑ PrintToFile – Boolean value indicating of the print job should be sent to a file and not output to a printer.

❑ SupportsColor – Boolean flag indicating if the referenced printer supports color printing.

❑ ToPage – Value indicating the last page to print in this print job.

A PrinterSettings object is created like a standard .NET object; however, this does not initialize it to a specific printer. Setting the PrinterName property to a valid installed printer will fill the object's properties with the associated values of that printer. The Boolean property IsValid can be used to first test to see if the supplied printer's name is in fact a valid installed printer.

How can we get a list of all the installed printers on a system, you ask? Easy – use the static property InstalledPrinters. This is a StringCollection object containing the names of all printers currently installed on the machine.

This class can be used in several different ways. The two most common ways are to query the capabilities of a printer or printers installed on the computer. Many of the properties above do not make sense in this context. We will be examining this mode next. Later we will examine using this object as it relates to a specific print job. In this mode the remaining properties come into play and can be used to control the printer settings for the user's specific print job.

Displaying Printer Settings

Let's look at an example of how to query the capabilities of the installed printers. The example below is located in the PrinterCaps1 directory in the online code.

Create a new C# Windows Form application called **PrinterCaps1**. Change the name of the main form to **frmMain**. Add the following code to the form's Paint event handler:

```
private void frmMain_Paint(object sender,
    System.Windows.Forms.PaintEventArgs e)
{
    PrinterSettings pSettings = new PrinterSettings();
    Font printFont = new Font("Arial", 10);

    //Position
```

```
        int nTextPosY = 0;
        int nTextPosX = 5;
        int nHeight = (int)printFont.GetHeight(e.Graphics);

        foreach(string sPtr in PrinterSettings.InstalledPrinters)
        {
          //pSettings.PrinterName = sPtr;
          pSettings.PrinterName = "BadName";
          //if(pSettings.IsValid)
          //{
            e.Graphics.DrawString(sPtr, printFont,Brushes.Black, nTextPosX,
                nTextPosY + 5);
            e.Graphics.DrawString("Can Duplex: "
                + pSettings.CanDuplex.ToString(), printFont,Brushes.Black,
                nTextPosX + 10, nTextPosY + (5 + nHeight));
            e.Graphics.DrawString("Is Default: "
                + pSettings.IsDefaultPrinter.ToString(),
                printFont,Brushes.Black, nTextPosX + 10, nTextPosY + (5
                + nHeight*2));
            e.Graphics.DrawString("Is Plotter: "
                + pSettings.IsPlotter.ToString(), printFont,Brushes.Black,
                nTextPosX + 10, nTextPosY + (5 + nHeight*3));
            e.Graphics.DrawString("Landscape Angle: "
                + pSettings.LandscapeAngle.ToString(),
                printFont,Brushes.Black, nTextPosX + 10, nTextPosY + (5
                + nHeight*4));
            e.Graphics.DrawString("Maximum Copies: "
                + pSettings.MaximumCopies.ToString(),
                printFont,Brushes.Black, nTextPosX + 10, nTextPosY + (5
                + nHeight*5));
            e.Graphics.DrawString("Maximum Page: "
                + pSettings.MaximumPage.ToString(),
                printFont,Brushes.Black, nTextPosX + 10, nTextPosY + (5
                + nHeight*6));
            e.Graphics.DrawString("Minimum Page: "
                + pSettings.MinimumPage.ToString(),
                printFont,Brushes.Black, nTextPosX + 10, nTextPosY + (5
                + nHeight*7));
            e.Graphics.DrawString("Supports Color: "
                + pSettings.SupportsColor.ToString(),
                printFont,Brushes.Black, nTextPosX + 10, nTextPosY + (5
                + nHeight*8));
            nTextPosY = nTextPosY + ((5 + nHeight*8) + nHeight);
          //}

        }

        return;
      }
    }
  }
```

The last thing we need to do before this application can run is to add a `using` statement to import the `System.Drawing.Printing` namespace. Add the following lines to the top of the `Form1.cs` file.

```
using System;
using System.Drawing;
using System.Collections;
using System.ComponentModel;
using System.Windows.Forms;
using System.Data;
```

```
//Need Printing namespace
using System.Drawing.Printing;
```

You are now ready to compile and run the application. If all goes well, when this application runs you should see a simple Windows form displaying the installed printers on your system. While the window may not be large enough to display them all, it can be resized to display more. Obviously each system will be different, but as an example, the output on my system looks like the following:

The main thing this application does is loop through the `PrinterSettings.InstalledPrinters` string collection and display the settings of the printers, using the `PrinterSettings` object. The following lines assign the printer name to the `PrinterSettings` object and then checks to see if the printer is valid. Since we have retrieved the names directly from the `InstalledPrinters` collection we can be confident that it is a valid printer; however, it is always good to check before assuming the printer is valid.

```
//Assign the name to the PrinterSettings object
pSettings.PrinterName = sPtr;
if(pSettings.IsValid)
{
    //Perform actions with the valid pSettings object
}
```

Once we are sure we have a valid `PrinterSettings` object referencing a printer, we can display the capabilities of the printer. Note that there are more properties in the `PrinterSettings` class than we display in this example. This is because the other properties are useful only when using the `PrinterSettings` object in the context of a print job. We will see this in a later example, and see how the additional properties can be useful in these situations. For now, the properties we display in this example are more general and relate to the entire printer.

Utilizing the `Graphics` object to output the text to the Window shouldn't be new. We covered writing to the screen using the `Graphics` class in the last chapter, and we are not doing anything new here. The only strange thing about this example is the math required to position each block of printer capabilities correctly on the page. To do this correctly we calculate the height of the font using the `Graphics` object and some extra math to calculate where each block should go.

PrintDocument

As we have discussed before, the `PrintDocument` class is the most important component in the .NET printing library. This is the object that translates calls from .NET to the Windows printing HAL, and where custom application logic is placed to facilitate printing within your Windows applications. While often used in conjunction with other objects we will discuss later, such as the `PageSetupDialog` and `PrintDialog` classes, the `PrintDocument` class is the one class absolutely required to perform any printing in the .NET Framework.

The `PrintDocument` class contains many important properties, methods, and events. These are described below.

Properties

❑ `DefaultPageSettings` – Gets or sets the `PageSettings` object that represents the default settings for each page in the document. The `PageSettings` class represents how a page is formatted and displayed, and the `DefaultPageSettings` property setting assigns the default `PageSettings` object to use if a page does not explicitly set one.

❑ `DocumentName` – Gets or sets the document name used to submit the document to the Windows printing API. Note that this property does not apply a title to the document or output any text; it is only an internal reference for Windows. This property is what is displayed as the name of the print job in the printer's job queue. The default is "document".

❑ `PrinterSettings` – Gets or sets the `PrinterSettings` object that contains information about the print job this document consists of. Initialized to the printer's defaults.

Methods

❑ `Print` – Initiates the printing process, which will eventually invoke the various printing events on this `PrintDocument`.

Events

❑ `BeginPrint` – This event is invoked when a printing request has been made (for example, the `Print` method is called or the document is assigned to a print preview dialog box), but before the `PrintPage` event is called for the first time.

❑ `EndPrint` – This is invoked after the last page has printed.

❑ `PrintPage` – This event is invoked for each page of printed output required. This is where the majority of custom application code will be placed, as this method provides the `Graphics` object required to output text and graphics to the printer.

❑ `QueryPageSettings` – This event occurs immediately before each `PrintPage` call, and exists to allow the user to override the default `PageSettings` object assigned to the entire `PrintDocument` object. This allows the application to provide custom page setup information on a page-by-page basis.

PrintPage

The key event in this object is the PrintPage event handler, as this is where you place code to actually write output to the printer. The event itself is passed an object of type PrintPageEventArgs, which contains the following members:

PrintPageEventArgs Properties

❑   Cancel – Boolean flag indicating if the current print job should be canceled. Can be set to true at any time to stop this print job.

❑   Graphics – Gets the Graphics object referencing the current printer page. This object can then be used to write text and draw graphics to the page.

❑   HasMorePages – Boolean flag indicating if the PrintPage event should be invoked again because more data exists to be printed. If this is true upon exiting, the PrintPage event will be raised again. Set to false by default.

❑   MarginBounds – Contains a rectangle object representing the page margin boundaries as set by the default page setup from the printer and any customization by the user.

❑   PageBounds – Contains a rectangle object representing the entire page boundaries.

❑   PageSettings – Gets the PageSettings object for the current page being printed.

The Graphics property is where the Graphics object is passed to your code to allow access to the drawing functionality. However, the other settings are important for printing as well. The two properties MarginBounds and PageBounds each provide a rectangular area representing the page. The values in these two objects must be understood and taken into consideration because they give you the dimensions of the available canvas you have to work with. This relates to what was discussed earlier about having to consider more when drawing to a printer – you need to take things like paper size and margins into consideration.

The following diagram displays what the two objects represent. Note that the PageBounds represents the entire paper, but few printers can actually write output from edge to edge. The MarginBounds represents the margins, as set by the user or by default settings from the printer, and care should be taken to display output within the margins.

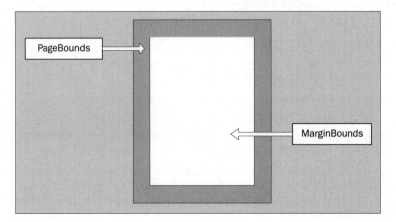

Print Preview

The .NET Framework contains a very useful class that enables developers to include print-preview capabilities in their application quickly and easily. We will be using this print preview dialog box for the rest of the samples in this chapter to ensure thousands of trees aren't wasted while we learn how to print.

To use the print preview dialog box simply instantiate an object of type `PrintPreviewDialog`. This is very much the standard dialog box classes we have seen throughout the book. This class has a `Document` property, which must be assigned the `PrintDocument` object you wish to print preview. Upon calling `ShowDialog` the `PrintDocument` will be printed to the window of the `PrintPreviewDialog`'s window, but the code will be executed in exactly the same manner as if the document were printing to a printer.

We will see plenty of samples using this functionality in the remaining examples, but here is a short snippet showing how to invoke the print preview functionality.

```
PrintPreviewDialog ppDialog = new PrintPreviewDialog();
// printDoc is an existing PrintDocument object
// with the PrintPage event handler defined
ppDialog.Document = printDoc;
ppDialog.ShowDialog();
```

Printing

Let's write some output to the printer using the `PrintDocument` class! We are going to write the `PrinterSettings` output to the printer, using the same formula we used in the previous example.

This example is included in the online code within the `PrinterCaps2` directory of this chapter's code.

Create a new C# Windows application titled `PrinterCaps2`. Add a single button to the main form and change the following properties so you have a small dialog box with a single button in the center.

Object	Property	Value
Form	Name	frmMain
	FormBorderStyle	FixedDialog
	Size	182, 118
	Text	Printer Caps
Button	Name	btnPrint
	Location	52, 28
	Text	Print

The `PrintDocument` object and the `PrintPreviewDialog` object can both be added to the form via the toolbox, just like a standard Windows Form control. Scroll to near the bottom of the toolbox and select the `PrintDocument` control. Drag this object onto the form; you should see it placed in the bottom of the screen where all non-visual components are placed. Add a `PrintPreviewDialog` control in the same manner. Change the names of these components to `printDoc` and `ppDialog`, respectively.

Note that I am illustrating how to do this in Visual Studio .NET, but all the functionality required is available from the .NET Framework itself, therefore you could easily write the code required to add a `PrintDocument` and a `PrintPreviewDialog` to a Windows Form by hand. You also have the option to create the `PrintDocument` and/or `PrintPreviewDialog` directly within the methods that require their use, thus avoiding keeping these objects in memory longer than required. All of these possibilities are left as exercises for the reader.

We are now ready to add the printing logic to the `PrintDocument` object. Remember the printing code is placed in the `PrintPage` event, which we can add through the Visual Studio .NET interface. Select the `printDoc` component and change the properties window to the **Event** view. Double-click on the `PrintPage` event to create a new event handler. Place the following code within the method:

```
private void printDoc_PrintPage(object sender,
    System.Drawing.Printing.PrintPageEventArgs e)
{
  PrinterSettings pSettings = new PrinterSettings();
  Font printFont = new Font("Arial", 12);

  //Use the Margins
  int nTextPosY = e.MarginBounds.Top;
  int nTextPosX = e.MarginBounds.Left;
  int nHeight = (int)printFont.GetHeight(e.Graphics);

  foreach(string sPtr in PrinterSettings.InstalledPrinters)
  {
    pSettings.PrinterName = sPtr;
    if(pSettings.IsValid)
    {
      e.Graphics.DrawString(sPtr, printFont,Brushes.Black, nTextPosX,
          nTextPosY + 5);
      e.Graphics.DrawString("Can Duplex: "
          + pSettings.CanDuplex.ToString(),
          printFont,Brushes.Black, nTextPosX + 10, nTextPosY + (5
          + nHeight));
      e.Graphics.DrawString("Is Default: "
          + pSettings.IsDefaultPrinter.ToString(),
          printFont,Brushes.Black, nTextPosX + 10, nTextPosY + (5
          + nHeight*2));
      e.Graphics.DrawString("Is Plotter: "
          + pSettings.IsPlotter.ToString(),
          printFont,Brushes.Black, nTextPosX + 10, nTextPosY + (5
          + nHeight*3));
      e.Graphics.DrawString("Landscape Angle: "
          + pSettings.LandscapeAngle.ToString(),
```

```
          printFont,Brushes.Black, nTextPosX + 10, nTextPosY + (5
          + nHeight*4));
       e.Graphics.DrawString("Maximum Copies: "
          + pSettings.MaximumCopies.ToString(),
          printFont,Brushes.Black, nTextPosX + 10, nTextPosY + (5
          + nHeight*5));
       e.Graphics.DrawString("Maximum Page: "
          + pSettings.MaximumPage.ToString(),
          printFont,Brushes.Black, nTextPosX + 10, nTextPosY + (5
          + nHeight*6));
       e.Graphics.DrawString("Minimum Page: "
          + pSettings.MinimumPage.ToString(),
          printFont,Brushes.Black, nTextPosX + 10, nTextPosY + (5
          + nHeight*7));
       e.Graphics.DrawString("Supports Color: "
          + pSettings.SupportsColor.ToString(),
          printFont,Brushes.Black, nTextPosX + 10, nTextPosY + (5
          + nHeight*8));
       nTextPosY = nTextPosY + ((5 + nHeight*8) + nHeight);
    }

  }

}
```

This is almost identical to the code we used to list out the printer capabilities to the screen in the last example. We have changed the code to account for the paper margins, however. Note that the nTextPosY variable, which is used to position each line of text vertically, is now set using the Top property of the MarginBounds object. Likewise, the nTextPosX variable, which is used to position each line of text in the horizontal direction, is set using the Left property of the MarginBounds object. This ensures the text output is within the margins as defined by the printer and the user.

We are associating this with the PrintDocument object, which means we can assign that PrintDocument object to the print preview dialog box to display what would be displayed if it was actually printed. To do this, add a Click event handler to the btnPrint button and add the following code.

```
private void btnPrint_Click(object sender, System.EventArgs e)
{
  try
  {
    ppDialog.Document = printDoc;
    ppDialog.ShowDialog();
  }
  catch(Exception ex)
  {
    MessageBox.Show(ex.ToString());
  }
}
```

This assigns the `PrintDocument` object to the print preview dialog box and tells the dialog box to display itself. If we were planning on printing directly to the printer, the following code could be used instead:

```
try
{
  printDoc.Print()
}
catch(Exception ex)
{
  MessageBox.Show(ex.ToString());
}
```

This code calls the `Print` method on the `PrintDocument` object directly, and tells the user if there were any errors printing.

Before this example will work we need to reference the `System.Drawing.Printing` namespace in the code. Add the following lines at the top of `Form1.cs`:

```
using System.Drawing;
using System.Collections;
using System.ComponentModel;
using System.Windows.Forms;
using System.Data;
```

```
//Need this namespace to access the Printing functionality
using System.Drawing.Printing;
```

We are now ready to run the application. The form is not very impressive – just a small dialog box with a single button. But when that button is pressed you should see a new dialog box displayed containing the output of the printer capabilities text. Again, this will be different on each system, but as a reference for those of you not actually running the samples, my output looks like the following:

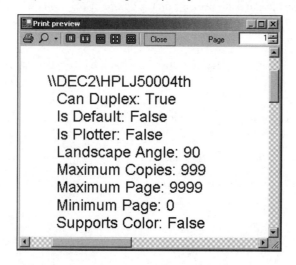

This dialog box is created from the `PrintPreviewDialog` class, and is the default view of the `PrintDocument` object's data. More importantly, this is how output can be generated with the `PrintDocument` object and sent to the printer.

Multiple Page Content

Most of the time your print jobs will consume more than a single page. Often multiple pages will be required to display a single report, or a long list of items will need to be displayed. The .NET Framework provides support for printing multiple pages through the `PrintPage` event and is entirely controlled by the application developer.

The `PrintPage` event will continue to be invoked as long as the `HasMorePages` flag of the `PrintPageEventArgs` object is set to `true` upon exiting. If it is `true`, the event will be raised again, with a fresh sheet of paper ready for printing. However, the architecture and plumbing required to support the transition to multiple pages must be handled by your code, and this can become rather tricky. Let's examine how to add multiple page support to our simple `PrinterSettings` application.

First, add a few printers to your system from the control panel. This should ensure the printing process will require more than a single page. Run the previous example and see the output in the print preview dialog. Note that the text is clipped to a single page, and there are no additional pages, even though there is more text than can be printed on a single sheet. This is because you must provide the implementation for multiple page printing.

PrinterCaps3

We are going to expand upon the last example to include printing multiple pages. In the online code this example can be found in the `PrinterCaps3` directory; however, you can simply extend the previous example as it will build upon the code we have already written.

We first need to add some way to track the current page being printed. Recall that the `PrintPage` event will continue to be invoked as long as our code tells it to, but the `PrintDocument` class does not keep track of the current page. Therefore we need to keep some state external to the `PrintPage` event handler. Since this application is outputting printer information, we will keep track of the current printer. We will do that with a private member variable, as shown below:

```
public class frmMain : System.Windows.Forms.Form
{
    private int m_nCurrPrinter;
```

We will initialize this value to zero when the print button is clicked, to ensure each print job starts at the beginning of the printer list:

```
private void btnPrint_Click(object sender, System.EventArgs e)
{
    //Set to default
    m_nCurrPrinter = 0;

    try
    {
        ppDialog.Document = printDoc;
        ppDialog.ShowDialog();
    }
    catch(Exception ex)
    {
        MessageBox.Show(ex.ToString());
    }
}
```

We will be changing the `PrintPage` method extensively, and we will cover each of the changes in detail. The complete method is shown below:

```
private void printDoc_PrintPage(object sender,
System.Drawing.Printing.PrintPageEventArgs e)
{
    PrinterSettings pSettings = new PrinterSettings();
    Font printFont = new Font("Arial", 12);

    //Use the Margins
    int nTextPosY = e.MarginBounds.Top;
    int nTextPosX = e.MarginBounds.Left;
    int nHeight = (int)printFont.GetHeight(e.Graphics);

    //Height of a printer block
    int nBlockHeight = 9 * nHeight;

    //Loop through using indexer now
    //Start with the previous index in m_nCurrPrinter
    for(int x = m_nCurrPrinter;x<
        PrinterSettings.InstalledPrinters.Count; x++)
    {
```

```
        pSettings.PrinterName = PrinterSettings.InstalledPrinters[x];
    if(pSettings.IsValid)
    {
        //Ensure this printer block can fit on the page
        if(nTextPosY + nBlockHeight < e.MarginBounds.Bottom)
        {
            //Print the caps of the printer
            e.Graphics.DrawString(PrinterSettings.InstalledPrinters[x],
                printFont,Brushes.Black, nTextPosX, nTextPosY + 5);
            e.Graphics.DrawString("Can Duplex: "
                + pSettings.CanDuplex.ToString(),
                printFont,Brushes.Black, nTextPosX + 10, nTextPosY + (5
                + nHeight));
            e.Graphics.DrawString("Is Default: "
                + pSettings.IsDefaultPrinter.ToString(),
                printFont,Brushes.Black, nTextPosX + 10, nTextPosY + (5
                + nHeight*2));
            e.Graphics.DrawString("Is Plotter: "
                + pSettings.IsPlotter.ToString(),
                printFont,Brushes.Black, nTextPosX + 10, nTextPosY + (5
                + nHeight*3));
            e.Graphics.DrawString("Landscape Angle: "
                + pSettings.LandscapeAngle.ToString(),
                printFont,Brushes.Black, nTextPosX + 10, nTextPosY + (5
                + nHeight*4));
            e.Graphics.DrawString("Maximum Copies: "
                + pSettings.MaximumCopies.ToString(),
                printFont,Brushes.Black, nTextPosX + 10, nTextPosY + (5
                + nHeight*5));
            e.Graphics.DrawString("Maximum Page: "
                + pSettings.MaximumPage.ToString(),
                printFont,Brushes.Black, nTextPosX + 10, nTextPosY + (5
                + nHeight*6));
            e.Graphics.DrawString("Minimum Page: "
                + pSettings.MinimumPage.ToString(),
                printFont,Brushes.Black, nTextPosX + 10, nTextPosY + (5
                + nHeight*7));
            e.Graphics.DrawString("Supports Color: "
                + pSettings.SupportsColor.ToString(),
                printFont,Brushes.Black, nTextPosX + 10, nTextPosY + (5
                + nHeight*8));
            nTextPosY = nTextPosY + ((5 + nHeight*8) + nHeight);
        }
        else
        {

            //Could not fit block on the page - need more pages
            m_nCurrPrinter = x;
            e.HasMorePages = true;
            return;
        }
    }


}
```

```
        //Last page if we reached here
        e.HasMorePages = false;
        m_nCurrPrinter = 0;
        return;
    }
```

This method has changed significantly, but we will examine each piece and understand why the changes were made. The first change is the calculation of the height of a printer block. This is simply the height of nine lines of text in the current font, because the application displays nine lines of printer settings for each printer. This is calculated using the following line:

```
//Height of a printer block
int nBlockHeight = 9 * nHeight;
```

We will use the nBlockHeight variable later in the method to determine if we should move to a different page, because we do not want to split a printer block among multiple pages. If you were printing something line by line, you could simply test if there were additional lines left to print instead of performing this calculation.

Note that we have also changed the very way we iterate through the InstalledPrinters string collection. Instead of using a foreach technique, we are now using a for loop with an integer indexer. This is because we need a way, on subsequent calls to this method, to set the beginning of the loop to the current printer. This will enable us to skip the printers that have already been output in the previous pages. In addition, we iterate until we reach the count property of the InstalledPrinters collection, as this represents the number of printers on the system. This all occurs in the following lines:

```
//Loop through using indexer now
//Start with the previous index in m_nCurrPrinter
for(int x = m_nCurrPrinter;x< PrinterSettings.InstalledPrinters.Count; x++)
{
    pSettings.PrinterName = PrinterSettings.InstalledPrinters[x];
```

Note that we use the current indexer (x) to get the printer's name and assign it to the PrinterSettings object.

The next section is the heart of the example.

```
//Ensure this printer block can fit on the page
if(nTextPosY + nBlockHeight < e.MarginBounds.Bottom)
{
    //Removed output to Graphics object
}
else
{
    //Could not fit block on the page - need more pages
    m_nCurrPrinter = x;
    e.HasMorePages = true;
    return;
}
```

The code first tests to see if the next printer block can still fit on the page. It does this by adding the current Y position of the text and the `nBlockHeight` variable (remember this is the height of a block of printer capabilities output) and tests to ensure this is less than the bottom of the margins rectangle (as represented by the `MarginBounds` property of the `PrintPageEventArgs` class). If the next output is indeed less, the code can print the next block of output.

If the text will not fit, then we need to tell the .NET Framework that there needs to be an additional page. We do this is by assigning the `HasMorePages` property of the `PrintPageEventArgs` class to true, and assigning the current printer (x) to the global placeholder `m_nCurrPrinter`. Now, when the `PrintPage` event is invoked again (which it will be because we told it to) the code will begin with the printer stored in the `m_nCurrPrinter` location, not at the beginning. However, if we fall out of the `for` loop normally, we know we have output all the printers, and we can set the `HasMorePages` property to `false`, as we are now done.

This application is now ready to run. If you have added several more printers to your system you should see output similar to the following:

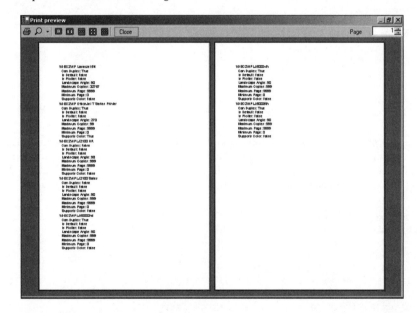

This example perhaps seems overly complex to simply print a few pages of text; however, remember that none of this is handled in a framework like MFC. You must provide all the printing apparatus, including making page breaks and pagination. This can quickly get complex, but much of the code required to perform the basic task of multiple page output to a printer is handled in this example.

GDI+ Calls

Text is not the only thing that can be output to the printer. Any of the many DrawX methods can be invoked through the Graphics object that is contained in the PrintPageEventArgs object. These calls are translated and sent to the printer as the correct graphical output on the printed page. We covered GDI+ calls extensively in the last chapter, so we will not reiterate all the capabilities of the Graphics class; however, we will add some pretty graphics to our PrinterSettings application as an example of some of the things that are possible.

We are going to add two things to the output of our application. This example application can be found in the PrinterCaps4 directory, but it expands upon the previous three examples.

We are going to modify the PrintPage event and add some graphical pizzazz in our printed report. First add the System.Drawing.Drawing2D namespace to the top of the Form1.cs file. This namespace is required for the gradient colors we need for the background of our report.

```
using System;
using System.Drawing;
using System.Collections;
using System.ComponentModel;
using System.Windows.Forms;
using System.Data;

using System.Drawing.Printing;
using System.Drawing.Drawing2D;
```

We are going to print a background for our report. I really like gradient textures and images, so I thought it would be neat to have a subtle gradient background for our report. However, I do not want it to obscure the actual text, so I am going to use the alpha blending capabilities built into the GDI+ subsystem. This is accomplished in the following lines:

```
//Height of a printer block
int nBlockHeight = 9 * nHeight;

//Print Background Graphic
LinearGradientBrush aBrush = new
    LinearGradientBrush(e.MarginBounds,Color.FromArgb(100,Color.LightBlue),
    Color.FromArgb(100,Color.Blue),LinearGradientMode.ForwardDiagonal);
e.Graphics.FillRectangle(aBrush,e.MarginBounds);
```

Here we are creating a gradient filled brush with which to fill the background of the page. The FromArgb method of the Color class can accept an existing color and an additional alpha transparency value to facilitate the creation of a new alpha blended color. This is very convenient and we use this to quickly create the transparent colors for the background. The alpha blending value can be a value from 0 (transparent) to 255 (opaque). We have selected 100 so that the color will display on the page, but will not obscure any of the important text of the report. The last parameter to the constructor merely states the direction the gradient should fill. This is an enumeration provided by the .NET Framework.

The last and easiest step is to call the `FillRectangle` method on the `Graphics` object. This passes in the newly created `Brush` object and the rectangle bounds, as provided by the `MarginBounds` property of the `PrintPageEventArgs`. With this completed we now have a slightly transparent, gradient-filled background ready for some text.

To illustrate another, commonly used, aspect of the `Graphics` class, we will add some additional drawing logic to the application. Specifically we will draw lines after each printer block, to further delineate each section from the next. As discussed in the last chapter, this process is very simple, and can be accomplished in just two lines of code.

```
//Draw line after each
e.Graphics.DrawLine(System.Drawing.Pens.Black,nTextPosX,nTextPosY,
                    e.MarginBounds.Right - 10,nTextPosY);
e.Graphics.FillEllipse(System.Drawing.Brushes.Black,e.MarginBounds.Right -
                    10,nTextPosY-5,10,10);
```

This should print a line ending in a small circle after each printer block. I know it isn't the most beautiful report you have ever seen, but it shows some basic GDI functionality. The GDI calls we added are pretty simple and don't contain anything new. Once all of these changes have been made to the code the application should print the report like the following screenshot. Note that this book is printed in black and white, so you can't see the beautiful color gradient, so I encourage you to actually download the code or create it yourself to see the amazing work of art we have created.

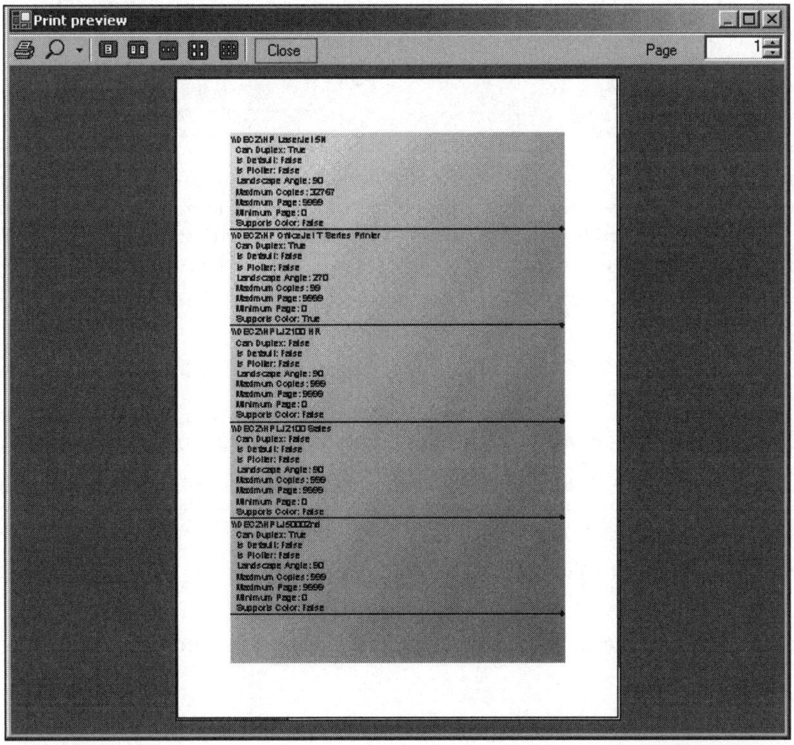

PrintDialog

The applications we have created so far have used the default printer assigned in Windows, and have not allowed the user to change any specific settings about the print job itself. This functionality can range from setting which printer to use to the number of copies to the start and end pages to print. Most Windows applications provide this functionality in the form of a common dialog box known as the print dialog. Applications written in the .NET Framework can access this same Windows dialog box through the `PrintDialog` class. For illustration purposes, this dialog box looks like the following screen:

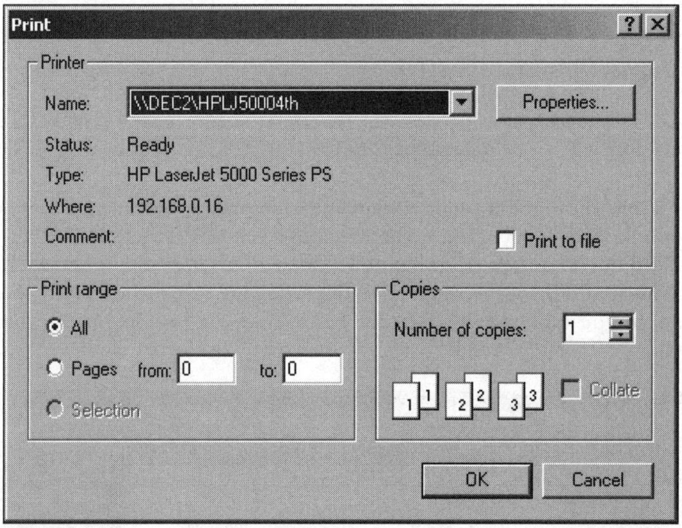

Note that many specific settings can be customized and enabled and disabled from within the application itself. These are set through the properties of the class, and are summarized below. If the `PrintDialog` object is added to the application through the Visual Studio.NET IDE, these will be available through the properties window and can be easily changed at design time.

PrintDialog Properties

- ❑ `AllowPrintToFile` – Boolean flag indicating if the **Print to file** checkbox option is available in the dialog box.

- ❑ `AllowSelection` – Boolean flag indicating if the **Selection** option button is available.

- ❑ `AllowSomePages` – Boolean flag indicating if the option to print a range of pages is available.

- ❑ `Document` – Represents the `PrintDocument` object this `PrintDialog` references.

- ❑ `PrinterSettings` – The `PrinterSettings` object this `PrintDialog` references and modifies.

- ❑ `PrintToFile` – Boolean flag indicating if the **Print to file** checkbox is checked.

❑   ShowHelp – Boolean flag indicating if the **Help** button is displayed. When a user clicks the **Help** button a HelpRequest event is raised and can be handled by the calling application to respond to the help request

❑   ShowNetwork – Boolean flag indicating if the **Network** button is displayed.

The method that displays the dialog box and requests input from the user is ShowDialog, just like any other dialog box in the .NET Framework. The result from this synchronous call should always be checked to ensure the user actually wants to continue to print and didn't click the **Cancel** button. The basic form of this would look like the following code:

```
if(oPrintDialog.ShowDialog() == DialogResult.OK)
{
    oPrintDoc.Print();
}
```

This class must be associated with a PrintDocument object, through the Document property. This PrintDocument acts as the base from which to query the PrinterSettings values, and as the user makes changes in the dialog box, this PrintDocument's settings are modified. This way, by the time your custom code in PrintPage is invoked, the custom settings specified by the user are available in the PageSettings.PrinterSettings property of the PrintPageEventArgs object.

Printing a Range of Pages

Note that the majority of settings specified in the PrintDialog's dialog box are settings that do not need to be managed by your application. Things like the printer used and the choice between printing to a file as opposed to printing to a printer. However there are things that must be managed by your application and will add an additional level of complexity to your printing logic.

The most obvious is providing the ability for users to select a range to print. Thus the user can select a beginning and ending page for the print job – and your code must manage printing only the selected pages. The .NET Framework does not do anything extra to help you – the same PrintPage event is raised for each page, and you must add the logic to query the correct values in the PageSettings.PrinterSettings object.

Sample Application – PrinterCaps5

To illustrate a basic example of how this works, let's add the print dialog support to our Printer Settings application. Once again, this example is contained in a separate directory (PrinterCaps5) in the online code, but you can simply modify your existing application as it builds upon the previous examples.

First, add a PrintDialog component from the toolbox to the main form in the design window of the Visual Studio .NET IDE. This will add a new PrintDialog object to the bottom of the window, with the existing PrintDocument and PrintPreviewDialog objects.

We are going to configure the `PrintDialog` object's properties through the IDE. Note that these can all be managed and changed within the code as well. Ensure the `PrintDialog` object is selected and switch to the properties window. Set the following properties:

Property Name	Value
Name	oPrintDialog
AllowPrintToFile	True
AllowSomePages	True

These changes will ensure the dialog box we receive will be tailored to the functionality desired. We want to give the user the ability to specify a print range as well as the ability to print to a file if desired. Now we just need to implement the ability to print a range of pages.

To do this, we will again be adding a private data member to the class to maintain state between the calls to `PrintPage`. This time we are going to add the current page being printed. Add the following line of code to add the data member to the class:

```
public class frmMain : System.Windows.Forms.Form
{
  private int m_nCurrPrinter;
  private int m_nCurrPage;
```

Again, as in the previous example, we will initialize this to a default value in the button-click event, to ensure it is the correct value every time a new document is printed.

```
private void btnPrint_Click(object sender, System.EventArgs e)
{
  //Set to defaults
  m_nCurrPrinter = 0;
  m_nCurrPage = 1;

  try
  {
    ppDialog.Document = printDoc;
    ppDialog.ShowDialog();
  }
  catch(Exception ex)
  {
    MessageBox.Show(ex.ToString());
  }
}
```

We will use this variable to ensure we only print the correct pages. Add the following code to the `PrintPage` method:

```
//Height of a printer block
int nBlockHeight = 9 * nHeight;
```

```
if(e.PageSettings.PrinterSettings.PrintRange == PrintRange.SomePages)
{
  while(m_nCurrPage < e.PageSettings.PrinterSettings.FromPage)
  {
    //Move printer to next page block
    m_nCurrPrinter += (int)(e.MarginBounds.Height / nBlockHeight);
    m_nCurrPage++;
    if(m_nCurrPrinter > PrinterSettings.InstalledPrinters.Count)
      return;
  }

  if(m_nCurrPage > e.PageSettings.PrinterSettings.ToPage)
  {
    //Don't print anything more
    return;
  }
}
```

```
//Print Background Graphic
LinearGradientBrush aBrush = new LinearGradientBrush(
    e.MarginBounds,Color.FromArgb(100,Color.LightBlue),
    Color.FromArgb(100,Color.Blue),LinearGradientMode.ForwardDiagonal);
e.Graphics.FillRectangle(aBrush,e.MarginBounds);
```

This code checks to see if the user has selected a range by checking the PrintRange property against the PrintRange enumeration. If they have, the code drops into a while loop that will continue to loop until the correct start page is found. Note that each time it skips a page it advances past the number of printers that can fit on a page. In your custom applications you will need a way to move to the next page in the data for exactly this reason. In addition, there is a check within the loop to ensure the user did not enter a page that was outside the range of the print job.

Finally, the code ensures it is not printing a page above the maximum selected by checking the e.PageSettings.PrinterSettings.ToPage property.

We need to add a final piece of code to invoke the PrintDialog. Add this code to the btnPrint_Click event handler:

```
private void btnPrint_Click(object sender, System.EventArgs e)
{
  //Set to defaults
  m_nCurrPrinter = 0;
  m_nCurrPage = 1;

  oPrintDialog.Document = printDoc;
  if (oPrintDialog.ShowDialog() == DialogResult.OK)
  {
    try
```

Once this code is in place the application can be executed and when the Print button is clicked a print dialog box will display. With the properties we set at design time, the dialog box should look like the following:

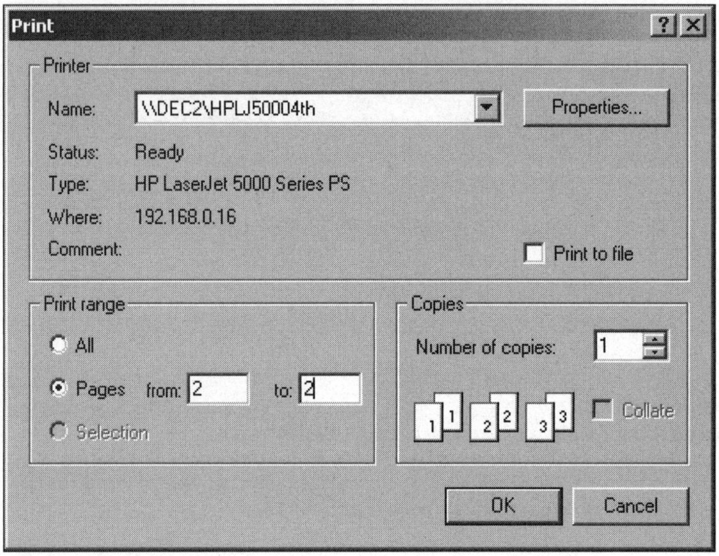

Select a valid range of pages (such as from page 2 to page 2), and click the OK button. You should see a print preview dialog box containing only the page with the printer settings in the range selected. For my system, this looks like the following:

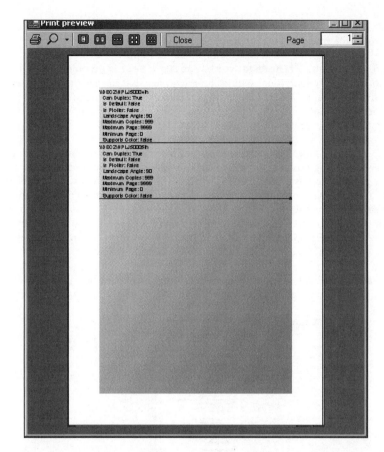

In summary, the PrintDialog is a class that encapsulates the functionality of the dialog box most Windows applications display as a result of the File | Print menu option. This dialog box allows the user to select the printer to use for the print job, the number of copies, and optionally the range of pages to print within the document. Much of this functionality is encapsulated within the .NET Framework, such as the number of copies and printer selection. However, some of the functionality is only a means to capture input from the user and you must provide all the actual functionality as it relates to your application. Allowing a user to select a range to print is an example of this, and we have examined how to implement this custom functionality within our example application.

PageSetupDialog

The PrintDialog class we just examined is used to specify settings for the entire print job – such as the specific printer to use and the number of copies to print. For individual page settings, the PageSetupDialog can be used. Much like the previous dialog, this class contains many public properties that can be set to customize the UI and functionality of the dialog box when it is displayed to the user. However, since a printing request is not persisted to the PrintDocument object automatically upon the closure of this dialog box, the settings chosen by the user must be saved and persisted elsewhere. This is done through the PageSettings class.

The PageSettings class specifies how an individual page will be printed, and when a document is ready to be printed the saved PageSettings object must be assigned to the PrintDocument's DefaultPageSettings property. These settings will now apply to every page, and can be retrieved in the PrintPage event in the PrintPageEventArgs.PageSettings object. Most business applications do not require individual settings for each page, but instead apply the page setup dialog box for the entire document. Document and page formatting-intensive applications, such as Microsoft Word, would need to maintain a collection of PageSettings objects for each page in the printed document, but most of the applications you create will be able to utilize a single PageSettings object.

The PageSettings and PageSetupDialog classes work hand in hand, and before displaying the PageSetupDialog dialog box the saved PageSettings object should be assigned to the PageSetting property to ensure the values previously selected by the user are reflected in the dialog box. Basically, the PageSetupDialog class acts as the way to collect page information from the user – which is then stored in the PageSettings class. This information is persisted to the PrintDocument object through the PageSettings class and applied to all pages in the document through the DefaultPageSettings property. We will examine both the PageSetupDialog and the PageSetting classes in this section, since they are intrinsically linked.

To illustrate what this dialog box looks like, the following is a screenshot of a PageSetupDialog window with the default settings configured.

PageSetupDialog Properties

Like the PrintDialog class, this class contains a set of public properties that configure both the look and feel of the dialog window and the functionality it exposes. These will normally be set during design time to ensure you offer the desired functionality to the user.

- ❑ AllowMargins – Boolean flag indicating if the margins section of the dialog box is enabled

- ❑ AllowOrientation – Boolean flag indicating if the orientation section of the dialog box (landscape as opposed to portrait) is enabled

- ❑ AllowPaper – Boolean flag indicating if the paper section of the dialog box, which displays the paper size and paper source options, is enabled

- ❑ AllowPrinter – Boolean flag indicating if the Printer button is enabled for the user

- ❑ Document – The PrintDocument object this PageSetupDialog class references to get and set page settings

- ❑ MinMargins – A value indicating the minimum margins the user is allowed to select, in hundredths of an inch

- ❑ PageSettings – The PageSettings object referenced by this PageSetupDialog

- ❑ PrinterSettings – The PrinterSettings object referenced by this PageSetupDialog

- ❑ ShowHelp – Boolean flag indicating if the Help button is available for the user

- ❑ ShowNetwork – Boolean flag indicating if the Network button is available for the user

Like the previous dialog, this class supports the ShowDialog method to display the dialog box to the user. This method returns synchronously with the DialogResult the user selected. It also exposes the HelpRequest event, which can be caught to respond to the user pressing the help button, if it is available.

PageSettings Properties

- ❑ Bounds – Returns a rectangle specifying the height and width of the page, in hundreds of an inch

- ❑ Color – Boolean flag indicating if the page should be printed in color

- ❑ Landscape – Boolean flag indicating if the page should be printed in landscape orientation; if this is set to false the page will be printed in standard portrait orientation.

- ❑ Margins – The Margins object that dictates the margins for this page

- ❑ PaperSize – The PaperSize object that represents the paper size for the page

- ❑ PaperSource – The PaperSource object that represents the page's paper source (for example, the printer's upper tray)

- ❑ PrinterResolution – The PrinterResolution object that represents the resolution for this page

- ❑ PrinterSettings – The PrinterSettings object that represents the printer settings for this page

PageSetupDialog Example

To illustrate how to utilize the `PageSetupDialog` and the `PageSettings` class, let's add support for them in our `PrinterSettings` application. To do this we are again going to add to the existing example we have been building on through this entire chapter. The code for the example is contained in the `PrinterCaps6` directory in the online code.

Most Windows applications will invoke the page setup dialog box through the File | Page Setup menu option. Since we do not have a menu in our sample application, we will invoke the dialog with an additional button. Besides, this chapter isn't about good user interface design! Add an additional button to the main form, changing the name to `btnSetup` and the text to Page Setup.

Next we need to add a `PageSetupDialog` object to the form. Like most of the other printing components we have worked with in this chapter, we can add this object through the toolbox in the IDE. Scroll down to the bottom of the toolbox and drag and drop the `PageSetupDialog` to the bottom tray area containing the other printing components for the application. Rename this object `oPageSetup`. Your IDE should now look like the following:

We need to add the `PageSettings` object to the `frmMain` class – to ensure the changes made to the page settings are persisted after the dialog box is invoked. Therefore, add the following line to the top of the `frmMain` class.

```
public class frmMain : System.Windows.Forms.Form
{
    //Saved PageSettings Object
    private PageSettings oPageSettings;

    private int m_nCurrPrinter;
    private int m_nCurrPage;
```

We will use this object when we display the page setup dialog, but first we need to ensure it is initialized properly. Therefore, in the constructor for the form, add the following initialization line:

```
public frmMain()
{
  InitializeComponent();

  //Create PageSettings object to store page information
  oPageSettings = new PageSettings();
}
```

We are now ready to add the code that actually invokes the dialog box and persists the configured settings to the PrintDocument object. Add a click event handler to the new btnSetup button and add the following code:

```
private void btnSetup_Click(object sender, System.EventArgs e)
{
  oPageSetup.PageSettings = oPageSettings;
  if(oPageSetup.ShowDialog() == DialogResult.OK)
  {
    oPageSettings = oPageSetup.PageSettings;
  }
}
```

This code assigns the stored PageSettings object to the dialog box object and displays the dialog box itself. If the user closes the dialog box by pressing the OK button, then any changes made are stored back into the PageSettings object for use later.

The code to associate the stored PageSettings object with the requested page setup information from the user to the PrintDocument object is very simple. Basically we are just assigning the stored PageSettings object to the DefaultPageSettings property of the PrintDocument object before calling Print, or assigning it to the print preview dialog box. This will make the PageSettings object the standard for all the pages in the document, but this can be changed in the QueryPageSettings event of the PrintDocument object. This event is raised for every page for which PrintPage event is invoked and provides a way for your application to change the PageSettings object, which would be needed if your application contained a collection of PageSettings objects for every page.

The one caveat to this is the fact that the PrinterSettings object is encapsulated within the PageSettings class; therefore any changes made through the PrintDialog will be lost at this point. The easy way to avoid this is to explicitly assign the PrintDocument's PrinterSettings object to the new PageSettings.PrinterSettings reference.

```
private void btnPrint_Click(object sender, System.EventArgs e)
{
  //Set to defaults
  m_nCurrPrinter = 0;
  m_nCurrPage = 1;

  oPrintDialog.Document = printDoc;
  if (oPrintDialog.ShowDialog() == DialogResult.OK)
  {
```

```
        try
        {
            //Ensure the correct PrinterSettings object is used
            oPageSettings.PrinterSettings = printDoc.PrinterSettings;
            //Assign PageSettings object to all pages
            printDoc.DefaultPageSettings = oPageSettings;
            ppDialog.Document = printDoc;
            ppDialog.ShowDialog();
        }
        catch(Exception ex)
        {
            MessageBox.Show(ex.ToString());
        }
    }
}
```

When you run this application, you can now set the page settings via the page setup dialog box. Click the Setup button and adjust the margins to .5 inches all around (or something similar in whatever your local measurements are set to). When you click the Print button you should see the print preview display has adjusted the printing to account for the user-defined changes. This is the reason to use the MarginBounds property of the PrintPageEventArgs class. You can play around with this example more – such as changing the orientation of the page to landscape – and see the result in the print preview window.

Example: Printing a DataGrid

We have now covered all you need to know to add printing support to your Windows applications. However, the previous examples in this chapter have been designed to illustrate specific pieces of the printing architecture, not to illustrate a real-world application. These can be very useful to understand how all the constituent pieces work; however, printing is a complex process and the previous examples do not provide answers for the multitude of complexities involved in printing an enterprise system.

Because of this, we are going to delve into a much more complex example and examine it thoroughly. The topic at hand is outputting the contents of a DataGrid to a printer. As discussed earlier, most Windows applications comprise controls and grids for data input and display, and the majority of reports are displayed on screen in a .NET DataGrid. We are going to build the component that will be useful when your boss asks, "Can we turn that grid into a hard copy report?"

Note that this will be a lengthy discussion and code walkthrough. The code we will be building will not be as simple as the previous examples, but will be designed to perform a real-world task and not simply to illustrate a printing concept. Because of this it is much more complex. I encourage you to download the source code and work through the code as we discuss the different pieces, to get the most out of this example.

Design Goals

The main goal with our component is reusability. I really don't like hard coding the printing logic into the form code (like the previous examples) and I would like to have a simple component that contains its own generic drawing logic. When combined with the data from a DataGrid this should create a passable report. The biggest difficultly will be trying to ensure the component is generic enough while still providing the functionality required. We also want to ensure clients can use this component easily and with a minimal amount of effort.

There will be a limitation on the component, at least for this book. This component will only print a single DataTable. A DataGrid can comprise multiple DataTables with relationships, and this can be easily implemented via the functionality of the DataGrid, but we will not display any sub-tables and linked data in our report. Such a report writer is possible, but it becomes much more complex and I believe this example will illustrate complex printing enough without the additional overhead of multiple DataTables. If you need this functionality, I encourage you to build on the example we create here.

GridPrinting

Enough talk – let's get to the code! We will be building this application from scratch, but the complete code is contained within the GridPrinting directory in the online code.

> Note, this example assumes you have access to the Northwind database installed by default on SQL Server 2000. Any data source will do; you will simply have to modify the data access section of the client application.

To begin with, create a C# Windows application called GridPrinting. First we will create the client application that contains the data to be printed. We are going to create a very simple application that displays some data from the Northwind database in a DataGrid. Once we have this in place we can begin to implement our grid-printing component.

Add the following controls to the form and set the appropriate properties:

Object	Property	Value
Form	Name	frmMain
	Text	Printing Grid Example
DataGrid	Name	dGrid
	Dock	Fill
MainMenu	Name	mnuMain
PrintPreviewDialog	Name	ppDialog
PrintDialog	Name	oPrintDialog
	AllowSomePages	True
PageSetupDialog	Name	oPageSetup

This will create a simple dialog box that contains a DataGrid. We will populate this DataGrid with data upon startup, and use our component to print the results when requested by the user. We have also added the various dialog boxes associated with printing, because we want to provide a full-featured Windows printing environment for our users.

We will now add the menu for the application, which will provide access to the printing dialogs as well as the actual printing functionality. Add the following five entries to the mnuMain object, through the Visual Studio .NET menu editor.

- ❑ File
- ❑ Page Setup...
- ❑ Print...
- ❑ Print Preview...
- ❑ (Separator line)
- ❑ Exit

The main form should now look like the following, with the menu expanded for illustration:

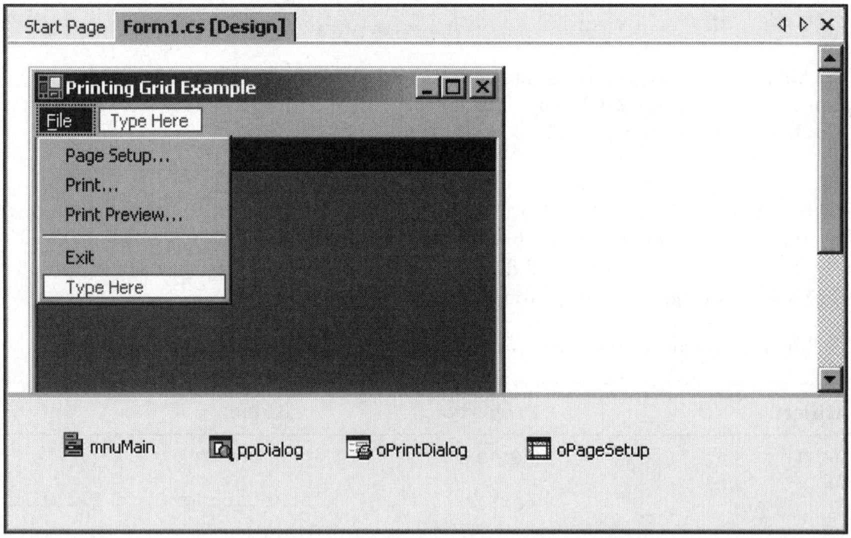

To get the basic functionality working, we are just going to add the data retrieval to the form load event and populate the DataGrid at that time. To do this, add the following code to the form load event:

```
private void Form1_Load(object sender, System.EventArgs e)
{
  try
  {
    //COnnection to database - get dataset
```

```
      SqlConnection aConn = new SqlConnection("data
          source=localhost;initial catalog=Northwind;integrated
          security=SSPI;");
      SqlDataAdapter sqlAdapter = new SqlDataAdapter("Select CompanyName,
          Address, City, Region, PostalCode, Country from
          Customers",aConn);
      DataSet aDataSet = new DataSet();
      sqlAdapter.Fill(aDataSet);

      //Assign dataset to Grid
      dGrid.DataSource = aDataSet;
      dGrid.SetDataBinding(aDataSet.Tables[0],"");
    }
  catch(Exception ex)
  {
    MessageBox.Show(ex.ToString(),"Error");
  }
}
```

Note that you will have to supply the name of the server containing the Northwind database to the connection string, as well as valid username and password if your login does not have permission to the database. This code is fairly common ADO.NET connect and query code, with the resulting dataset being bound to the DataGrid. This should not be new to you, and if it is I would suggest reading *Professional ADO.NET* from Wrox Press (ISBN: 1-86100-527-X).

If you run the application at this point you should have a simple window that displays a grid of data from the Northwind database. The data displayed is a sampling of customer information – you can customize the query if you wish.

PrintGridDocument

We are now ready to begin working on our actual grid-printing component. To satisfy the design goals of reusability and ease of use, this component is going to be a class that derives from the PrintDocument class. This will allow the client code to utilize it as if it were a PrintDocument, and it can still be assigned to the various printer dialog boxes, but deriving a custom class will allow us to place the grid-printing logic inside the derived class without touching client code at all.

Eventually this component could be moved to a separate class library DLL, but for now we will just add it directly to the application. Migrating this to a separate project should not be difficult, but I have left it as an exercise for the reader.

Add a new class to the project. Name the file PrintGridDocument.cs. You will be presented with an empty class file to begin working your magic on. First things first; let's add the required namespace declarations and derive the class from PrintDocument. Note that I have also removed the various comments Visual Studio .NET adds to the newly created class file.

```
using System;
using System.Drawing;
using System.Windows.Forms;
using System.Data;
using System.Drawing;
```

```
using System.Drawing.Printing;

namespace GridPrinting
{
  public class PrintGridDocument : PrintDocument
  {
    public PrintGridDocument()
    {

    }
  }
}
```

We need to provide a way for the client application to pass in the DataGrid to print. Since this is so fundamental to the component, and without a DataGrid this class could not function, we are going to modify the constructor to accept a DataGrid object and assign it to a private variable. Since this is a derived class, we are also going to add a call to the base class constructor, to ensure anything that needs to be initialized has a chance to be so. This is especially important when deriving a custom class from a Framework class, as we have no idea exactly what occurs within the Framework constructor.

```
public class PrintGridDocument : PrintDocument
{
  //Data Members
  private DataGrid m_oDataGrid;

  public PrintGridDocument(DataGrid aGrid): base()
  {
    //Default Values
    m_oDataGrid = aGrid;
  }
```

We are also going to need a measure of the total columns and rows in the DataGrid. We will extract that data in the constructor by accessing the underlying DataTable structure in the DataGrid. Besides this, we will also initialize some private variables that will be useful later in our printing logic. These include the current page number, and the current row.

Note that we are also going to expose the ability to set the Font used to create the text of the report. Unlike the previous variables, this will be public, as the client must be able to set it directly. However we will provide a default font if the client fails to set this. In addition we will provide a Title public property that represents the name of the report. We will print this out on the top of the first page, enabling an easy way to title the report.

```
//Data Members
private DataGrid m_oDataGrid;
private int m_nCurrPage;
private int m_nCurrRow;
private int m_nColumns;
private int m_nRows;

//Properties
public Font PrintFont;
public string Title;
```

```
public PrintGridDocument(DataGrid aGrid) : base()
{
  //Default Values
  m_oDataGrid = aGrid;
  m_nCurrPage = 0;
  m_nCurrRow = 0;

  //Get total number of cols/rows in the data source
  m_nColumns = ((DataTable)(m_oDataGrid.DataSource)).Columns.Count;
  m_nRows = ((DataTable)(m_oDataGrid.DataSource)).Rows.Count;
}
```

We are now going to override the OnBeginPrint method. As discussed previously, this event is raised before each print job, and acts as a means to initialize data structures before the actual printing. The reason we did not use this for much of the initialization previously, and why we will only be using it for font creation now, is because the method is not passed a Graphics object or MarginsBounds object. Without these it is impossible to calculate the initialization data required. We will see how to get around this in the OnPrintPage method.

Basically all we are doing in the OnBeginPrint method is calling the base class method and creating the Font object we will use for printing the report. We create the object here if the user has not created a Font object yet.

```
//Data Members
private DataGrid m_oDataGrid;
private int m_nCurrPage;
private int m_nCurrRow;
private int m_nColumns;
private int m_nRows;

//Properties
public Font PrintFont;
public string Title;

public PrintGridDocument(DataGrid aGrid) : base()
{
  //Code excluded for brevity
}
```

```
//Override OnBeginPrint to set up the font we are going to use
protected override void OnBeginPrint (PrintEventArgs ev)
{
  base.OnBeginPrint(ev);
  //If client has not created a font, create a default font
  // Note: an exception could be raised here, but it is deliberately not
  // being caught because there is nothing we could do at this point!
  if(PrintFont == null)
    PrintFont = new Font("Arial", 9);
}
```

We are now ready to add the `OnPrintPage` method, which will contain the bulk of the code for this component. This is the method that raises the `PrintPage` event for the client code to respond to. By placing our custom code within this class, we free the client from having to write any printing logic in their applications.

```
//Override the OnPrintPage to provide the printing logic for the document
protected override void OnPrintPage(PrintPageEventArgs e)
{
  //Call base method
  base.OnPrintPage(e);
}
```

There are going to be some things we need to calculate the first time a print job is requested but do not need to calculate every time the method is invoked. Remember that this method is called for every page that is printed, therefore any amount of unnecessary code we can avoid executing will be a performance gain. However, we need to perform this initialization within this method because we have access to the actual `Graphics` and `MarginBound` objects, which are crucial to calculating page layout and size. Because of this, we are going to add an initialization section to this method, and only drop into it on the initial call.

```
private int m_nRows;
private bool m_bInitialized;
private int m_nLinesPerPage;
private int m_nTotalPages;

//Properties
public Font PrintFont;
public string Title;

public PrintGridDocument(DataGrid aGrid) : base()
{
  //Default Values
  m_oDataGrid = aGrid;
  m_nCurrPage = 0;
  m_nCurrRow = 0;
  m_bInitialized = false;
  //Get total number of cols/rows in the data source
  m_nColumns = ((DataTable)(m_oDataGrid.DataSource)).Columns.Count;
  m_nRows = ((DataTable)(m_oDataGrid.DataSource)).Rows.Count;
}

//OnBeginPrint excluded

//Override the OnPrintPage to provide the printing logic for the document
protected override void OnPrintPage(PrintPageEventArgs e)
{
  //Call base method
  base.OnPrintPage(e);

  //Get the margins
  int nTextPosX = e.MarginBounds.Left;
  int nTextPosY = e.MarginBounds.Top;
```

```
   //Do first time initialization stuff
   if(!m_bInitialized)
   {
     // Calculate the number of lines per page.
     m_nLinesPerPage = (int)(e.MarginBounds.Height /
        PrintFont.GetHeight(e.Graphics));
     m_nTotalPages = (int)Math.Ceiling((float)m_nRows /
        (float)m_nLinesPerPage);

     //Set flag
     m_bInitialized = true;
   }
 }
```

Within the initialization block we calculate two very important numbers – the number of possible lines per page and the total pages required, based on that number. The generate these numbers the `MarginBounds` property is used, as well as the `Graphics` object – to query the correct height of the font based on the `Graphics` settings. To get the correct number of maximum pages we need to take the next highest integer than the result of dividing the number of rows by the lines per page. For example, if there are 90 total lines, but only 60 can fit on a page, we want the result to be two pages, not 1.5. We cannot simply round because even a result of 1.1 must equal two pages. To get the result we want the `Math.Ceiling` method is used to return the next highest real number.

Note that in addition to the initialization block we have also added two lines that store the margin's left and top position. We did a similar thing in the earlier examples, and we will be using these variables in the same manner. They will give us a starting position when we begin to actually output the data.

But before we get to the actual output of data to the page, we are going to add some cosmetic enhancements to our report. These will include a title on the first page and a page number on every page. This code is fairly complex, but only because of the positioning logic required. The basic idea is that we want the title in the center of the page directly above the margin boundary (it is the title after all). The page number we want in the lower right corner, within the boundary of the margins.

```
     //Set flag
     m_bInitialized = true;
   }
```

```
//Move to next page
m_nCurrPage++;

//Print Title if first page
if(m_nCurrPage == 1)
{
  Font TitleFont = new Font("Arial",15);
  int nXPos = (int)(((e.PageBounds.Right - e.PageBounds.Left) /2 ) -
     (e.Graphics.MeasureString(Title,TitleFont).Width / 2));
  e.Graphics.DrawString(Title,TitleFont,Brushes.Black,nXPos,
     e.MarginBounds.Top - TitleFont.GetHeight(e.Graphics) - 10);
}

//Draw page number
```

```
string strOutput = "Page " + m_nCurrPage + " of " + m_nTotalPages;
e.Graphics.DrawString(strOutput,PrintFont,Brushes.Black,
    e.MarginBounds.Right - e.Graphics.MeasureString(
    strOutput,PrintFont).Width,e.MarginBounds.Bottom);
```

> **Note that we have arbitrarily picked a font and size for the title. It would not be difficult to add the ability to customize this from client code, but I thought this example was convoluted enough!**

As I said, this code is beginning to get unreadable, largely because of the calculations required to position the strings in the correct places. The first block of code is basically calculating the location where the title string should be placed. It must take into account the size of the font and the fact that we want the title centered on the page.

The next block of code generates the page location string, and outputs this string in the lower right hand corner of the page. Again, the code looks convoluted, but it is essentially just calculating the position based on the size of the font and the width of the string.

Ready to actually output the data of the grid yet? Well – you are going to have to wait a little while longer. We could go the easy route here and just loop through the data and print it off, but how would be deal with the limitations on the size of the paper? Obviously we want to stay within the margins of the page, so how can we ensure we print all the relevant data while still staying on the page?

The solution to this problem involves determining the boundaries required for each column of data and clipping text that lies outside of that boundary. The first step is to loop through the data within each column and determine the largest line of text. This is the widest the column must be. We then must check to see that no column is above the maximum allowed size for the page, which is the width of the page margins divided by the number of columns. Therefore, if any of the maximum column widths are greater than this value, the column width is reset to the maximum allowed value.

The above paragraph describes the algorithm used to generate the bounding rectangles for each column. These bounding rectangles are used to clip the text to ensure that all the data can fit on the page, even if some of it is cut off. Note that this may not be appropriate for your custom reports. Perhaps you need a way to define custom maximum sizes based on certain fields. Again, the code we develop in this chapter can serve as a guide in designing a new custom printing solution. The following code implements the algorithm described above; it iterates through the data and generates the bounding rectangle for each column.

```
//Do first time initialization stuff
if(!m_bInitialized)
{
  // Calculate the number of lines per page.
  m_nLinesPerPage = (int)(e.MarginBounds.Height  /
      PrintFont.GetHeight(e.Graphics));
  m_nTotalPages = (int)Math.Ceiling((float)m_nRows /
      (float)m_nLinesPerPage);

  //Create bounding box for columns
  m_nColBounds = new int[m_nColumns];
```

```
//Calculate the correct spacing for the columns
for(int nCol = 0;nCol<m_nColumns;nCol++)
{
  //Measure the column headers first
  m_nColBounds[nCol] = (int)e.Graphics.MeasureString(
      ((DataTable)(m_oDataGrid.DataSource)).Columns[nCol].ColumnName,
      PrintFont).Width;

  for(int nRow=0;nRow<m_nRows;nRow++)
  {
    //Compare data to current max
    if(e.Graphics.MeasureString(
        m_oDataGrid[nRow,nCol].ToString(),PrintFont).Width >
        m_nColBounds[nCol])

      m_nColBounds[nCol] = (int)e.Graphics.MeasureString(
          m_oDataGrid[nRow,nCol].ToString(),PrintFont).Width;
  }
  //Just use max possible size if too large
  if(m_nColBounds[nCol] > e.MarginBounds.Width / m_nColumns)
    m_nColBounds[nCol] = e.MarginBounds.Width / m_nColumns;

  //Can't be less than column width
  if(m_nColBounds[nCol] < (int)Math.Ceiling(e.Graphics.MeasureString(
      ((DataTable)(m_oDataGrid.DataSource)).Columns[nCol].ColumnName,
      PrintFont).Width))

    m_nColBounds[nCol] = (int)Math.Ceiling(e.Graphics.MeasureString(
        ((DataTable)(m_oDataGrid.DataSource)).Columns[nCol].ColumnName,
        PrintFont).Width);
}

  //Set flag
  m_bInitialized = true;
}
```

In addition to the previous code we need to add the declaration for the column array in the declaration section of the class.

```
public class PrintGridDocument2 : PrintDocument
{
  //Data Members
  private DataGrid m_oDataGrid;
  private int m_nCurrPage;
  private int m_nCurrRow;
  private int m_nColumns;
  private int m_nRows;
  private Font PrintFont;
  private bool m_bInitialized;
  private int m_nLinesPerPage;
  private int m_nTotalPages;
  private int[] m_nColBounds;
```

The code added to the initialization block within the OnPrintPage method is complex, but it follows the logic described previously. The end result of the code is that the m_nColBounds array is filled with the correct width of each column. When it comes time to printing out the data we will use this to position each block of text in exact column lines, and we can be sure all of the data will be on the page.

We are now ready to add the central part of any print logic – the part that actually prints the data to the printer device. We are going to add a routine that loops through the data from the DataGrid and prints it using the previously defined column boundaries. This will clip some of the text, but again, ensure that all of it can fit on a single page. We will also ensure all of the text is within the margin boundaries of the page, and we must implement correct multiple page printing. We saw how to do this earlier in the chapter, and we will be using a very similar model in this component. We will check the current row against the previously computed max lines per page; once that is reached we need to exit from the PrintPage method after setting the current row to a class variable and telling the Framework to print more pages.

```
//Draw page number
string strOutput = "Page " + m_nCurrPage + " of " + m_nTotalPages;
e.Graphics.DrawString(strOutput,PrintFont,
  Brushes.Black,e.MarginBounds.Right -
  e.Graphics.MeasureString(strOutput,PrintFont).Width,
  e.MarginBounds.Bottom);

//Utility rectangle - use for many drawing operations
Rectangle aRect = new Rectangle();

//Loop through data
for(int nRow=m_nCurrRow; nRow < m_nRows; nRow++)
{
  //Loop through each column
  for(int nCol=0; nCol < m_nColumns; nCol++)
  {
    //Set the rectangle to the correct position
    aRect.X = nTextPosX;
    aRect.Y = nTextPosY;
    aRect.Width = m_nColBounds[nCol];
    aRect.Height = (int)PrintFont.GetHeight(e.Graphics);

    //Print the data
    e.Graphics.DrawString(m_oDataGrid[nRow,nCol].ToString(),
        PrintFont,Brushes.Black,aRect);
    //Advance the x Position counter
    nTextPosX += m_nColBounds[nCol];
  }

  //Reassign the x position counter
  nTextPosX = e.MarginBounds.Left;
  //Move the y position counter down a line
  nTextPosY += (int)PrintFont.GetHeight(e.Graphics);

  //Check to see if we have reached the line limit - move to a new page if so
  if(nRow - ((m_nCurrPage-1) * m_nLinesPerPage) == m_nLinesPerPage)
  {
    //Save the current row
```

```
      m_nCurrRow = ++nRow;
      e.HasMorePages = true;
      return;
   }
 }
```

Note that the Rectangle object is used repeatedly to set the bounds of the column. The correct settings are set for each column of data and then passed to the DrawString method. This ensures the data is printed, but clipped to the correct length.

Note that after each row of data is printed the code checks the current row against the maximum rows per page limit. If this is reached the current row is saved to the m_nCurrRow class variable and the HasMorePages property is set to true, telling the .NET Framework to call the PrintPage event again. When this method is called next it will use the stored value in m_nCurrRow to print the next page in the correct location. Note we must advance the row position before storing it, to represent the fact that it has not been advanced for the current row of data. After these things are done the method returns.

We now have basic printing capabilities for outputting a DataGrid to a page, but I want to improve the formatting. What I really want to add is alternating rows of shading. This makes large grids of data easier to read and more pleasing to the eye. Since we already have a framework in place for iterating through the rows of data, it is fairly easy to add a formatting change like this to our printing component.

```
//Loop through data
for(int nRow=m_nCurrRow; nRow < m_nRows; nRow++)
{
   //Draw the current row within a shaded/unshaded box
   aRect.X = e.MarginBounds.Left;
   aRect.Y = nTextPosY;
   aRect.Width = e.MarginBounds.Width;
   aRect.Height = (int)PrintFont.GetHeight(e.Graphics);

   //Draw the box
   if(nRow%2 == 0)
     e.Graphics.FillRectangle(Brushes.LightGray,aRect);

   e.Graphics.DrawRectangle(Pens.Black,aRect);

   //Loop through each column
   for(int nCol=0; nCol < m_nColumns; nCol++)
```

Note that this code is placed between the two for loops. This is because it must run once for every row of data in the grid.

The code utilizes the same rectangle we use later for the text output. This rectangle is positioned to the current row of data. Then, for every other row of data, light gray shading is applied. However, at every row a black outline is drawn around the rectangle. This gives each row a clear delimitation, and looks nice as well. Note that we fill the rectangle before any text printing is done because the rectangle would obscure any text printed underneath it. Therefore we will now draw the text on top of the shaded rectangle.

An additional formatting downfall is the fact that this output does not contain any header for the columns. Without this, how can the user know what kind of data they are examining? To output the headers requires very similar code to what we examined earlier. It comes from a different source, however, so it must be contained in a different loop:

```
//Draw page number
string strOutput = "Page " + m_nCurrPage + " of " + m_nTotalPages;
e.Graphics.DrawString(strOutput,PrintFont,Brushes.Black,
   e.MarginBounds.Right -
   e.Graphics.MeasureString(strOutput,PrintFont).Width,
   e.MarginBounds.Bottom);

//Utility rectangle - use for many drawing operations
Rectangle aRect = new Rectangle();

//Draw the headers
for(int nCol=0; nCol < m_nColumns; nCol++)
{
  aRect.X = nTextPosX;
  aRect.Y = nTextPosY;
  aRect.Width = m_nColBounds[nCol];
  aRect.Height = (int)PrintFont.GetHeight(e.Graphics);

  e.Graphics.DrawString(((DataTable)(m_oDataGrid.DataSource))
      .Columns[nCol].ColumnName, PrintFont,Brushes.Black,aRect);

  //Advance the x Position counter
  nTextPosX += m_nColBounds[nCol];
}

//Reassign the x position counter
nTextPosX = e.MarginBounds.Left;
//Move the y position counter down a line
nTextPosY += (int)PrintFont.GetHeight(e.Graphics);

//Loop through data
for(int nRow=m_nCurrRow; nRow < m_nRows; nRow++)
```

This code basically just loops through the headers and outputs them to the page in using the same technique we used previously. It uses the rectangle to determine the spacing and position, and outputs the text to the correct location. Note that after we have finished we must reset the two variables, nTextPosX and nTextPosY, so the central loop that outputs that data will be positioned correctly.

We only have one more thing left to do! Since we will be allowing the user to select a range of pages to print, we need to add support for this within the method itself. We saw how to do this earlier as well, and the technique will be very similar. This code should be added to the initialization block of the OnPrintPage method:

```
//Calculate the correct spacing for the columns
for(int nCol = 0;nCol<m_nColumns;nCol++)
{
```

```
  //Code removed for clarity
}
```

```
//Move to correct starting page
if(this.PrinterSettings.PrintRange == PrintRange.SomePages)
{
  while(m_nCurrPage < this.PrinterSettings.FromPage-1)
  {
    //Move to next page - advance data to next page as well
    m_nCurrRow += m_nLinesPerPage;
    m_nCurrPage++;
    if(m_nCurrRow > m_nRows)
      return;
  }

  if(m_nCurrPage > this.PrinterSettings.ToPage)
  {
    //Don't print anything more
    return;
  }
}
```

```
//Set flag
m_bInitialized = true;
```

This code is very simple, and it should be familiar from the previous code for multiple page printing. Basically, if a subset of pages has been requested, it loops until it reaches that starting page. Each time it advances past a page, the current row variable is advanced by the number of possible lines on the page. In addition, the code checks to ensure the current page is less than the requested maximum page.

We are now done with this custom grid-printing component, and we are ready to finish out the functionality in the Windows Forms application.

Since we are going to allow the user to customize the page setup with the page setup dialog box, we need to add a PageSettings object to the Form class. This is very easy to do, and only requires the following code:

```
public class frmMain : System.Windows.Forms.Form
{
  //Stored Page Settings object
  private PageSettings oPageSettings;

  //... Extra code removed for clarity

  public frmMain()
  {
    InitializeComponent();

    oPageSettings = new PageSettings();
  }
```

Now that we have this in place we can provide support for the **Page Setup** menu option. Add the click event to this menu choice and add the following code. This code should be very familiar by now, as it is exactly the code we used earlier in the previous examples.

```
private void menuItem3_Click(object sender, System.EventArgs e)
{
    oPageSetup.PageSettings = oPageSettings;
    //Show the Page Setup dialog
    if(oPageSetup.ShowDialog() == DialogResult.OK)
    {
        //Save the results
        oPageSettings = oPageSetup.PageSettings;
    }
}
```

To add the actual printing command, add the following code to the click event of the **Print** menu item. This will utilize the previously saved `PageSettings` object, as well as display the `PrintDialog` for the user.

```
private void menuItem4_Click(object sender, System.EventArgs e)
{
    //Setup the document to print
    PrintGridDocument aDoc = new PrintGridDocument(dGrid);
    aDoc.Title = "Employee Report";
    oPrintDialog.Document = aDoc;
    if (oPrintDialog.ShowDialog() == DialogResult.OK)
    {
        //Display the print preview dialog
        aDoc.DefaultPageSettings = oPageSettings;
        try
        {
            //Print the document
            aDoc.Print();
        }
        catch(Exception ex)
        {
            //Display any errors
            MessageBox.Show(ex.ToString());
        }
    }
}
```

Note that we are creating a `PrintGridDocument` object instead of a `PrintDocument`. The `PrintGridDocument` is our custom class that we have just created. Recall that it inherits from `PrintDocument`, meaning it can be used anywhere that requires a `PrintDocument` class, such as the `Document` property of the print dialog box or print preview dialog box.

Finally, we can add print preview support to our application through the now familiar `PrintPreviewDialog` class we have used so much throughout this chapter. Add the following code to the click event of the **Print Preview** menu option.

```
private void menuItem2_Click(object sender, System.EventArgs e)
{
   //Setup the document to print
   PrintGridDocument aDoc = new PrintGridDocument(dGrid);
   aDoc.Title = "Employee Report";
   oPrintDialog.Document = aDoc;
   if (oPrintDialog.ShowDialog() == DialogResult.OK)
   {
     //Display the print preview dialog
     aDoc.DefaultPageSettings = oPageSettings;
     ppDialog.Document = aDoc;
     ppDialog.ShowDialog();
   }
}
```

We are finally finished! Run the application and you should have a Window containing a sampling of data from the Northwind database. Selecting the Print Preview menu option will display the following print preview dialog box, which is generated from our custom component.

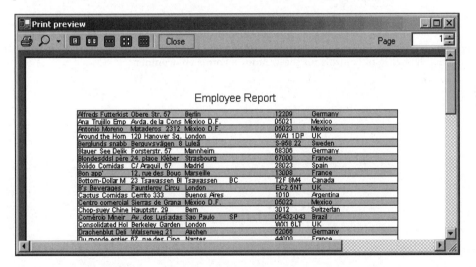

Hopefully this has shown you how to create a real-world printing solution in the .NET environment. We have walked through creating a custom printing component that can print out the data contained in any DataGrid. While it could be expanded to contain additional functionality, it accomplished the basic design goals we started out with well. Most importantly, walking through its creation has demonstrated how to develop with and around the .NET printing architecture.

Summary

This chapter has covered how to access and use the printer in the .NET Framework. We have covered the `System.Drawing.Printing` in detail and looked at all of the major classes contained within. In addition to this we took a real-world example and showed how to apply the generic knowledge we learned by building a reusable component that can print out the content of any `DataGrid` control.

In this chapter we have examined:

- ❑ How the basic printing architecture functions in .NET
- ❑ The key classes contained in the `System.Drawing.Printing` namespace
- ❑ Querying the installed printers and obtaining the printing capabilities of a printer
- ❑ Utilizing the `PrintDocument` class to output text and graphics to the printer
- ❑ Accessing the functionality of the various printing dialog boxes, including the print, page setup, and print preview dialog boxes
- ❑ Building a generic `DataGrid` printing component

In the next chapter we are going to learn how to further customize our Windows applications, and examine building custom controls for the Windows Forms environment.

Custom Controls

There will be times when we have a task where the controls and components that ship with Visual Studio .NET just don't seem to fit our needs. Fortunately, we can always make our own. Maybe we just want to make minor tweaks to one of the existing standard controls, or maybe we need to make an extremely customized control from the ground up.

Extending existing controls in .NET is a snap with inheritance. Even if we need to build a fully customized control, the .NET Framework provides us with a robust 'grounding' in the form of the `System.Windows.Forms.Control` base class.

The term 'custom' is often used in a broad context to describe all types of controls we build ourselves. However, in this chapter we'll use the following terms to describe the three major classifications of control examples we will be building:

- **Extended Control** – Inherits directly from an existing control. In our example we'll extend an existing `TextBox`.

- **Composite Control** – Inherits directly from the `UserControl` class and is actually composed of other controls. In our example, we'll create an address control.

- **Custom Control** – Inherits directly from the `Control` base class and is completely responsible for producing its own custom user interface. We'll create a round button control in our example.

It is vital that we never forget that the controls we author will be consumed on two levels. Developers will consume our controls at design time as they create solutions, and then true end users will consume our controls at the run time of those solutions. Consequently, we should strive to make our controls as attractive at design time as they are at run time.

Rather than wading through a hierarchical list of topics regarding control creation, this chapter takes a example-based approach and will seem more like several miniature case studies. Rather than showing disconnected snippets of code here and there on various topics, we will actually author three controls and discuss relevant issues as they arise during the course of development. We will also carry some topics across examples as we discuss basic concepts in one control, and then cover some advanced aspects of the topics in the next control (where it makes sense to employ them).

We have a lot of ground to cover; so there are a few topics that we simply couldn't do justice to in this chapter; namely, control licensing, extender providers, or numerous topics involving custom serialization and code generation. Hopefully you'll be inspired to investigate these topics further as you push the boundaries of custom controls and components.

Finally, we should note that this chapter will be Visual Studio .NET-centric since the extensible design time architecture in the .NET Framework was built with VS.NET in mind and vice versa. While nothing prevents you from building all these controls with a text editor and the command line, we won't spend much time at all detailing this. Even if you plan to do all your development without VS.NET, you will need to know the design-time architectural issues we cover in this chapter if you expect your controls to be robust when consumed by others who do employ the VS.NET environment. This would be wise since a large majority of .NET developers will likely be VS.NET users.

Over the course of the chapter our examples will gradually introduce and expound on several ways to improve the Visual Studio .NET design-time qualities of our controls. We'll see how XML documentation and attributes can enhance metadata, control member visibility, and specify certain elements of design-time behavior. We'll see how to build a custom control designer that can specify in even more detail how Visual Studio .NET should interact with our control. We'll also explore custom `TypeConverters` and custom `UITypeEditors` that further enhance design time integration with the Properties window.

> *Even though we might not list every single line of code related to the controls we build (we'll omit redundant code for reasons of space), the complete source for this chapter's samples is available in the code download for this book, which is available at http://www.wrox.com*

Extended Controls

If we want to add some functionality to an existing Windows Forms control or alter its current functionality, we can create a new control that inherits from the existing control. Even though we are talking about visual controls here, don't be confused, everything is ultimately just another class, and the standard .NET rules of inheritance still apply. Our new control would inherit all the functionality of the base control. Let's see this in action.

Creating an Extended TextBox Control

In our first example, we'll extend the standard `TextBox` control. We'll alter the functionality of the `ReadOnly` and `BackColor` properties to change the control's appearance when user input is disabled. We'll also add an `IsRequired` property, as well as an associated `propertychanged` event to provide notification when the value of the `IsRequired` property changes.

When we wish to stop user input in a TextBox, we can set its ReadOnly property to true. This has several advantages over setting the Enabled property to false. While both tactics will prevent users from changing the value of the Text property via input, using ReadOnly instead of disabling the control will still allow the TextBox's contents to be selected and copied to the clipboard. Clipboard contents, however, cannot be pasted into a TextBox whose ReadOnly property is true.

Another reason we may not want to completely disable the TextBox is that when we do, the font is automatically changed to a light color that it is barely readable. Setting the ReadOnly property to true, however, does not cause the TextBox to lose its original legible font color. It would be helpful if there was some kind of clear visual change to indicate that editing was no longer allowed, though. In this example we will make the TextBox's background color change to gray when the ReadOnly property is set to true. This gives us the best of both worlds: a font that is still legible and a background color that indicates the control will not accept input.

When it comes time for a consumer of our control to do validation processing, wouldn't it be handy to have an IsRequired property that allows our control to be marked as required or optional? While we could use the already present Tag property for such a task, I can always seem to find other uses for that Tag property, and I bet you can too. Also, since the Tag property is of type object, by defining a specific Boolean IsRequired property here we avoid having to constantly cast the object to a bool.

First we need to create and set up the project in Visual Studio .NET. (*These steps will obviously differ depending on your chosen IDE, or especially if you are using the command-line compiler.*) Begin by creating a new **Class Library** project in Visual Studio .NET. Notice we are starting a new **Class Library** project rather than a new **Windows Control Library** project. Although the compiler output for both types is the same, **Class Library**, it's often more efficient to start a simple, non-container control (like our extended TextBox) as a common **Class Library** and add any necessary references as we go. The **Windows Control Library** project template is a great starting point for building a UserControl, but it adds references and code we won't need for our simple control. Now take the following steps:

- ❑ Choose **Project | Properties** and change the **Assembly Name** to **ExtendedTextBox** and the **Default Namespace** to **Wrox.Samples.GUI**.

- ❑ Add references to System.Windows.Forms.dll and System.Drawing.dll – the regular class library project does not contain references to the forms and graphics namespaces we will need to use. Do this by selecting **Project | Add Reference**, and then looking for the filenames on the .NET tab of the **Add Reference** screen:

❑   Change the name of the class from `Class1` to `ExtTextBox`.

Now we can enter our code as follows:

```
using System;
using System.Drawing;
using System.Windows.Forms;
using System.ComponentModel;

namespace Wrox.Samples.GUI
{
  /// <summary>Simple extension of a Windows Forms TextBox</summary>

  public class ExtTextBox : System.Windows.Forms.TextBox
  {
    private Color mHoldColor;
    private bool mIsRequired;
    private System.EventHandler onIsRequiredChanged;

    /// <summary>
    /// Initializes a new instance of the Wrox.Samples.GUI.ExtTextBox class
    /// </summary>
    public ExtTextBox()
    {
    }

    /// <summary>
    /// Gets or sets a value indicating whether text in the
    /// control can be changed or not.
    /// </summary>
    /// <remarks>
    /// Replaces the ReadOnly property of TextBox. When ReadOnly
    /// is true, the BackColor is grayed out as a visual cue to the user.
```

```
/// </remarks>
[Category("Behavior"), DefaultValue(false),
Description("Gets or sets a value indicating whether text in the " +
"control can be changed or not. Also adjusts the BackColor property " +
"accordingly as a visual cue to the user.")]
new public bool ReadOnly
{
  get {return base.ReadOnly;}
  set
  {
    if (base.ReadOnly != value)
    {
      if (value)
      {
        // Push BackColor to hold color
        // before actually changing
        mHoldColor = base.BackColor;
        base.BackColor = SystemColors.Control;
      }
      else
      {
        // Pop BackColor from hold color
        base.BackColor = mHoldColor;
      }
      base.ReadOnly = value;
    }

  }

}
}
```

New Implementations For Existing Properties

First, let's discuss the code for the two properties we are changing from the base class, ReadOnly and BackColor.

If ReadOnly is being set to true, we store the control's background color in mHoldColor, then change the control's background color to SystemColors.Control – by default a shade of gray. If ReadOnly is being set to false, we want to set the background back to its original color. Note that we only do either of these things if the property is changing from its previous value – otherwise we want to leave BackColor and mHoldColor as they are. Finally, regardless of what action was taken above, we call the base class's ReadOnly property accessor – which will do everything that changing the ReadOnly property of a TextBox would normally do.

We also want to prevent the control's consumer from changing the BackColor property while the control is in read-only mode. We can do this by adding the following code to simply intercept the BackColor property set and store the color in mHoldColor for possible later use when the ReadOnly property is set to false.

```
/// <summary>
/// Gets or sets the background color of the control.
/// </summary>
/// <remarks>
/// Overriden from TextBox. If the ExtTextBox's ReadOnly
/// property is true, the BackColor is not actually changed, but is
/// saved until such time as the ReadOnly property is set to false.
/// </remarks>
[Category("Appearance"), DefaultValue(typeof(Color), "Control"),
Description("Gets or sets the background color of the control.")]
public override Color BackColor
{
  get {return base.BackColor;}
  set
  {
    if (base.ReadOnly)
    {
      // Push Color value to hold color since
      // ReadOnly BackColor should stay LightGray
      mHoldColor = value;
    }
    else
    {
      // We are free to actually change the color
      base.BackColor = value;
    }
  }
}
```

The BackColor property is declared as public override, whereas the ReadOnly property is declared as new public. Let's discuss the reason for this. Because the BackColor property of our TextBox base control was itself an overridden property from its parent class (System.Windows.Forms.TextBoxBase), we can happily override BackColor again here in our ExtTextBox class. We cannot, however, simply override the ReadOnly property because the property is not marked as virtual, abstract, or override in our TextBox base class. We can determine this by looking in the **Object Browser**, .NET Framework documentation, or ILDASM.EXE. Because of this we use a feature called **hiding** with the ReadOnly property by preceding our declaration with the new keyword and abandoning the override keyword:

```
new public bool ReadOnly
```

Just because we are implementing custom versions of these properties in our extended control, we're not required to completely reinvent them. We can, and should, still use the functionality of the base TextBox class where appropriate. As you see, after all the custom color trapping and swapping logic, we finally call the TextBox base class property get and set accessors:

```
return base.ReadOnly;        // called in our ReadOnly get
base.ReadOnly = value;       // eventually called in our ReadOnly set

base.BackColor = value;      // sometimes called in our BackColor get
return base.BackColor;       // called in our BackColor get
```

The Importance of XML Documentation and Attributes

As we mentioned before, the design-time behavior of a custom control should not be forgotten in the zeal to develop cool run-time behavior. XML documentation and attributes are some of the simplest ways of enhancing a control consumer's design-time experience in RAD tools such as Visual Studio .NET and others that adhere to the .NET designer architecture.

XML Documentation

I think that as developers, most of us would agree that doing documentation is a pretty dreary task. We should definitely use XML documentation liberally because it feeds information to **Object Browser** and the IntelliSense help system in the editor. Would we appreciate having to use a component that did not provide any of this help we have come to rely on so much in a RAD environment? Of course not, and neither would the eventual consumers of our control.

With XML documentation, the .NET Framework goes a long way to lighten the burden of documentation. In our example we've already keyed in source that is sprinkled with information contained in XML documentation tags (items preceded by / / / instead of the regular C# comment prefix of / /). When we finally build our control, we can instruct the compiler to generate an XML document for us that contains all the information we have tagged throughout our source code.

> *The XML documentation files Microsoft produced with the regular .NET Framework assemblies reside in the same directory as the assemblies themselves (possibly in \WINNT\Microsoft.NET\Framework\v1.0.3705 depending on the particulars of your installation).*

We won't look at all the available tags, but the following table lists some of the more frequently used tags.

Tag	Description
<summary>	Specifies a summary of the class or member.
<remarks>	Specifies a longer description of the class or member.
<param>	Specifies the name and description for a parameter of a method.
<returns>	Specifies a description of the return value of a method.
<example>	Specifies an example of how to use a member.
<code>	Identifies the contained text comment as code. Commonly used within an <example> section to provide sample code for a member.
<exception>	Specifies which exceptions a class can throw.

One nice feature provided by Visual Studio is a mechanism to browse these XML documentation files in a pleasant style. Selecting the **Tools | Build Comment Web Pages** option produces a handy set of pages for our control in the directory of our choosing. Overleaf is a sample from the pages generated for our finished ExtTextBox control.

Industrious and generous people have already developed XSLT (stylesheet transformation) files and utilities for the .NET XML documentation schema that they have made freely available to the .NET community. See http://ndoc.sourceforge.net and the archives at http://www.discuss.develop.com.

Visual Studio-Friendly Attributes

Attributes are markers we can supply within brackets above classes and members. The Properties window in Visual Studio .NET is mainly composed of a `PropertyGrid` object. The grid relies heavily on attributes to provide a rich design time experience with control and component members so we should make use of attributes with each of our custom properties and events. Some of the more frequently used attributes are described in the following table.

Attribute	Description
Category	Defines the category grouping for the property or event in a `PropertyGrid`
DefaultValue	Defines a default value for a property
Description	Defines a description for the property or event
Browsable	Defines whether the `PropertyGrid` should display a property or event
DefaultEvent	Designates an event as the default event of a component
DefaultProperty	Designates a property as the default property of a component

The preceding table lists only a few of the nearly 30 attributes available in the `System.ComponentModel` namespace. Later in the chapter we'll see two more, `Designer` and `Editor`, in action. Also it is important to note that the `DefaultValue` attribute will only work for simple types. In our composite control example later in the chapter we'll show another way to specify defaults in circumstances where you have a property that is a complex type, like a `Font`, for instance.

Yes, even with these nice shiny new tools, documentation is still tiresome. We'll see some of the design-time behavior fruits of this labor a bit later though when we use our control in an application. It will be evident then that failing to make use of attributes and XML documentation in controls and components built for .NET RAD is unconscionable.

Adding Our Own Properties and Events

Well, we've modified a couple of properties from our base control, but while we have the hood open let's explore adding our own properties and events. Let's implement an IsRequired property and associated change notification event by adding the following highlighted lines of code to our control.

```csharp
public class ExtTextBox : System.Windows.Forms.TextBox
{
  private Color mHoldColor;
  private bool mIsRequired;
  private System.EventHandler onIsRequiredChanged;

  public ExtTextBox() {}

  new public bool ReadOnly  {// Code Omitted for clarity}

  public override Color BackColor  {// Code Omitted for clarity}
```

```csharp
  /// <summary>
  /// Occurs when the ExtTextBox.IsRequired property value changes.
  /// </summary>
  [Category("Property Changed"), Browsable(true),
  Description("Occurs when the IsRequired property value changes.")]
  public event EventHandler IsRequiredChanged
  {
    add {onIsRequiredChanged += value;}
    remove {onIsRequiredChanged -= value;}
  }


  /// <summary>
  /// Raises the ExtendedTextBox.ExtTextBox.IsRequiredChanged event.
  /// </summary>
  /// <param name="e">
  /// A System.EventArgs object that contains the event data.
  /// </param>
  protected virtual void OnIsRequiredChanged (EventArgs e)
  {
    if (onIsRequiredChanged != null)
    {
      onIsRequiredChanged(this, e);
    }
  }


  /// <summary>
  /// Gets or sets a value indicating whether the control is required.
  /// </summary>
  [Category("Behavior"), DefaultValue(false),
  Description("Gets or sets a value indicating whether the control " +
  "is required.")]
  public bool IsRequired
  {
    get {return mIsRequired;}
    set
    {
      if (!mIsRequired.Equals(value))
```

```
        {
            mIsRequired = value;
            OnIsRequiredChanged(EventArgs.Empty);
        }
    }
}
}
```

We declare a private `System.EventHandler` delegate named `onIsRequiredChanged`. Next we create the publicly visible event named `IsRequiredChanged`. Note that this public member uses the explicit `event` keyword. Much like a property with its `get` and `set` accessors, an `event` has its own custom accessors named `add` and `remove`. We use these accessors to link the event to our underlying private `onIsRequiredChanged` delegate. This allows consumers of our control to subscribe to and unsubscribe from the event.

The `OnIsRequiredChanged` method actually raises the event by invoking the delegate. We check to see if the `EventHandler` delegate `onIsRequiredChanged` is empty (`null`). If it is not null, then it means there are some subscribed handler methods so we invoke the delegate to call the methods in the delegate's list. We populate the first parameter, `sender`, with the object `this` (meaning our control). For the second parameter, `EventArgs`, we simply pass along the `EventArgs` object that was passed into the `OnIsRequiredChanged` method. By marking our `OnIsRequiredChanged` method as protected and virtual, we follow the pattern set in the standard `Windows.Forms` controls. This way, controls that inherit from our `ExtTextBox` control will have the ability to override the method if desired.

Finally we get to our actual `IsRequired` property implementation. In the `set` accessor, we check to see if the value being passed in is different from the current value of our private property value holder. If it is indeed different, then we change the value of our private holder and then call our `OnIsRequiredChanged` method to actually raise the event.

Building a DLL

Before building our `ExtTextBox` control, let's add a bitmap to our project that will display with our control in the Visual Studio **Toolbox**. We must be sure the bitmap is named the same as the class of our control (we'll need `ExtTextBox.bmp`) Choose **Add Existing Item** in our project and select the bitmap. Be sure to choose **Embedded Resource** as the **Build Action** of the bitmap properties. (`ExtTextBox.bmp` is included with the code download for this chapter.)

Next, even though we have added all manner of nice XML documentation to our source, the compiler will ignore it unless we specify an output file. The default build configuration is debug mode so the DLL file will be placed in the \bin\debug directory under the project. So let's go into the Project | Properties for our project and specify the full pathname and ExtendedTextBox.xml for our documentation file (see following image). This will place the XML file and the DLL file together.

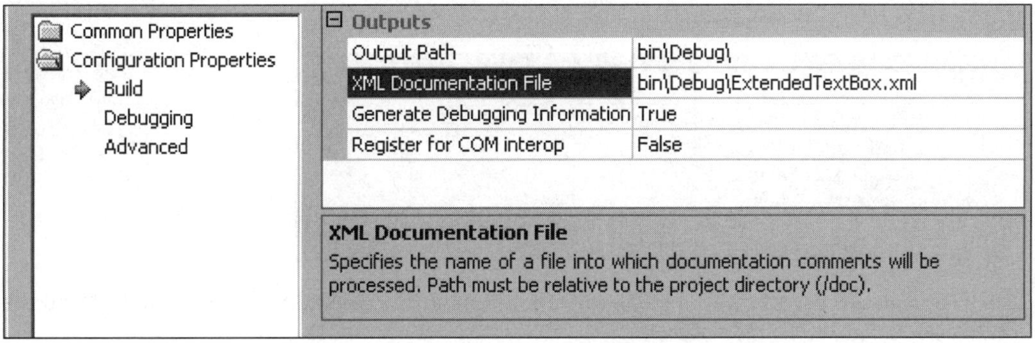

Now we can build the ExtendedTextBox project. The following lines show an example of the switches necessary to create our control with the command line compiler

```
csc /target:library /out:bin\Debug\ ExtendedTextBox.dll
/doc:bin\Debug\ExtendedTextBox.xml ExtendedTextBox.cs
```

The full source for this control is in the ExtendedTextBox *project of the chapter code download.*

Consuming Our Extended TextBox Control

It's time to build a simple Windows Application project to put our ExtTextBox control through its design-time and run-time paces. When we built our control project, we created an assembly called ExtendedTextBox.dll. It is possible to simply add a reference to the DLL in our new project and then begin using Wrox.Samples.GUI.ExtTextBox in code. But what about letting the Visual Studio .NET IDE host our control in the designer's Toolbox where we can drag and drop it like a standard control?

After creating a new C# Windows Application project, right-click on the Windows Forms tab in the Toolbox and select Customize Toolbox. Now, in the .NET Framework Components tab of the Customize Toolbox dialog box, select the Browse button and find the file ExtendedTextBox.dll in the \Bin\Debug directory of the earlier ExtendedTextBox project. Once selected, ExtTextBox and our simple bitmap appear in the Toolbox list (following image on the left):

Click OK and now our ExtTextBox control is conveniently located in the Toolbox on the Windows Forms tab (image on the right above).

> *The full source for this consumer form is in the* frmMain.cs *file of the* ExtendedControlTest *folder in the chapter code download.*

Add the following controls to the main form:

- ❑ One ExtTextBox control named myExtendedTextBox
- ❑ One Button control named btnBackColor
- ❑ Three CheckBox controls – named chkEnabled, chkReadOnly, and chkIsRequired
- ❑ One ColorDialog component named myColorDialog

Arrange the controls as desired; the preceding screenshot offers an example configuration.

Next, add the following to the form's constructor:

```
public frmMain()
{
  // Required for Windows Form Designer support
  InitializeComponent();

    this.chkEnabled.CheckedChanged +=
        new System.EventHandler(ToggleEnabled);
    this.chkReadOnly.CheckedChanged +=
        new System.EventHandler(ToggleReadOnly);
    this.chkIsRequired.CheckedChanged +=
        new System.EventHandler(ToggleIsRequired);
    this.btnBackColor.Click +=
        new System.EventHandler(ChangeBackColor);
    this.myExtendedTextBox.IsRequiredChanged +=
        new System.EventHandler(NotifyRequiredChange);

    this.chkEnabled.Checked = myExtendedTextBox.Enabled;
    this.chkReadOnly.Checked = myExtendedTextBox.ReadOnly;
    this.chkIsRequired.Checked = myExtendedTextBox.IsRequired;
}
```

Having done that, add the following methods to the form class:

```
private void ToggleEnabled(object sender, System.EventArgs e)
{
  myExtendedTextBox.Enabled = ((CheckBox)sender).Checked;
}

private void ToggleReadOnly(object sender, System.EventArgs e)
{
  myExtendedTextBox.ReadOnly = ((CheckBox)sender).Checked;
}

private void ChangeBackColor(object sender, System.EventArgs e)
{
  ColorDialog myColorDialog = new ColorDialog();
  myColorDialog.AllowFullOpen = false;
  myColorDialog.Color = myExtendedTextBox.BackColor;
  myColorDialog.ShowDialog();
  myExtendedTextBox.BackColor = myColorDialog.Color;
}

private void ToggleIsRequired(object sender, System.EventArgs e)
{
  myExtendedTextBox.IsRequired = ((CheckBox)sender).Checked;
}

private void NotifyRequiredChange(object sender, System.EventArgs e)
{
```

```
    MessageBox.Show(this, "Changed To: " +
        myExtendedTextBox.IsRequired.ToString(), "IsRequired Has Changed");
}
```

The code in this form is not complicated; we merely create some event handler methods and subscribe to the events of our `Button` and `CheckBox` controls. We try to exercise all the custom events and properties we implemented in our `ExtTextBox` control.

Now build and run the project. We can see that selecting the **Read Only** box will gray out the `ExtTextBox`'s background, while leaving a nice, legible black font. Clicking the **BackColor** button will invoke a standard `ColorDialog` so we can select a new color. Provided the `ExtTextBox` is not in read-only mode, the `BackColor` property will be changed. If the textbox is in read-only mode then color changes will be held in reserve and take effect once read-only is turned off:

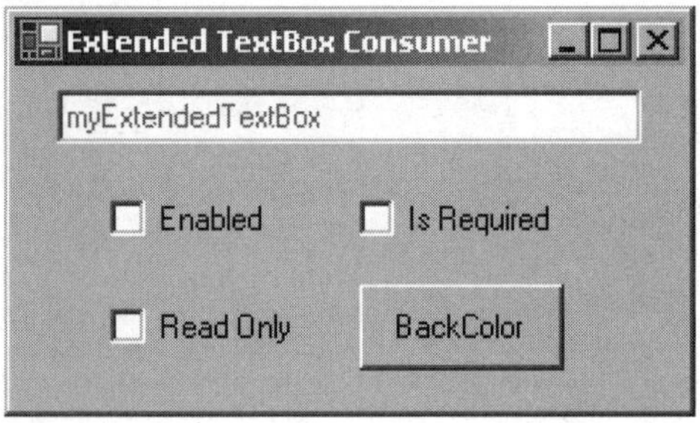

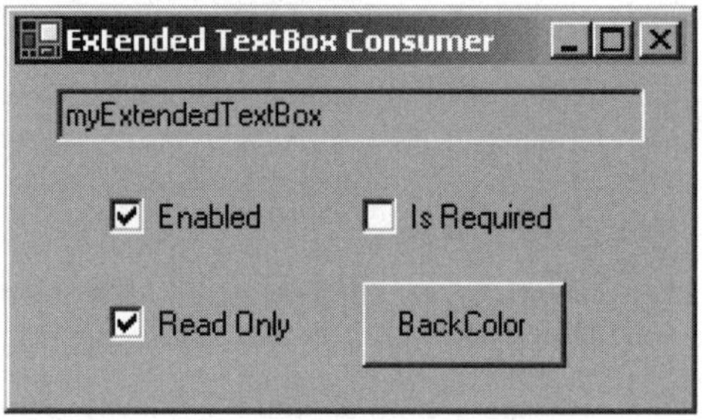

Checking the `Enabled` box will allow for a quick comparison to prove that our custom read-only user cue is indeed a superior implementation of communicating the fact that the control will not allow any changes by the user.

Checking the **Is Required** box will display a `MessageBox` proving to us that the consumer form is successfully subscribed to our custom `ExtTextBox.IsRequiredChanged` event.

Attributes and XML Doc in Action at Design Time

After stopping the application, look back on the form design surface and select our `myExtendedTextBox` control. Now look in the **Properties** window. The bottom of the following screenshots show the `PropertyGrid` displaying the `Description` attributes we specified for the `IsRequired` and `ReadOnly` properties. We can also see that the `Category` (`"Behavior"`) attribute that we associated with the `IsRequired` property has caused the `PropertyGrid` to include the property under the **Behavior** heading.

We also decorated both the `IsRequired` and `ReadOnly` properties with `DefaultValue(false)` attributes. We can see that the `PropertyGrid` does not display these property values in bold unless we change them to `true`. We can also look at the designer-generated `InitializeComponent` method in code to see that the designer serializes neither of these properties unless we change their value to `true` in the **Properties** window.

Clicking on the lightning bolt icon on the `PropertyGrid` toolbar will display events instead of properties and allow us to confirm that our `IsRequiredChanged` property and its description are correctly displayed in the `PropertyGrid`.

Let's use the **View | Other Windows | Object Browser** option to see how our XML documentation efforts turned out. Look at the `extendedtextbox` assembly and find our `Wrox.Samples.GUI.ExtTextBox` control. By viewing the `BackColor` member, we can see the results of our `<summary>` and `<remarks>` tags (screenshot overleaf).

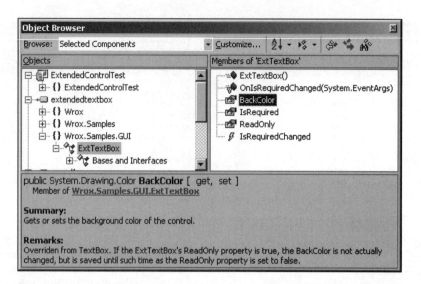

Also, while keying in the code for this test consumer project in Visual Studio .NET, you may have noticed and taken for granted the editor IntelliSense member list, statement completion, and tooltips for our control. This IntelliSense experience would not be nearly as robust had we not taken the time to produce the XML documentation for our control. Just like the Object Browser, IntelliSense will interrogate our control and its XML documentation file to retrieve relevant information.

```
ColorDialog myColorDialog = new ColorDialog();
myColorDialog.AllowFullOpen = false;
myColorDialog.Color = myExtendedTextBox.BackColor;
myColorDialog.ShowDialog();
myExtendedTextBox.BackColor =  myColorDi
```

[property] System.Drawing.Color ExtTextBox.BackColor
Gets or sets the background color of the control.

Well, that wraps up our example of extending an existing common control. We can see that extending an existing control, even when providing thorough metadata and XML documentation, is a relatively easy task with C# and the .NET Framework. Now let's look at using several of our ExtTextBox controls as building blocks in a larger composite control.

Composite Controls

Extending existing common controls is fine for the case of a single control. If we want to combine several controls and treat them like one, however, the System.Windows.Forms.UserControl class should be our base. Both the Form class and the UserControl class are derived from System.Windows.Forms.ContainerControl so they can encapsulate other controls and components. An address control consisting of Street, City, State, and Postal Code textboxes is an obvious candidate for an example. Let's explore composite controls by building a robust UserControl-derived address control whose core is composed of several of the extended TextBox controls we created in our first example. We'll selectively expose certain aspects of these constituent controls, encapsulate address validation within the control itself, look deeper at using attributes to hide unwanted members, then finally implement a custom designer to provide greater control over the design-time experience for consumers of our control.

Creating a Composite AddressControl

First, let's start a new **Windows Control Library** project and name it `CompositeControl`.
Just as we can for a `Form`, we can view either the code or a designer surface for the `UserControl1`
class. When we create this project the all too familiar constructor, `InitializeComponent` method,
and `Dispose` method we're accustomed to with forms are also added to the `UserControl1` class for us.
Let's go ahead and change the `Name` property of the `UserControl` to `AddressControl`.

> If you haven't already added the finished **Wrox.Samples.GUI.ExtTextBox** control to
> the Visual Studio Toolbox (see the previous control example) then you'll want to do so
> now. At the very least, we'll need to add a reference to the finished
> **ExtendedTextBox.dll** residing in the **\Bin\Debug** directory of the previous
> control project.

❑ Add five `Wrox.Samples.GUI.ExtTextBox` controls named `txtLine1`, `txtLine2`,
`txtCity`, `txtState`, and `txtZipCode`

❑ Add four standard `Label` controls named `lblAddress`, `lblCity`, `lblState`, `lblZip`. Now
set the `Text` properties of the lables to **Address**, **City**, **State**, and **Zip** respectively.

Arrange the controls in a similar way to the screenshot above. We should go ahead now and set the
`TabIndex` property of each address `ExtTextBox` control to the proper order. This is a good time to
point out that once we have our finished address control running as part of an application, the control
itself will never accept focus. Anytime a `UserControl` would receive focus, it defers to the tab order of
its constituent controls and shifts the focus to one of them.

The full version of the `AddressControl` source included in the chapter code download is over 800
lines of code. This code listing alone would take up about 11 pages in its entirety, even without
discussion or explanation. While I can't stress enough how important it is to include those XML
comments for the consumers of our controls and components, for the sake of brevity, clarity, and sanity,
we'll omit them in the chapter text here as we display code.

As we build up the features of our control example, we'll also be adding many properties and events for
our text and label controls that provide exactly the same functionality, just for different constituent
controls. In those cases we will show only one of these redundant members in the chapter text as a
guide for you to implement the other similar members.

*The full source, including the designer-generated code region and all XML documentation tags can
be found in the `AddressControl.cs` file of the `AddressControl` project in the chapter
code download.*

To get started coding, change the designer-generated code so it matches the listing below.

```csharp
using System;
using System.Collections;
using System.ComponentModel;
using System.ComponentModel.Design;
using System.Drawing;
using System.Drawing.Design;
using System.Reflection;
using System.Text;
using System.Windows.Forms;

namespace Wrox.Samples.GUI
{
  [Description("Composite Control Example")]
  public class AddressControl : System.Windows.Forms.UserControl
  {
    private Wrox.Samples.GUI.ExtTextBox txtLine1;
    private Wrox.Samples.GUI.ExtTextBox txtLine2;
    private Wrox.Samples.GUI.ExtTextBox txtCity;
    private Wrox.Samples.GUI.ExtTextBox txtState;
    private Wrox.Samples.GUI.ExtTextBox txtZipCode;

    private System.Windows.Forms.Label lblAddress;
    private System.Windows.Forms.Label lblCity;
    private System.Windows.Forms.Label lblState;
    private System.Windows.Forms.Label lblZip;

    private System.ComponentModel.Container components = null;

    public AddressControl()
    {
      InitializeComponent();
    }

    protected override void Dispose( bool disposing )
    {
      if( disposing )
      {
        if( components != null ) components.Dispose();
      }
      base.Dispose( disposing );
    }

    //< Omitted Component Designer generated code>
  }
}
```

Providing Access to Our Constituent Controls

Select any of the `ExtTextBox` and `Label` controls we have added to our `UserControl`. Look at the `Modifiers` property in the **Design** section of the **Properties** window. Notice the default value is **Private**. It is best practice to leave this as **Private**, and in fact it is hardly ever a good idea to change this to **Public**. Instead we should write explicit public accessor properties and methods to selectively expose certain aspects of our constituent controls to the consumers of our composite control.

Later, we'll see that we want certain properties of our groups of controls to stay synchronized, but certainly there is a need for the `Text` property of each of our constituent controls to be unique. First, let's implement a property named `AddressLine1Text` to give public access to the `Text` property of our `txtLine1` control.

```
[Category("Address"),
Description("Gets or sets the text in the Address Line 1 Control.")]
public string AddressLine1Text
{
  get {return this.txtLine1.Text;}
  set {this.txtLine1.Text = value;}
}
```

Next, instead of exposing an event and an `OnPropertyNameChanged` method (refer back to the `OnIsRequiredChanged` method in of the `ExtTextBox` control itself), for simplicity's sake we can just provide an appropriately named public accessor to our `txtLine1.TextChanged` event delegate. Here we name it `AddressLine1TextChanged`.

```
[Category("Property Changed"),
Description("Occurs when the AddressLine1Text property value changes.")]
public event EventHandler AddressLine1TextChanged
{
  add {this.txtLine1.TextChanged += value;}
  remove {this.txtLine1.TextChanged -= value;}
}
```

Now that we've exposed our `txtLine1` control, we can add similar property and event implementations for each of our other `ExtTextBox` controls: txtLine2, txtCity, txtState, and txtZipCode. By implementing AddressLine1Text, AddressLine2Text, CityText, StateText, and ZipCodeText properties and textchanged events, we provide access to the contents of each of the `ExtTextBox` controls that make up the heart of our control. The `Label` controls are static, so there is no need to expose their `Text` properties.

So far we have specifically exposed selected unique members of our `ExtTextBox` controls. Now we'll create some `AddressControl` members that pertain to all the `ExtTextBox` controls as a group. Let's start with a `Clear` method to blank out the text in the address entry boxes.

```
public void Clear()
{
  SetAddressProperty("Text", null);
}
```

Since we plan to have several of these group-level members, we don't want to constantly repeat txtLine1, txtLine2, CityText, StateText, and ZipCodeText. We can build a private method for our AddressControl to use internally to set a specified property for these constituent controls. The GetProperty method of a Type returns a PropertyInfo object we can utilize for numerous controls of that type. The SetValue method of the PropertyInfo class allows us to specify the object whose property we want to set and the value we want assigned to that property. Here in the SetAddressProperty method we assign the same value to a specified property for all the ExtTextBox controls that make up our address.

```
private void SetAddressProperty(string PropertyName, object NewValue)
{
  PropertyInfo pi = (typeof(ExtTextBox)).GetProperty(PropertyName);
  pi.SetValue(this.txtLine1, NewValue, null);
  pi.SetValue(this.txtLine2, NewValue, null);
  pi.SetValue(this.txtCity, NewValue, null);
  pi.SetValue(this.txtState, NewValue, null);
  pi.SetValue(this.txtZipCode, NewValue, null);
}
```

Now we can utilize this method to ensure that the BackColor and ForeColor properties of all our address boxes remain in sync.

```
[Category("Address"), DefaultValue(typeof(Color), "Window"),
Description("Gets or sets the background color used to display text "
+ "in all Address ExtTextBoxes displayed by the control.")]
public Color AddressBackColor
{
  get {return txtLine1.BackColor;}
  set {SetAddressProperty("BackColor", value);}
}

[Category("Property Changed"),
Description("Occurs when the AddressBackColor property value changes.")]
public event EventHandler AddressBackColorChanged
{
  add {this.txtLine1.BackColorChanged += value;}
  remove {this.txtLine1.BackColorChanged -= value;}
}
```

Wait a minute, if this AddressBackColor property is supposed to be for all our address boxes, why is it reading a value from only txtLine1 in the get accessor? Well, we could have gone to the trouble to maintain a private property field in our control and set it before calling the SetAddressProperty method, but that would just be extra overhead. We are providing controlled access to these properties and enforcing that they are all the same value. When we need to query a property value for the whole group why not just pick one of the address boxes and let it be the spokesperson for all the others? We'll also just provide a public accessor to the txtLine1.BackColorChanged event delegate to represent the entire group of controls.

Now we can follow the pattern of AddressBackColor/AddressBackColorChanged and define property/propertychanged members for AddressForeColor/AddressForeColorChanged.

Let's also implement a ReadOnly property for our AddressControl. We aren't naming the property AddressReadOnly because the property's context does essentially apply to the whole control since our address ExtTextBox controls are the only constituent controls in our UserControl that support editing and a ReadOnly property.

We can just follow the pattern of our AddressBackColor and AddressForeColor properties (and their associated PropertyNameChanged events).

```
[Category("Behavior"), DefaultValue(false),
Description("Gets or sets a value indicating whether the Address can be "
+ "changed by the user or not.")]
public bool ReadOnly
{
  get {return txtLine1.ReadOnly;}
  set {SetAddressProperty("ReadOnly", value);}
}

[Category("Property Changed"),
Description("Occurs when the ReadOnly property value changes.")]
public event EventHandler ReadOnlyChanged
{
 add {this.txtLine1.ReadOnlyChanged += value;}
 remove {this.txtLine1.ReadOnlyChanged -= value;}
 }
```

Let's also override the ToString method of our UserControl base. If we simply allowed our AddressControl to inherit the ToString functionality of the base then the method would return the namespace and control name. This isn't very helpful, so we use ToString to provide a relevant string representation of the value of the object. In this case, we use a StringBuilder to create a formatted address from the current values of our address ExtTextBoxes.

```
public override string ToString()
{
  StringBuilder myText = new StringBuilder(txtLine1.Text + "\n");
  if (!(txtLine2.Text.Length == 0))
  {
    myText.Append(txtLine2.Text + "\n");
  }
  myText.Append(txtCity.Text + ", ");
  myText.Append(txtState.Text + "  ");
  myText.Append(txtZipCode.Text);
  return myText.ToString().TrimEnd("\n, ".ToCharArray());
}
```

Well, that's about all the time we can devote to the address ExtTextBox controls; now let's add some properties and methods for our Label controls. Again, using our address property implementations as a model, let's provide a mechanism for consumers of our control to change all label background and foreground colors. We'll use the first Label control, lblAddress, for our LabelPropertyName get and event accessors just as we used txtLine1 for our address box controls earlier.

```
[Category("Labels"), Description("Gets or sets the background color of "
+ "the text in all labels displayed by the control."),
DefaultValue(typeof(Color), "Control")]
public Color LabelBackColor
{
  get {return lblAddress.BackColor;}
  set {SetLabelsProperty("BackColor", value);}
}

[Category("Property Changed"),
Description("Occurs when the LabelBackColor property value changes.")]
public event EventHandler LabelBackColorChanged
{
  add {this.lblAddress.BackColorChanged += value;}
  remove {this.lblAddress.BackColorChanged -= value;}
}
```

Earlier we implemented a SetAddressProperty method to apply a common property value to all our ExtTextBox controls. In the following code we'll implement a SetLabelsProperty method to do the same for our Label controls.

```
private void SetLabelsProperty(string PropertyName, object NewValue)
{
  PropertyInfo pi = (typeof(Label)).GetProperty(PropertyName);
  pi.SetValue(this.lblAddress, NewValue, null);
  pi.SetValue(this.lblCity, NewValue, null);
  pi.SetValue(this.lblState, NewValue, null);
  pi.SetValue(this.lblZip, NewValue, null);
}
```

Follow the pattern of LabelBackColor/LabelBackColorChanged and define a property/propertychanged pair for LabelForeColor/LabelForeColorChanged.

Now let's expose a Font property for all our labels too. The LabelBackColor and LabelForeColor implementations were so similar, we only showed one, but we'll look at a LabelFont implementation in detail because we have an interesting situation with design time property serialization.

```
[Category("Labels"), Description("Gets or sets the font of the text in all "
+ "labels displayed by the control.")]
public Font LabelFont
{
  get {return lblAddress.Font;}
  set {SetLabelsProperty("Font", value);}
}

[Category("Property Changed"),
Description("Occurs when the LabelFont property value changes.")]
public event EventHandler LabelFontChanged
{
  add {this.lblAddress.FontChanged += value;}
  remove {this.lblAddress.FontChanged -= value;}
}
```

Well, that looked wearily familiar, except that we didn't specify a `DefaultValue` attribute. So far the attribute has served us well to define a value to guide designers like Visual Studio .NET in determining whether they should or should not generate code in the `InitializeComponent` method. We mentioned earlier that the `DefaultValue` attribute was only good for simpler types (`bool`, `string`, `System.Drawing.Color`, etc.). With a more complex value like a `Font`, we have to take another approach.

If the designer does not find a `DefaultValue` attribute for a property, it then searches for methods named `ShouldSerializePropertyName` and `ResetPropertyName` to determine whether to generate code and whether to enable the right-click **Reset** option in the **Properties Window**. The `ShouldSerializePropertyName` method returns a boolean value that specifies whether the current value is the same as the default value. The `ResetPropertyName` method provides an implementation to actually reset the property value to the default value. Below we implement these methods using the static `DefaultFont` property value of `System.Windows.Forms.Control` to insure we get the desired designer behavior.

```
private bool ShouldSerializeLabelFont()
{
  return (LabelFont != Control.DefaultFont);
}

private void ResetLabelFont()
{
  LabelFont = Control.DefaultFont;
}
```

Encapsulating Validation

Another common benefit of a composite control is the ability to hide validation relating to the constituent controls within the black box of the `UserControl`. We might load some complex validation rules from an XML file, but for ease of illustration, we'll just hard-code some validation rules. The point is that the rules are enforced within the control itself, and consumers need only be aware of any public methods, properties, or events we choose to expose regarding validation.

Let's go back to the constructor of our `AddressControl`. We'll initialize the `IsRequired` property for each of our `ExtTextBox` controls by adding the following code right after the `InitializeComponent` method call. Remember the `IsRequired` property was an enhancement we added when we extended the regular `TextBox` in our previous chapter example. Not all addresses need a two line street address, so we'll mark the second line entry as not required. We'll also place a meaningful description of each control's contents in its `Tag` property for later use in error messages.

```
public AddressControl()
{
  InitializeComponent();

  txtLine1.IsRequired = true;
  txtLine2.IsRequired = false;
  txtCity.IsRequired = true;
  txtState.IsRequired = true;
  txtZipCode.IsRequired = true;
```

```
    txtLine1.Tag = "Address Line 1";
    txtLine2.Tag = "Address Line 2";
    txtCity.Tag = "City";
    txtState.Tag = "State";
    txtZipCode.Tag = "Zip Code";
}
```

We'll make a Boolean method that takes an `ExtTextBox`, checks its `IsRequired` property, and returns `false` if the field is required and empty. If the `displayErrors` argument is `true`, then we change the focus to the invalid control, and use that `Tag` property we set earlier to return a little more user-friendly message pointing out which control is invalid.

```
// Validate an ExtTextBox if IsRequired == true
private bool IsExtTextBoxValid(ExtTextBox boxToTest, bool displayErrors)
{
  if (boxToTest.IsRequired && boxToTest.Text.Length == 0)
  {
    if (displayErrors)
    {
      boxToTest.Focus();
      MessageBox.Show(this, String.Format("The {0} field is required.",
                      boxToTest.Tag), "Invalid Field");
    }
    return false;
  }
  return true;
}
```

Now we can make a Boolean `ValidateAll` method to check each of our address boxes. This method takes a `bool` parameter as well, so it knows whether to pop up a message or quietly just return a Boolean value to its caller. This way, we can use the method in a property and a method we will craft.

```
// Validate all concerned ExtTextBoxes
private bool ValidateAll(bool displayErrors)
{
  if (!IsExtTextBoxValid(txtLine1, displayErrors))
  {
    return false;
  }
  if (!IsExtTextBoxValid(txtLine2, displayErrors))
  {
    return false;
  }
  if (!IsExtTextBoxValid(txtCity, displayErrors))
  {
    return false;
  }
  if (!IsExtTextBoxValid(txtState, displayErrors))
  {
    return false;
  }
  if (!IsExtTextBoxValid(txtZipCode, displayErrors))
```

```
  {
    return false;
  }
  return true;
}
```

We expose an `IsAddressValid` bool property that calls our `ValidateAll` method, suppressing any pop-up messages so we simply get `true` or `false`. Notice we set the `Browsable` attribute to `false` so this property with a run-time context will not be shown in the design-time **Properties** window. Our `ValidateAddress` method calls the `ValidateAll` method with the parameter set to cause notification of which entry is invalid.

```
[Category("Address"), Browsable(false),
Description("Gets a value indicating whether the Address information "
+ "passes all specified validation rules. Returns a simple true or "
+ "false value without displaying any exception messages.")]
public bool IsAddressValid
{
  get {return this.ValidateAll(false);}
}

public void ValidateAddress()
{
  this.ValidateAll(true);
}
```

Hiding Members

Although we can't really get rid of an unwanted member we have inherited, we can hide the member from IntelliSense much in the same way we have already hidden some properties from view in the **Properties** window. We have hidden members with the `Browsable` attribute so far in our examples, but now we will use the `EditorBrowsable` attribute.

Possible values for this attribute are in the `EditorBrowsableState` enum: Never, Always, or Advanced. `Always` is default, `Never` is also obvious, but what about Advanced? Advanced is a setting that an editor can choose to show or suppress depending on options. In the **Tools | Options | Text Editor | C# | General Statement Completion** section, for example, there is a checkbox to **Hide advanced members**.

Let's add the following code to our `AddressControl` class to hide some properties.

```
[EditorBrowsable(EditorBrowsableState.Never)]
new public Control.ControlCollection Controls
{
  get {return base.Controls;}
}

[EditorBrowsable(EditorBrowsableState.Never)]
new public Color ForeColor
{
  get {return base.ForeColor;}
```

```
    set {base.ForeColor = value;}
  }

  [EditorBrowsable(EditorBrowsableState.Never)]
  new public System.Drawing.Font Font
  {
    get {return base.Font;}
    set {base.Font = value;}
  }
```

Here the only reason we implement these properties is to add this attribute so we simply defer the implementation back to the base for all circumstances.

Even with this "hiding", a user of our control can find out that the property exists and simply type it into the code editor to use it. In the real world we can't rely on some consumer to not fool around with these members, but we could add some XML documentation tags to alert consumers that these members are either not used by our control (Font and ForeColor), or not meant to be used directly by consumers (Controls).

Implementing a Custom ControlDesigner

Now we'll look at creating a custom designer for our AddressControl. In the .NET Framework, a designer is a class that manages the design-time appearance and behavior of a component. For instance, the System.Windows.Forms.Design.UserControlDocumentDesigner associated with the UserControl class provided the means for us to drag and drop our ExtTextBox and Label controls on the UserControl design canvas. Of course, each constituent control we site on the UserControl has its own designer to manage its behavior within the design container.

What will our custom designer do? At first we'll concentrate on hiding some properties and events we inherited from UserControl. We've accomplished some of this type of member filtering already with EditorBrowsable and Browsable attributes. However, one reason we might want to implement member filtering with a custom designer instead of with attributes is that we would not be required to actually add a custom implementation of a member to our control solely so we can decorate it with an attribute.

System.Windows.Forms.Design.ControlDesigner is the base designer from which most other control designers are derived. Because we did not specify a designer for our ExtTextBox control, it simply inherited the System.Windows.Forms.Design.TextBoxBaseDesigner associated with its base TextBox control. For our AddressControl, we'll use the basic ControlDesigner as our base to implement a custom designer named AddressControlDesigner.

Why not derive our AddressControlDesigner from UserControlDocumentDesigner since our AddressControl itself is derived from UserControl? We have to keep focused on just which design-time we are talking about: the one we are in right now, or the one we'll be in later when we are consuming our AddressControl. As we discussed earlier, the UserControlDocumentDesigner is actually governing our design-time experience as we assemble our AddressControl from other controls.

The base `ControlDesigner` is appropriate for us because when our `AddressControl` is a finished deployed component being used by consumer projects it will function as a single control in design time and run time. If we were actually building a control that acted as a container of other controls both at design time and run time then `System.Windows.Forms.Design.ParentControlDesigner` or one of its derivatives might be appropriate.

We'll need to add a reference to `System.Design.dll` in our `AddressControl` project in order to access `System.Windows.Forms.Design.ControlDesigner`.

Earlier in the chapter we discussed attributes, but we alluded to the `Designer` attribute. Now we'll see it in action as we associate our `AddressControl` class with the custom designer we are about to create. Add the following line after the `Description` attribute of our `AddressControl` class:

```
[Description("Composite Control Example"),
Designer(typeof(AddressControl.AddressControlDesigner))]
public class AddressControl : System.Windows.Forms.UserControl
{
  // AddressControl code omitted for brevity
}
```

We specify the designer type as `AddressControl.AddressControlDesigner` because we will actually implement our designer as an internal class within the `AddressControl` itself. This is just for simplicity. Nothing prevents us from actually implementing designers as a fully separate class, or even in a separate DLL as long as our `Designer` attribute contains the proper type reference. Let's go ahead and add the following code to the end of our `AddressControl` class:

```
internal class AddressControlDesigner :
             System.Windows.Forms.Design.ControlDesigner
{
  public AddressControlDesigner()
  {
  }

  protected override void PostFilterProperties(IDictionary Properties)
  {
    Properties.Remove("ForeColor");
    Properties.Remove("Font");
    base.PostFilterProperties(Properties);
  }

  protected override void PostFilterEvents(IDictionary Events)
  {
    Events.Remove("ForeColorChanged");
    Events.Remove("FontChanged");
    Events.Remove("TextChanged");
    base.PostFilterEvents(Events);
  }
}
```

These two filter methods hail from the System.ComponentModel.Design.IDesignerFilter interface that is implemented by ComponentDesigner and ControlDesigner. The following table lists the IDesignerFilter methods.

IDesignerFilter Method	Description
PostFilterAttributes()	Change or remove attributes exposed by the control
PreFilterAttributes()	Add attributes exposed by the control
PostFilterEvents()	Change or remove events exposed by the control
PreFilterEvents()	Add events exposed by the control
PostFilterProperties()	Change or remove properties exposed by the control
PreFilterProperties()	Add properties exposed by the control

All these methods are passed an IDictionary interface to a collection of members of the control being designed. Our implementation of the PostFilterProperties method removes the Font and ForeColor properties from the collection. We filter out their associated change events in our PostFilterEvents implementation. The UserControl class already hides the Text property with attributes, but doesn't hide its associated TextChanged event. We'll go ahead and take care of that here in our designer.

Notice in both our methods we call the base implementation after our custom removals. For the set of Post methods like we use in our example, it is best practice to execute our custom code first and then call the base method. For the set of Pre methods, it is best practice to call the base method first and then execute our custom code. This keeps the filtering process orderly, and allows all designers to have their proper turn at applying changes.

Speaking of the Pre methods, what are they for anyway? They add members to the **Properties** window that aren't implemented in the actual control. Why would we ever want to do this? If we look at the Design category in the **Properties** window for a constituent control during design, we will see the Locked and Modifiers properties as examples. These properties aren't part of the actual control class itself, but are added at design time. The Locked property is used by the designer to restrict movement and resizing of the control in the designer canvas. The Modifiers property is used by code generation methods to set the access modifier when serializing the declaration of the control within its container.

In addition to hiding properties, another excellent use for pre filtering is **shadowing**, that is intercepting properties and simply changing their design-time behavior. Think about the Visible property. When we set its value to false at design time we certainly don't want to actually make the control disappear off of our designer surface; however, we do want this value to be serialized.

Although we don't do this in our example, it is worth mentioning that we can shadow a property by implementing a new version of it in our designer. This new version can simply persist its value in the ControlDesigner.ShadowProperties collection (its get and set accessors access the shadow collection instead of passing the value to the actual control property). Then the PreFilterProperties can substitute our designer version of the property in place of the actual control property.

Another method we don't customize here but is worth mentioning is `DoDefaultAction`. Earlier in the chapter in our discussion of attributes, we mentioned we could designate a default event with the `DefaultEvent` attribute. The `DoDefaultAction` method actually takes this designated event and produces lines of source code. This is what inserts events for us when we double-click on a control in the design surface.

Finally, let's mention the `ControlDesigner.OnPaintAdornments` method. This method is called when the control is finished painting in the designer surface. We could override this event to produce our own design-time cues on the control. An example of this is the grid dots painted on a `Form` or `UserControl` control surface at design time.

Now, on to another designer topic we are implementing in our example; `DesignerVerbs`. Verbs are design-time action commands we can implement for a control. They appear like `LinkLabels` at the bottom of the **Properties** window and also on the right-click context menu for the control.

Let's add a verb to clear all our address `ExtTextBoxes` at design time. Add the following private `DesignerVerbCollection` declaration at the class level of our internal `AddressControlDesigner` class:

```
private DesignerVerbCollection mVerbs = null;
```

This is our internal collection to hold our verbs. Now add the following method and property:

```
private void OnVerbClearAddress(object sender, EventArgs e)
{
  ((Wrox.Samples.GUI.AddressControl)Control).Clear();
}

public override DesignerVerbCollection Verbs
{
  get
  {
    if (mVerbs == null)
    {
      mVerbs = new DesignerVerbCollection();
      mVerbs.Add(new DesignerVerb("Clear Address",
              new EventHandler(OnVerbClearAddress)));
    }
    return mVerbs;
  }
}
```

In the method, we simply retrieve the control being designed with the `Control` property and then cast it into an `AddressControl` so we can call the `Clear` method we defined earlier in the chapter. The `Verbs` property accessor adds a new verb associated with our `OnVerbClearAddress` method. The user will actually see **Clear Address** as the commands on the screen at design time.

This way, if the user keys in new values for the `AddressLine1Text`, `AddressLine2Text`, `CityText`, `StateText`, and `ZipCodeText` properties at design time and then changes their mind, they could clear them all at once with one click using the verb. If this isn't clear now, we'll see it in action shortly as we finally build and consume our `AddressControl`.

Consuming Our AddressControl

Before building our `AddressControl`, let's add a **Toolbox** bitmap for it as we did to our `ExtTextBox` control earlier in the chapter (refer back to the build instructions for that example if you need a reminder). Now let's build our `AddressControl` and look at a new project to consume it.

We'll consume our control by creating a new **Windows Application** project called `CompositeControlTest`. We can add our `AddressControl` to the **Toolbox** as we did in our earlier `ExtTextBox` example by using the **Customize Toolbox** option and browsing for the `AddressControl\Bin\Debug\AddressControl.dll`.

Site the following controls on our consumer form:

❑ One `Wrox.Samples.GUI.AddressControl` – name it `ctlAddress`. Notice how our control is treated as one control in the designer (following screenshot). The individual constituent controls now have no real identity outside of the context of the composite control.

❑ One `ListBox` control – name it `lstMsg`.

❑ Three `Button` controls – name them `BtnToString`, `BtnValidate`, `BtnClearAddress`

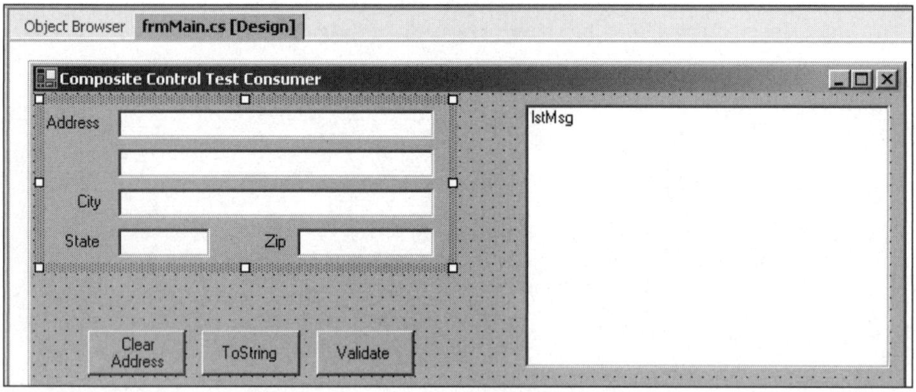

Design-Time Behavior

Even before adding any code, we can examine some of the design-time behavior of our control by looking at the Properties window for ctlAddress. We can see our custom public accessors in the Address and Labels categories.

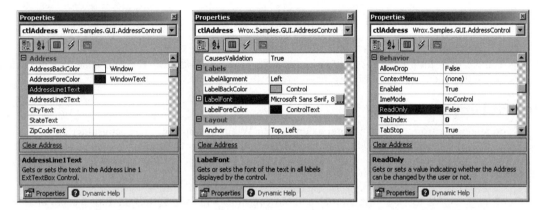

Notice the link command for the **Clear Address** DesignerVerb we created in our AddressControlDesigner is visible. Go ahead and type in some values in the **AddressLine1Text**, **CityText**, **StateText** and **ZipCodeText** properties and try out the **Clear Address** verb to reset those values to null.

Now let's add the following code to the constructor of the form in our consumer project.

```
btnToString.Click += new System.EventHandler(ShowToString);
btnValidate.Click += new System.EventHandler(ValidateAddress);
btnClearAddress.Click += new System.EventHandler(ClearAddress);
```

Now we'll add the following handler methods:

```
private void ShowToString(object sender, System.EventArgs e)
{
  MessageBox.Show(ctlAddress.ToString(),
    "AddressControl's Custom ToString Implementation");
}

private void ValidateAddress(object sender, System.EventArgs e)
{
 ctlAddress.ValidateAddress();
}

private void ClearAddress(object sender, System.EventArgs e)
{
  ctlAddress.Clear();
}
```

Select our ctlAddress again. Get into the **Events** view of the **Properties** window and double-click on the ReadOnlyChanged event to hook up the following event handler method. Then we can add the following highlighted line to provide visual notification of the event.

```
private void ctlAddress_ReadOnlyChanged(object sender, System.EventArgs e)
{
    this.lstMsg.Items.Add("ReadOnly Changed");
}
```

We could repeat this process for all of our custom PropertyNameChanged events (changing the string we add to the ListBox appropriately, of course) if we so desire.

The PropertyGrid Control

If you remember from our first chapter example, our Windows application test consumer for the ExtTextBox included a **BackColor** Button whose subscribed event handler method implemented calling a ColorDialog with the existing ExtTextBox.BackColor property setting, then updating that property with the user's new color choice.

Our AddressControl is a huge animal, and our consumer's PropertyNameChanged event handler test methods were enough of a pain to insert and cut and paste, we sure don't want to have to write cumbersome code to exercise all the properties of our control at run time. We can simply type in the entry boxes and hit our **ToString** button to test the properties tied to our address boxes, but what about all the other properties?

Control authors everywhere should be grateful that Microsoft has included the PropertyGrid control for our use. This is the same control that produces the design-time **Properties** window, and it is available for our use at run time as well. It is available, but it is not included in the **Toolbox** by default. Again we need to add it by looking on the **.NET Framework Components** tab of the **Customize Toolbox** dialog. There is no need to browse for a DLL, however, since the PropertyGrid is in the System.Windows.Forms namespace. It is already in the list so we simply need to select it by checking it.

Let's site a PropertyGrid toward the bottom of our consumer Form. Now we'll set the PropertyGrid's Dock property to Bottom and set its SelectedObject property to ctlAddress.

This now has the makings of a decent little test rig for our `AddressControl`. Let's build and run our consumer project now. We can test our control's custom methods with our buttons. We can try out setting all our custom properties with the `PropertyGrid`, all the while seeing confirmation that our property change events are being raised appropriately and calling their subscribed handler methods.

When it comes to building test applications for our complex custom controls, the `PropertyGrid` is an excellent tool. It is certainly better than writing tons of code from scratch to exercise all our properties and events.

Now let's delve into our third custom control – a truly custom control in the sense that it has a completely customized owner-drawn appearance.

Custom Drawn Controls

When looking for a solution where a standard control just won't suffice, we should try to either extend existing controls or build a composite control to meet our needs if possible. If neither of these approaches will meet our needs, however, then it is nice to know that the .NET Framework provides us the infrastructure to rather easily create a control with a completely custom appearance.

In this example we will look at creating a simple round button control by inheriting directly from `System.Windows.Forms.Control`. This class is the base for all the controls in the `System.Windows.Forms` namespace, and it is a very robust starting point. It would seem logical to use the `Button`, or even the `ButtonBase` class as a base for a custom button control; however, these classes are very rectangular-centric. We'll save ourselves some grief by just dropping down to the `Control` class and starting there. We'll also implement a simple interface, `IButtonControl`, to get our control back up to regular "button" standards.

Building our RoundButton Control

Lets start by creating a brand-new **Class Library** project in Visual Studio .NET. Choose **Project | Properties** and change the **Assembly Name** to `RoundButton` and **Default Namespace** to `Wrox.Samples.GUI`. Next we need to add references to `System.Windows.Forms.dll` and `System.Drawing.dll`.

Now let's change our class so it looks like the following code listing. Once again, we're omitting XML tags and attributes in the chapter text, but don't forget them in a real-world control.

> *The full source including all XML documentation tags can be found in the* `RoundButton.cs` *file of the* `RoundButton` *project in the chapter code download.*

```
using System;
using System.Collections;
using System.ComponentModel;
using System.Drawing;
using System.Drawing.Drawing2D;
using System.Windows.Forms;

namespace Wrox.Samples.GUI
{
  public class RoundButton : System.Windows.Forms.Control
  {
    private ButtonState  mButtonState;

    public RoundButton()
    {
```

```
      mButtonState = ButtonState.Normal;
    }

    protected override void OnPaint(PaintEventArgs p)
    {
      base.OnPaint(p);
      PaintStandard(p.Graphics);
    }
  }
}
```

We've already covered GDI+ in Chapter 6, so we'll concentrate more on our control plumbing here than on explaining every line of graphics code. Our private `ButtonState` variable allows us to keep up with whether the button should be drawn as pressed or just normal.

When overriding the `OnPaint` method, we should always call the base `OnPaint` method so that any delegates in the base class will be properly invoked. Next we call our `PaintStandard` method to do all painting for our control. It's named `PaintStandard` because our `RoundButton` sample only implements standard 3D-style painting. If we enhanced the control to support `Flat`, `Popup`, and `System` sytles in the future, we could add routing logic in our `onPaint` method to call a `PaintFlat`, `PaintPopup`, or `PaintSystem` method as appropriate.

Next we add the implementation of our `PaintStandard` method. We take a `Graphics` object as a parameter. Our `onPaint` method passes the `PaintEventArgs.Graphics` property so we have the appropriate drawing surface for the control.

```
private void PaintStandard(Graphics g)
{
  g.SmoothingMode = SmoothingMode.AntiAlias;
  Rectangle myRect =
          new Rectangle(2, 2, this.Width - 4, this.Height - 4);
  if (this.Focused)
  {
    //Shrink the rectangle to allow room for the focus border
    myRect.Inflate(-2,-2);
  }
  PaintButtonBackGround();
  Draw3DBorder(myRect, g);
  DrawText(myRect, g);
  if (this.Focused)
  {
    DrawFocus(g);
  }
}
```

Since our control is going to be oval, we'll define the rectangle myRect a couple of pixels smaller than the full width and height of our control so the outside edges of our border ellipse will not be flattened. This rectangle will define the boundaries we will use for drawing our borders and text. We also check to see if our control has the focus so we can shrink the rectangle a bit to allow us room to implement an extra focus border.

Next we'll paint our background with the call to our `PaintButtonBackGround` method (see below). Since our control doesn't require us to paint anything later except borders and text, our background actually serves as our interior as well. This is where we actually break the shackles of the rectangular world and make our control truly oval. We use a `GraphicsPath` object to build a template of the shape we want for our control by drawing an ellipse the full size of the control. Now we can create a new `Region` object with our `GraphicsPath` object. Finally, we assign this new `Region` object to the `Region` property of our control.

```
private void PaintButtonBackGround()
{
  GraphicsPath myPath = new GraphicsPath();

  //Region is full width and height of control
  myPath.AddEllipse(0, 0, this.Width, this.Height);
  Region myRegion = new Region(myPath);
  this.Region = myRegion;
}
```

Changing the `Region` is not only important for looks, but is critical to ensure we get appropriate behavior at run-time. Later we'll see that our oval control will not respond to mouse clicks outside the `Region`. This means the corners of the control's bounding rectangle that are not within the `Region` do not behave as part of the control, which is the behavior we want. We don't want a mouse click near our oval button, but not actually on it, to actually be processed by our control.

Next, we draw our regular border. Standard rectangular controls have discrete sides to which they can apply shadowing technique, but since we do not, one way we can achieve this effect is with a gradient. If the button is currently not pushed, we draw an ellipse with a gradient that fades from white at top left to black at bottom right. If the button is currently pushed, then we draw a dark border so it will appear sunken a bit.

```
private void Draw3DBorder(Rectangle r, Graphics g)
{
  if (mButtonState == ButtonState.Pushed)
  {
    Draw3DBorderPushed(r, g);
  }
  else
  {
    Draw3DBorderNormal(r, g);
  }
}

private void Draw3DBorderNormal(Rectangle r, Graphics g)
{
  LinearGradientBrush myBrush =
      new LinearGradientBrush(r, Color.White, Color.Black,
                              LinearGradientMode.ForwardDiagonal);
```

```
    Pen myPen = new Pen(myBrush, 3);
    g.DrawEllipse(myPen, r);
    myPen.Dispose();
}

private void Draw3DBorderPushed(Rectangle r, Graphics g)
{
    Pen myPen = new Pen(SystemColors.ControlDarkDark, 3);
    g.DrawEllipse(myPen, r);
    myPen.Dispose();
}
```

Our routines to draw our Text property value on our control must not only consider whether the button has been pushed, but must consult the Enabled property. If the control is disabled, the text is simply drawn twice, once with **white**, and once with **system gray** slightly offset to achieve that familiar shadowed look standard buttons exhibit when they are disabled. If the control is enabled, then the text is always drawn with the control ForeColor; however, it is drawn a bit offset if the button is pushed so as to produce movement.

```
private void DrawText(Rectangle r, Graphics g)
{
    StringFormat myFormat = new StringFormat();
    myFormat.Alignment = StringAlignment.Center;
    myFormat.LineAlignment = StringAlignment.Center;

    if (this.Enabled)
    {
        if (mButtonState == ButtonState.Pushed)
        {
            r.Offset(1, 1);
        }
        g.DrawString(this.Text, this.Font,
                    new SolidBrush(this.ForeColor), r, myFormat);
    }
    else
    {
        r.Offset(1, 1);
        g.DrawString(this.Text, this.Font,
                    new SolidBrush(Color.White), r, myFormat);
        r.Offset(-1, -1);
        g.DrawString(this.Text, this.Font,
                    new SolidBrush(SystemColors.GrayText), r, myFormat);
    }
    r.Offset(0, 0);
}
```

Finally, we want to support another user cue drawn by standard buttons. When we click on a button and the focus remains there, an extra border is drawn around the control to denote that it has the focus. Remember we are only calling this method if we are repainting the control when it has focus.

```
private void DrawFocus(Graphics g)
{
    //Focus rectangle the full width and height of the control
    Rectangle myRect =
            new Rectangle(1, 1, this.Width - 2, this.Height - 2);
    Pen myPen = new Pen(Color.Black, 2);
    g.DrawEllipse(myPen, myRect);
    myPen.Dispose();
}
```

Now it's time to start overriding other standard `Control` methods to provide our own implementation. When the left mouse button is down, we give our button the focus, signal that our control has captured the mouse, set our buttons state flag to pushed, invalidate our control, and then cause our control to be repainted. Don't forget to call the base `OnMouseDown` method for scenarios where we are not providing a replacement implementation.

```
protected override void OnMouseDown(MouseEventArgs m)
{
    if (m.Button == MouseButtons.Left)
    {
        this.Focus();
        this.Capture = true;
        mButtonState = ButtonState.Pushed;
        this.Invalidate();
        this.Update();
    }
    else
    {
        base.OnMouseDown(m);
    }
}
```

The `Invalidate` method informs Windows that the client area of our control is no longer valid and needs to be repainted. This is sufficient in some circumstances where we can be patient because any other queued up events being processed may cause a delay in the actual call to `OnPaint`. Calling `Update` makes an immediate call to `OnPaint`, which paints any invalid areas.

When the left mouse button is released while our button is in a pushed state we want to signal that our control has no longer captured the mouse, set our button state flag to normal, then cause our control to be repainted.

```
protected override void OnMouseUp(MouseEventArgs m)
{
    if ((mButtonState == ButtonState.Pushed)
        && (m.Button == MouseButtons.Left))
    {
        this.Capture = false;
        mButtonState = ButtonState.Normal;
        this.Invalidate();
        this.Update();
    }
```

```
        else
        {
            base.OnMouseUp(m);
        }
    }
```

Now we just override a series of methods where we want to either patiently request a repaint or demand a more immediate repaint if events have drastically changed our control.

```
    protected override void OnGotFocus(EventArgs e)
    {
        this.Invalidate();
        base.OnGotFocus(e);
    }

    protected override void OnLostFocus(EventArgs e)
    {
        this.Invalidate();
        base.OnLostFocus(e);
    }

    protected override void OnSizeChanged(EventArgs e)
    {
        base.OnSizeChanged(e);
        this.Invalidate();
        this.Update();
    }

    protected override void OnTextChanged(EventArgs e)
    {
        base.OnTextChanged(e);
        this.Invalidate();
        this.Update();
    }
```

We could build our project now and have a decent control, but let's add a tiny bit more functionality. Since we derived our control from `System.Windows.Forms.Control` instead of from `Button` or `ButtonBase` we are not implementing a standard interface that the framework expects a button to support.

The `IButtonControl` interface allows a control to act as the `AcceptButton` or `CancelButton` for a `Form`. This small interface consists of the `DialogResult` property plus the `NotifyDefault` and `PerformClick` methods.

First, add the interface to the declaration of our control class:

```
    public class RoundButton : System.Windows.Forms.Control, IButtonControl
```

Next, we give ourselves a couple of Boolean flags under the private ButtonState declaration at the top of our class:

```
private ButtonState  mButtonState;
private DialogResult mDialogResult;
private bool mIsDefault;
```

Now we move on to our implementation:

```
[Category("Behavior"), DefaultValue(DialogResult.None),
Description("Gets or sets the value returned to the parent form " +
            "when the button is clicked.")]
public virtual DialogResult DialogResult
{
  get {return mDialogResult;}
  set {mDialogResult = value;}
}

public void NotifyDefault(bool value)
{
  mIsDefault = value;
  this.Invalidate();
  this.Update();
}

public void PerformClick()
{
  this.OnClick(EventArgs.Empty);
}

protected override void OnClick(EventArgs e)
{
  base.OnClick(e);
 ((Form)this.TopLevelControl).DialogResult = mDialogResult;
}
```

When a control supports this interface, it will appear in the drop-down editor for a form's AcceptButton and CancelButton properties. If the control is assigned to one of these duties, then our DialogResult property value will be set to DialogResult.OK or DialogResult.Cancel as appropriate. Although we don't really do much of anything with the NotifyDefault method here, we must implement it. We could use this default notification and flag to do something like draw an extra thick border around our control.

The PerformClick method provides a standard way for callers to generate a Click event for our control. Speaking of clicks, in order to actually use the DialogResult value our control was assigned by its parent form, we need to actually customize the OnClick. After calling the base implementation, we must also assign this value to the DialogResult property of our control's parent.

Consuming Our RoundButton Control

Let's go ahead and build our `RoundButton` control so we can use it in a test application.

Again, there is a simplistic bitmap (RoundButton.bmp) in the chapter code download if you wish to add it to the project as an embedded resource before building.

We'll consume our control by creating a new Windows Application project. We should add our `RoundButton` to the Toolbox so we can drag and drop onto the form.

It's pretty simple to test a button so we won't show the boring code from this project. Instead we'll just look at some screenshots.

The full source is included in the chapter code download under the CustomControlTest project.

The example consumer project has several buttons in gray and white so we can compare the `RoundButton` appearance and behavior to that of a standard `Button` in various states. The only `CheckBox` enables or disables all the buttons together.

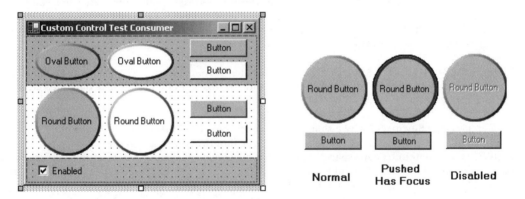

We can also verify that our `IButtonControl` implementation includes our `RoundButton` controls in the drop-down property editor for `AcceptButton` and `CancelButton`.

If we designate one of our RoundButton controls as an accept or cancel button, we can look at the designer generated InitializeComponent method and confirm that the value is properly serialized to the DialogResult property we implemented.

If they were intimidating before, hopefully owner drawn controls aren't anymore now that we have the robust infrastructure provided by the .NET Framework.

Deeper into the PropertyGrid

Now that we've finished our three controls, let's revisit the PropertyGrid that we interact with so much in the design time **Properties** window. We'll see that the extensible .NET design time architecture allows for more customization of behavior that just the attributes we've seen so far.

Custom TypeConverters

As we've seen, control properties aren't always simple types. One way the PropertyGrid handles editing these properties is expandable/collapsible view support right within the grid. The Size property of a control is a great example of an expandable type. We can key in the height and width separated by a comma ("640, 480"), or we can expand the property in the window and key in individual values for the **Height** line and for the **Width** line.

This is possible because the Size class has an associated custom TypeConverter to parse the string into the individual Height and Width members and conversely to build a comma delimited string from the members.

To add this capability to a class, we should create a new converter that inherits from either TypeConverter or ExpandableObjectConverter (both can be found in the System.ComponentModel namespace). The ExpandableObjectConverter is a robust choice for a base class from which to implement a custom TypeConverter. It already provides GetProperties and GetPropertiesSupported methods that support expandable types.

The sample code below shows the shell of a hypothetical custom TypeConverter that would support converting an object of type OurType to and from an object of type string.

```
public class OurTypeConverter : ExpandableObjectConverter
{
  public override bool CanConvertFrom(ITypeDescriptorContext context,
                                      Type sourceType)
  {
    if (sourceType == typeof(string))
    {
      return true;
    }
    return base.CanConvertFrom(context, sourceType);
  }

  public override object ConvertFrom(ITypeDescriptorContext context,
                                     CultureInfo culture, object value)
```

```
    {
        // Make sure that the incoming value object is a string, convert it if
        // possible, and return a new object of OurType. If conversion fails
        // then raise an exception.

        // If the incoming object is not a string then see if the base can
        // handle it as follows:

        return base.ConvertFrom(context, culture, value);
    }

    public override object ConvertTo(ITypeDescriptorContext context,
                                     CultureInfo culture, object value,
                                     Type destinationType)
    {
        // Make sure that the incoming value object is of type OurType and
        // that the incoming destinationType is of type string.
        // If so, then convert the value and return a new string.
        // If not, then see if the base can handle it as follows:
        return base.ConvertTo(context, culture, value, destinationType);
    }
}
```

To associate our custom converter with the OurType class we would simply decorate the class with a TypeConverter attribute using our custom converter as the value.

```
[TypeConverter(typeof(OurTypeConverter))]
public class OurType
{
}
```

Custom UITypeEditors

Look at any standard control's Font property in the design-time PropertyGrid to see a good example of not only an expandable property edit view, but also a custom editor. The button at the far right of the Font property top line invokes the familiar Font modal dialog edit form. This dialog form is an example of a custom UITypeEditor of style UITypeEditorEditStyle.Modal.

We can also see excellent examples of custom drop-down style editors in action by looking at the standard Anchor and Dock properties (see following screenshots). As their name implies, UITypeEditorEditStyle.DropDown style editors behave much like a ComboBox dropdown and are displayed within the area of the PropertyGrid itself.

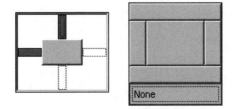

How can we designate a custom editor for a property? Below we create a custom control named SimpleControl by simply extending a common Label and overriding its Text property so we can decorate it with the Editor attribute and link it to a custom editor named SimpleTextEditor.

```
public class SimpleControl: System.Windows.Forms.Label
{
  public SimpleControl() {}

  [Category("Appearance"), Browsable(true),
  Editor(typeof(SimpleTextEditor),
         typeof(System.Drawing.Design.UITypeEditor))]
  public override string Text
  {
    get {return base.Text;}
    set {base.Text = value;}
  }
}
```

Yes, creating a custom editor for the Text property is ridiculous since it is a simple string, but it will serve to illustrate the basic plumbing necessary. Armed with this knowledge, you will then be able to experiment with implementing editors for more and more challenging types.

> *The full source for the control and custom editor can be found in the SimpleControl project of the chapter code download. A basic consumer project is also provided in the SimpleConsumer project.*

To actually create the custom modal editor, SimpleTextEditor, we need at least two classes. First we need to inherit the System.Drawing.Design.UITypeEditor class and create our SimpleTextEditor class itself. Next, we must provide custom implementations of the GetEditStyle and EditValue methods.

The second class we need is the actual dialog editor form that is just like any other Windows Form-derived class. For ease of development, we can simply add a new Windows Form to our project and use the visual designer to create our editor dialog as we would any regular form.

Now we can take the source from the form class (SimpleTextEditorForm in the following code listing) and copy it as a nested class inside the SimpleTextEditor class. We should change the declaration of the nested Form class from public to protected and then delete the original Form class source file we copied from. It's possible you may have to deal with some resource file merging issues with this procedure when dealing with robust forms. (Make a backup copy of your Form's **resx** file just in case.) We could avoid this complexity by keeping the SimpleTextEditorForm class separate instead of nesting it inside the SimpleTextEditor class, but it would be exposed to the outside world.

```
using System;
using System.Windows.Forms;
using System.Windows.Forms.Design;
using System.Drawing.Design;
using System.ComponentModel;

namespace SimpleControl
{
```

```csharp
public class SimpleTextEditor : System.Drawing.Design.UITypeEditor
{
  public SimpleTextEditor() {}

  public override UITypeEditorEditStyle
               GetEditStyle(ITypeDescriptorContext context)
  {
    return UITypeEditorEditStyle.Modal;
  }

  public override object EditValue
      (ITypeDescriptorContext context, IServiceProvider sp, object value)
  {
    string OriginalValue = (string)value;
    SimpleTextEditorForm frm = new SimpleTextEditorForm(OriginalValue);
    IWindowsFormsEditorService EdSvc = (IWindowsFormsEditorService)
                    sp.GetService(typeof(IWindowsFormsEditorService));

    if (DialogResult.OK ==  EdSvc.ShowDialog(frm))
    {
      OriginalValue = frm.EditedValue;
    }
    frm.Dispose();

    return OriginalValue;
  }

  protected class SimpleTextEditorForm : System.Windows.Forms.Form
  {
    private System.Windows.Forms.Label label1;
    private System.Windows.Forms.Button btnOK;
    private System.Windows.Forms.Button btnCancel;
    private System.Windows.Forms.TextBox txtTextValue;
    private System.ComponentModel.Container components = null;

    public SimpleTextEditorForm(string OriginalText)
    {
      InitializeComponent();
      this.txtTextValue.Text = OriginalText;
    }

    public string EditedValue
    {
      get {return this.txtTextValue.Text;}
      set {this.txtTextValue.Text = value;}
    }

    protected override void Dispose( bool disposing )
    {
        // omitted for brevity
    }

    #region Windows Form Designer generated code
    private void InitializeComponent()  { // omitted for brevity  }
```

```
        #endregion
    }
  }
}
```

The following screenshots show the results of the previous code listing. The editor form itself is simple: an OK button, a Cancel button, and a TextBox for actually editing the string. The code listing above omitted the designer-generated InitializeComponent method for clarity.

Even though the full source is available for download with the chapter examples, we should point out that the OK and Cancel buttons have been assigned to the Form's AcceptButton and CancelButton properties. This ensures that an appropriate DialogResult property value will be returned to the IWindowsFormsEditorService.ShowDialog method that is called in the SimpleTextEditor.EditValue method.

The following screenshots show the SimpleControl sited on a consumer form at design time. The PropertyGrid would show the editor activation button at the far right of the Text property line. We also see the extremely simple custom dialog editor form we created.

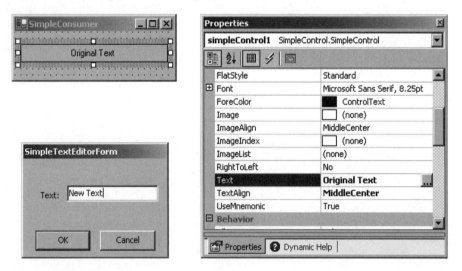

Summary

We've covered a lot in this chapter, but the topic of custom controls is a large one since the .NET Framework provides a powerful and extensible supporting architecture for producing controls that are as attractive at design time as they are at run time.

First, we looked at simply extending existing controls by inheriting from a standard `System.Windows.Forms.TextBox`. We added custom implementations by overriding and even hiding some inherited members, and we also added some new members. We saw how important XML documentation and attributes are to the design-time experience. We built our control into a DLL, and then built a test consumer project to see how our control fared both at design time and at run time.

Next, we explored composition in addition to inheritance as we derived an `AddressControl` from the `System.Windows.Forms.UserControl` and built up a control that was an aggregation of several of the controls from our first example. We saw the importance of encapsulating our constituent controls and providing public access to them in purposely constrained ways. We also added functionality to make the control self-validating. We discussed additional attributes to make unused members less obvious to our design time consumers in the Visual Studio .NET Properties window and code editor. We described how to build a custom control designer that also allowed us to remove members from view at design time, add our own design-time-only properties, and shadow existing properties to modify their design-time behavior. Again we looked at both the design-time and run-time behavior of our control in a test consumer project. In this consumer project we also saw how we can make use of the `PropertyGrid` control to save ourselves a ton of effort when building applications to test and debug our custom controls.

Next, we created a round button control with a truly custom-drawn appearance. We not only covered issues related to painting and the various states of our control, but we also implemented the `IButtonControl` interface so our custom button could be treated like a standard button in many ways.

We briefly explored the principles of custom `TypeConverters` and custom `UITypeEditors` to further enhance design time `Properties` window behavior.

Optimizing Windows Applications

Up until now this book has primarily been focused on building feature-rich Windows applications including graphics, printing, and user input. Detailing Windows Forms programming with only these aspects of development relating to the UI would not enable Windows applications to be optimized for performance. There will be many occasions where Windows applications may have to produce and display results for complex data queries or complex calculation. Given this, extending our knowledge somewhat to allow us to develop applications that are optimized for performance, using many .NET features would round off our understanding.

Conceptually, we have to address the idea that many applications need the processor to do work for them. In this way we must ensure that any desktop application we write isn't "resource hungry". For example, most of you will at some point have come across an application that freezes the system when it's tasked to do some data-access work or connect to a remote server on the network, leaving the form to turn white on the desktop. This is how not to write applications!

This chapter is primarily concerned with issues that affect application performance and respect the needs of the many other applications on the system, as well the users' needs.

In this chapter we'll cover:

- ❏ Multi-threaded Windows Forms programming
- ❏ Asynchronous programming
- ❏ Optimizing Windows Forms programming
- ❏ Optimizing for client-server and other models of programming
- ❏ Event Accessors

Basic Threading Issues

Every time we click on an executable file (such as any of the executables we have created throughout this book) Windows will load the code into a process address space and create a block defining relevant information to enable the security context, various initialization times, structures containing the amount of memory and virtual memory used by the process etc. The native executable code will be loaded into the process address space and then a single thread will be created (a main thread) in order to run the code in the executable.

A thread is nothing more than a unit of execution. Each process must have at least one thread. Threads, as we will see, allow us to distribute work so that more than one task within an application can be accomplished simultaneously. The processor can obviously only process one task at a time, so on a single processor system, we can use Windows to distribute the tasks that an application has to do over the one processor by creating a number of threads and 'scheduling' each thread so that different tasks can occur, and appear to be occurring concurrently by giving each thread within a process a small portion of the processor's time (a quantum). This will allow a form to update the UI on one thread and on a separate thread to do a complex calculation. As we will see later, using a single thread for everything can be detrimental to an application, which may 'lock up' since it doesn't have the resources to update the UI while a complex calculation is taking place.

The process of shifting between threads is known as a "context switch". A context switch occurs when the details and "state" of the old thread is swapped for the new thread (which will have a small proportion of the processors time). This swap will repeatedly occur between all the threads in all the processes.

In the diagram above, eight threads are shown, each having three units of processor time. The context switch occurs in the spaces between the threads. One of the problems here is that the more threads we have overall in the system, the more context switches we have and the more time we waste between context switches. There will come a point where the amount of time that the processor is giving to each thread and the context switches between them may result in degradation in the performance of the system (and specifically the application). As we see later, this is a very important factor that we must bear in mind when developing multithreaded applications. There are an optimal number of threads that we can use for the application – too many threads may be detrimental to the performance of our application.

A good deal of material in this chapter will center on the concept of programming multithreaded Windows applications. Visual C++ developers should need no introduction to developing a multithreaded application. Developers who have made the leap from VB to .NET may have not used threads in their applications before. Visual Basic only exposed the developer to single threaded applications (although building Windows applications in VB6 could be done using the CreateThread API – albeit not a good development model). .NET has exposed a multithreaded programming model, which we can use with great ease. This model has great advantages over the traditional threading models exposed through COM applications.

Many early applications were single-threaded, which meant that all method calls to every object that was created by the COM server (either an ActiveX EXE or DLL) would be done using the same thread. Obviously for the EXE server this would rely on a call to another process, so in order to be able to create an object and call a method on that object, a proxy object had to be created within the process of the calling EXE. This proxy object would make calls to a stub in the ActiveX EXE process using Remote Procedure This process is known as marshaling.

The second type of COM threading model is the apartment threading model, which allows each COM object to be created in its own thread. The only stipulation is that only the creating thread can be used to access the object's method and properties. In this way all calls from other threads will have to use a proxy object. This threading is automatically thread-safe as threads do not share objects and as such threads are not able to interact with each other. This issue, as we will see later, is very important as with .NET we may have to apply this level of protection ourselves to ensure that global variables of the object retain the correct value when the object is being accessed by many threads.

The free threading COM model was not available to Visual Basic developers but C++ developers could quite easily implement this model (supported through ATL libraries and wizards). This differs from the other two models in that all threads can access all objects. With respect to threading it is important to understand the consequence of this. Any global variables being shared by threads may be changed by one thread and in turn the wrong value being read by another thread obscuring the results needed by the second thread. We shall cover this in greater detail later in the chapter.

This chapter is also concerned with how we build desktop applications. Each problem poses a unique challenge but solutions can fit into a variety of categories. In this first example we'll look at the use of a simple form and resolve difficulties with the form being "locked up" and unable to process anything interactively while the form is doing a complex calculation. In doing so we'll address how it is possible to use multithreaded techniques to avoid situations like this. Networked computing has meant that there are now a variety of methods available to us in the creation of desktop applications that release load from the client and centralize distribution on a server so that client install are much smaller.

Within the scope of this chapter we'll take a quick look at various solutions: standalone, two-tier, and multi-tier applications and when each one should be used. The design of the model that we use affects the overall design of a desktop application and its performance can be improved through the use of a distributed model. Towards the end of the chapter we'll look at when to use distributed models over standalone models.

With .NET comes a new concept called Application Domains. A thread in one process cannot directly invoke a method on a thread in another process. In effect, the thread is confined to a particular process. Each Windows Form application exists within an **Application Domain**, or **AppDomain**, and this restriction doesn't apply to it– a thread in an AppDomain can invoke a method on another thread in the same AppDomain. The AppDomain lives inside of the process and this enables all the functions of a process that we would normally expect (such as fault tolerance) but will also enable threads in other AppDomains to invoke methods. Process isolation and the inability of one process to directly invoke code in another process led to the use of inter-process communication between application processes through the operating system, for example, pipes, mail slots, etc. Application Domains allow the same level of isolation as separate processes but allow different 'applications' – each loaded into an AppDomain – to call methods on each other (via their respective threads) without the use of inter-process communication techniques.

The following code uses the AppDomain class to create a new AppDomain named library. Any objects created that come from the assembly loaded into this new AppDomain will be subject to the process isolation we described above.

```
AppDomain libraryDomain = AppDomain.CreateDomain("library");
libraryDomain.ExecuteAssembly("library.dll");
```

Application Locking

The first example demonstrates something that many of us will be familiar with. When a single-threaded application is involved in some heavy processing it must finish doing work before it releases control back to the user. This means that the application is effectively 'locked' until the work is done. While the application is busy running a task the window may not repaint – this is indicative of a single threaded application. Additionally we may be unable to move the form as the single thread is blocked doing the calculation.

When the button is pressed the click event is handled by a method that continues to count and print the result in the Debug window.

```
private void TakeTime()
{
  for(int i=0;i<320000000;i++)
  {
    System.Diagnostics.Debug.Write(i);
  }
}
```

Attempting to exit the application while the calculation is being processed will result in the following dialog (on Windows XP machines):

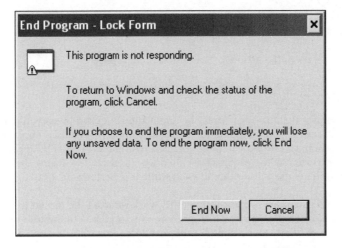

The problem has been "dumbed-down" into its simplest form. Real-world examples may involve calls to a database that run complex queries, waiting for a response from a file read or write operation or waiting for a response to an RPC or message request within a distributed system. Of the many ways that we can handle the problem of the UI not updating and not allowing the user any interactivity, we can simply break up the application calculation into smaller parts or keep checking for messages after certain parts of a calculation are completed. This can be more complicated to code, however, and may not be of any use for distributed operations like database or RPC calls, which cannot be broken up like the calculation (we have to wait for the response in these two cases). In order to prevent this locking, we have to introduce another thread into the application. This thread will handle the calculation and the other thread (UI thread) is going to be free to respond to user input.

If we now extend the UI by adding a textbox and pressing the start button and trying to get the focus of the textbox to type something in, we'll find very quickly that this is not possible. If we add the code to the event handler to call the TakeTime method (shown at the start of this section) instead of calling the method directly, we can first create a new thread that can then be used to call the method.

```
private void butWasteTime_Click(object sender, System.EventArgs e)
{
  Thread t = new Thread(new ThreadStart(TakeTime));      t.Start();
}
```

Just to recap slightly, a delegate represents a 'safe' function pointer, which can be used to represent a method with exactly the same signature. Signature effectively means the parameter list and return type. The TakeTime method takes no parameters and returns void. This is the signature needed for the ThreadStart delegate above. When we wish to create a new Thread, the method that is going to be executed by this thread is passed by name to the ThreadStart delegate, which in turn is used in the Thread class's constructor.

The Thread class's constructor takes a ThreadStart object, which in turn is a delegate taking a method with a signature of a void return type and no parameters that will be invoked when the thread is started.

The Start method must be called on the Thread before the TakeTime method will be invoked.

The Thread class resides in the System.Threading namespace.

```
using System.Threading;
```

One noteworthy point is that this time when the application is exited (even while the background thread is running) we don't see the "not responding" dialog and the form is closed apparently smoothly. The second thread that we have created will be terminated with the process. This thread and other subsequent threads created by the process are called worker threads. Closing the form will unconditionally terminate the worker thread even while it is performing a task.

In order to be alerted when the thread completes its work we want the thread to interrupt us when it has finished the calculation. The easiest way is to present a message box to the user letting them know that the work has been done. This can be done by simply adding the following line of code to the end of the TakeTime method:

```
MessageBox.Show ("Finished");
```

A more complex approach to display a message box would be to allow the user to have more control over the application. In general, threads can exist in many states. In the application, we have just identified a running state. However, if we allowed the user to interrupt the calculation we could suspend the worker thread or even terminate it. The methods on each Thread object could be used to this effect.

Thread.Abort aborts the referenced thread and frees the resources used by it. It does this by raising a ThreadAbortException. Thread.Suspend can be used to suspend execution of the thread until Thread.Resume is called. In the examples later in the chapter we'll also use the ThreadState enumeration, which represents the possible states of the thread, for example, whether the thread is suspended, waiting, aborted, or running.

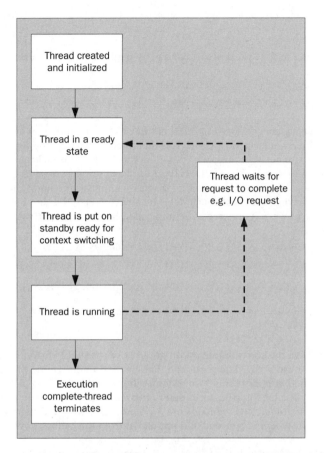

The use of threads in this context demonstrates an **asynchronous operation,** meaning that the operation will proceed independently from the interactive user thread and will return at a later time (in other words, the user will not have to wait for a response before continuing to use the application). Now that we've introduced the topic of threads we'll discuss how to program a Windows Form to access methods asynchronously. This involves a slightly different style of programming but allows for greater flexibility (as we will see later).

> *Using asynchronous programming is especially useful for developing multithreaded applications. The term "fire and forget" is almost applicable since when the operation returns the user can be alerted that the work has been done. The main thread may forget about the task being done by the worker thread and will simply be alerted when it is complete.*

We begin by defining an asynchronous result interface that will be used to hold the return values for the method being called asynchronously. Asynchronous programming is supported by File IO, Stream IO, networking, web services, and asynchronous delegates (like the ThreadStart delegate below). Methods can be invoked by specifying the method call as a parameter to the ThreadStart delegate as we did before. However, when the task is complete we can be alerted through the use of a callback method, which can be used to alert the user.

```
private System.IAsyncResult m_EndInvoke = null;
```

When the button on the form is pressed the TakeTime method is invoked using an asynchronous call.

```
ThreadStart threadstart = new ThreadStart(TakeTime);
m_EndInvoke = threadstart.BeginInvoke(new AsyncCallback(MethodBeginInvoke), null);
```

The ThreadStart delegate is declared in the same way as before and takes a single parameter-less method argument with a return type of void. It is then used, by calling the BeginInvoke method. This method is called synchronously (in this case) but allows us to set an **asynchronous callback** method that will allow a method to be invoked when the calculation has finished processing. As such it would be a good idea to put the MessageBox we wished to display within this method. The first argument of BeginInvoke is the **AsynchronousCallback** delegate and the second is an object that we'll set to null. When the thread returns we will now see a method called MethodBeginInvoke called:

```
private void MethodBeginInvoke(System.IAsyncResult ar)
{
    if(ar.CompletedSynchronously)
        MessageBox.Show("TakeTime() called synchronously");
    else
        MessageBox.Show("TakeTime() called asynchronously");
}
```

The method should have the above signature; in other words, it should take a parameter of type IAsyncResult and return void. The result can then be used to determine the current state of play within the thread – whether it has completed among other things. The CompletedSynchronously property returns a bool value allowing us to determine the nature of the call (synchronous or asynchronous). The variable ar that contains the AsyncResult will hold the same value as the m_EndInvoke variable, which is returned and populated from the callback operation.

In this example there has been a distinct absence of thread creation. In the first two examples, we created a Thread object and started it, but in this case we didn't actually need to do that and still managed to create a thread. .NET manages the thread creation process for asynchronous programming by using a thread from a **thread pool**, which is owned by each process. The .Net Framework automatically provides services that allow us to avoid the practice of creating and managing threads within an application. This is why in the above code we haven't had to explicitly create the threads needed for the task. .NET has done this for us implicitly. We shall see a lot more about thread pool programming later in the chapter.

When developing multithreaded Windows Forms applications, the Threads window in Visual Studio .NET becomes an invaluable companion. This window will monitor the number of threads within the application and will account for the current thread.

The window can be displayed within Visual Studio .NET by choosing the Debug menu option and then choosing the Threads submenu option from the Windows menu. Threads will only be viewable within the window when a breakpoint is reached.

As well as a `BeginInvoke` method on the `ThreadStart` delegate we have an `EndInvoke` method. Calling `EndInvoke` will block the main thread until a completion signal has been returned to acknowledge that the thread has done its work. Using `EndInvoke` following `BeginInvoke` will again tie up our UI. It seems then that using `EndInvoke` will return us to our single threaded non-responsive UI.

```
IAsyncResult m_EndInvoke2 = null;
ThreadStart threadstart = new ThreadStart(TakeTime);
m_EndInvoke = threadstart.BeginInvoke(new AsyncCallback(MethodBeginInvoke),
String.Copy("test"));

ThreadStart threadstart2 = new ThreadStart(TakeTime);
m_EndInvoke2 = threadstart.BeginInvoke(new AsyncCallback(MethodBeginInvoke),
null);

threadstart.EndInvoke(m_EndInvoke);
threadstart.EndInvoke(m_EndInvoke2);
```

This code uses two separate calls to `ThreadStart` for the same operation – running it helps us understand more about threads in that each one (remarkably) takes the same time to run. We can also check to see whether the thread has completed its work. To do this we can use the `IsCompleted` property of the `IAsyncResult` object we created earlier. This object will carry the signal that lets us know when the thread has completed its task and returned from executing the method. If we poll this property consistently with the main thread (at intervals – maybe every 3 seconds) we can check to ensure that the operation has finished.

To block the main thread we can use the following, which will signal the main thread when the operation has completed. Using this technique will place us at no greater advantage, however, than if we simply used a single thread in the application.

```
m_EndInvoke.AsyncWaitHandle.WaitOne();
```

It may be applicable, however, to allow the user to check when the asynchronous operation has completed. The user can simply press a button that will check the `IsCompleted` property and, if applicable, check for results from the operation and display them. Unlike using the thread creation and management approach earlier asynchronous programming will not allow the asynchronous operation to be aborted directly.

```
if (!m_EndInvoke.IsCompleted) { ... }
```

Thread Performance

All in all, the ease with which we can now write multithreaded Windows Forms applications is an absolute blessing for us. It means that we can distribute a number of pieces of work to be undertaken concurrently by the same form application. One of the things that we must understand with this new use of powerful programming is what effect 'overdoing it' will have on our application. It could be that too many threads are too much of a good thing. As we said earlier in the chapter, too many threads may affect system performance since each one has a small time slice of the processor and the more threads that there are the more context switches need to occur – and as a result the less scheduled time for each thread to perform work.

We should be able to check what effect adding additional threads has on our application by taking some measurements. In the ThreadDare application we do exactly this by monitoring the latency of the overall completion per thread as each one invokes the TakeTime method.

To begin with we'll declare a struct containing a ThreadStart delegate and a DateTime object.

```
struct _threadstart
{
  public ThreadStart threadstart;
  public DateTime dt;
}
```

an array of type _threadstart (the struct above) then we'll declare in the class.

```
_threadstart[] th;
```

The user will enter a value into a textbox, which allows them to suggest the number of threads that they want to create, and this number will be used to create an array of structs (of the user-defined size). The program will start when the user clicks on the **Start** button. The event handler contains the following code:

```
private void btThreadStart_Click(object sender, System.EventArgs e)
{
  th = new _threadstart[Convert.ToInt16(txtNoOfThreads.Text)];


  for(int i = 0; i < th.Length; i++)
  {
    th[i].threadstart = new ThreadStart(TakeTime);
    th[i].threadstart.BeginInvoke(new AsyncCallback(ThreadFinished), i);
    th[i].dt = DateTime.Now;
  }
}
```

When the **Start** button is pressed the current time is recorded so that when the asynchronous call has finished the call time can be calculated.

The `for` loop is used to loop through the empty array and populate it with values by creating a new `ThreadStart` delegate and calling the `BeginInvoke`, method which can be used to provide the asynchronous callback method – this method is called `ThreadFinished` in this example. If we look at the number of parameters being passed to the `BeginInvoke` method we'll notice an extra one – in order to be able to identify the thread (which would be anonymous without this feature) we can pass an argument of type `object` – which means that we can create any object (including a custom class instance) and pass it to the callback method. The current `DateTime` is recorded using the `DateTime.Now` property, which returns a `DateTime` object containing the current time.

The `callback` method, which we came across in the last section, looks like this:

```
private void ThreadFinished(IAsyncResult ar)
{
    int i = (int)ar.AsyncState;

    // Put something into the listbox
    lbThreads.Items.Add("Thread "+(i+1)+" finished - " +
(DateTime.Now.Subtract(th[i].dt)));
}
```

When the `ThreadFinished` method is invoked we can retrieve the `int` we passed into the `BeginInvoke` method by requesting the `AsyncState` property and casting it to an integer. This number can then be used to determine which thread has just finished work and use the integer returned to check the array variable holding the start time so that the time taken for the thread to finish executing can be worked out.

What I've done above is not good! The only reason it may work is because of Windows XP, which will happily handle bad programming practice. The main application thread, however, should be the only one that handles the UI updates. In order to update the UI safely we can use any of the `Invoke` methods (either `Invoke`, `BeginInvoke`, or `EndInvoke`), which will marshal the call to the main thread and update the UI – each of these methods is 'safe' to call rather than updating the UI directly via a worker thread.

The property `InvokeRequired` on the Control will return `true` if the control needs to be invoked through the creating thread which is the main thread. We can use the delegate `ItemAdd` to call our `UpdateListbox` method through `Invoke`, which will update the listbox. If the control returns `false` to `InvokeRequired` then we can just update the Control via the current thread.

```
void UpdateListbox(string listboxText)
{
  lbThreads.Items.Add(listboxText);
}

delegate void ItemAdd(string item);
private void ThreadFinished(IAsyncResult ar)
{
    ItemAdd ia = new ItemAdd(UpdateListbox);
    int i = (int)ar.AsyncState;
    string state = "Thread "+(i+1)+" finished -
"+(DateTime.Now.Subtract(th[i].dt)).ToString();
```

```
    //put something into the listbox
    if(lbThreads.InvokeRequired)
    {
      lbThreads.Invoke(ia, new Object[] {state});
    }
    else
    {
      lbThreads.Items.Add(listboxText);
    }
}
```

We should be able to calculate the average time per thread by recording the total elapsed time (as each thread object is created at the same time albeit, on standby) and dividing it by the total number of threads. We should first declare the start and end times as member variables.

```
DateTime dtStart;
DateTime dtEnd;
```

Then we must record the start time as the variable dtStart. This is done in the button event handler as the first thread is created. After this we must add some code to the callback function ThreadFinsihed.

```
if(i==(th.Length-1)) lbThreads.Invoke(ib, new Object[]{""});
```

The `ib` variable is the delegate we defined earlier pointing to the `FinalCallback` method.

```
void FinalCallback(string blank)
{
  dtEnd = DateTime.Now.Subtract(new TimeSpan(dtStart.Ticks));
  lbThreads.Items.Add("Total Thread Time:
"+((dtEnd.Minute*60)+dtEnd.Second).ToString()+" seconds");
  lbThreads.Items.Add("Average Thread Time:
"+(((dtEnd.Minute*60)+dtEnd.Second)/th.Length)+" seconds");
}
```

The figure above shows that 18 threads have run with an overall 'finish all work' time of 78 seconds. At first glance this doesn't appear to be that noteworthy but when examined in the context of increasing numbers of threads it does become very significant. We can add simple checks like this to our applications while in development to check for the point when the number of threads reaches saturation and the total time elapsed increase to such an extent that we begin to see more overhead for every extra thread we add.

Using too many threads can degrade the performance of a Windows Forms application. There will be a point related to the work we're actually doing where we achieve diminishing returns to scale. We have to bear in mind that the more threads that we use in our applications the more **context switches** will occur, which will increase the delay time where the processor isn't actually doing any work but swapping in and out management of the thread. It is important to understand that some of the best-written desktop applications using only a small number of threads to get the job done. Threads can be very powerful if used correctly but can destroy an application if not. Threads give us benefit on multiprocessor systems where more than one operation can occur concurrently and also directly in our applications where we need several things to occur apparently simultaneously (for example, user input, data access, and network access).

Writing Multithreaded Applications

In order to address all the things we haven't referred to yet regarding threads for developing Windows applications, we'll discuss and create two applications that are both multithreaded and describe some of the issues that occur in these applications as well as some of the features we can use in .NET to help us understand and contain these issues.

A database application

The first application will continually check a database for updates and present the user with values on the screen, and the second will be a peer-to-peer networking application allowing two clients to talk to each other. Although there are many uses for threads in Windows Forms development, these are two common Windows programming scenarios.

The first application we'll look at is a pricing application with three textboxes representing prices of commodities. I've chosen gold, coffee, and tea to price. In a high-risk environment such as bank software where a trader or commodity broker needs instant price feed information, it is imperative to use techniques in our Windows applications to get the most up-to-date information – without the user noticing any performance degradation in the UI updates – threading can obviously be a key solution to this problem.

For the purposes of this example, I'll store the prices of the three goods in a SQL Server database table (the database creation script is included in the download). There are only three rows in the table: Each row has a unique type:'C' for coffee, 'G' for gold, and 'T' for tea. For this simple application we'll assume that each commodity has only one price (in reality there will be several changing numbers including bids, offers, spreads, etc.).

We'll begin by declaring all of the instance variables that we'll be using be using within the application.

```
private int lastCoffeePrice = 0;
private int lastTeaPrice = 0;
private int lastGoldPrice = 0;
private int noOfUpdates = 0;
```

The variables `lastCoffePrice`, `lastTeaPrice` and, `lastGoldPrice` will hold the old value of the commodity price so that daily price change quantity can be calculated on an ongoing basis. Each of these prices will be tested for changes on each trip to the database and if changed, then the `noOfUpdates` variable will be incremented.

```
private System.Threading.Timer t1 = null;
private System.Threading.Timer t2 = null;
private System.Threading.Timer t3 = null;
```

We also need to declare the `System.Threading.Timer` objects as instance variables (not to be confused with `System.Windows.Forms.Timer` – this is why we need to use fully qualified references here to avoid any ambiguity). This class is immensely useful and can be used to call back a method at a specific interval. As you can imagine, it's great for invoking code that continually needs to be repeated in an application. This is exactly what we need here, as we're going to have to check for updates at regular intervals:

```
t1 = new System.Threading.Timer(new TimerCallback(PriceCheck_Callback), 'C', 0,
                                500);
t2 = new System.Threading.Timer(new TimerCallback(PriceCheck_Callback), 'T', 1,
                                500);
t3 = new System.Threading.Timer(new TimerCallback(PriceCheck_Callback), 'G', 2,
                                500);
```

For the purposes of the chapter we've overemphasized the use of `Timers` in this example. It is possible that in a real-world application a single timer would be used to check these values and possibly generate events if they have changed so that any subscribers could use the events to update the screen values.

The three timers are initialized and specify the same callback method to use. The first parameter of the `Timer` constructor is a `TimerCallback` delegate, which in all three cases uses the same method to call back to. The second parameter is something that we can pass to the callback delegate to represent an input parameter. The signature is such that it has one parameter, which is of type `object`: `PriceCheck_Callback(object state)`. The third parameter is a delay to calling the method. A one-millisecond delay offset has been specified. The last parameter (`500`) is the delay interval, which is the number of milliseconds after which the call repeats, meaning that the function will be invoked by three separate threads no sooner than 0, 1, and 2 and 500, 501, and 502 milliseconds past initial code execution. This will schedule the thread calls almost sequentially allowing them to be executed (probably) in a distinct order.

The `PriceCheck_CallBack` method is shown below:

```
protected void PriceCheck_Callback(object state)
{
    ThreadPool.QueueUserWorkItem(new WaitCallback(GetData), state);
}
```

This method introduces the idea of thread pools that we touched on earlier. The `ThreadPool` class represents a managed pool of threads that the application owns. Each thread can be given work and then queued until the current worker thread context switches. Threads can generally be in one of the following states:

❑ Running

❑ Stopped

❑ Suspended

Running threads are threads currently doing work. If a thread is stopped, it is left idle until it is needed again in the application – in which case it will begin its work all over again once started. Suspended threads can be resumed at any time and pick up where they left off from in terms of the work they were doing. Threads can also be put to sleep for any duration of time. In fact, one agreed way of halting the execution of a Windows application is by calling the `Thread.Sleep(500)` method, which will cause the current thread (the main application thread) to sleep for 500 milliseconds before being in a state ready for rescheduling.

This state of sleep is common for programs with many threads. This is where the `ThreadPool` class becomes immensely useful as it manages the group of threads – code that would have to be written anyway for applications with large numbers of threads. Threads within the pool are called "worker threads" and the pool itself has a separate thread that monitors all the other threads that are queued in the thread pool and their signal states (each thread returns a signal when it has completed, which is used to control the state of the thread – when the signal that the task is completed occurs it will return to the pool) – thus managing callback function invocations.

As each process implicitly has a pool of threads, it is not necessary to instantiate the `ThreadPool` class. All the methods that are supplied by the class are static.

The method `ThreadPool.QueueUserWorkItem(new WaitCallback(GetData), state)` is used to get another thread from the pool (if a free thread is available – otherwise it will wait until the pool can give it a free thread) and queue the callback request. In our application, each thread invokes the same method passing a different state variable to the method. As is probably evident, the `WaitCallback` delegate has the same method signature as the `TimerCallback`, enabling us to pass specific thread information to the method as part of the thread method call. The variable `state`, remember can have one of three possible values – C, T, or G.

Instead of using the `QueueUserWorkItem` method we could have accomplished the same using a `threadpool` thread via the `RegisterWaitForSingleObject` method. this would allow us to use the `Callback` method in the same way as the `Timer` and to call it at regular intervals. An `AutoResetEvent` object is used in the code below. This class inherits from `WaitHandle` and can provide a signal state for the object. This class resets the signal state automatically when the thread returns from the callback function. The converse is a `ManualResetEvent` where the signal state (whether it is still waiting or not) has to be set by us.

```
AutoResetEvent are = new AutoResetEvent(false);
ThreadPool.RegisterWaitForSingleObject(are, new WaitOrTimerCallback(GetData), 'C',
                                       500, false);
```

The `GetData` method is reproduced in part below:

```
string priceType = (char)type;

string sql = "SELECT Price FROM tblPrices WHERE Type='" + priceType.ToString() +
             "'";

SqlConnection cn = new SqlConnection("Server=localhost; Database=Prices;
                                     Integrated Security=SSPI");
cn.Open();

SqlCommand cmd = new SqlCommand(sql, cn);
int retVal = (int)cmd.ExecuteScalar();
```

The `GetData` method begins with some simple code to create a database connection based on using the SQL Server managed provider.

> **We'll cover this very briefly for those that haven't done any data programming with .NET, but a more complete description can be found *in Professional ADO.NET Programming (ISBN: 1861005-27-X)* by Wrox Press.**

The SQL statement uses the `type` method parameter to construct the `WHERE` clause. A `SqlConnection` object is then created, which is set to use integrated security on the database (which means that it will effectively use Windows authentication to authenticate to SQL Server – this should be set up on SQL Server and the logged-in user should have sufficient permission to run `SELECT` statements against the database). Calling the `Open` method then opens the connection to the database.

A SqlCommand object actually executes the SQL text, passing it to the database and returning the result from the database. It needs to be aware of which connection to use – this is why we pass the SqlConnection to the constructor of the SqlCommand.

The ExecuteScalar method is invoked and simply reads the first record and first value (as we're only interested in one record – since there can never be more than one row returned from our query). The letter character is the primary key in the table, so only one row with the character defined in the WHERE clause of the query will exist. In a different implementation of this, we would probably read the three rows together and then update them rather than use three separate queries to the database. In a real-world application using a stored procedure would allow slightly better performance as well.

Synchronization

There are many things that need to be addressed when writing multithreaded applications. Although threads offer many powerful features and a level of efficiency that makes complex applications optimize far easier to, there are several issues that need to be addressed with multithreaded applications. One extremely important issue is that of **thread synchronization**. Up until now we've assumed that all instance variables will be unaffected by the multithreaded nature of an application. Unfortunately, this is not the case.

Synchronization is a necessary aspect of thread handling, and involves making sure that two threads don't have simultaneous access to the same variable. One of the problems of threads is that the existence of shared resources such as instance variables invariably requires resources to maintain their integrity. To avoid two threads concurrently operating on the same value we can use several synchronization techniques.

The problem occurs when one thread attempts to access a variable to get its current value but then a context switch occurs, the value is then changed by a second thread, and when the first thread is running again and gets the value of that variable, it will now be an incorrect value. The problem can be understood by thinking of each method call that the thread does as a series of machine code instructions. In the example code below, the simple additions and comparisons are compiled into several machine code instructions and if the context switch occurs between threads within this process it's very possible that a new value will be present when the context switch back to the original thread occurs. There are a number of errors that can take place, as it's also possible that the variable will contain a null value, causing an error or grave miscalculation.

```
switch(priceType)
{
  case 'C':
    lastCoffeePrice = Convert.ToInt32(txtCoffeePrice.Text);
    txtCoffeePrice.Text = retVal.ToString();
    break;
  case 'T':
    lastTeaPrice = Convert.ToInt32(txtTeaPrice.Text);
    txtTeaPrice.Text = retVal.ToString();
    break;
  case 'G':
    lastGoldPrice = Convert.ToInt32(txtGoldPrice.Text);
    txtGoldPrice.Text = retVal.ToString();
    break;
}
allUpdates++;
```

Using the `lock` keyword is an easy way to ensure that if the current context thread is in the middle of an operation then no other thread can have access to that variable until the sequence of instructions within the lock is executed. Unsurprisingly, `lock` works by "locking" an object – in fact it uses a kernel object called a **mutex** – a mutually exclusive lock to ensure that the variable is unaffected by any other operation until the bracketed code is executed. In the code below I've locked the pointer to the current object, the current object (our form) as form `this` as the lock requires a reference type. In order to test this example out and understand how locks work we must change the `retVal` int variable that holds the value of the price for a particular commodity to a member variable. This will mean that the variable is now shared between all worker threads. If we now run the application again we will see many of the values skewed. The textboxes will periodically contain the wrong values since some threads will overwrite the `retVal` value and when the context switch occurs to the initial worker thread it will now use an incorrect `retVal` value.

```
lock(this)
{
  retVal = (int)cmd.ExecuteScalar();
  switch(priceType)
  {
    case 'C':
      lastCoffeePrice = Convert.ToInt32(txtCoffeePrice.Text);
      txtCoffeePrice.Text = retVal.ToString();
      break;
    case 'T':
      lastTeaPrice = Convert.ToInt32(txtTeaPrice.Text);
      txtTeaPrice.Text = retVal.ToString();
      break;
    case 'G':
      lastGoldPrice = Convert.ToInt32(txtGoldPrice.Text);
      txtGoldPrice.Text = retVal.ToString();
      break;
  }
}
```

Adding the `lock` keyword has blocked all other worker threads until this section of code has been completed by the first worker thread that reaches it (the problem that this cures is called a race condition). It will protect the value of `retVal` until it leaves this section of code irrespective of the number of context switches that occur in between.

The immediate way to test this application is to execute some SQL. A tool comes with the SQL Server distribution called Query Analyzer that will allow SQL to be executed against a database.

By using the following SQL, we can update the value of one of the commodity prices – it should immediately filter through to the Windows form values:

```
USE PRICES
GO
UPDATE TBLPRICES SET PRICE = 23 WHERE TYPE = 'C'
```

The result is the virtually immediate process updating on the UI. The `ThreadPool` worker threads will ensure that the database is constantly being monitored for changes and delivers them to the UI.

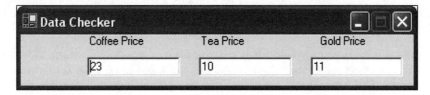

One important message that should be defined now with respect to using synchronization and locking resources is the possibility of **deadlocks.** Deadlocks occur when two threads compete for the same resources and are unable to continue execution because each thread has a dependency on a resource locked out by the other. For example:

Thread 1:

```
lock(message)
{
    hidden += temp;
}
```

Thread 2:

```
lock(hidden)
{
    message += temp;
}
```

In this example a deadlock can occur as each thread can potentially lock an object required by the other. If `Thread 1` locks message and then context switches and then `Thread 2` locks hidden and tries to access `message` it will be unable to until `Thread 1` releases the lock. However, it is apparent that this will never happen because hidden is locked so both threads will be unable to proceed. Careful programming and analysis of what resources are locked out at any one time can avoid deadlocks. Locks add significant overhead to multithreading and should be avoided where possible.

Another point to bear in mind is that applications with many threads that use significant number of locks can cause a large degradation in performance as each thread has to wait in a queue until an object is freed. A better way to write applications is to use locks when atomic behavior needs to be used (a sequence of events must be performed by a thread without interruption).

In this section we should detail some of the other ways that we can protect global variables from concurrent access by threads. The `Monitor` class can be used in exactly the same way as `lock` above. We could replace the `lock` encapsulating the code between the `Monitor Enter` and `Exit`.

```
Monitor.Enter(this);

Monitor.Exit(this);
```

This code will now be "locked".

Similarly Monitor.TryEnter can be used to set a lock on a particular object for a TimeSpan value after which the lock will be released. This can be a very good way to avoid deadlocks in code (but potentially adding extra overhead by specifying a larger than necessary time value).

Another useful class is the Mutex class. When a thread requires signaling as to whether something has occurred, a Mutex object can be used. Each thread can check and be signaled as to whether the Mutex has been released. This means that if two threads call two methods explicitly they can both be used to check the state of the Mutex or many Mutex objects. In each method we may use this code to create a Mutex object:

```
Mutex m = new Mutex();
```

This code halts execution of the running thread until the Mutex is released.

```
m.WaitOne();
```

and this releases the Mutex and signals to all waiting threads to continue:

```
m.ReleaseMutex();
```

An array of Mutex objects can be used and threads can suspend execution until all or any of the array items is released.

```
Mutex[] mutex = new Mutex[3];
Mutex.WaitAny(mutex);
Mutex.WaitAll(mutex);
```

Mutex classes can be used in conjunction with AutoResetEvents described earlier to produce some very good multithreaded applications that allow signals to be generated when one or all threads have completed and/or one or all Mutexes have been released. A Mutex can thus be used like a lock stopping all threads from using locked resources until the current worker thread releases the Mutex.

A Networking Application

One other very common use of multithreaded forms applications in a business environment is a peer-to-peer networking application – as the simplest form of distributed system involves only message passing, it is not uncommon to find networked business clients that use proprietary protocols to access networked services on a range of TCP ports. Each application can have a single thread per network connection and an extra thread for the work that has to be done by the UI – however, this is a non-scalable architecture – a much better implementation of this uses I/O Completion ports, which provide a way for networked services to switch to another thread when a thread processing a client is blocked and waiting for an I/O request to complete – this ensures that a thread is always actively processing a client request. This example will show a client-to-client application. We will consider a client-server application in a different light later in the chapter.

The Chat Application is a peer-to-peer chat sample program that is set to run in **loopback** (on a single machine). The Chat Application is modeled on the old UNIX program `talk`. It allows a user to input any information that will be received on any networking endpoint (as long as there is a path to another client application). This application won't distinguish between clients; so many clients can connect to it (using TCP sockets) and receive messages. It could be used to control the endpoint – currently the endpoint has been set to **localhost**, but to use the application on a network the list could be generated from a `startup` file or something similar, and each client host could be populated. Then the client could specify where the message should go. An IP address or hostname is a valid value for this.

The Windows form has two significant declarations:

```
private PeerConnection p = null;
internal System.Windows.Forms.ListBox listBox1;
```

The first is a `PeerConnection` object that will do all the thread handling and the networking, and the second variable is the `listbox` control that will be populated by the `PeerConnection` object.

Using the constructor of the Windows form, we create the following `PeerConnection` object, passing it the network port on which we want the server service to run, and the `Handle` to the current Windows form so that the `PeerConnection` instance can find the form to update the `listbox` control.

```
p = new PeerConnection(4048, Handle);
```

The `PeerConnection` class contains the following declarations:

```
private System.Net.Sockets.TcpListener peerListener = null;
private System.Net.Sockets.TcpClient peerClient = null;
private System.Net.Sockets.NetworkStream netStream = null;
private Thread t1 = null;
private ListBox lb;
private int port = 0;
private bool clientEnabled = true;
```

I'm not going to delve too much into networking speak – only enough to explain how it's communicating to the other client. Again, the focus here is the combined use of thread pools and management threads as a way of developing Windows applications. It's very easy to understand from this example and the previous one that well-written multithreaded applications follow a distinct "template" in the way they're written.

Above we declare a `TcpListener` object, which is used to listen for any messages on a predefined port. In this application, I set this to 4048 (it's good practice to set this above 1024 as anything above can be for user-defined purposes but those in the range of 1-1024 may have associated services running already, and it's not possible to listen on the same port as another service). The `TcpClient` class will create the actual **socket** to the listener and send the message. The `NetworkStream` class is used to send and receive information to and from client sockets. The stream buffers messages that arrive to and from the client. The application will just read this buffer and retrieve the value. The `ListBox` is used to hold a reference to the listbox on the form "ChatApplication" so that we can add an item to it from the `PeerConnection` object. The `bool clientEnabled` (as we'll see later) can be checked in order to suspend the listener and stop receiving messages for an unspecified period of time.

```
public PeerConnection(int port, ListBox formHandle)
{
    this.port = port;
    this.formHandle = formHandle;

    t1 = new Thread(new ThreadStart(CreateListener));
    t1.Name = "Listener Thread";
    t1.Priority = ThreadPriority.AboveNormal;
    t1.Start();
}
```

The `ThreadPriority` enumeration is used to identify which threads the scheduler should give greater priority to in terms of task completion and scheduling. Normally real-time systems will need to run threads with `ThreadPriority.Highest` whereas other threads that process batch jobs (and may not be very important compared to the real-time tasks) will have `ThreadPriority.Lowest` as their priority. By default when .NET creates a thread object all new threads are created with `ThreadPriority.Normal`. Other values include `AboveNormal` and `BelowNormal`.

The constructor creates and starts a thread that calls the CreateListener method to set up the listener on port 4048. The thread that calls CreateListener is named by setting the Name property. This makes it much easier to identify our threads. Returning to the **Threads Windows** will show the thread with the name **Listener Thread** allowing us to differentiate between threads that are used by the TcpClient and the single thread that is used to listen and read messages.

CreateListener declares the following variables at the top of the method:

```
Socket tc = null;
peerListener = new TcpListener(port);
peerListener.Start();
```

This starts the application listening on the specified port number (4048).

```
CallbackListbox clb = new CallbackListbox(SetListboxString);
while(true)
{
  tc = peerListener.AcceptSocket();
  byte[] byMessage = new byte[256];
  Thread.Sleep(500);
  int iLength = tc.Receive(byMessage, 0, byMessage.Length, SocketFlags.None);
  if(iLength>0)
  {
    string message = System.Text.Encoding.Default.GetString(byMessage);
    try
    {
      if(lb.InvokeRequired) lb.Invoke(clb, new object[]{message});
    }
    catch(Exception e)
    {
      message = e.Message;
    }
    finally
    {
      System.Diagnostics.Debug.WriteLine(message);
    }
  }
}
```

The server continually listens for messages on the port by never breaking out of the while loop. The thread of execution is blocked when it reaches the AcceptSocket method since it is waiting for a client to connect and send a message. The thread will resume execution on connection by the client and, using the Receive method of the Socket class, will populate an array using the byte array buffer. There is an upper-limit of 256 bytes on this, so data transmitted that is longer than this will be truncated by the application.

The byte array is then converted into a string and a handle is obtained to the ChatApplication class (the Windows form) and an item is added to the ListBox via the Invoke technique described earlier and used to marshal a call from the worker thread to the UI thread.

While this is occurring, one or many clients may be connecting across a network and the requests will be queued by the listener on the listener thread.

When the user wants to send a message and clicks on the **Send** button, everything in the textbox will be read and sent across to the listener:

```
private void btSend_Click(object sender, System.EventArgs e)
{
    p.Write(txtMessage.Text);
}
```

The `Write` method is called on the `PeerConnection` object and the message is passed to it:

```
internal void Write(string message)
{
    ThreadPool.QueueUserWorkItem(new WaitCallback(CreateClient), message);
}
```

Here we see the use of the `ThreadPool` class again, which means that the pool is managing the client connection and our listener thread is being managed by the application. The `ThreadPool` class is used here to manage client connections so that the chat application can have concurrent connections and send messages to many other chat applications independent of the network latency or the response time for locating the host and accepting of the connection etc. – in this way the application can send as many concurrent messages as necessary. The **callback** method `CreateClient` looks like this:

```
peerClient = new TcpClient();
peerClient.Connect(cmb.SelectedText, port);

netStream = peerClient.GetStream();

StreamWriter sw = new StreamWriter(netStream);
sw.Write((string)message);
sw.Flush();

peerClient.Close();
```

The `TcpClient` object is created and connects to `localhost` at 4048 (this value is pulled from the currently selected `ComboBox` value – I only have `localhost` in the `ComboBox` currently but this can be replaced or added to with a `NetBIOS` or `DNS` name). The `NetworkStream` is returned and the `StreamWriter` object is used to stream a string to the listener instead of a byte array (which is how a `NetworkStream` is used). When the message has been written to the `Stream` and the `Stream` has been flushed to the server, the client connection is closed, as all it needs to send is a single message.

Finally, when the checkbox is checked, the `Enabled` property on the `PeerConnection` object is set and will stop the server from listening until its unchecked:

```
private void chkSuspendClient_CheckedChanged(object sender,
                                             System.EventArgs e)
{
    p.Enabled = chkSuspendClient.Checked;
}
```

The `Thread` methods `Suspend` and `Resume` are used here.

```
internal bool Enabled
{
   set
   {
      if (t1.ThreadState == ThreadState.Suspended && value)
         t1.Resume();
      else if (t1.ThreadState != ThreadState.Suspended && !value)
         t1.Suspend();
      clientEnabled = value;
   }

   get
   { return clientEnabled; }
}
```

The `ThreadState` property is checked to see if the thread has been suspended already, and also the `bool value` is checked. In this way the property can determine whether to `Resume` or `Suspend` the thread. If the thread is suspended, execution of the listener app will stop until it is resumed. With the `ThreadState` enumeration and property, we can check whether the thread being referenced is currently running, suspended, stopped, aborted, or sleeping. We can also check to see whether the thread is a `background` thread or not (this is a user-defined value and can be set by `Thread.IsBackGround = true`). A background thread is identical to a foreground thread except that it doesn't stop a process from terminating. When all foreground threads have been destroyed the process can terminate calling `Abort` on any background threads.

Different Windows Forms Programming Models

There has been a significant shift in the way that Windows applications are being written and designed via the .NET Framework. The web services model has allowed distributed client-server desktop applications to flourish again where they had been all but replaced with thin-client web applications since the Internet/intranet revolution. In this section I want to discuss the approach to design and the issues involved in choosing single or multiple-tiered models for our Windows Forms applications. In order to understand some of the issues involved in the choices, we'll review several possible ways of creating and consuming services from Windows Forms applications.

These will include:

- ❏   Building fat-client forms applications

- ❏   Building client-server applications

- ❏   Building client front ends to web services

By **fat client** I refer to the use of wholly solitary, completely non-distributed clients. The application shown earlier in the chapter, which pulled data from the database using a single form and a single executable, was an example of something so self-contained. However, this is not always the best means of doing something. Sometimes the application is too functional to place on the client – requiring vast calculations – and it also may need access to resources that the client cannot see directly since only a single point on the network has a route to these resources.

Client-server is a fantastic model for distributing load from a client application. Using RPC the business logic can be set in another tier on a server. This is preferable for rolling out new applications. As many client applications are just a window onto data, it makes sense to include the business rules in a separate layer, so that any updates will be visible to all clients and won't require new versions of the client to be rolled out to hundreds of desktops. The new RPC model for .NET, which is a great improvement on DCOM, is .NET Remoting that allows clients to call servers on the network through either a binary protocol or a SOAP protocol. Either way, the entire TCP port range is available for RPC use. .NET Remoting is far more flexible than DCOM and can be used in internet scenarios as well as over an internal network.

The last entry in the list is what we'll discuss now, including some of the issues of programming using this new model. Since the inception of web services, Microsoft has provided a rich development environment in Visual Studio .NET and has been very keen to see them consumed not only in a web environment, but also using form-based clients. This has given rise to the term "**Smart Client**", which is a client used to consume web services.

We'll gloss over the subject of web services briefly, as there is a great deal of literature and an even greater deal of VS.NET that which aids in development of web services and makes them a really easy option. What we're interested in now is to how to use web services in an economical way.

A brief description of web services could be that they are network services that are accessible through the use of common standardized web protocols such as SOAP and HTTP. They are deployed to a web server and have a published interface in an XML dialect called WSDL. A client can read this and obtain a full description of what is available through the web service (methods, types, etc.).

We'll talk through the creation of a color picker web service, which returns a random color that will be used to change the background color of the Smart Client form. This is a very simple example, but there is really no limit to what the web service can do. Two examples would be a web service to store the message left by people using the chat client earlier, so that the chat client pumped messages to the service and left them there so that the client could periodically check the service for chat messages; or a web service that emulated the commodity pricing form and returned data from a database that could be displayed on the form in the same way as before. These uses will become more and more widespread as web services permeate application development. One consideration, which should be apparent from the content in the rest of this chapter, is the need to invoke web services efficiently and in a non-UI blocking manner. This introduces the idea of multithreaded web service clients – it is essential that these be written with non-blocking UIs in mind, since they will have the extra overhead of network latency to the web service.

First we'll create the web service. In this case, we'll use the VS.NET project wizard. Select **ASP.NET Web Service** and type in the name of the project. I've called my web service `TextWebService`. A virtual web directory is created in the root of the IIS web server.

In VS.NET, it is possible to add web references in the same way as we would normally add a locally installed component reference – once the service is created, we would wish to add a web reference to the client application that will enable IntelliSense for the web service classes. Choosing **Add Web Reference** brings up a dialog box requesting the location of a WSDL file. This file is created implicitly following an HTTP request to IIS. In the dialog box, if we browse to http://localhost/TextWebService/service1.asmx?WSDL (`service1.asmx` is the default project filename VS.Net will display the service and give us the option to add a reference to this service). The WSDL query string enables the WSDL to be constructed and delivered via an ISAPI filter in IIS. When the web reference is set in the client, a C# proxy is built "on the fly" containing a number of methods that relate the web service methods:

```csharp
[WebMethod]
public string ColorPicker()
{
    string color = null;
    System.Random rnd = new Random(DateTime.Now.Second);
    int retVal = rnd.Next(5);
    switch(retVal)
    {
        case 0:
            color = "white";
            break;
        case 1:
            color = "red";
            break;
        case 2:
```

```
        color = "black";
        break;
    case 3:
        color = "green";
        break;
    case 4:
        color = "blue";
        break;
    }
    return color;
}
```

Rather than show and discuss the whole web service class (this is not the focus of this diversion), we'll just look at the method we're interested in – the code is available in the associated web download from http://www.wrox.com.

The attribute above the method specifies that this is a web method enabling it to be accessed using web service protocols as opposed to common RPC protocols. The method simply calculates a random number using a seed value and returns a color string to the client.

```
private localhost.Service1 loc = new localhost.Service1();
private System.IAsyncResult iSync;
private System.Windows.Forms.Label lblNoOfTimes;
private int noOfTimes = 0;
private System.Timers.Timer timer;
```

The form begins with the above declarations, the most important of which is the `localhost.Service1` declaration, which refers to the web services type `Service1`.

```
string color = loc.ColorPicker();
this.BackColor = Color.FromName(color);
timer = new System.Timers.Timer(10000);
timer.Enabled = true;
timer.Elapsed += new System.Timers.ElapsedEventHandler(timer_Elapsed);
```

Initially the `ColorPicker` method is called synchronously on the web service and returns one of five colors, which is then set to the form `BackColor`. The `Timer` object is created and set to repeat at an interval of ten seconds. The `ElapsedEventHandler` delegate `timer_Elapsed` will then be called every ten seconds, when it will call the web service `ColorPicker` method asynchronously:

```
protected void timer_Elapsed(object sender, System.Timers.ElapsedEventArgs e)
{
    iSync = loc.BeginColorPicker(new AsyncCallback(callback), noOfTimes);
}
```

The above **BeginXxx** method should look very familiar by now. The C# web service proxy class creates one for every method along with the equivalent **EndXxx** method. The `AsyncCallback` method is set to a method named `callback`:

```
private void callback(IAsyncResult iSync)
{
    BackColor = Color.FromName(loc.EndColorPicker(iSync));
    noOfTimes++;
    lblNoOfTimes.Text = Convert.ToString(noOfTimes);
}
```

The callback function `callback` uses the string that is returned from the `EndColorPicker` method. The return type is always returned from the web service method, so if the web method returned an `int`, the `EndColorPicker` would also return an `int`. The return string is then used to set the `BackColor` property of the form, and a count is kept of the number of color changes and printed in a label in the bottom left corner of the screen.

The button pressed is handled by the following:

```
private void btGetColor_Click(object sender, System.EventArgs e)
{
    iSync = loc.BeginColorPicker(new AsyncCallback(callback), noOfTimes);
}
```

This does exactly the same thing as the timer method but as this is invoked asynchronously control is returned to the UI so the button can be pressed constantly any number of times and the form will remain "unlocked".

Using P/Invoke

P/Invoke or **Platform Invoke** is how we are able to use APIs from .NET. Any exposed API functions including the Win32 API can be used from .NET by loading the DLL library and referencing the function that we want to call. In C++ these functions are exposed through header files and written using `__stdcall` notation. In Visual Basic they are referenced using `Declare` statements within a VB module. In C# it is just as easy to reference an API.

In order to demonstrate the use of P/Invoke, I've included an application called `FibersTest` which is a C# Windows Forms application that makes calls to the Win32 API using P/Invoke. The most common use of P/Invoke will probably be for Windows API calls to `kernel32.dll` or `user32.dll`. We call the code being executed in these DLLs "unmanaged".

`FibersTest` uses a Windows object that the .NET Framework doesn't expose, so in order to create this object we have to use a Windows API call. The object in question is called a `Fiber`. Fibers can be considered as lightweight threads that can be scheduled by our application rather than the operating system. In fact unlike threads they are invisible to the Windows `kernel`. Fibers are generally not used in application development since they require a fair amount of scheduling code and generally the performance of application that use fibers can be matched using efficient multithreaded apps (threadpools and possibly I/O completion ports). That said SQL Server, which is a very heavy load application, is written using `Fiber` objects.

The `FibersTest` application (shown below) simply uses six fibers to append an item to a listbox switching between each of them to do work. Each `Fiber` maintains its own stack like its parent thread and runs in the context of this thread. Fibers can be scheduled within code as we will see but the parent thread will continue to be context-switched like all other threads in the system. Fibers have the benefit of being able to do work and not be registered with the Windows kernel (so that no context switching need occur).

The code below shows how the Windows API functions are declared in the C# program. Each method must be marked both `extern` and `static`. The method is decorated with an attribute called `DllImport` that takes the name of the DLL that must reside in a Windows system path (or a fully qualified path must be used to non-Windows DLLs). In order to use `DllImport` we must use the `System.RunTime.InteropServices` namespace.

```
[DllImport("kernel32.dll")]
extern static IntPtr ConvertThreadToFiber(int fiberData);

[DllImport("kernel32.dll")]
extern static IntPtr CreateFiber(int size, System.Delegate function, int
fiberData);

[DllImport("kernel32.dll")]
extern static IntPtr SwitchToFiber(IntPtr fiberAddress);

[DllImport("kernel32.dll")]
extern static void DeleteFiber(IntPtr fiberAddress);

[DllImport("kernel32.dll")]
extern static int GetLastError()
```

Three of the functions above return a System.IntPtr type that can hold a reference handle to an object (the size of this type is dependent on the system – on a 32-bit system this struct is 32 bits). In each case above the IntPtr references a handle to a Fiber object.

The ConvertThreadToFiber function takes a value that can be used as an input argument for that fiber. This function is used to turn the current thread into a fiber, which must be done prior to creating many fibers for work (using the thread). Once this is done the CreateFiber method is used to create any number of fibers and initialize them. The size parameter holds the size of the fiber stack in bytes. The System.Delegate represents a delegate of the method to call and fiberData represents an argument to the fiber. The System.Delegate argument is used in place of a pointer but the call is marshaled via the runtime.

The SwitchToFiber function starts the fiber (effectively scheduling the fiber to do work). The DeleteFiber method frees all resources associated with the fiber. These two functions use a pointer to the Fiber as their input parameter.

GetLastError will return the last error of the current thread being run (this will be applicable to all the fibers as they are run in the context of the creating thread and all that is apparent to the kernel is this thread). The value returned can be checked against a lookup table in the Platform SDK documentation (under the System Error Codes section).

```
System.IntPtr obj;

void NewThreadToFiberExecution()
{
  try
  {
    SetTextOutputToEventLog stof = new SetTextOutputToEventLog(OutputLog);

    obj = ConvertThreadToFiber(0);
    long l1 = GetLastError();
    System.IntPtr retVal1 = CreateFiber(500, stof, 1);
    System.IntPtr retVal2 = CreateFiber(500, stof, 2);
    System.IntPtr retVal3 = CreateFiber(500, stof, 3);
    System.IntPtr retVal4 = CreateFiber(500, stof, 4);
    System.IntPtr retVal5 = CreateFiber(500, stof, 5);
    if(GetLastError()!=0) throw new Exception("Create Fiber failed!!");
    IntPtr fiber1return = SwitchToFiber(retVal1);
    IntPtr fiber2return = SwitchToFiber(retVal2);
    IntPtr fiber3return = SwitchToFiber(retVal3);
    IntPtr fiber4return = SwitchToFiber(retVal4);
    IntPtr fiber5return = SwitchToFiber(retVal5);

    if(GetLastError()!=0) throw new Exception("Create Fiber failed!!");

    DeleteFiber(retVal1);
    DeleteFiber(retVal2);
    DeleteFiber(retVal3);
    DeleteFiber(retVal4);
    DeleteFiber(retVal5);
  }
  catch(Exception e)
```

```
    {
        throw e;
    }
}
```

The `ConvertThreadToFiber` method is called to turn the current thread into a fiber. Then, five threads are created using `CreateThread` and five different `int` values are passed into them along with an initial stack size of 500 bytes and the delegate `stof` pointing to the `OutputLog` method. As each `SwitchToFiber` is called on each fiber respectively, the fibers invoke the method `OutputLog`. When the work is done (and if no errors have occurred) then all five fibers are deleted. The thread then continues executing and exits the method. It then exits too – it can also be changed back into a `Thread` using the API call `ConvertFiberToThread`.

This method is invoked by a worker thread created by the main thread in the form's constructor.

```
Thread t1 = new Thread(new ThreadStart(NewThreadToFiberExecution));
t1.Start();
```

The `OutputLog` method is called by each fiber in turn passing an `int` value (1-5) into it and calling the listbox delegate to update the items in the listbox.

```
void OutputLog(int fiberNumber)
{
    this.Invoke(new AddToListBox(SetText), new object[]{fiberNumber});
    SwitchToFiber(obj);
}

void SetText(int message)
{
    lstFibers.Items.Add("Fiber "+message.ToString()+" added this");
}

delegate void AddToListBox(int message);
```

One important thing to note about the `OutputLog` file – which is common to the behavior of fibers – is the additional call to the `SwitchToFiber` function. If this doesn't occur then the first fiber won't return from the `OutputLog` method. The reason this is occurs is that the fibers must be scheduled by the code, unlike thread objects the management is done by us. This call will return to the original fiber `obj` in the `NewThreadToFiberExecution` method.

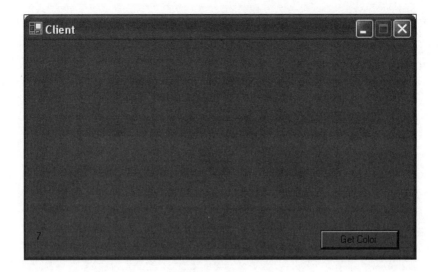

Event Accessors

Highlighted in this chapter are many issues regarding Windows Forms development. This last section focuses on a topic that can be used to optimize the performance of applications that have large numbers of events raised.

Throughout this book we've seen examples of events being published and subscribed to by classes. Generally the following syntax is used to subscribe to an event:

```
button.Click += new EventHandler(handler);
button.Click -= new EventHandler(handler);
```

In this case the button control is called `button` and the event handler that handles the `Click` event is called `handler`. We should analyze what is actually happening here, though, as it all too easy in practice to churn out code in parrot fashion without understanding what is occurring behind-the-scenes. It is especially relevant in this case as it isn't apparent from what we can deduce of events and delegates.

In this case the Windows Form `EventHandler` delegate is being used with the `+=` operator. We can think of this `+=` operator as shorthand for `Delegate.Combine`. The static method `Combine` will add the event handler method to a list of methods that are called sequentially whenever the event is triggered. It follows therefore that we should expect the `-=` operator to call the `Delegate.Remove` method.

In reality neither of these methods is called directly. Instead, methods called `add` and `remove` are used to control access to the delegate (as you probably know, these are two reserved words in C#). Each of these methods is an accessor method for the particular event. As each event in an application involves a delegate being declared large Windows Forms programs may expend unnecessary resources on delegates for each event they subscribe to. It would be far more efficient to write a better implementation for a class that has many events.

The following example involves a form requesting the user's login name. When the form initializes it subscribes to a single login event twice.

```
public class LoginAuditInserter
{
  public delegate void LoginAuditHandler(string username);
  private AccessorContainer container = new AccessorContainer();
  private static int key = 0;
  public event LoginAuditHandler LoginAudit
  {
    [MethodImpl(MethodImplOptions.Synchronized)]
    add
    {
      container.Add(key, value);
    }
    [MethodImpl(MethodImplOptions.Synchronized)]
    remove
    {
      container.Remove(key, value);
    }
  }

  protected void OnLoginAudit(string username)
  {
    LoginAuditHandler loginAudit = (LoginAuditHandler)container.Get(key);
    if(username!=null)
    {
      loginAudit(username);
    }
  }

  public void AddAuditEntry(string username)
  {
    OnLoginAudit(username);
  }
}
```

The LoginInserter class contains a definition of an event that exposes the add and remove accessors. The attributes decorating this event are found in the System.Runtime.CompilerServices namespace and are used to stop concurrent access to the accessors (thread synchronization as we saw earlier in the chapter). The variable container is of type AccessorContainer, which uses a collection object internally to store the delegate subscriber methods. Instead of calling Delegate.Combine and Delegate.Remove directly, we can use the Add and Remove methods of the container class to manage a collection of delegates.

```
public class AccessorContainer
{
  private ArrayList arrayAccessor = new ArrayList();
  public Delegate Get(int key)
  {
    return ((Delegate)arrayAccessor[key]);
  }
```

```
  public void Add(int key, Delegate ptr)
  {
    try
    {
      arrayAccessor[key] = Delegate.Combine((Delegate)arrayAccessor[key], ptr);
    }
    catch(ArgumentOutOfRangeException)
    {
      arrayAccessor.Add(ptr);
    }
  }

  public void Remove(int key, Delegate ptr)
  {
    arrayAccessor.Remove(Delegate.Remove((Delegate)arrayAccessor[key], ptr));
  }
}
```

The `AccessorContainer` class uses an `ArrayList` internally to manage the storage of a collection of delegates. This class can be used by any number of classes to store delegates relating to events. Each class must use a unique key value, though, to index a new `ArrayList` element.

We can now declare the `LoginInserter` class as a member variable in our form.

```
LoginAuditInserter la = new LoginAuditInserter();
```

In the form constructor we can subscribe to the event twice using two delegates.

```
la.LoginAudit += new LoginAuditInserter.LoginAuditHandler(AddAuditEntry);
la.LoginAudit += new LoginAuditInserter.LoginAuditHandler(AddEventLogEntry);
```

The two event handlers add a line to the Debug window in VS.NET and add an entry to the Application event log respectively.

```
static public void AddAuditEntry(string username)
{
  System.Diagnostics.Debug.WriteLine(username);
}

static public void AddEventLogEntry(string username)
{
  string applicationName = "Login Audit";
  EventLog ev = new EventLog("Application");
  ev.Source = applicationName;
  ev.WriteEntry("Login Attempted.", EventLogEntryType.Information);
}
```

When the button on the form is pressed, the `AddAuditEvent` method is called in the `LoginAuditInserter` class, which will raise the `LoginAudit` event if the username is not an empty string. To get a handle back to the delegate(s) references in the `ArrayList` it will use the key value in the `LoginAuditInserter` class.

The importance of this technique of using collection storage for each new delegate becomes paramount, as an application gets larger. One of the consequences of subscribing to many events means that the compiler generates code that will contain a private delegate field for each event. As we have access to the event accessor methods we can circumvent this and avoid extra delegate declarations, thus saving space. This is especially relevant for Windows Forms development as controls may have hundreds of events (and not all of them being subscribed to either). A delegate field for each of these takes up storage space, which will have a detrimental effect on the performance of our program. Using the described collection class or a similar technique would increase the efficiency of the application and save storage space.

Summary

This chapter covered many aspects of multi-threaded programming of Windows Forms and asynchronous programming. When these principles are understood good design of desktop applications for a high-octane business environment can follow. Many Windows Forms team developers at Microsoft adhere to the adage that 90% of poorly performing applications follow bad design principles and not poor coding standards.

In this chapter we addressed:

- Problems with single threaded applications
- Writing multithreaded applications
- Using synchronization
- Using the `ThreadPool` class
- Asynchronous programming
- Developing multithreaded data and networking apps
- Building asynchronous web service clients
- Using P/Invoke
- Using Event Accessors

10

Deploying Windows Applications

Deploying Windows applications has become a very interesting topic with the emergence of the .NET Framework. In this chapter, we will look at the features provided by .NET to facilitate different deployment scenarios, and see how we can take advantage of these. The topics covered in this chapter include:

❑   Using and configuring the Windows Installer

❑   Web Setup projects

❑   Using CAB files

❑   Using Merge Modules

❑   Code Access Security

❑   Assemblies and the GAC

❑   Distributing the .NET Framework Runtime with projects

However, before we look at what .NET has to offer in the way of setup and deployment features, let's review the history of application deployment and why we need ever more complicated setup projects to install a Windows application.

In the days of DOS, applications didn't need to be installed by an installation package; a simple XCOPY statement would copy all the relevant files and directories from a source disk – usually a floppy disk or CD – to the destination hard drive (XCOPY is synonymous with a directory drag-drop operation in Windows Explorer) . Early Windows applications used the PATH environment variable to locate DLLs that were to be loaded into the process space of an executable. In this way, DLLs could be copied to any directory referenced by the path statement, although most installers would copy DLL files into the Windows system directory (rather than extend the PATH environment variable).

This simplistic form of deployment, however, could not be used effectively to install distributed enterprise applications or applications that used language-independent technologies such as COM. COM demands that components need to be registered so that the COM runtime can locate the classes needed, load the DLL, and execute the function. As a result, installing a software product got slightly more complicated.

Before we elaborate on the new deployment features of the .NET Framework, it's worth mentioning that deployment has once again come full circle to the idea of XCOPY. Unlike the COM runtime (which has to locate a DLL through a **ProgID**), the .NET Runtime doesn't have to locate a DLL in the same way – it just has to be resident in the application folder. In effect, this is the best of both models. The functional aspects of COM are preserved, coupled with the deployment simplicity of an API DLL (this type of DLL contains nothing more than a quantity of functions that could be loaded into the current process). As .NET assemblies contain metadata and are self-describing, unlike COM they don't need separate type libraries to be registered to describe the DLL. .NET addresses the problem of "DLL hell" which was prevalent in COM application installations. This occurs when a higher version COM DLL file is registered and overwrites a previous file, breaking the contract between the COM client and server. As a client is tied to the server and a higher version has been installed, binary compatibility will be broken and the client will stop working. As we shall see, .NET supports side-by-side execution, which allows many servers to be installed, as each client references a particular server version, so many client EXE programs can use many DLL assemblies of the same type (thus avoiding DLL hell).

In order to demonstrate how to deploy our Windows applications, we first need an application to deploy. We'll use a very simple application called TextReader for this purpose; the code for this application is available as part of the downloadable code for the book. This application consists of a form with two buttons that invoke methods in a class in a separate DLL assembly:

The TextReader application offers a good example of the advantages of XCOPY deployment. The DLL and EXE files will be stored in the TextReader executable directory on a floppy disk (or some other medium). In a subdirectory called src we could have the source files of C# application which could be distributed with the application. We could deploy the application simply by scripting a batch file to use XCOPY to copy the contents from the floppy disk or CD to the client machine. An example XCOPY statement (which would be present in the batch file) may look like this. The /Y and /E switches tell the XCOPY program to copy all subdirectories and to overwrite files if a file with the same name exists at the destination:

```
XCOPY a:\ c:\textreader /Y /E
```

It should be noted, however, that the XCOPY command has a few drawbacks and shouldn't be used for anything other than very simple deployments. Unfortunately, XCOPY just copies from one directory to another, so it may overwrite files that are necessary for one application with files that are needed for the current application. Also, XCOPY can't check the version number of files and deploy higher versions, add an uninstall mechanism, or create a start menu shortcut. For something a bit more complex, there are many alternatives that are discussed in this chapter.

You may have already noticed that Visual Studio .NET, unlike its predecessor, contains setup project types within the IDE. In Visual Studio 6, the Setup and Deployment wizard was accessed separately from the VS environment. The integration of deployment projects with the IDE means that solutions can contain setup projects that are accessible when the solution is opened in VS.NET – this allows a single point of reference for all applications. There are also third-party installers such as WISE and InstallShield that add even richer sets of features than the installer types available through VS.NET. These normally cost in license fees and for both development and distribution of software products.

Using Windows Installer

Windows Installer is not a new product. It has been in existence for some time, and comes as standard with Windows operating systems (for NT4 and 9x, which were written before Windows Installer, downloads and service pack updates can be used to install Windows Installer to the desktop). All Windows versions other than XP have to have the Windows Installer upgraded to version 2 (XP has v2 as standard).

Windows Installer runs as a background process, normally as a service (if the Windows version supports services). When the Windows Installer package is executed, the Windows Installer process is used to add the application to a database of applications so that it can be uninstalled. Windows Installer packages can be created and then distributed on any medium, including download over a network.

Visual Studio .NET includes a Windows Installer deployment project that allows us to create a set of activities that are needed to install the application. As we will see soon, there are many supplementary things that can be done at install time that Windows Installer setup projects support.

Important features of Windows Installer include the way that failed installations can be recovered, installed products can be uninstalled, and incomplete installations can be rolled back. This obviously should leave the system unaffected from a partial installation.

Windows Installer packages contain all the installation files that, when executed, will provide a series of screens that can be used to unpackage and install the application, including changing configuration settings, registering COM components, and/or registering .NET assemblies in the GAC. Each package has the extension .msi. It should be stressed that the Windows Installer project type is not dependent on the .NET Framework, so it's altogether possible to create a project within VS.NET that doesn't involve the installation of a Windows Forms application. In fact, any application can be installed using the Windows Installer. An unmanaged API exists for this as part of the Platform SDK, which can be used to create Windows Installer projects from C++.

In order to install the TextReader application shown above, we'll create a Windows Installer project using the Setup wizard and add several settings to the project to demonstrate some of the advanced installation features of Windows Installer.

The Setup Wizard

The easiest way to create an installation program for our assembly is by adding a **Setup Wizard** project to an existing solution in Visual Studio .NET. We do this by choosing **Add Project** from the **File** menu, and selecting the **Setup Wizard** project type in the **Setup and Deployment Projects** folder. This starts the **Setup Wizard**. The first screen is just a flash screen, so click on **Next**. The next step allows us to choose which type of setup project we wish:

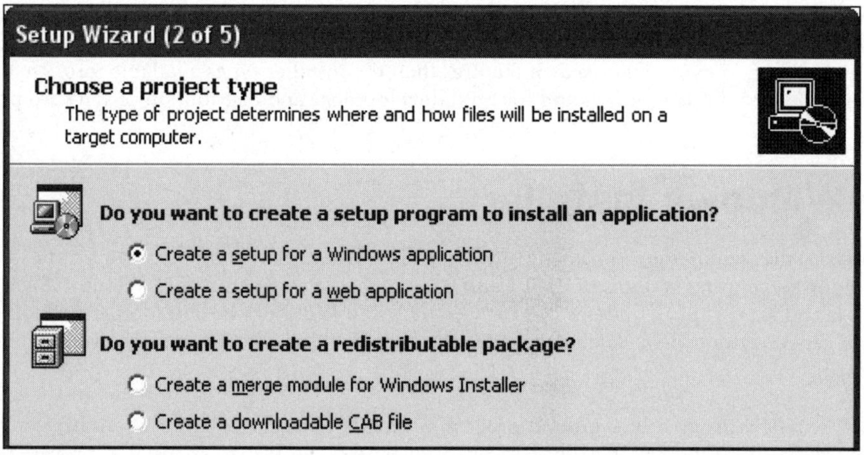

In this case, choose the **Create a setup for a Windows Application** option, as we're only interested in Windows applications in this book.

The next step in the wizard detects which projects we have in our solutions and puts up a checkbox requesting the type of files we want to distribute with the package:

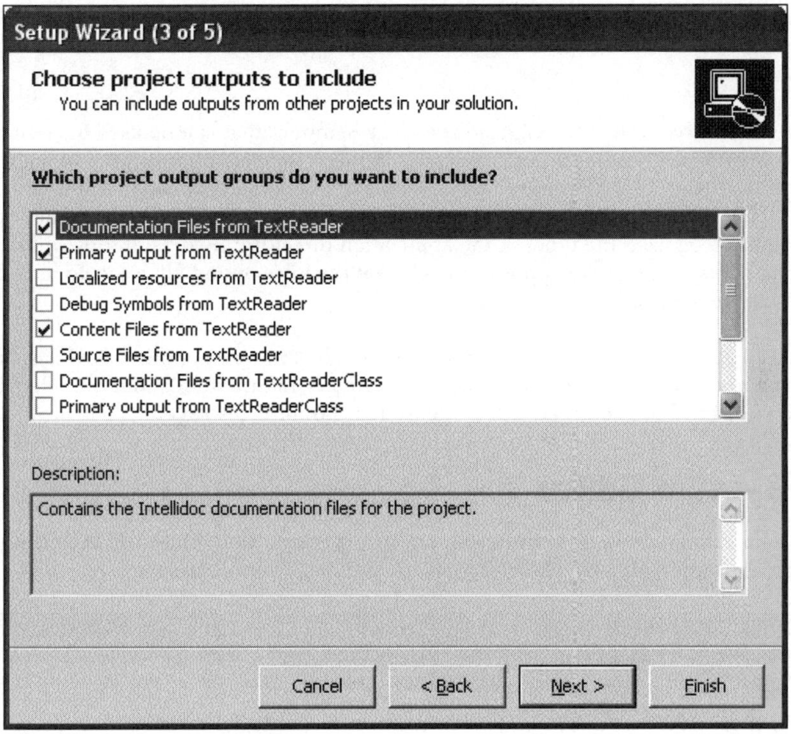

Note that we will only see these options if we added the setup project to a solution containing the application we wish to deploy.

There are several options for each existing project in the solution:

- ❑ Documentation files
- ❑ Primary output
- ❑ Localized resources
- ❑ Debug symbols
- ❑ Content files
- ❑ Source Files

The **Documentation files** option refers to the auto-generated XML documentation files generated by the C# compiler from XML tags within special comments. These document the application and can be viewed through the browser. This is beyond the scope of this chapter but more information on this type of documentation can be found in Chapter 8. A sample XML documentation file has been included with the code download so that this can be installed with our Windows Forms project.

Primary Output refers to the DLL or EXE files generated for each project. This should be added to the installer package – if this isn't included then the main program files won't be included in the installer package!

The **Localized Resources** refers to language-specific assemblies that can be used to create multilingual applications. If we're distributing source code, the **Debug Symbols** option is used to allow us to distribute the associated PDB (Program Debug Database) with the installation – this can be handy for distributing debug configuration settings (for example, breakpoints). The **Content Files** option can include all other recognized file types in the application directory; by default, this will include all .ico files if nothing else specific to the application. The **Source Files** option allows us to include the C# source code files in the installation package.

The next screen allows us to add any external files (which aren't part of our VS.NET solution) to the installation package, and the final screen displays summary information about the selections we've made. Once the wizard has completed, the File System Editor is displayed.

The File System Editor

The File System Editor allows us to install files to specific important folders on the client machine. These folders are represented by virtual folders in the File System Editor:

In the screenshot above, the left-hand pane represents the file system on the client machine (where we will deploy our application). By default, the pane shows three virtual folders (although we can add other folders):

- The Application folder is the folder that will contain the project binaries and any other application-specific files; typically, this will be C:\Program Files\[Company Name]\[Application Name].

- The User's Desktop folder allows us to place a shortcut link on the user's desktop; this would map to C:\Documents and Settings\[username]\Desktop on a Windows 2000 machine.

- The User's Programs Menu allows us to place program shortcuts in the Start Menu; this folder maps to C:\Documents and Settings\[username]\Start Menu\Programs.

> Note that the names of these folders may vary according to the language version of
> Windows installed on the client. This is why we should never hard-code folder names.

We can create a shortcut to a file or folder by right-clicking on the item in the right-hand pane, and
selecting **Create Shortcut to XXX**. We can then drop the shortcut that's created into one of the other
folders – for example, if we want to place a shortcut to our application on the desktop, we would drop
the shortcut into the **User's Desktop** folder in the left-hand pane.

We can also get our installation program to copy files to a particular folder by right-clicking on that
folder and selecting to **Add** a file; this will bring up a dialog box where we can define what executable
we want to add. In this way, if we want to add other items such as help files or other applications to our
package, then we can place shortcuts from a folder in the name of our software company. This can be
done in any of the folders, but it makes sense to use the **User's Programs Menu** to reference help and
other files, as this allows us to group the application and its support files.

If you look at the properties window for one of the files, you'll see that there is a **Register** property for
each file added to the package, which can be set to one of five enumeration values. These values default
to the type of file (for example, COM DLL or .NET Assembly) that is being added to the setup project.
In this way, the application will know what to do with the file. If a COM file is included, this will be
registered as part of the setup process. The possible values are:

❑ `vsdrpDoNotRegister` – the item does not need to be registered (the default for .NET
    assemblies)

❑ `vsdrpCOM` – the item needs to registered as a COM component

❑ `vsdrpCOMRelativePath` – the item will be registered as an isolated COM object

❑ `vsdrpCOMSelfReg` – the item will self-register as a COM object

❑ `vsdrpFont` – the item will be registered as a font file

Adding Extra Folders

If you right-click on **File System on Target Machine** above all of the folders, you will see that many
other folders can be added to the Installer Package. These are (the default values are listed in brackets
after the virtual folder name):

❑ **Common Files Folder** (`C:\Program Files\Common Files`)

❑ **Fonts Folder** (`C:\Windows\Fonts`)

❑ **System Folder** (`C:\Windows\System32`)

❑ **User's Application Data Folder** (`C:\documents and
    settings\[username]\Application Data`)

❑ **Program Files Folder** (`C:\Program Files`)

❑ **Favorites Folder** (`C:\Documents and Settings\[username]\Favorites`)

❑ **Personal Data Folder** (`C:\Documents and Settings\[username]\UserData`)

- ❑ **Send To Folder** (`C:\Documents and Settings\[username]\SendTo`)

- ❑ **Start Menu Folder** (`C:\Documents and Settings\[username]\Start Menu`)

- ❑ **Startup Folder** (`C:\Documents and Settings\[username]\Start Menu\StartUp`)

- ❑ **Template Folder** (`C:\documents and settings\[username]\Template`)

- ❑ **Windows Folder** (`C:\Windows`)

- ❑ **Global Assembly Cache Folder** (`C:\Windows\Assembly`)

Many of these folders should be obvious and should give an indication of the configuration power of the Windows Installer. I'll briefly describe some of the folders that can be used with our applications to enhance the user experience and enable deployment of all types of application. It may be necessary to add fonts with an application that uses multilingual fonts, so the font file can be added to the Windows **Fonts** folder. The **System** folder can be used to add DLLs so that they can be loaded by an application and functions contained within can be called – this should no longer be necessary with .NET, and should really be avoided if at all possible. The **Send To** folder obviously will allow us to add our application shortcut to the **Send To** menu in Windows Explorer, which allows the user to choose from a list of applications to open a file. The **Startup** folder is used to make sure that the application is started every time the machine reboots. The **Global Assembly Cache** folder we'll look at in more detail later in the chapter (as this is relevant to the way that we write our applications).

Other Editors

So far, we've been looking at the File System Editor, but there are many other editors that enable us to make different configuration changes to the system during our installation. We can toggle between the editors by right-clicking on the setup project in the Solution Explorer pane, selecting the **View** menu, and choosing the different editors; or by clicking on the project and switching between the representative editor icons at the top of the Solution Explorer pane:

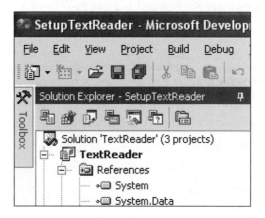

These icons allow us to toggle between the following editors:

- ❑ File System Editor
- ❑ Registry Editor
- ❑ File Types Editor
- ❑ User Interface Editor
- ❑ Custom Actions Editor
- ❑ Launch Conditions Editor

The Registry Editor

The Registry Editor provides an interface (not dissimilar to Regedit.exe) to allow us to create registry keys specific to our application:

This window exposes the HKEY_CURRENT_USER and HKEY_LOCAL_MACHINE hives and automatically references the Software key that is used in this instance to add a key value for either the current user's registry, or for all users. The HKEY_CURRENT_USER hive will be loaded for the user who is currently logged on, so any registry values added here aren't available machine-wide. So if users who didn't install the application use the machine, they will not be able to read the registry values for the application. To read values back for all users, put the key under HKEY_LOCAL_MACHINE.

The HKEY_CLASSES_ROOT enables developers to add the necessary keys to register a COM component (the equivalent of what Regsvr32.exe does). Now that we have a message value the application can reference it later to get application configuration information once installed.

The next editor window after the Registry Editor is the File Types Editor.

The File Types Editor

The File Types Editor can be used to create associated actions for certain file types. For example, if we create a file type with the extension .wrox that could be loaded into an application and parsed when the file is clicked on in Windows Explorer, we could use this editor to associate the file with an application and a command (usually Open or Run). Once we have done this, clicking on the file in Windows Explorer will start the application and load the contents of the .wrox file into it. The File Types menu can be viewed from Windows Explorer by clicking on Tools | Folder Options and choosing the File Types tab.

We can create a new file type in the File Types Editor by right-clicking on File Types on Target Machine and selecting Add File Type. Once we've created a new file type, we can set the extensions associated with it in its Properties window. Multiple extensions for a single file type should be separated with a semi-colon. Notice that we don't need to prefix the extensions with a period (.).

Once we've added the file type, VS.NET will automatically add the Open command as the default action, which will be perform when the user double-clicks on the file in Windows Explorer. For each action, we need to set the Verb (the command such as Open or Run that will be used to open/execute the file), and any additional arguments.

The UI Editor

The UI Editor can be used to arrange the installation screens or modify the properties or order of the screens by adding custom graphics to the screens or adding new screens to the setup process. There are several pre-built template screens that allow the complete customization of the UI sequence for application deployment. The default screen flow is as follows:

❑ Welcome

❑ Installation Folder

❑ Confirm Installation

❑ Progress

❑ Finished

The UI Editor also presents an Administrative screen flow that can be used to deploy an application from the network. The setup image can be run from the network, allowing all functions including uninstall and recovery to run from the same place.

Dialog boxes can be added at any stage of the screen flow (but always before the dialog to confirm installation). We'll consider in this section some of the very general ways that we can improve the application install. These very general suggestions should be sufficient for most of our application distributions:

❑ Showing the user a license agreement

❑ Giving the user a serial number screen to ensure that they are entitled to use the installation

❑ Displaying a registration screen

❑ Showing users a custom screen that allows them to add information that can be used by another part of the setup process

By right-clicking on the three possible stages of the project (start, progress, and end) we can choose to add a custom dialog from an installer predefined template:

Adding a License Agreement

To begin we'll choose the License Agreement option – adding it to the start stage of the install process. Notice that when a dialog is added to the project, it will disappear from the Add Dialog box – so we can't add several instances of the same dialog to the setup screens).

If we right-click on the added dialog in the VS.NET main window, we can adjust its properties. We can also drag the dialog to another position in the list, and the change the order in which the dialogs are presented to the user. Let's now add a license file to our License Agreement dialog; this is a two-stage process:

❑ Go back to the File System Editor that we looked at earlier in the chapter, right-click on the Application Folder, and choose Add, followed by File. Select the .rtf file containing the license agreement text to display on this screen. This file has now been added to the application folder and will be installed to this location. (We can use the exclude property to prevent installation of the file; by default, this is set to false, but it can be changed to true, in which case the file will be used and referred to during the setup process, but will not be deployed to the target machine.)

Return to the UI Editor Window and highlight the license file form. In the Properties window on the right-hand side of the screen, choose the license file by selecting the Application Folder and browsing to the file. The license file has now been added to this screen.

This screen will appear as below when the user runs the actual setup process:

The license agreement shown above is from a Rich Text Format file. During the installation, users must choose the I Agree radio button in order to enable the Next button (like all license agreements, this imposes a legal obligation on users, and they must now respect the terms and conditions packaged with the product).

The next screen we'll be adding is the **Customer Information screen** that allows the user to enter their Name, Company Name, and Serial Number. The serial number can be used to validate whether the user was given a product key or not. Product keys are normally distributed when a product has been purchased to enable unlocking and installation of that particular piece of software. The serial number validation algorithm is not particularly complex, but will help us to secure the product by providing a series of needed values. These values may or may not be parsed by the validation process (ignorance about where these validated numbers occur is the key to locking the product, as otherwise anybody could use the published algorithm to derive the digits needed to unlock the product).

The SerialNumberTemplate property in the properties window contains the following value (for this to be shown on the dialog, the ShowSerialNumber property must be set to true):

```
<###-%%%%%%%-^??%>
```

The template can contain the following symbols: <, #, -, %, ^, ?, and >. These represent different substitutable values. The < character is the start of the serial number; anything before this value in the `SerialNumberTemplate` property will be discarded. The # value signifies that a digit has to be entered at this location, but this value is only checked to see if it is digit. If so, then no additional validation occurs on it. The - character is used to denote a break in the serial number string, which is highlighted by placing a - character on the screen in between textboxes. The % character is used to enforce a digit being present in this location that will be checked by the validation algorithm (which will be described later). This is the only character that is enforced by the validation algorithm. The ^ character requires either an upper-case value or a digit, but is not subject to the validation algorithm. The ? character is used to denote an alphanumeric character that is not used by the validation algorithm. The last character is the companion to the first; the > character denotes the end of the serial number string, and all values after this in the template will be discarded.

Now let's return to the serial template value:

```
<###-%%%%%%%-^??%>
```

A valid serial number that corresponds to this would be:

```
111-7777777-A117
```

The only numbers that are of any concern are the 7s, as each of these is denoted by the % character in the `SerialNumberTemplate`. The validation algorithm checks that all of the % values add up to a multiple of 7. In this case, there are eight % values and eight 7 values. As all the numbers are 7, the total must be a multiple of 7 also, and so the validation succeeds and allows the user to continue to the following screen.

There are a set number of screens that can be used by the installer application. The screens we haven't discussed include custom dialog boxes that enable the user to enter information at install time, and for this information to be used at some other point within the installation application. In the download with this chapter we've shown the use of one of the three types of screen that can be used (up to three of each can be used in the installation procedure). These are checkbox screens, radio button screens, and textbox screens. The textbox screen is shown below:

Using the textbox, radio button, or checkbox screens allows us to elect whether to show up to four of these visual objects on one screen. The results of the user input in this screen (which uses only one textbox) can then be used in a following section, either as a condition or as text. In the example above, the text will be used as a registry value.

Installation Conditions

We can generally use any values from these screens by treating them as Windows Installer "environment" variables. In the Properties window for this screen, there are four named textboxes that can be displayed by toggling the VISIBLE property of each of the textboxes. Each box is given a property name, for example we've named the above textbox WELCOMETEXT. This name can then be used to add the text from this textbox to a registry key value by using the following syntax:

```
[WELCOMETEXT]
```

If the name occurs in the Value property of a registry key as it is shown above, then the textbox value will be substituted for the environment variable.

Each registry key within the Windows Installer model has a Condition property attached to it that will ensure that key will only be created if the registry variable condition is met. This is really meant to be used with the radio button or the checkbox screens, as each of these screens will return a Boolean value depending on whether the item was checked or not. In this way the Condition property will generally only have the name of the environment variable as the property value, for example:

```
[CHECKBOX1]
```

These values can be used in all parts of the installation process; for example, we can decide whether to install files by putting the environment variable name in the condition property. As we'll see later in the chapter, we also need to use these to use Custom Actions and Launch Conditions.

Most everyday pieces of software come with some sort of user registration program that allows the user to register for support online. Windows Installer provides a screen for user registration that will allow us to execute a program and pass argument details through to the program. Most programs will send details across to a web database so that the user can be registered for that particular product. Details will vary, but at a minimum the username and installation date will be sent to the server. A web service would provide an appropriate endpoint for a request to the web server with the details.

In the Properties window of the Register User dialog, we can define the path to the program that will be used to register the user (this will be in the Application folder, and so has to be added to it in the same way that we added the license file earlier). We can also define command-line arguments (separated by spaces) that will be passed to this program. For example, if we're using a C# program to complete the registration, this may have a Main() method as shown below. This program will be invoked when the external program is spawned from the Register User screen. A space-separated list of "environment" variables can be passed to this program and accessed through the args array:

```
static void Main(string[] args)
{
    Application.Run(new RegisterUser(args[0]));
}
```

We can use the [USERNAME] environment variable that we populated from the serial number template screen (from the name textbox). A space-separated list can be added to the Arguments property, and this can be used to provide values for the args array in our RegisterUser application.

The Register User screen appears with a "Register User ... " button. When this is clicked, the program defined to register the user details will be executed.

The Custom Actions Editor

In the last section, we looked at the UI editor. Even though this has a great deal of flexibility, in that we should be able to present the user with every eventuality throughout the installation process, there are two things it doesn't cater for. The first is the introduction of unique screens, which can be built up by the developer and dropped into a Windows Installer package, and the second is the use of custom screens when the application is being repaired or removed. This can be circumvented by using a third-party tool to create a Windows Installer package that will allow us create custom screens. The MSI file format doesn't specify these limitations – it is the VS.NET Installer builder that doesn't support these features.

Custom Actions can bridge this gap, though, through VS.NET. Even though there are no screens that can be added as part of the installer process, Custom Actions allow us to define a program (EXE or DLL) or a script file (in VBScript or JScript) that can be used to present the user with different messages or custom program actions based on an event. The events that we can use are:

- ❑ Install
- ❑ Rollback
- ❑ Commit
- ❑ Uninstall

Rollback and Commit represent the two transactional states that can occur if the product is successfully installed (in which case the software is committed), or if the Cancel button has been pressed or a problem occurred during installation (in which case the installation will be rolled back to the beginning and everything that was configured or installed will be removed from the system).

In much the same way as all the other programs (or scripts) that can be used throughout the installation process, each of the executables or scripts used here can have a Condition property populated using the data from the custom textbox screens or any other environment variables. They also have a property that enables us to pass program arguments to them.

A VBScript file has been included with the download for this chapter, which simply puts a Message Box up on the screen. This file has been added to the Uninstall event, and so will be triggered when the package is uninstalled. In order to add the script, we have to right-click on the Uninstall folder in the Custom Actions pane. From the context menu we must select the Add Custom Action... option and navigate to the script file or executable file we wish to associate with this event.

The Launch Conditions Editor

To round off our explanation of the different editors of the Windows Installer VS.NET project, we have one more that is potentially the most important of all the editor screens. The Launch Conditions editor provides us with the ability to check various conditions and determine whether we should install the package or not. There are two tabs on the screen:

- ❑ Search target machine
- ❑ Launch conditions

The former allows us to add the following searches before we deploy the product:

- ❏ Add File Search
- ❏ Add Registry Search
- ❏ Add Windows Installer Search

The File Search will allow us to check whether a file exists, and if so use this to decide whether to install something from our application folder or another folder by adding a condition referencing the property name in the search. We can do the same thing by checking to see if a registry key exists. The Windows Installer search defines whether something has been installed through Windows Installer. Each Windows Installer Package has a GUID value that enables it to be located through this search. Therefore this option can determine whether another Windows Installer Package has been installed, and if so, use that fact as a launch condition. As these searches return true or false, the names of the "environment" variables can be used in other points in the installation process to affect the outcome of the installation.

The Launch Conditions tab can be used to check that other software is installed. By right-clicking on the root tree node, Requirements on Target Machine we should be able to see five predefined options for launch conditions. These values won't be used in the same way as the searches, but if any returns false then the installation will halt and a message in the Message property will be displayed to the user. The launch conditions are:

- ❏ Add File Launch Condition
- ❏ Add Registry Launch Condition
- ❏ Add Windows Installer Launch Condition
- ❏ Add .NET Framework Launch Condition
- ❏ Add Internet Information Services Launch Condition

A registry launch condition could be used to check whether a piece of software has been installed (on which the current installed package depends). The Windows Installer launch condition could be used to determine whether a certain Windows Installer package was present in the installer database. The .NET Framework may need to be present on the target machine for the software to work, so this check can halt execution and present a message with a download URL for the .NET Framework. A code example package containing could exploit the IIS launch condition to determine whether to deploy a web site to the target machine or to halt execution of the package.

Repairing and Removing

Once the package has been installed, if the .msi file is executed again, it will result in the Repair and Remove screen. It can either be executed by clicking on the original file, or by using the Add/Remove Programs menu in the Control Panel and selecting Remove (or also by right-clicking on the .msi file and choosing the appropriate option from the context menu).

Redistributing the .NET Framework

One important thing to ensure when installing the `.msi` package and deploying a .NET application is that the .NET Runtime files are currently on the system. As the final release of .NET has been available for less than a year, it is reasonable to assume that most users won't have the .NET Runtime installed as part of their desktop build. One of the problems with attempting to redistribute the .NET Framework is its sheer size – most users won't want to download and install something so large to simply run an application. However, it is still practical to redistribute the framework redistributable and the application package installer via some other media, such as on CD.

In Solution Explorer, there is a folder under the project called Detected Dependencies that shows the .NET Framework runtime files. This is automatically excluded from the project, and must not be included. If this is included, when the project is installed an error is shown to the user and execution is halted. The .NET Redistributable is a merge module – we shall be looking at Merge Modules later in the chapter. However, the .NET Redistributable package can be downloaded from the following URL and the files can be integrated into the Windows Installer package:

http://msdn.microsoft.com/downloads/default.asp?url=/downloads/sample.asp?url=/msdn-files/027/001/829/msdncompositedoc.xml

By right-clicking on the **Setup Project** file and choosing the **Properties** pages for the **Setup** project, we should see a property called **Bootstrapper**. When the Windows Installer package is created, an associated `setup.exe` file is created as well, in order to "bootstrap" the installation. It is this `setup.exe` file that should be run, which will then bootstrap the installation process of the Windows Installer package. This should be done first, since the target machine may not contain a recent (or any) version of the Windows Installer. The `setup.exe` will check to see if the Installer is present, and if not install the correct installer that is generally distributed with each Windows Installer package. By changing this from **Windows Installer Bootstrapper** to **None**, we can modify and use the redistributable package setup example from the following MSDN web page. Setting this property to **None** will allow us to specify our own bootstrapper – which can then be used to install the .NET Framework Runtime files if they are not present:

http://msdn.microsoft.com/downloads/default.asp?url=/downloads/sample.asp?url=/msdn-files/027/001/830/msdncompositedoc.xml

This URL will allow us to download an example `setup.ini` file and an example `setup.exe` that can be used and slightly modified to provide a bootstrap for the redistributable .NET Framework package and also for our Windows Installer package. The .NET Runtime redistributable is an executable file called `DotNetfx.exe`; this contains the Windows Installer redistributable, and so will install this prior to installing the .NET Runtime files if .NET is not present on the target machine. Once the `setup.exe` is run, it will check to see whether the runtime files exist on the target machine, and if not it will install them before using the information in the `setup.ini` file to install our package. The code changes to the sample `setup.ini` file are shown below:

```
[Bootstrap]
Msi=SetupTextReader.msi
```

If the .NET Runtime has already been installed, `setup.exe` will automatically bootstrap the Windows Installer package.

Installing to the GAC

The Global Assembly Cache (or GAC) can be used to include shared assemblies. We may want to register class libraries that are available to all clients on the machine – this was easy with COM, since the COM runtime would automatically find the COM component for us through registry details that were set when the component was registered with the system. However, if we want to install a component that will be available to every application that we deploy and which won't need to be copied into each application directory then we should use the GAC. The **References** menu of VS.NET automatically detects GAC assemblies – all of the runtime libraries such as `System.IO` have been registered with the GAC.

The class library we developed earlier will now be installed to the GAC, and we will reference the GAC version of the class library in our project. In order to create a GAC assembly, we need to sign the assembly with a strong name. This can done using `sn.exe` from the .NET Framework command prompt. For example:

```
sn.exe -k C:\key.snk
```

This would create a file called key.snk in the root of the C directory. This file uses a cryptographic private-public key pair to create a strong name so that the assembly can be registered with the GAC. We can associate this key file with our assembly by slightly amending the AssemblyInfo.cs file in the class library project. When the keyfile is referenced in the [AssemblyKeyFile] attribute (shown below), on the next compilation of the project the compiler will sign the assembly with the private key to verify authenticity and embed the public key in the assembly manifest. Aside from being able to use the Windows Installer to install an assembly to the GAC, we can also use a supplied .NET Framework command-line tool called gacutil. The GAC embodies the principle of side-by-side execution, which allows multiple versions of the same assembly to be registered and even to run on the same machine simultaneously. In this way, a client can reference a particular version of the assembly without being affected by GAC updates to that assembly. This is something that was unsupported by the COM runtime and led to the problem of DLL Hell (although Windows XP now boasts side-by-side execution for COM components).

```
[assembly: AssemblyKeyFile("C:\\key.snk")]
```

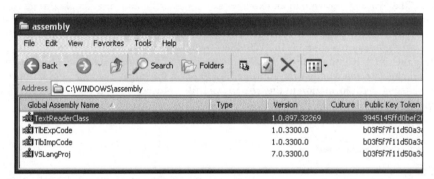

In the above screenshot, the GAC is visible showing assemblies registered with strong names. This view was taken after compiling the TextReaderClass project with the referenced key file and then adding the Global Assembly Cache folder to the File System Editor of the Windows Installer project. Now all the client projects installed in future can reference the GAC version of the class library instead of the application folder version of the class library. When the GAC version of the assembly needs to be updated, new client installations will contain the updated version that can exist side-by-side in the GAC with former versions of the same class library. As each client library references a particular version of the class library within the GAC, some clients can use the former version without being affected while others can use the current version.

Using Windows Installer Over the Web

Before discussing the other project types listed at the beginning of the chapter, it's worth discussing how Windows Installer can be bootstrapped from the Web. Bootstrapping from the Web is simplicity in itself; all it takes is a change in the property pages for the installer project from Windows Bootstrapper to Web Bootstrapper. By pressing the configuration button, details can be entered that enable us to identify the URL for the Internet download folder. This value will be used by the setup to work out the URL path to the .msi file. The setup.exe project that is created is downloaded to the client browser and run seamlessly by downloading and running the TextReaderSetup.msi file. Any other files, such as the .NET Framework and the Windows Installer, will be downloaded as and when needed. This is obviously very efficient in that it avoids downloading anything that is not essential to the installation.

There is an optional section that allows the user to select a URL for a Windows Installer upgrade download. This URL should contain the two files that are produced through all the bootstrap setups: `InstMsiW.exe` and `InstMsiA.exe`. The former represents a Unicode implementation of Windows Installer v2, and the latter an ANSI implementation (the latter will only be applicable for operating systems such as Windows 98 that store strings internally as ANSI strings).

The screenshot above shows what happens when the web setup package is downloaded and run. Before the actual download occurs, a digital signature is sent down to the client. Essentially, the installer package is signed using Authenticode – if this is not present then the browser will show a dialog box warning the user that the file is not signed. Authenticode certificates can be obtained from companies like **Verisign** and can be used in conjunction with private keys and hashing functions to provide a means for the user to verify that the software company has been verified by a Certificate Authority (and that the software hasn't been tampered with – ensuring that the user is installing the original product).

Merge Module Projects

Merge Module projects allow us to componentize the installation process. In an object-oriented world where some key business aims include the production of reusable software components, it also follows that we should be able to componentize the installation packages we use so that we don't have to add the same files to several projects, or define conditions, or perform any other operations necessary for the install process. It makes more sense to use a Merge Module that can be integrated into a Windows Installer project. The Merge Modules that have been added to the project are visible in the **Detected Dependencies** section in the Solution Explorer. Merge Modules cannot be used in their own right – they can only be used as part of a Windows Installer project.

Using the **File System Editor** on the Windows Installer setup project `TextReaderSetup` that we created earlier, we can add the new merge module – we do this by right-clicking on the background and selecting **Project Output...** from the context menu:

The Merge Module is an .msm file that can be reused again and again in any number of Windows Installer projects. I have chosen the most common usage to illustrate the way that a merge module will function, but it can be used to distribute anything to the target machine. There is actually no limit to the number of Merge Modules that can be incorporated into a Windows Installer project, so it follows that larger projects will benefit from being redistributed as Merge Modules based on different sets of distributions. Indeed, this will probably work quite well for products that are segregated into standard, professional, and enterprise builds.

The image above shows a Merge Module being added to a Windows Installer project. This actually is a list of all the projects that can be added – if you remember this can be used to include the binaries of an application project. In this case, since a Merge Module project is selected from the drop-down list, the Windows Installer project will automatically recognize that this is a Merge Module project and identify it as such in the Project Output listbox.

CAB Files

CAB Files should need little introduction. They are distributed with almost all Microsoft media. They are essentially compressed files and folders that are unpacked by installation programs. CAB (short for cabinet) files have an extra use that enables them to be downloaded over the Internet and extracted into a temporary folder.

CAB files used for deployment purposes normally contain ActiveX controls that can then be run using the browser as a container. ActiveX controls provide a way of using rich client-side functionality within the web browser (but at the cost of having very little security). They are essentially resuable controls that can be embedded in a container such as a web browser or a VB6 form (or, as we saw in Chapter 3, a .NET Windows form). Malicious ActiveX controls can be scripted to cause damage to the file system of the client. Most configured corporate desktops will in any case have security settings that disable ActiveX controls. As we saw before with web downloads, ActiveX controls can be signed using Authenticode to allow a user to make an informed decision whether to download and run them, if they have their browser security settings set to prompt them to trusted ActiveX control download.

To package an ActiveX control in VS.NET, we can select a **Cab Project** from the **Setup and Deployment Projects** menu. When this is done, an ActiveX control can be added to the Cabinet file by browsing to an `.ocx` file and adding it to the CAB. The `.ocx` file should be registered on our machine so that we can add it a web form. In order to create a CAB project that can be used to deliver an ActiveX control to the browser, follow the steps below:

- ❑ Create a new ASP.NET Web Application

- ❑ Right-click on the toolbox and click Customize Toolbox

- ❑ Under the **COM Components** tab check the component **Calendar Control 8.0**

- ❑ When this appears in the toolbox, drag this onto the form

- ❑ Add a new project (this time a Cab project)

- ❑ Right-click on the Cab project in Solution Explorer and select **Add | File**

- ❑ Choose the **Calendar Control** (the path can be found from the **COM Components** tab earlier – the file is called `MsCal.ocx`, and lives in the Windows `System32` folder)

- ❑ Build the Cab project and add the CAB file to the web project by selecting **Add | Existing Item** and browsing to the location of the cabinet

- ❑ In the **Properties** window for the ActiveX **Calendar Control** on the web form, type in the set the `codebase` property to the name of the `Cabinet` file

- ❑ When this is delivered over the web, the ActiveX control will be deployed in the browser and unpacked on the client from the CAB

When ActiveX controls are downloaded by a supporting browser such as IE, the CAB file will be downloaded and unpacked, and the controls will be placed into a local cache.

CAB files are not used solely to distribute ActiveX controls. Many large software producers use CAB files (Microsoft especially) to package their applications, enabling them to be shrunk to a fraction of their size. This is possible as CAB files are essentially archives that use compression schemes such as Zip. In this way, the archive can be expanded during the installation and the files stored in temporary directories and then installed.

Trickle Deployment

We've decided to save the best until last. The best in this case is the new security model that comes with bootstrapped assembly downloading. This is possibly the most useful feature of all the ways of deploying applications through the .NET Framework. An assembly download process begins on the client that makes a request for an assembly on a web server. The assembly can download onto the user's system and the bootstrap process that began the download can show a form application that is executed and subject to the normal security constraints defined by the download zone – was it downloaded from the Internet, intranet, or localhost (or some other defined domain)? Was the zone trusted or untrusted? These are all issues that are referred to as code access security, a term that we'll meet in greater detail later in the chapter.

To kick off what's called the "trickle" download process, we need something that is already executing on the client machine. This can be one of two things. The first is a form application that is set up from a web setup bootstrapper that we looked at earlier. This would download and install a Windows application that would enable us to download assemblies "on the fly" and keep getting assembly updates for that particular software application over the Web (these assemblies would be stored in a local cache on the target machine). This can be done in many elegant ways; one way is to get the user to download a setup program that when installed is just a splash screen. The splash screen loader will retrieve the assembly from the Internet and the splash screen will continue to show until the new application has been downloaded and the form executed.

The way that I'll describe begins with a process called "no touch deployment" that allows us to embed .NET Windows Forms Controls into a web browser – these controls would normally be downloaded as part of a web page, and would execute in the client browser when the page has successfully downloaded. It's not a new concept for controls to be downloaded and executed in the browser. As we described earlier, ActiveX controls did exactly the same thing – as we shall see, the difference with .NET controls is that there is a security model in place to enable safe execution that cannot touch the file system or local services.

This is not the only way that we can use the trickle concept to download an assembly; we can also use a Windows form. The important point, though, is that there is a bootstrap process that executes on the client side initiating the download of the assembly that can then be used to create a Windows application.

The assembly is downloaded into an area known as the download cache that can be found at `C:\Windows\assembly\download`.

We'll start by looking at "zero touch deployment" in the browser. This can consist of any .NET Windows Forms control downloaded into the web browser. The only browser that currently supports embedded .NET controls is IE5 (or greater).

The **UserDetector** project is a custom Windows control, derived from the `UserControl` class. This control can be embedded in a container programmatically in much the same way as the ActiveX control we looked at earlier. To create the Windows Control Library, select the **New Project** option from the File menu in VS.NET and choose **Windows Control Library**. We won't go into detail about creating custom controls here, as that is covered thoroughly in Chapter 8.

The user interface for our control is very simple; it allows the user to enter a username and password to log in to a site:

Here is the sequence of events that will allow the assembly containing the Windows Form to be downloaded into the cache on the client and executed:

❑ The user requests a web page that contains an embedded control showing a login prompt

❑ The user enters a username and password

❑ The username and password are sent to a web service

❑ The web service checks the validity of these credentials against an MD5-hashed value in the User database

❑ If the user exists in the database, they are allowed to download the assembly

❑ The assembly is used to create the Windows Form, and it is shown in the foreground

There is a skeleton ASP.NET Web Application using VS.NET called DetectUser that is used to deliver the Windows Control. In order to embed the control into the ASP.NET page, the following syntax is used:

```
<object id="UserDetector"
        classid="UserDetector.dll#UserDetector.UserDetector"
        width="600" height="300" VIEWASTEXT>
</object>
```

The classid attribute contains the name of the DLL followed by the type of the control (this is the class name preceded by the namespace). It's important to understand that that the DLL is being referenced in the object tag from the virtual web root, so it must be copied into the web directory. The settings for the virtual directory must be changed to allow script permission only, and not execute and script permission. If execute permission is given too, the web application will attempt to execute the DLL rather than simply downloading it.

The `UserDetector` DLL has the following code for the button event handler:

```
try
{
    localhost.Identity id = new localhost.Identity();
    if (id.ValidateUser(txtUsername.Text, txtPassword.Text, false))
    {
        // ...
    }
    else
    {
        MessageBox.Show("Login failed!!");
    }
}
catch(Exception ex)
{
    MessageBox.Show(ex.Message);
}
```

When the user enters information into the username and password textboxes, a web service is used and the `ValidateUser()` method is invoked to check the user's credentials. Should the credentials be accepted by the web service and a `true` value be returned to the client, the assembly will download. The implementation code to retrieve the assembly is not shown here – we'll return to this later after looking at how the web service validates the user credentials.

As can be seen in the code above, the web service method `ValidateUser()` is invoked from the control client where it can be used to validate the username and password information. The reference to `localhost.Identity` is due to the fact that the web service class is called `Identity`. The reference to `localhost` is used since in the course of creating a client we have to set a web reference that involves downloading a WSDL document describing the web service. The .NET Framework provides a filter that enables the dynamic generation of WSDL (Web Service Description Language describes the types and methods on the web service, the parameters that methods take, and the types that methods return). By using the following syntax the WSDL can be returned for our web service. Any web service can have the WSDL generated for it by appending `?WSDL` after the `.asmx` page name (all ASP.NET web services are `.asmx` files):

```
http://localhost/ValidateIdentity/service1.asmx?WSDL
```

In order to use the web service from our Windows Control project, we have to right-click on the project in Solution Explorer to bring up the context menu and select the **Add Web Reference** option. The URL above should be entered into the address bar of the dialog, and the **Add Reference** button should pressed:

The web reference works in much the same way as normal class library references for the purposes of this example. Suffice it to say that a reference is set from an assembly where type information can be obtained and a web reference from a WSDL document where type information on the web service can also be obtained.

So now we can add a web reference to our user control (to the `Identity` web service). When the WSDL document is imported into the project, a tool provided with the .NET Framework (`WSDL.exe`) is used to generate a C# proxy class, which can be used to convert method calls and returns between SOAP and calls that C# can understand natively.

The `Identity` web service class is declared as below (inheriting from `WebService`):

```
public class Identity : System.Web.Services.WebService
```

The definition for the web service method we'll be calling is as follows:

```
[WebMethod]
public bool ValidateUser(string username, string password,
                         bool bIntegratedSecurity)
{
    MD5CryptoServiceProvider md5 = new MD5CryptoServiceProvider();
```

```
        string b64string = Convert.ToBase64String(md5.ComputeHash(
                            Encoding.Default.GetBytes(username+password)));
    SqlConnection cn = new SqlConnection(
                "server=localhost;database=Users;integrated security=SSPI");
    cn.Open();
    SqlCommand sq = new SqlCommand("SELECT COUNT(*) FROM tblUsers " +
        "WHERE USERNAME='" + username + "' AND HASH='" + b64string + "'", cn);
    SqlDataReader sr = sq.ExecuteReader(CommandBehavior.CloseConnection);
    sr.Read();
    if(sr.GetInt32(0) > 0)
        return true;
    else
        return false;
}
```

The ValidateUser() method is used to check whether a user exists in the database. If so, a value of true is returned to the client; otherwise false is returned. The username and password are concatenated together and then hashed using an MD5 message digest. The result is then converted to a Base64 string. (Base64 ensures that no non-printable character will be present, as each character will no longer be a full byte 0-255. In the Base64 encoding scheme the string is treated as a bit stream, so each 6-bit chunk is taken and used to form a character defined by the Base64 alphabet (the Base64 alphabet has 64 characters represented by the byte values 0 – 63. A Base64 string is always terminated by an equals sign.) This technique is common as a security mechanism to avoid storing plaintext usernames and passwords together – by only storing the username, if database security is compromised only 50% of what is necessary to login will be known by the intruder. For the purposes of the code download example, the login can be tested using the username richard with a password of newuser. The Base64 MD5 hash for this stored in a SQL Server Database table is:

```
jaPB3FQwHj2odCkOkU/wbw==
```

The Users database is checked using the SQL statement and the row count is checked to ensure that it is greater than 0. If so, the entry has been found in the database. Otherwise a value of false is returned to the client.

Here is the DDL statement used to create the tblUsers table where the username and hash value is stored. The complete DDL commands for generating the Users database for this project are included in the code download.

```
CREATE TABLE [dbo].[tblUsers] (
    [username] [varchar] (50) COLLATE Latin1_General_CI_AS NOT NULL ,
    [hash] [varchar] (50) COLLATE Latin1_General_CI_AS NULL
) ON [PRIMARY]
```

When a successful login occurs, the code below is invoked. We first load an assembly from the web server – this address is a localhost address, which means that we will be using our local web server in loopback, but it can equally be any navigable internet or intranet URL. In order to use this example the path to the DLL relative to the web root should be /dll/ViewPubs.dll.

When we obtain a handle to the assembly through the `Assembly` object, we cast this to the class we want to get from the assembly by using `GetType()`. As we now have a type reference, an object can be created and returned to us as the generic `object` type.

An instance of this type is created from the assembly using the `Activator.CreateInstance()` method. An object is returned from this operation that is then cast to a form. Calling the `Form.Show()` method will display the form on screen in the desktop foreground:

```
Assembly formAssembly = Assembly.LoadFrom
                    ("http://localhost/dlls/ViewPubs.dll");
Type frmAssembly = formAssembly.GetType
                ("Wrox.WindowsGUIProgramming.Chapter10.pubs", true);
object objView = Activator.CreateInstance(frmAssembly);
Form assembly = (Form)objView;
assembly.Show();
```

The `pubs` form is shown below. This form has been downloaded from an application directory on the web server, which has similar permissions to the directory that contains the control:

title_id	title	type	pub_id	price	advance	royalty	ytd_sa
BU1032	The Busy Exe	business	1389	19.99	5000	10	4095
BU1111	Cooking with	business	1389	11.95	5000	10	3876
BU2075	You Can Co	business	0736	2.99	10125	24	18722
BU7832	Straight Talk	business	1389	19.99	5000	10	4095
MC2222	Silicon Valley	mod_cook	0877	19.99	0	12	2032
MC3021	The Gourmet	mod_cook	0877	2.99	15000	24	22246
MC3026	The Psycholo	UNDECIDED	0877	(null)	(null)	(null)	(null)
PC1035	But Is It User	popular_com	1389	22.95	7000	16	8780
PC8888	Secrets of Sili	popular_com	1389	20	8000	10	4095
PC9999	Net Etiquette	popular_com	1389	(null)	(null)	(null)	(null)
PS1372	Computer Ph	psychology	0877	21.59	7000	10	375
PS2091	Is Anger the	psychology	0736	10.95	2275	12	2045
PS2106	Life Without F	psychology	0736	7	6000	10	111

The form simply lists a table from the sample `pubs` database in SQL Server and uses a `DataGrid` control to display the result set:

```
private void btTitles_Click(object sender, System.EventArgs e)
{
    SqlConnection cn = new SqlConnection(
                "server=localhost;database=pubs;Integrated Security=SSPI");
    cn.Open();
    SqlDataAdapter sda = new SqlDataAdapter("SELECT * FROM TITLES", cn);
```

```
    DataSet ds = new DataSet();
    sda.Fill(ds, "titles");
    dg.SetDataBinding(ds, "titles");
}
```

The button handling code shown above uses a query to return the contents of the `titles` table and then fills a `DataSet`. The `DataSet` is then bound to the `DataGrid` that enables it to display the contents in grid form.

Every time an assembly is requested from a remote point on the network, the bootstrapper process doing the download will check the cache (`C:\Windows\assembly\downloads`) to see if the web version is the same as the version in the cache. If the version is higher than the version in the cache, the new version is placed in the cache and run; otherwise, the current cache version is run. In this way, software updates can be distributed transparently to the user. This is a very cool feature.

Looking at the cache will reveal that a collection of the same assemblies exists with differing version numbers. Old DLLs remain in the cache indefinitely but can be deleted using the `gacutil` tool and specifically using the following command:

```
gacutil /cdl
```

Code Access Security – Protecting the Client

We have already established that one of the problems with ActiveX controls was the fact that they don't have an inbuilt security manager enabling them to access local resources on a machine. This has led to ActiveX controls that can be maliciously scripted to enable access to the user's hard drive.

Code Access Security has a model that is similar to (but far more granular than) the Java sandbox model, which enables users to download Java Applets and run them in the browser without fear of them utilizing resources on the local machine.

Code Access Security enforces policies on assemblies that have originated from the local machine and assemblies that have originated from the Internet or intranet. There are fives possible zones from which an assembly can originate:

❑ Locally (MyComputer)

❑ Intranet

❑ Internet

❑ Trusted sites

❑ Untrusted sites

Assemblies that have originated from the local machine can run with full trust and access all local resources. Intranet and Internet zone assemblies cannot access local file and registry resources. Trusted sites have similar permissions to the Internet zone by default. Assemblies from untrusted sites will not be able to execute on the local machine at all.

Any assembly can have its trust levels increased through the .NET Framework wizards that exist in the Administrative Tools program folder. These Wizards provide an application called Trust an Assembly that can be used to add or remove trust to or from a particular assembly by defining the URL from where the assembly originated:

The Trust an Assembly wizard is very straightforward, so we won't provide a screen-by-screen walk-through. The first choice is whether to change the assembly's trust level for the current user, or for all users of the machine. We are then asked for the path or URL to the assembly. Finally, we can assign the trust level for the specified assembly on a sliding scale from full trust to no trust.

Code Access Security was intended to secure implementation of downloaded applications by stopping them from maliciously using the local resources. By stopping use of the file systems and registry, we are effectively limiting the application to a similar role to a web page. However, distributing rich-client applications in this way will make it far easier for Windows Forms developers to deploy applications. It will also make it far easier to make a case for development of Windows Forms applications, as a single change can be rolled out to users immediately, just like changes to a web site.

Many things can be adjusted via the wizards and configuration utilities provided with the .NET Framework. In particular trust can be selectively added or removed for particular assemblies or permissions can be changed for download zones to re-enable local .NET policies allowing applications from different zones to have different levels of security applied to them.

Summary

This chapter looked at how to use VS.NET setup projects to deploy a .NET application. We compared all the different needs of the user, from a web download to building a redistributable Windows installer packages. We described how to transparently redeploy packages using the Web and bootstrap deployment using "no-touch deployment" downloads.

All of the examples we used centered on creating projects with Visual Studio .NET. This is very convenient for us, but possibly not optimal for large products, which may span one or more whole CDs. The tools we have been given with Visual Studio .NET do indeed allow us to create fairly thorough deployment solutions, but third-party tools such as InstallShield and WISE have similarly developed more functional installation agents that can be used from the Visual Studio IDE. Using packages such as these adds virtually complete control over the deployment process and allows more functional Windows Installer packages to be built. As a first step, however, Microsoft has provided a good series of integrated deployment solutions to suit virtually all of our development needs.

In summary, throughout this chapter we covered:

- Deploying applications using the Windows Installer
- Merge Module projects
- Using CAB Files
- Deploying to the GAC
- Using the Web Setup package
- The download cache
- Deploying a Windows application over a network
- Code Access Security

Index

A Guide to the Index

The index is arranged hierarchically, in alphabetical order, with symbols preceding the letter A. Most second-level entries and many third-level entries also occur as first-level entries. This is to ensure that users will find the information they require however they choose to search for it.

M

Q

quality settings
graphics state, 229
QueryPageSettings event
PrintDocument class, 271, 293
queue-based messages, 12
NON-queued messages and, 12
QueueUserWorkItem method
ThreadPool class, 376, 384

R

RadioButton control, System.Windows.Forms, 99
CheckBox and, 99
CheckedChanged event, 99
properties, 99
Appearance, 99
AutoCheck, changing state automatically, 99
BackColor, 99
Checked, getting/setting state, 99
FlatStyle, 99
Image/~Align, adding/aligning image, 99
ReadOnly property
Address Composite control, 333
DefaultValue attribute, 327
Description attribute, 326
DomainUpDown control, 91
ExtendedTextBox control, 314
changing property from base class, 317
hiding property, 318
Receive method
Socket class, 383
Rectangle structure
Contains method, 247
Inflate method, 242
Offset method, 242
printing DataGrid control example
formatting printout, 305
System.Drawing namespace, 241
transformations, 241
Union method, 246
RectangleF structure
System.Drawing namespace, 246
Refresh method
invoking event handlers for Paint event, 227
Regedit.exe
compared to Registry Editor, Visual Studio .NET, 407
Region class
Exclude method, 246
GetBound method, 247
GetRegionScans method, 246
Intersect method, 246
IsInfinite method, 247
IsVisible method, 247
paths, 244
System.Drawing namespace, 241, 244
transformations, 241
Union method, 246
Xor method, 246
Region property
RoundButton custom control, 348
Regional options
internationalizing the keyboard, 197
Windows operating system, 197
regions

GDI+, 237, 246
Register property of files
File System Editor, Visual Studio .NET, 405
list of values, 405
Register User option, adding
customizing deployment using UI Editor, 413
RegisterClass function, 15
RegisterWaitForSingleObject method
ThreadPool class, 376
Registry Editor, Visual Studio .NET
compared to Regedit.exe, 407
HKEY_CLASSES_ROOT, 407
HKEY_CURRENT_USER, 407
HKEY_LOCAL_MACHINE, 407
Windows Installer, 407
registry keys, Windows Installer, 413
Condition property, 413
installation conditions, 413
Value property, 413
Registry Launch Condition option
Launch Conditions Editor, Visual Studio .NET, 415
Registry Search option
Launch Conditions Editor, Visual Studio .NET, 415
relations, DataTables
see DataRelations.
ReleaseMutex method
Mutex class, 380
Remove method
AccessorContainer class, 394
BindingContext class, 140
Delegate class, 393
Items collection, DomainUpDown control, 91
Event accessors, 393
IList interface, 156
RemoveAll method
ToolTip class, 218
RemoveAt method
BindingManagerBase class, 142
IList interface, 156
RemoveIndex method
IBindingList interface, 174
RemoveSort method
IBindingList interface, 174
ResetPropertyName method
setting properties to default value, 335
ResizeRedraw value
ControlStyles enumeration, 226
Resume method
Thread class, 366, 385
ResumeBinding method
BindingManagerBase class, 142
ResumeLayout method, 31
Form Designer's login Form, 31
RichTextBox control, System.Windows.Forms, 82
inherited Form, 39
properties, 84
DetectUrl, 84
Rtf/Selected~, recognizing RTF codes, 83
SelectedText/SelectionColor/~Font, 84
Text property, 59
ZoomFactor, 85
RTF, displaying document as, 82
LoadFile(), loading text, 82
output, 83
Split(), separating code from text, 83
Right value
MouseButtons enumeration, 216

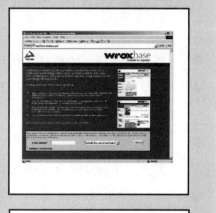
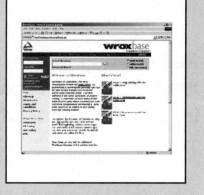

Professional Windows GUI Programming using C# – Registration Card

Name _____

Address _____

_____

_____

City _____ State/Region _____

Country _____ Postcode/Zip _____

E-Mail _____

Occupation _____

How did you hear about this book?

❏ Book review (name) _____

❏ Advertisement (name) _____

❏ Recommendation _____

❏ Catalog _____

❏ Other _____

Where did you buy this book?

❏ Bookstore (name) _____ City _____

❏ Computer store (name) _____

❏ Mail order _____

❏ Other _____

What influenced you in the purchase of this book?

❏ Cover Design ❏ Contents ❏ Other (please specify):

_____

How did you rate the overall content of this book?

❏ Excellent ❏ Good ❏ Average ❏ Poor

What did you find most useful about this book? _____

_____

What did you find least useful about this book? _____

_____

Please add any additional comments. _____

_____

What other subjects will you buy a computer book on soon?

_____

What is the best computer book you have used this year?

_____

Note: This information will only be used to keep you updated about new Wrox Press titles and will not be used for any other purpose or passed to any other third party.

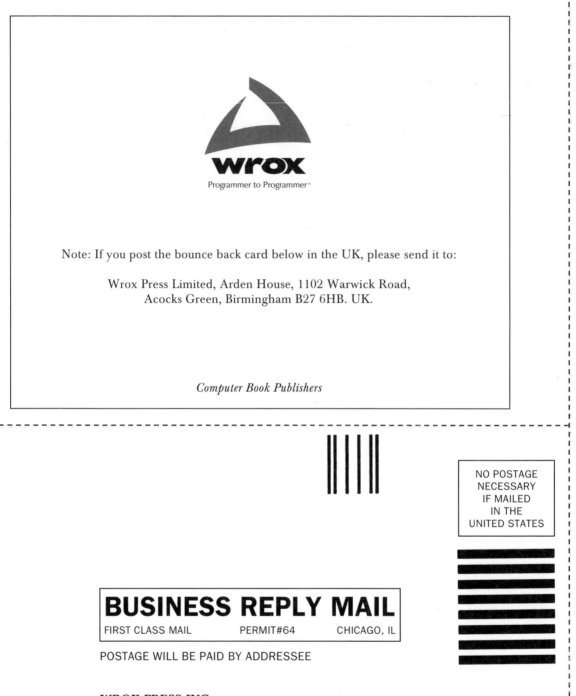

wrox

Programmer to Programmer™

Note: If you post the bounce back card below in the UK, please send it to:

Wrox Press Limited, Arden House, 1102 Warwick Road,
Acocks Green, Birmingham B27 6HB. UK.

Computer Book Publishers